Agility
Right from the Start

*The ultimate training guide to
America's fastest-growing dog sport*

By Eva Bertilsson and Emelie Johnson Vegh

Photography: Eva Bertilsson, Mette Björne, Annika Clerselius, Tommy Hagström, Lone Hellesvik, Tom Espen Hellesvik, Jenny Johansson, Emelie Johnson Vegh, Michaela Kartler, Gunnar Lindgren, Nina Mortensen, Johanna Strandner, and Hans Wretling. Unless otherwise noted on page 440, all images were taken by Nina Mortensen.
Photo preparation: Nina Mortensen, www.ad-meliora.se
Editor: Nini Bloch, www.ninibloch.com
Book design: CoDesign, Boston MA USA www.codesignco.com

Agility Right from the Start
The ultimate training guide to America's fastest-growing dog sport

Karen Pryor Clickertraining
Sunshine Books, Inc.
49 River Street
Waltham, MA 02453
www.clickertraining.com

For information about special discounts for multiple-copy purchases please contact KPCT Sales at 1-781-398-0754 or wholesale@clickertraining.com.
Library of Congress Control Number 2009943280

ISBN 978-1-890948-41-2
Manufactured in the United States of America

10 9 8 7 6 5 4 3 2

We dedicate this book to
our much-loved companions and teachers:
Sickan, Misty, Soya, Tizla, Kicki,
Nilla, Flox, My, Gaia, and Scout.

Contents

Exercises

Exercises are one of the ways we have chosen to describe practical training. Much of our training also relies on shaping behaviors that are not easily explained in step-by-step descriptions. So the list here doesn't represent our entire program, but it does give a good sample of the kinds of skills we train.

We've numbered the exercises to make them easier for you to find in the book and to see progressions. For a detailed overview of our whole program and one-sheet versions of the exercises you can take with you to practice, visit www.AgilityRightFromTheStart.com.

A note from the publisher

For years I've been looking for just the right book on clicker training and agility. When I go to an agility trial and see dogs make mistakes, I know some training is missing. When I see handlers get upset or stop focusing on their dogs, I know some training is missing. People need access to more clicker skills.

Now here's the book I was looking for. Swedish authorities Eva Bertilsson and Emelie Johnson Vegh have created a modern guide to agility based entirely on reinforcement technology. With this book any competitor can qualify sooner, with fewer errors and faster runs. With this book any dog owner and dog, competing or not, can reach new levels of teamwork and understanding.

Why is this book so different? It's the most logical by far. Nothing is left to chance. The authors build a rock-solid foundation of dog and human skills and reliability before going anywhere near an obstacle. Dozens of brief intense exercises, liberally illustrated with photos, guarantee progress and success.

Every one of these quick little exercises has multiple benefits. You might be training "over, under, around, or through," using a wheelbarrow or kitchen chairs for obstacles. Meanwhile, however, your dog is also learning speed, energy, and focus, and you are sharpening your timing and learning to deliver clicks, cues, and rewards with ever-increasing precision.

Bertilsson and Vegh have provided occasional TAGteach™ or "click the human" exercises, so a friend can help you out with such skills as throwing tug toys far and accurately with your non-dominant hand. They've also included many ingenious new training ideas, such as teaching a dog to knock over piles of clattering objects, so he learns to like sudden noises instead of finding them daunting—handy on the agility field and in everyday life, too.

I love the hundreds of wonderful action photographs that show you what this training looks like. You can't help but notice the intense focus and the visible teamwork; but I think what I like best are the radiantly joyful faces of people and of dogs. Above all, what they are doing is FUN. This is training the way it ought to be. I hope you try it out and think so too.

Karen Pryor

Foreword

I first met Eva and Emelie at a faculty dinner during one of Karen Pryor's Clicker Expos. They were full of great questions and amazing enthusiasm. I remember thinking, "Wow! These Swedish girls are the most energetic and inquisitive trainers I have met in years!" But it was clear to me at that first meeting that they had a deep understanding of the science and a great passion for training. *Agility Right from the Start* demonstrates both that passion and that grasp of the science.

The sport of agility has the unique capacity to be fun for the animal, the trainer, and the spectator—which may explain its popularity. The best agility competitors are capable of a very complex series of behaviors. The enthusiasm that a well-trained dog displays when running an agility course can lead some trainers to believe that agility training is easy because the dogs appear to enjoy it so much. While it is true that the best-trained dogs do seem to find agility very reinforcing, that is usually the result of a skilled trainer teaching agility to the dog in a systematic manner. That is what this book does so well; it takes the reader through a truly systematic approach to agility training.

I believe this book will prove valuable to far more than just those with an interest in agility. The book is split into three sections: theory, foundation skills, and putting it all together. The first two sections give the reader a great introduction to the benefits and science of clicker training as well as a focus on the importance of foundation skills. While these skills are critical to good agility training, I believe all trainers will also find the practical approach in these sections extremely valuable.

I particularly like the way Eva and Emelie ask and answer three questions:

1. *What does the behavior look like?* They ask this question repeatedly throughout the book and describe in detail what the behavior should look like when it's done correctly. Every trainer should ask himself this question when developing a shaping plan, and *Agility Right from the Start* models this well for the reader.

2. *How do you train it?* This book takes a step-by-step approach to explaining how the authors would train the behavior being described.

3. *What could/might go wrong?* Frequently the authors include sidebars that describe common challenges and give suggestions about how to mitigate those potential problems.

As if that weren't enough, Eva's and Emelie's style of writing is fresh and appealing. I enjoy their use of unique analogies and terms while still using good science. You will find concepts like the "tiered cake of reinforcers," "the Bermuda triangle," or "staying in the training bubble." The use of these terms makes reading the book enjoyable and helps convey the message and meaning behind the concepts. *Agility Right from the Start* is a thoroughly enjoyable and extremely useful training book. I am pleased to add it to my library of references.

Ken Ramirez
Vice President of Animal Collections and Training, Shedd Aquarium, Chicago.
Author/editor: *Animal Training: Successful Animal Management Through Positive Reinforcement*

Preface

We first met and got to know each other in 1998 when we both were competing during a week of agility trials here in Sweden. The days were full of runs, taking care of the dogs, soaking up the sun, and generally having a good time, and the nights were full of yet more socializing and games. We soon realized we share a true love for training and analyzing.

We both were seasoned competitors, getting a thrill out of the competitive side of agility, but we were even more passionate trainers.

At the time when we first met, we each had been involved in agility and teaching agility classes for several years. We both had only recently discovered the joy and efficiency of clicker training, however, so our minds were transitioning to clicker training mode. In each other, we found the perfect match.

In the earlier days (early 1990s) when we started out, our classes were rather typical and traditional: While we did use reward-based training, neither of us had heard of clicker training, so we used lots of lures and body language to get the dogs to do what we wanted. The obstacles were our focus, and the goal of our beginners' classes was basically to get the dogs to do all the obstacles so that our students could go out and run courses. We added cues early on in the training process, and the handling was pretty rudimentary.

As we got to know each other, applying the principles of clicker training to agility quickly became our obsession. We discussed and analyzed every aspect of agility training, from how to train a perfect start-line stay to how to explain to students why their reward delivery affects their dog's weaving. Our passion for training brought us together and eventually inspired us to try teaching together. In the summer of 2001, with Emelie hugely pregnant and waddling around the agility field, we gave our first classes together. Teaching together was like love at first sight—it just clicked, and we've never looked back. A couple of years later we wrote our first article together, and since then we've just kept doing what we love: teaching, writing, training, discussing, analyzing, and learning.

The dimension of being two adds a lot of flavor to our teaching. We live 400 kilometers apart, so we've worn out our keyboards and run up our phone bills with our discussions. Most of the time it feels as if large parts of our brains are somehow connected, with one of us finishing the thoughts of the other. When we're away teaching, for instance, we often are dead tired when evening falls. But then one of us sparks an intense discussion that keeps going until we fall asleep mid-sentence. Something happens when the two of us are out on that training field, be it on an actual field or just in our minds, and we love that dynamic.

In the process of teaching, training, and writing, we've realized that how we teach agility differs somewhat from what other instructors do. We decided to write down our approach to agility training and share it with you in this book.

First, we use the science of learning to train dogs in the best possible way. We build behavior step by step using positive reinforcement. We split the training into small, digestible pieces—foundation skills—that our students practice one at a time. We make sure the dogs are well rewarded. The principles of clicker training suffuse all our training and lie behind everything we describe in this book.

Second, we work hard at instilling a mind-set and work structure in our students to ensure that everything in and around the training situation happens in a manner that's appropriate to training agility. Through our years of teaching and training together, we've increasingly come to appreciate how important it is that focus, intensity, and a devotion to following your handling system at all times pervade every aspect of your training. We refer to these principles as Good Agility Practices. By always keeping Good Agility Practices in mind, you'll be able to make the very best out of every training session.

Third, we emphasize developing your skills as well as your dog's. Your knowledge and skills determine how far the training will go and what the results will be. We want to teach people the same way we train dogs: splitting exercises into pieces, working on the foundation skills one at a time, making sure to give precise, positive feedback, and so on. And we want you to treat yourself with kindness during the learning process, setting yourself up for success and allowing yourself to make mistakes. Therefore we try to break down each task into digestible components, and we do extensive hands-on training with just the people, without their dogs. When teaching people we often employ TAGteach™ (Teaching with Acoustical Guidance, clicker training for people), to provide precise instructions and exact feedback. You can read more about TAGteach later in the book, and you'll find lots of references to TAGteach to help improve your own skills.

Finally, we focus on principle over method. Clicker training principles and Good Agility Practices are our guiding stars, and adhering to them will give you a happy and confident agility dog. The particular training methods you choose aren't the most important thing; what's more important is that the methods you choose comply with the main principles. So even though this book encompasses lots of detailed descriptions of what you can train and how you can train it, the bigger picture is what we really wish to get across! Our aspiration is to assist you in determining your goals and to help you on your journey toward them.

Are you a beginner? This book will provide you with the opportunity to get into agility the right way from the start, and a good foundation in dog training in general. We wish that we'd hear fewer people say, "Oh, I wish somebody had told me that in the beginning!" When you're a beginner, there's so much to do and keep in mind. We've written this book to keep you and your dog happy and confident throughout the process. Are you a seasoned competitor? This book is also written for the competitor who wants to build stellar performance, keeping the spotlight on the details. We want you to take responsibility for the learning process and to focus on your own and your dog's skills and knowledge, building and honing an excellent agility team.

Whether you're a beginner or a pro, we want to help you use the clicker training principles in your agility training, making it both fun and efficient. We want you and your dog to enjoy working with all the foundation details that make up the core of agility. We want you to let Good Agility Practices permeate all your training. We want you to focus on developing your own skills as well as your dog's. And we really want you to take principle over method to heart, making you the very best trainer for yourself and your dog.

We wish you happy training days!

Eva Bertilsson
Emelie Johnson Vegh

Part I
Training fundamentals

1

Introduction

Agility truly is the ultimate dog sport! It combines speed and precision, teamwork and independence, dog training skills and handler finesse in a wonderfully complex mix. Agility has the capacity to give both you and your dog innumerable moments of joy and excitement. In this book we wish to inspire you to make the most, and the best, of your agility training.

Our training program

What is it about agility that appeals to you? Why do you want to do agility with your dog? We often raise these questions in our classes, and although the answers vary, most groups come up with lists that look something like this:

- Fun
- Cooperation
- Brainwork
- Enrichment
- Nice social community
- Competitive
- Always room for improvement
- Want to do something with my dog
- Like to teach my dog stuff
- Physical exercise

Agility is all of these things, and more. We find these lists so useful that we usually leave them on the whiteboard during class, so that we can easily refer to them. The list of reasons to train agility helps keep matters in perspective, which in turn makes your life as a trainer and perhaps as a competitor easier. For example, using training methods based on positive reinforcement is the obvious choice if one of the reasons you train agility is to have fun with your dog. In the same fashion, it's a good idea to really teach your dog skills—not just let him run around the course—if you want your agility training to provide brainwork for your dog.

Let's enjoy this game together!

In our training program we don't differentiate between agility-just-for-fun and competitive agility. Our entire program rests on building good foundation skills for you and your dog, something that is as important for the backyard trainer as it is for the world cup team. There's no contradiction between "having a ton of fun" and "well-planned and thoughtfully executed training." Even if you have no intention of ever competing, clear goals and thorough planning will help you make training fun and fair for your dog. And if you want to reach the highest competitive level, you obviously will benefit from careful planning and step-by-step progression toward your highest goals—but it's equally important for your future success that both you and your dog have a blast every time you train.

Our goal: a happy and confident dog

We strive toward one major goal in all our training: a happy and confident dog! We picture a dog that is focused, works intensely, embarks on any given task with great enthusiasm, and enjoys both the exercises and the rewards. The objective of having "a happy and confident dog" makes sense for all kinds of dogs and handlers and all levels of training, whether you just do a little agility in your backyard or strive to make it onto a world-class team.

And since agility is about dogs and people alike, your happiness and confidence is of equal importance. You'll both get the most out of your agility training when you know what to do and enjoy doing it.

In addition to happiness and confidence, we also picture a dog and handler team that can get around any course with flow, speed, and precision. Our training program seeks to create a dog that knows exactly what to do whenever he gets to a piece of equipment and that smoothly follows your handling between the obstacles. We like to say that you and your dog have different responsibilities on the agility course: your job is to tell your dog where to go, and your dog's job is to perform the obstacles correctly without help from you.

We strive to teach the dog all the behaviors he needs to master to be able to independently get to, perform, and leave each obstacle in the best possible fashion. Our teaching stresses independent obstacle performance for several reasons. If your dog can perform the obstacles on his own, that leaves you free to focus on directing his path. Basically it all boils down to happiness and confidence: your dog will be happier and more confident when he really knows what to do and gets rewarded for it, and you'll be happier and more confident when you can count on your dog to get it right without you having to babysit him. Having a dog that can negotiate the obstacles at full speed gives you a competitive edge, and the very process of learning those skills works your dog's brain and enriches his life.

We also strive for each dog and handler team to learn a system of handling—a limited repertoire of handling signals that are used consistently and that fit together without contradictions. Your handling system is your steering wheel, enabling you to direct your dog between obstacles at full speed. To build good habits for yourself and your dog, you need to be consistent in your body language throughout your agility training. The system you use to handle your dog should therefore carry through when moving your dog to and from exercises, directing him to a good spot to start each exercise, providing him with a sense of direction through the exercises, and throughout your reward procedures.

Building blocks for agility

Our goal—a happy and confident team that can get around the agility course with flow, speed and precision—informs and influences our training, our teaching, and the structure of this book.

1. **You need to develop your theoretical understanding and knowledge of dogs, training, and agility.**

   As your dog's teammate and teacher, you're in charge of the training process: The path to a happy and confident dog goes through you. The more you know and understand about dogs, training, and agility, the easier it will be to decide what to train (both what your ultimate goals are, and which steps you can take to get there) and how to train.

   All our training is based on the principles of clicker training. Derived from the laws of learning, clicker training provides us with a clear outline for how to train: focus on behavior, use positive reinforcement, and build behavior step by step. Foundation training thus becomes our top priority because that is where both you and your dog get to work on one aspect at a time, which enables you to gain success right from the start. Throughout this book we aim to provide you with an understanding of the underlying principles of clicker training and how to use them in your agility training. The more you learn about positive reinforcement training, the better equipped you'll be to design your own training program, reach your goals, and resolve any problems that might arise during the process.

All our training is also based on our conviction that everything in and around the training situation should happen in a manner that is appropriate to agility. No matter what you're training at the moment, you should always make sure to work with maximum focus and full intensity, and to follow your system of handling. We refer to these rules as Good Agility Practices. Along with the principles of clicker training, Good Agility Practices provide the framework for our training.

Accordingly, the first part of this book addresses the theoretical underpinnings that guide our training.

2. **You and your dog need to learn foundation skills.**

The most important part of practical agility training is laying a solid foundation. It's like building a house or learning arithmetic: The genius is in the details, which means that you need to start with the basics. Foundation skills form the core of agility, so you'll revisit them over and over throughout you agility career to refresh, maintain, and refine them.

What kind of foundation training are we talking about, then? For you, it entails acquiring the skills needed to train your dog so that you can get the behaviors you want, and establishing the basics of handling so that you can move around smoothly with your dog during and between exercises. Applying the principles of positive reinforcement, we employ TAGteach to help you learn these basic skills. (TAGteach is discussed further in Chapter 3.)

For your dog, foundation training is all about learning to love the game of agility. He'll learn to work with focus and intensity, offering behaviors and earning rewards. Some examples of foundation skills you might work on during your agility training are: reward procedures (like running to a treat bowl or playing tug); working on both your left and your right sides; going between, over, and under things; developing body awareness; and liking and creating noise and movement. You can practice foundation skills virtually anywhere, and the good news is that you need neither a lot of space nor any formal agility equipment to do it.

We know that the equipment on the agility course can be very tempting! To maximize happiness and confidence throughout the training process, however, it's best to split your training into smaller segments and work on one thing at a time, building a proper foundation. There's no denying that thorough work on the basics will delay your first try at running a full course, but proper grounding in the basics is the only way to ensure that both you and your dog will get it right from the start, avoid rehearsing bad habits, have fun, and be successful all through the process. Later, when you start working on handling maneuvers and teaching the different obstacles (and eventually begin running obstacle sequences and courses), you'll easily put the pieces together and reap the fruits of your excellent foundation work.

The second part of our book presents an array of basic skills that will give you and your dog the foundations necessary to play agility. Because you are the path to your dog's learning, we start with you. Once you have the methods and mechanics of training and handling under your belt, we move on to your dog.

From foundation skill to final obstacle performance with happiness and confidence

3. **You need to put it all together.**
   Soon enough the time will come for dog and handler to get onto the agility field and start working on handling maneuvers and obstacles. This is where all your foundation training really pays off!

   If you've built a strong foundation, you'll be amazed at how quickly your dog becomes proficient on the various pieces of agility equipment. Because you've already established your own training and handling mechanics, you'll be able to keep up with your dog's progress. Before you know it, you and your dog will be zooming through obstacle sequences—your dog performing each piece of equipment independently and you directing his path between the obstacles.

   The third part of the book shows you how to combine all those foundation skills to teach your dog to follow your handling and to perform the agility obstacles in sequences.

So let's get started! As you've probably gathered by now, principle is more important to us than method. Accordingly, we'll first discuss the laws of learning—the basic theories that govern all our training.

2

Learning theory

You and your dog are entering the world of agility together, as a team—and you, the team coach, are in charge of the training process. Having a solid base of knowledge regarding dogs and training will make it possible for you truly to become your dog's teacher, making informed decisions about how to train. When you focus on behavior and make use of the laws of learning, you make it possible for both you and your dog to excel!

Behavior and learning

Dogs possess many qualities that make them well suited for agility. But dogs aren't born with any knowledge of the sport of agility. *We* know that agility requires the dog to be fully focused on following the handler's directions while executing the various obstacles with precision at high speed, and ignoring whatever might be going on around him (smells, sounds, other dogs, and so on). *The dog,* however, doesn't know this.

This means that

1. Dogs that sniff, pee, or interact with other dogs on the agility course aren't doing anything bad or wrong—they're just being dogs.
2. Agility is something we have to *teach* our dogs. We know what the game is about and our dogs don't. Therefore the responsibility is all ours. It's up to us to create situations where our dogs learn to do the things we want them to do.

As your dog's teacher, it's your job to create clever learning situations.

Behavior is what matters

As dog trainers we need to focus on *behavior*—in other words, what the dog *does*—and let go of what we believe the dog thinks or knows. We can never say for sure what a dog "knows" or "understands." Frankly, it's not important; trying to figure out what's going on in your dog's mind won't help your training. Instead, focus on what a dog actually *does.* It's the behavior that matters!

Learning alters behavior

Whenever your dog's experiences lead to a lasting change in his behavior, he's *learned* something. Learning is a *change in an individual's behavior,* the change is due to *previous experiences,* and it is a *lasting change.* As dog trainers we're in the business of altering behavior. Our job is to set the environment so that our dogs learn the things we want them to learn. As your dog's teacher, your job is to create situations where the desired learning process is likely to take place. So whenever you wish to teach your dog anything, it pays to know the laws that govern learning. You need to understand both *classical conditioning* (the form of learning that governs *involuntary* responses) and *operant conditioning* (which explains how consequences govern *voluntary* behavior).

Classical conditioning

More than a century ago, Russian scientist Ivan Pavlov discovered that if he always rang a bell before feeding his dogs, eventually the dogs drooled whenever he rang that bell, whether or not they actually got fed. Pavlov had unintentionally stumbled upon a phenomenon that's now known as classical (or Pavlovian) conditioning.

Unconditioned responses

Your dog's body reacts in different ways to different events. When your dog eats, salivation increases. When he chases a bunny, his body secretes stress hormones. When he lolls on the sofa, his body releases oxytocin (the "peace-and-quiet" hormone). We often describe these reactions in terms of emotions: the dog becomes happy, aroused, angry, scared, hungry, calm, sleepy, and so on. The autonomic nervous system controls these bodily reactions; they happen spontaneously and are beyond the dog's control, hence involuntary. No thinking or decision making are involved.

The taste of dog food, the sight of the fleeing bunny, and the feeling of quiet on the couch are called *unconditioned stimuli,* and the spontaneous reactions (salivation, stress, and calmness) are called *unconditioned responses.* Things that by themselves do not trigger such spontaneous reactions in your dog's body (like a bell, a cabinet door, or an open field) are *neutral stimuli.*

Conditioned responses: learned expectations

If you consistently feed your dog the same way—for example, you always open the hall cabinet, fill up the bowl, and give it to your dog—your dog eventually will start drooling in anticipation as soon as you open the cabinet door. His body now expects food. Opening the door is no longer a neutral stimulus: it has become a *conditioned stimulus* that triggers a *conditioned response* (drooling). In the same way, the ringing bell came to predict food for Pavlov's dogs. This pairing of stimuli is called *classical conditioning* (or *respondent,* or *Pavlovian, conditioning*).

"The agility field is my happy place!"

Changing already learned expectations

Classically conditioned responses are involuntary: the dog doesn't choose to respond and therefore cannot make a conscious choice to respond differently. You can change such responses in the following two ways:

1. *Extinguish the body's expectations.* If you start opening the cabinet door without feeding your dog, eventually he'll stop drooling when you open the cabinet door. And if your doorbell rings randomly, without anyone ever coming through the front door, your dog will eventually cease to react to the doorbell.

2. *Create new pairings.* Imagine that every time the doorbell rings your dog charges and barks in anticipation of a wild greeting ceremony. If, instead, you shower your dog with treats when the doorbell rings, he'll start expecting food when he hears the doorbell. So instead of triggering excitement about a greeting ceremony, the doorbell might cause your dog to drool and expect food. You can use such *counterconditioning* to alter any classically conditioned response, and it often proves a faster and more effective approach than merely trying to extinguish the response.

What does this have to do with agility?

Classical conditioning occurs all the time and everywhere, whether you're aware of it or not. Involuntary responses to earlier associations happen—on the agility field and off. Because of the way classical conditioning works, it's important that you avoid using harsh training methods. If, for example, you yell at your dog or yank his leash (for whatever reason), you might get him to behave the way you want him to, but he also might associate your anger with you and/or with the training context. In a similar situation, then, his body might start reacting *as if* you're yelling at him (he'll become stressed, perhaps insecure, or overly excited) even when you aren't. In a similar fashion, a dog that gets frustrated when trying to learn the weave poles will start feeling uneasy as soon as he approaches them.

To make training as easy and pleasant as possible, you want your dog to have positive associations to you, to agility training, and to all the gadgets and obstacles we use in training. So use classical conditioning to your advantage. Make sure all aspects of your agility training trigger happy and pleasant responses in your dog's body.

Operant conditioning

If your actions have a good outcome, you'll probably do the same thing again. If the outcome is bad, you'll most likely try something else next time. This is a fact of life—and it's also the basis for the learning theory called *operant conditioning*, which involves *voluntary* behavior (muscle movements controlled by the cerebrum). The term "operant" refers to the individual being active and "operating" on his environment. Operant conditioning is what is at play whenever a creature through the consequences of its actions learns which behaviors to repeat and which to avoid.

What does operant conditioning have to do with agility training? Just about everything! Training entails building and strengthening certain behaviors and weakening others, and this is exactly what operant conditioning is all about.

Reinforcement, punishment, and extinction

The terms *reinforcement, punishment,* and *extinction* refer to the possible effects that a consequence can have on a behavior. These three concepts form the cornerstones of operant conditioning.

THE PREMACK PRINCIPLE

When Grandma told you, "*First* eat your vegetables, *then* you get dessert," she was employing the Premack Principle to get you to eat your peas. The Premack Principle states that a more likely behavior (here, eating dessert) can function as a reinforcer for a less likely behavior (here, eating vegetables) and thus strengthen the weaker behavior.

When training your dog you can apply the same principle by employing your dog's favorite behaviors (the more likely behaviors) as rewards. Just consider what your dog is most likely to do in each situation, and use that behavior as a reward for what you're trying to train. If your dog is keener on running than on standing still, "go" is perfect for reinforcing his stay at the start line. If your dog enjoys playing more than eating, use a game of tug as a reward after he has swallowed a treat. And if your dog is more eager to greet the approaching dog than to look at you, you can reinforce eye contact by then letting him go greet that dog.

"When I carry the little ball to her, yummy pieces of chicken appear. Great! I'd better bring her things more often." This is a good example of positive reinforcement.

1. If the consequence of a behavior increases the likelihood of that behavior being repeated, that consequence is said to reinforce the behavior. The behavior will be strengthened because it produces desired effects. Reinforcement is what builds and maintains behavior.

2. If the consequence of a behavior decreases the likelihood of that behavior being repeated, that consequence is said to punish that behavior. Note that punishment is a purely technical term here, describing a consequence that weakens the behavior in the future.

3. If a behavior produces no consequence at all, that behavior will decrease and eventually disappear. This process is called extinction.

This chart describes five possible consequences of a behavior. In operant conditioning lingo, when something is added, it's labeled *positive*. When something is removed, avoided, or missed out on, it's labeled *negative*.

	Positive	**Negative**
Reinforcement (the behavior increases)	**Positive reinforcement = Something is added, which increases the behavior** "Hooray, it paid off!" If your dog gets a cookie when he watches you, he'll watch you more. You *add* a cookie, which *increases* the likelihood of your dog looking at you in the future: *positive reinforcement*	**Negative reinforcement = Something is removed or avoided, which increases the behavior** "Ah, what relief!!" If your dog avoids getting a jolt in his sore back by jumping off the teeter before it hits the ground, he'll probably bail again. Your dog *avoids* pain, which *increases* the likelihood that he'll jump off the teeter in the future: *negative reinforcement*
Punishment (the behavior decreases)	**Positive punishment = Something is added, which decreases the behavior** "Ouch, oh, help!" If your dog gets stung by a bee while weaving, his weaving behavior will deteriorate. Bee sting is *added,* which *decreases* the likelihood of your dog weaving correctly in the future: *positive punishment*	**Negative punishment = Something is removed, which decreases the behavior** "Darn!" If your dog's foot target is briefly removed when he tries to mouth it, he'll be less likely to grab it with his mouth again. Your dog *misses* out on the opportunity to put his foot on the target and earn rewards, which *decreases* the likelihood that he'll grab the target with his mouth in the future: *negative punishment.*
Extinction (the behavior decreases)	**Extinction = No consequence at all, which eventually extinguishes the behavior** "Huh"? If your dog never gets a response from staring at your treat pocket, his "pocket-staring behavior" will eventually disappear. There is *no consequence,* which *decreases* the likelihood of your dog staring at your pocket in the future: *extinction*	

Dogs do what works: In this case a dog has learned that making a commotion gets rewards and is devilishly good fun.

Operant conditioning in your agility training

Just like classical conditioning, operant conditioning is in play all the time. Your dog is always learning, whether you intend for him to or not. In your training (and in your everyday life) you need to pay close attention to what you reinforce. Dogs are economical egocentrics; they do what pays off. They never do "bad" things to spite you; nor do they do "good" things to please you. They do what works.

In our training, we're biased toward working only with certain parts of the operant quadrant: We add and withhold/remove nice things. Thus we apply *positive reinforcement* (rewards) to the behaviors we wish to strengthen, and we apply *extinction* (nothing happens) and some *negative punishment* (the opportunity to be rewarded disappears) to behaviors we wish to weaken. This approach assures efficient learning without harmful side effects.

The better you are at applying the principles of learning in your agility training, the more efficient and easier training will be for both you and your dog. If you keep the basic principles of classical and operant conditioning in mind, you can teach your dog to do anything. Just make sure to set up the environment for good associations, reinforce the behaviors you want, and avoid reinforcing the behaviors you don't want. That's all there is to it! We discuss the finer details in the next chapter, which focuses on clicker training.

Clicker training: science-based dog training

Clicker training is derived from the laws of learning. By using positive reinforcement, you can teach any animal anything it is physically or mentally capable of doing. You just need the knowledge and the skills to do it!

The basics of clicker training

In the 1930s, B.F. Skinner's pioneering work with operant conditioning initiated a major shift in animal training toward techniques based on science and positive reinforcement. Skinner fought all his life for the use of positive reinforcement in training, for two reasons: Positive reinforcement makes training efficient and reliable, and it avoids the many downsides of aversive training (such as escape or avoidance reactions and aggression). Today Skinner's training ideas have been popularized as *clicker training*. When we say that we're clicker trainers, we simply mean that we apply scientific learning principles, that we use strategic positive reinforcement, and that we avoid aversives. We also use a marker (such as the clicker) when it aids our training—but the clicker isn't the important part; the principles are.

It's not just a yummy treat—it's a reinforcer! Here, the behavior being reinforced is "climbing onto an overturned chair."

Training by clicker training principles

Clicker training uses strategic positive reinforcement to show the dog which behaviors "work," providing him with clear feedback. For your dog, rewards are more than yummy treats; they are motivation for future behavior. From the *trainer's* perspective, it's all about "catching the dog being right": When you focus on what you want and reinforce what you want, you get the behaviors you want. From the dog's point of view, *he* controls the reinforcements. Whenever your dog earns a reward he also gathers a piece of information—"Aha! This behavior works." And he learns that by offering different behaviors, he can make rewards happen—"I'll try this because it has paid off before!"

Basically, clicker training boils down to this:
- Reward what's "right."
- Ignore what's "wrong."
- Create situations where your dog is likely to get it right.

Clicker training is the perfect way to train agility. Remember the goals of our agility training? *We picture a happy and confident dog that is focused, works intensely, embarks on any given task with great enthusiasm, and enjoys both the exercises and the rewards. We also picture a dog that can get to, perform, and leave each obstacle in the best possible fashion, and that follows your handling between the obstacles.* Clicker training is the ultimate way to train toward these goals. Happiness and confidence come with the extensive use of rewards, the absence of aversives, and setting up the dog for success. Accurate and independent obstacle performance comes from carefully building behavior step by step, exploiting your dog's own initiative, and using rewards as information.

We firmly advocate that you teach your dog to offer behaviors voluntarily—without any prompting from you. If your dog learns to offer behaviors on his own from the beginning, think how much easier it will be to teach him to perform agility obstacles on his own. Your training thus never aims merely to get your dog to "do" something. Instead, you create situations where your dog is likely to do whatever it is you want him to do and then you reward the behaviors you like. Clicker training will turn your dog into a "learning junkie," a dog who is eager to offer behaviors and to experiment to get you to reward.

To make training efficient and successful, we
- split behaviors into tiny pieces and work on one little part at a time.
- keep training sessions short and focused.
- work with the dog's own initiative.
- reinforce desired behaviors and ignore unwanted responses.
- raise the level of difficulty bit by bit, in step with the dog's progress.
- strive to find as many opportunities as possible to reward the dog.
- use rewards both for building new behaviors and for maintaining established ones.
- often use a marker (the sound of a clicker, for example) to inform the dog, "That's right; that behavior produces a reward."

Aversives are banned. In a positive reinforcement program there simply is no need for aversives. When you're proactive instead of reactive and when you build behavior in small-enough steps, corrections become unnecessary. You, the trainer, are responsible for the results, and if something goes wrong, there's no point in blaming your dog. Your dog will get all the information he needs from the contrast between reinforcement and no reinforcement.

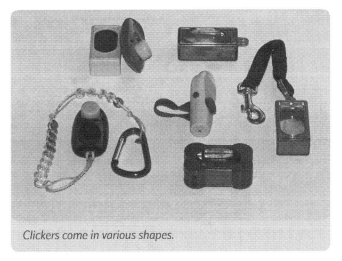

Clickers come in various shapes.

The marker signal

A marker signal (such as a clicker, or some other specific stimulus) is a fantastic training tool that helps you reinforce your dog as he performs the behavior you want. Like a camera, the marker takes a snapshot of a specific response. Your dog will learn that the marker means "that response just earned you a reward." The marker isn't the reward per se; it precedes the actual reward but tells the dog precisely which behavior is working, and should always be followed by a tangible reward, such as a treat or a toy.

We often tell our students that if they had a device like a doggie backpack with a tube going directly to the dog's mouth, or a ball-throwing device on the dog's back, those would be the perfect setups to deliver reinforcement at exactly the right time. But since we don't have such devices (and since they probably wouldn't be precise enough anyway), we use the marker to bridge the gap between the behavior and the tangible reward.

We don't always use a marker—sometimes delivering the reward on its own works just fine. But a marker is invaluable in many situations when you're aiming to reinforce a specific response; while shaping a new behavior, for example, or problem solving (using your marker to pinpoint exactly the response you wish to strengthen)

When it comes to pinpointing specific responses, the clicker is invaluable.

You'll soon notice that your dog gets excited when he hears the marker. This is classical conditioning at work; the marker is paired with treats or toys, and the association triggers an involuntary pleasant response. So the marker will have double value: It always triggers a happy response, and it's always followed by a "real" reward.

There are several reasons why a clicker makes an excellent marker:

- Your dog can easily distinguish the click from other sounds in the environment.
- The clicker sounds the same every time so it's easily recognizable.
- The click is black and white: either there's a click or there isn't. No gray areas!
- With some practice you'll be able to click with great precision, marking at exactly the right moment.

That said, it's also a good idea to condition a special word (a short "yes," for example) as a verbal marker for the times when you want to mark a specific response but don't have a clicker handy or don't have a hand free to hold a clicker. In theory, the verbal marker functions in the exact same way as the clicker. Practically, the clicker is more precise and more unambiguous and thus works better.

Note that there's a difference between a verbal marker and verbal praise. A verbal *marker* signals your dog "Correct. Reward is coming." Verbal *praise*, if you choose to use it, is part of your reward procedure, which follows the marker signal. Your marker signal should remain precise and consistent, but your praise can be as vigorous and as varied as you like.

Rewarding without marking

Simply rewarding (without marking first) plays a big role in agility training. Like a click, a well-timed reward reinforces behavior; however, it tends to be more global (it reinforces chunks of behavior rather than tiny responses) than a click. In that sense, rewarding without marking is perfect for reinforcing your dog's attending to your handling, running at top speed, or completing a sequence.

Here the remote reward is waiting for the dog at the end of the sequence

Consider these instances where we usually don't use a marker:

- When rewarding an entire obstacle performance (for example, reinforcing a correct weave pole performance with a tug toy as the dog leaves the weaves).
- When rewarding with a specific cue, such as the release cue at the start line or at the table. Here the cue itself is the reward because the dog gets to dash off.
- When using remote rewards. We often use treats and toys set at a distance, with the double function of giving the dog a direction to work in and a reward to run to. We then want the dog to keep going to his reward as soon as his task is completed.
- When rewarding while handling sequences. Agility is all about the flow between responding to handling and performing obstacles in a series of linked behaviors called a chain. Rewards can appear at any point during the handling sequence and tend to reinforce all the behaviors (links) in that chain.

Five keys to successful clicker training

There are five key factors that guide successful training:

1. **Criteria.** Decide exactly which response you're going to reinforce. Since each reward provides information for your dog, it's vital that you establish clear criteria. If you're not sure which behavior you're looking for or which aspect or criterion you should focus on first, most likely you'll reward various behaviors and confuse your dog. Setting criteria is a fine art: You should set the criteria low (easy) enough for your dog to be able to succeed quickly, and raise criteria according to your dog's progress.

2. **Timing.** Make sure you reward at the exact right moment, while your dog is doing whatever it is you want to reinforce. You either have to deliver your reward with exquisite timing, or use your marker to pinpoint the correct response. Your timing is crucial: If you reward too early or too late, your dog will probably be doing something other than what you intended to reinforce. You'll then be rewarding (thus strengthening) the wrong behavior instead.

3. **Rate of reinforcement.** Reward often! Set up for success, so that your dog manages to meet criteria and get reinforced most of the time, and make sure you reward *every* time your dog gets it right. Your dog learns from reinforcement, so the more rewards you can give your dog, the more information he'll get, and the faster he'll learn. Maintaining a high rate of reinforcement also keeps your dog's focus and reduces the risk of his rehearsing "garbage" behaviors. If your dog makes a lot of mistakes (which means that your rate of reinforcement drops), the exercise is obviously too difficult and needs to be broken down into smaller steps.

4. **Quality of reward.** Use rewards that your dog truly values. Anything your dog loves and is willing to work for can function as a reinforcer, but treats and toys generally are the most practical to use since you control them and can vary them infinitely to

suit every aspect of your agility training. You can tell by your dog's behavior if the reward is good enough. Remember: If the behavior doesn't increase, it hasn't been reinforced. Think of rewards as paychecks: Aren't you more willing to keep working if you get properly paid?

5. **Placement of reward.** Be aware of *where* you deliver the reinforcer. As a general rule for all your agility training, deliver the reward in the direction you want your dog's nose to point. Your placement of the reward will further enhance the position or direction you want your dog to work toward (for example, you can reinforce running ahead by throwing a ball in the direction your dog is heading). In our agility training, we usually make rewards turn up in accordance with our handling. That way your dog will automatically learn that by following your handling *and* by offering the behavior you're looking for, he'll get great rewards.

Reinforcers

In a training regime built on positive reinforcement, the reinforcers (the rewards) are your most important training tool. Reinforcement is what drives behavior, which is why you need rewards both when building new behaviors and when maintaining and refining old behaviors. Attractive stuff appearing—or not appearing/disappearing—is what clicker training is all about!

Anything your dog wants—and is willing to put some effort into getting—can function as a reward. This goes for both physical things and desirable events. Rewards for agility training fall into three major categories:

1. Various treats and toys (often the most obvious and useful rewards)
2. Social interaction and play, mostly in combination with treats and toys
3. The opportunity to perform desired behaviors

Even things you may normally think of as distractions have built-in reward potential: As long as your dog wants it, it can function as a reward. You just have to gain control over all the potential rewards so that they can be delivered or withheld as you see fit.

Treats and toys are versatile rewards that can be delivered whenever, wherever, and however you see fit.

Treats and toys

Treats and toys are your most useful rewards. First of all, they are (or will be, after some work) valuable to your dog. Second, you control where and how they appear. Third, you can vary them infinitely so you can always find a reward that suits your training purposes.

The more your dog wants all kinds of rewards, the easier it will be to train him. That means it's worth every effort to find the perfect treats and toys and to develop exciting reward procedures.

Some dogs are picky, challenging both your creativity and your training skills, but you can always increase a dog's interest in toys or treats. Be imaginative and try to figure out what your dog loves. If your dog likes food treats but isn't really into toys, you can disguise a tasty treat so that it can function as a toy—perhaps a chicken breast tied into an old sock, or one of the commercially available pockets or toys (usually with a Velcro closing) that allow you to stuff treats inside.

Furthermore, using the Premack Principle (discussed in Chapter 2, page 12), you can *teach* your dog to enjoy treats or toys he at first shows little interest in. If your dog likes footballs much better than treats, you can use "football playing" as a reward for "treat eating" and thus increase your dog's interest in treats. If your dog is food crazy, you can teach him to play tug—just use yummy treats to reward the tiniest tendency to tug. That way you can build reward procedures just as you build any other behavior.

Invest yourself in the game and have fun!

WHAT'S FUN?

Remember that *your dog* decides what is rewarding, so be aware of how your dog reacts to your interactions. Many dogs aren't that crazy about "Good dog" praise or sweet-talking, and some seem wary or insecure if a handler tries to pat and cuddle them during training or suddenly starts clapping, cheering, and jumping around. If your dog lowers his head, pulls his ears back, and licks or gasps, these are signs that he isn't having fun, so observe your dog closely. If you and your dog are not accustomed to playing with each other, it might take some getting used to—for both of you—but it's worth the effort. Think back to your dog's puppy days, watch how dogs play with each other, and experiment.

Social interaction and play

Social interaction can be whatever you and your dog find amusing: invitations to play (such as hunching, creeping, play bows, and silent glances followed by sudden movement), chasing each other, rolling around in the grass together, or getting a good back rub. By adding treats and toys to the game, the possible variations become endless.

Social interaction and play, however, aren't the best choice for reinforcing specific responses in your training. Treats and toys are much handier when you wish to reward frequently and quickly, or when you need to place a reward in a specific spot.

So our suggestion is that whenever there's a specific behavior you wish to reinforce, primarily use toys or treats to get the precision you want with your reward. Social interaction and play is best used similarly to the way you use praise—as an extra spice to your reward, something that happens after you've marked and/or delivered your reward with precision.

Opportunity to perform desirable behaviors

Remember Premack? The Premack Principle holds that the opportunity to perform a desired behavior will reinforce the performance of a less-preferred behavior. In our agility training we explicitly make use of this principle when training start-line stays; first you teach your dog to love exploding away on your start cue, and then you can use that magic start cue to reward him for standing still. Since your dog really wants to hear that start cue, he'll quickly learn that he can make you say it by staying perfectly still. Premack is also at play in all rewards: the reward procedure (playing, eating, and so on) is a "desired behavior," working to reinforce other behaviors.

As your dog grows to love the game of agility, you might start believing that the opportunity to keep working is all the reward your dog needs. And, in the spirit of Premack, to keep working could function very well as a reward. There's one major complication though: If the opportunity to keep working becomes the dog's most precious reward, then that opportunity would have to be removed whenever the dog does something undesirable. Since we never ever want you to withdraw your attention and your handling cues from your dog during training and leave him in limbo, we don't stop a dog from working if he makes a mistake. Instead, we give him precise feedback about which behavior is correct by adding or withholding the clicks and treat and toy rewards.

3. Specific reinforcement

2. Good Agility Practices

1. Agility is always safe and fun

The tiered cake illustrates how we work: We reward behaviors we want and ignore behaviors we don't want, while always sticking to Good Agility Practices and making sure the agility training throughout is a pleasant experience.

Bottom tier = Pavlov: Only nice things happen around agility training, which classically conditions your dog to enjoy all aspects of training.

Middle tier = Good Agility Practices: By maintaining focus and intensity, and sticking to your handling system, you keep your dog busy and give him a direction to work in, which, in turn, strengthens his focus, intensity, and ability to follow your handling.

Top layer = distinct reinforcement of specific behaviors: The clicker, treat and toy rewards, and the start line/contact release cue explicitly reinforce particular behaviors.

Rewards as distractions and distractions as rewards

All potential rewards are also potential distractions, since anything your dog wants can easily draw his attention from the task at hand. In the same fashion, any distraction is also a potential reward—and the more the dog wants it, the more powerful a reward it is.

We love to see a dog that is pestering his owner to get whatever it is he wants, jumping around and trying to steal out of pockets. A dog that really wants something is far easier to train than one that isn't excited by the available rewards—as long as you maintain control of those rewards. Let the dog figure out that stealing *doesn't* work but that offering you a desired behavior *does* work. For example, if your dog glances up at you to see why trying to pry the meatball out of your pocket isn't working, right there you have a rewardable moment! Never mind *why* he looked at you; the point is that he chose to look away from the meatball, and that is a great start. In the same spirit, if your dog gets so eager that he nips your finger as he goes for his treat, the treat just magically disappears. The same goes if he jumps up and tries to steal the toy out of your pocket; just hide the toy or hold on to it so he can't get it. He'll learn that he can take toys only when you say so; they simply aren't available at other times.

Marvelous smells on the ground, playing dogs, squirrels, or bitches in heat all have the potential for sabotaging your training. But if they are that attractive to your dog, they are also great reward material! Use the Premack Principle to take control, and make your dog believe that doing what *you* want is his best chance of getting access to what *he* wants. Bitches in heat or squirrels, of course, aren't the most practical rewards in your agility training, but by using distractions as rewards for nice behavior in other situations you'll turn your enemies into your best friends. If your dog gets into a system in his everyday life where he actively works with you to get a chance to get to whatever-it-is, there's a much better chance that he'll stay focused when training agility as well. Then you can use a brief dash at those squirrels as an occasional special reward if you like.

How to get behavior

So how do you find—or get—the behaviors you wish to reinforce? As clicker trainers, we never force or intimidate our dogs to do things. Neither do we nag, beg, or bribe. Instead we plan our training so that we can begin with a very small, simple response and gradually build from there. We set up clever training situations where the dog is likely to get it right, we constantly look for reinforceable responses, and we reward the behaviors we want to see more of.

Basically, a clicker training session boils down to just four steps:
1. Decide which behavior you're looking for.
2. Arrange a situation where the behavior is likely to occur.
3. Mark the desired behavior as it happens. (This step is optional but often preferred.)
4. Reward.

Your most important job as a trainer is to provide consequences to what your dog does so that he learns which behaviors are most profitable. Reinforcing a behavior means that it becomes stronger in the future, giving you something to build on—it doesn't necessarily mean that you'll see major progress right away. Working with small pieces of a behavior, reinforcing the tiniest tendencies toward the desired goal, can be counterintuitive for a time-fixated, results-oriented human being, whose first impulse often is to use any means available to get the dog to do stuff. But truly teaching your dog to do the little things and building step by step—instead of just getting him to do the big things right away—is a sure route to success and forms a cornerstone in our training program.

MAKING THE DOG DO SOMETHING, OR TEACHING HIM TO DO IT

Notice the difference between *making* your dog do something, and *teaching* him to do it. For example, if you need your dog to be on a table, you can just put him there (lift him up, lure him with a cookie, whatever, as long as he's comfortable with it). If you want to teach him to jump up on the table when you ask him to, however, you're looking for a learning process to take place. Remember the definition of learning: It's a lasting change in the behavior, due to previous experience. Thus you need to train your dog. You need to consider what your goal is, how to break down the training into small pieces, which method to use to get the behavior, what your criteria should be, if you're going to use a marker, what to use as a reward, where to place the reward, how to fade any helping aids, and so on.

Different ways to get behavior

There are as many ways to get behaviors as there are trainers to think them up! Capturing, free shaping, targeting, luring/prompting, and social facilitation are some main strategies.

Capturing: By simply watching your dog and reinforcing the behaviors you like, you can *capture* behaviors as they occur. Capturing is an excellent training tool that enables you to reinforce what your dog just happens to do. We strongly recommend that you stay alert and reward good behaviors whenever they happen. If your dog sits quietly beside you at ringside while someone else is running agility, for example, catch the moment and reward it. Just put on the right glasses, and you'll find countless rewardable moments. Remember that these opportunities pop up even if you're training something else: If you're working on your dog's jumping skills, for example, and he offers superb focus in face of some distraction, make sure to reward his attention.

Most agility behaviors, however, are rather complex and require a more elaborate approach. You need to break down the behaviors and train one small step at a time, successively progressing toward your goal. Such an approach is called *shaping,* since you shape the dog's behavior toward a desired goal.

Free shaping: When *free shaping* you work totally hands-off, forming new behaviors by reinforcing the tiniest increments of the desired behavior and building it from there. The timing and placement of the rewards will guide your dog through the shaping process. Free shaping teaches *you* a lot about training and will greatly improve your training skills, and it teaches *your dog* to be creative and to actively offer behaviors. The more clicker-savvy you and your dog become, the faster the shaping process will proceed.

The following pointers will help you get the most out of the free-shaping process:
- Look for the tiniest possible response that might eventually lead to the goal behavior.
- Understand that the response you're looking for must be within your dog's present repertoire—the starting point must be something that your dog already does.
- Markers provide information to your dog, so mark and reward every time you see the desired response.
- Gradually ask for more by rewarding only the best attempts, advancing step by step toward the goal behavior.
- Don't "help" or assist your dog in any way. Let your dog offer behaviors voluntarily, figuring it out for himself.
- Keep in mind the keys to successful training: criteria; timing; and rate, quality, and placement of reward.

A free-shaping exercise, using the procedure we call Aim for it.

Left: Choose a good starting point quite close to the object in question.
Center left: Click for nose pointing in the correct direction—toward the object.
Center right: Reward toward the object.
Right: Shape toward your final goal—in this case, all four feet on top of the object.

In our agility training, we use a specific free-shaping procedure to teach the dog to aim at something and continue to work in that direction. We call this procedure *Aim for it* (presented in detail in "Two strategies to get behavior," page 129). It involves giving your dog a perfect starting position, immediately rewarding him for pointing his nose in the right direction, and delivering the reward in front of your dog. It all goes very fast (nose pointing forward–click–reward ahead of dog–nose pointing forward–click, and so on). Each reward enhances your dog's aiming ahead while it simultaneously gives him a perfect starting position from which to continue working.

Targets come into use in our contact training.

Targeting: You can also use a *target* as a tool in shaping behavior. A target is an object you teach your dog to move toward and touch—for example, a plastic lid to put his paw on, or the palm of your hand to press his nose against. You can then place your target wherever you want your dog to go and eventually fade it away (remove it in successive stages).

In our agility training we use targets for teaching the dog where to place his paws on the contact obstacles (the A-frame, dogwalk, and teeter).

Luring and prompting: Another way of getting behavior is to use treats, toys, body language, and gestures to *lure* or *prompt* your dog to perform a desired behavior. We generally advocate against lures, since they often make for slow and inefficient learning. In particular, we don't teach equipment by letting the dog follow a treat in your hand, although that's how many people do it. In our experience, that simply isn't the best path to a happy and confident dog that works independently and performs with flow, speed, and precision.

We do use lures in specific situations, however. One example is the procedure we call *Race to reward* (presented in detail in "Two strategies to get behavior," page 142). In short, you begin by teaching your dog to race to a treat or toy that is set at a distance and

Running between two buckets toward a treat bowl.

eventually add tasks for your dog to do (for example, performing an obstacle) on his way to the reward. The remote reward then gives your dog a direction to work toward—in other words, it lures or prompts the direction—but to actually get the reward, the dog has to perform something on his way toward it.

Social facilitation: Social facilitation (what happens when your dog notices how you, other people, or other dogs react to the environment) also affects your dog's behavior. If you look intently at an object, for example, your dog will notice it and get interested. By looking wherever you want your dog to focus, then, you can redirect his attention. Social facilitation can work against you as well. For example, if you're in the habit of looking at things that happen around you while you're training, your dog will learn to do the same and easily become distracted.

In agility training, we use social facilitation to affect the dog's attitude. By remaining focused and working intensively, and by keeping a happy and positive attitude throughout training, your focus and your joyous spirit will rub off on your dog!

THE LURE OF LURING

Luring with a treat in your hand seems like an easy way to get a behavior, but that is deceptive. Since your dog follows the lure, he doesn't focus on what he's doing, so he's not learning a specific behavior. Making the transition from lured to independent behavior thus often is a painstaking process. Shaping a behavior is usually much more efficient even though it might seem slower at the start. Another major drawback with lures is that they tend to reinforce passivity: Whatever your dog does when you bring out the treat will be reinforced (standing still, sniffing in the grass, or whatever). On top of that, he eventually gets the reward for following the lure, rather than for thinking and acting on his own. If you do choose to lure a behavior, remember that the lure is merely an aid. Rewarding the correct response is what changes the dog's behavior.

When and how to advance

How do you know when and how to move on in your training? What you need to do is to evaluate whether the criteria you've set are being met most of the time: Does your dog mostly succeed? As a rule of thumb, if you're reinforcing your dog for at least 80 percent of his attempts for any given exercise, then it's time to move on.

As you ask for more of your dog, remember:
- Constantly advancing in baby steps is the best way to go.
- When you increase the difficulty in one area, make it simpler in others.
- Watch your dog's behavior! As long as the behavior is progressing in the way you want, you're on the right track. If it isn't, you need to make some changes.

You want to avoid both taking big jumps forward and getting stuck. Trying to progress too fast always causes a backlash and may confuse your dog and undermine his confidence; progressing too slowly will inhibit your dog's learning and cement the present level of performance. There are several aspects to upping the ante, which we describe briefly here. We'll give you detailed descriptions about how to advance when we go through different skills in Part II, *Foundation skills for you and your dog* and Part III, *Putting it all together*.

Raise criteria

The most obvious way to up the ante is to ask for more behavior. In a shaping process, where you alter your dog's behavior step by step, raising criteria simply means that you stop reinforcing the weakest or poorest responses and keep rewarding the best responses, constantly expecting your dog to do a little bit more. That way, the behavior will improve step by step. Raising criteria might also mean making the exercise more difficult to negotiate, for example by using a thinner or wobblier log to balance on or by elevating a jump bar.

Fade your aids

If you've used any targets, prompts, lures, or other helping aids, you eventually have to get rid of them or your dog will come to rely on them to perform the behavior. Note that once the aid is gone, your dog might view the exercise as completely different, so reward him lavishly for all attempts in the right direction. It's often easiest to fade aids gradually, making them less and less noticeable. Another possibility is to remove the aid "cold" and rely on your shaping skill and well-timed rewards to keep the behavior going.

Continually introduce new variations in your training. Here, a sweater alters the look of the jump.

Add variations and distractions

Your dog needs to learn that the behavior works (earns rewards) in different contexts and situations. In other words, gradually he needs to *generalize* the behavior. For example, if your dog has learned to start from your left side and dive under a kitchen chair, that doesn't guarantee that he'll go under other objects in other situations. He needs to learn that going under things works *even if* he starts from your right side, *even if* it's a park bench to go under instead of the chair, *even if* there's another dog close by, *even if* it's raining, and so on. As a rule, dogs don't generalize well, so it's a good idea to train the behavior in all the contexts where you want it to work. On the other hand, once your dog starts to generalize his behavior in many different situations, his performance will become really solid. Humans' fondness for doing things the same way all the time makes generalization a bit of a challenge for you as well. It helps to begin varying things just slightly early on in training: put on sunglasses, change your posture, wiggle your fingers, train in another room. The more tiny variations and distractions you work through, the stronger the behavior will get.

Add duration to the behavior

If you want to lengthen the period that your dog performs a behavior (for example, keeping eye contact, or holding on to a toy, or standing perfectly still at the start line), you need to gradually increase the time. The best way to train duration is to vary how much time elapses before you reinforce your dog. First, wait a fraction of a second; if he's still offering the behavior, reward! Then increase the period to half a second, one second, back to a fraction of a second, up to two seconds, and so on. If you ping-pong up and down with the time this way, your dog never knows when the reward will come but will learn that it *will* come sometime.

Add distance to the behavior

You want your dog to run ahead to the tunnel, sprint over the entire dogwalk to the contact zone, and so on. Wait until the behavior that you're working on is really strong (for example, your dog shoots through the tunnel as soon as he gets the opportunity), and then start stretching the distance inch by inch. If you add distance too soon, the behavior will deteriorate. If the behavior is rock solid at a short distance, adding distance will be a cinch.

Vary the reward ratio

If you want your dog to be able to perform a behavior several times in a row (without any reward in between), you need to vary the reward ratio. When you start training a new behavior, you reward *every* successful attempt. When the behavior is strong and consistent, consider letting your dog perform it two times in a row for one reward. After some training you can vary how many times your dog needs to perform the behavior before you reinforce. This is known as a *variable ratio* of reinforcement. For example, when you have taught your dog to jump through a tire and he happily does so as soon as he gets the chance, you might let him jump through two or three tires (or the same tire two or three times) for one reward.

VERBAL CUES IN OUR AGILITY TRAINING

In our agility training, we use mostly nonverbal handling cues and environmental cues. The handler's direction will tell the dog where to go, and the equipment itself tells the dog what to do (to jump over jump bars, to nail the weave entry and slalom through the poles, and so on). Therefore there is no need for verbal cues most of the time. The only verbal cue we're really particular about training is the start cue that releases your dog from the start line, from the contact zones, and from the table.

That doesn't mean you should never add any verbal cues. If you want to, you can name both obstacles and other behaviors, for example, to help your dog discriminate between two adjacent obstacles (like a tunnel under a dogwalk), or to enhance your handling (like a "go on" cue for just racing straight ahead). But we always make sure the dog knows the behavior solidly first, before adding any cue.

Notice, though, that your dog has to be able to keep offering behaviors without verbal cues. Even if you choose to add a verbal cue (saying "weave," for example), you'll still want your dog to be able to offer weaving when you're quiet.

"Name" the behavior

In much of our agility training we actually don't name behaviors at all. The handler's direction and the nature of the equipment tell the dog all he needs to know. For instance, your facing the tire will tell the dog both where to go (tire) and what to do (jump through).

If you wish to name a behavior, wait until the behavior is as good and as strong as you want it to be. Then add a cue just as the dog is about to perform the behavior. After some repetitions, the dog will connect the cue to the behavior. For example, when teaching your dog to start on cue (a verbal cue you *do* need), you set up a situation where you're sure that your dog will explode ahead, and then you say your "go" cue just as your dog starts off. After a while, your dog will explode away whenever he hears the "go" cue.

Humans are a verbal species that want to tell our dogs what to do, so trainers are often too eager to add verbal cues. But in dog training, your words (or even worse, your nagging) are of no help to your dog while he's trying to figure out what he needs to do. Let the rewards do the talking so your dog can learn the behavior completely and reliably. If you add the verbal cue too early, it will only frustrate your dog or accidentally name the wrong (or incomplete) behavior.

DISCRIMINATION, CUES, AND STIMULUS CONTROL

Since you obviously don't want your dog to offer every behavior he knows in every possible situation, you need to teach him when to perform which behavior. This is the realm of *discrimination, cues,* and *stimulus control.*

Discrimination is the process where the dog learns that a behavior works if, and *only if,* certain conditions are met, as opposed to generalization, where the dog learns to perform a behavior *even if* contexts change. Dogs are excellent discriminators—they always try to use the context as a clue to whether a behavior is worth attempting.

A *cue* is a stimulus that tells the dog when a specific behavior is going to work. Cues can be verbal, hand signals, other examples of body language, flashing lights—in short, anything the dog can notice. For example, your saying "go" will become a cue for your dog to explode away from a start line or a contact. Your pointing your shoulders in the direction of a piece of equipment will cue your dog to take that piece of equipment. And the nature of the equipment will be an environmental cue for your dog to perform a specific behavior at that piece of equipment (for example, jump *over* bars but run *through* tunnels). After the cue, the cued behavior—and only that behavior—stands a chance to get reinforced. Note: A cue is not a command or an order; it's simply a stimulus signaling that offering a specific behavior may earn a reward.

When the behavior always happens after a specific cue, and only after that cue, we say we have *stimulus control.* Stimulus control involves both discrimination (starting only pays off after the start cue—not after other cues, and no other behaviors pay off after that cue) and generalization (the dog always starts on the start cue, even if the context differs).

Form a behavior chain

One final way to advance is to put well-trained behaviors together in a chain: a sequence of behaviors where the "real," tangible reward happens only at the end. Agility is all about chains—on the agility course your dog will perform long strings of behaviors, seamlessly linked together. And since no chain is stronger than its weakest link, you have to make sure that you've trained each little part really well using positive reinforcement.

When building a chain it's often wise to start at the end and add one previous behavior at a time, so that the dog always is working toward a well-known behavior. This practice is known as *back-chaining.* In our agility training we constantly employ back-chaining, so you'll get countless examples of this process throughout the book. One example is the way we teach start lines, a two-part chain consisting of the stay behavior and the start behavior: First teach the dog to start on cue, and then teach him that he has to freeze in a stay in order to get that precious start cue so he can dash off the start line.

What to do when mistakes happen

Mistakes are a natural and unavoidable part of training—and of learning. You'll make some, and your dog will make some. These mistakes are valuable information, so don't cringe when they happen. Welcome them, try to figure out why they're happening, and alter your training program accordingly.

Whenever your dog does something other than what you were hoping for (for instance, knocking a bar, running by the A-frame, or losing his focus), the best you can do is to ignore the mistake, keep working, and make sure to reward when your dog gets it right.

- Ignore the behaviors you do not want.
- Keep working if a mistake happens.
- Increase the rate of reinforcement for the behaviors you *do* want.

Most people find it hard not to react when a mistake happens, but it's pointless to tell your dog that he did something "wrong." The mistake has already happened, you can't erase it, and the best solution usually is to ignore it (so it has no consequence). So just try to keep working! Don't stop short and try to "fix" the mistake, don't fall apart like a bad soufflé, don't resort to aversives—simply withhold the reward, move on, and find something else to reinforce. If you have to start over, do so as smoothly as possible.

The reward appearing or not appearing is the most vital information.

Remember, training is about *building* behavior by reinforcing it. The better you are at focusing on rewarding the behaviors you want (instead of agonizing over how to get rid of behaviors you don't want), the more successful you'll be in your training.

In general, your agility training should be quite smooth and error-free. If there are a lot of unwanted behaviors and thus your rate of reinforcement drops, you need to change something. Maybe the exercise is too complex, maybe you have set your criteria too high, maybe your timing is off, maybe your rewards are not valuable enough, and maybe there are too many distractions. If you can keep your rate of reinforcement high, your dog will be right-right-right, and he'll not have time for undesired behaviors.

Good management

Many potentially undesirable behaviors (such as greeting other dogs) are very reinforcing in themselves. Unwanted behaviors being reinforced is something you want to avoid, and steering clear of this trap is one of the most challenging parts of training. The key to solving this dilemma is good management: be proactive and control the environment.

Set up for success by planning your training sessions so that undesired behaviors don't happen. Keep the leash on, move farther away from distractions, train in shorter sessions with better rewards—do whatever you need to increase the likelihood of success. Keep in mind that it's no big deal if a mistake happens. Carry on training if possible, otherwise take a break and start over later. Remember that to have nice things happen near agility is always better than to have bad things happen near agility—even if some undesired behaviors accidentally get reinforced in the process. You'll learn to plan differently the next time. *You* are learning all the time, too. If you're well prepared and handle your dog and your training with care and thoughtfulness, both "ordinary" unwanted behaviors and emergencies are less likely to happen. Be proactive, not reactive.

THE TROUBLE WITH AVERSIVES

When we refer to "aversives" we are referring to all levels of unpleasant events added to training—anything from electric shocks to scruff grabs to verbal "ah-ahs." Trainers who use aversives as a consequence of an undesired behavior are working within a negative reinforcement/positive punishment regime. If the dog performs the desired behavior, he avoids the aversive (negative reinforcement). If he performs an undesired behavior, the trainer adds the aversive (positive punishment). Grabbing the dog and putting him back in place if he breaks at the start line, or giving a displeased "ah-ah" when he knocks a bar, are two examples of using aversives to correct undesired behaviors. Aversives can also be used to produce a desired behavior. For example, an "ah-ah" might cause the dog to slow down a bit before a difficult weave entry. Some call this "correction-based" training.

As a trainer, you always have a choice. You can choose to work only with reward-based strategies or you can choose to use aversives to some degree. Just don't let anyone tell you that you must use aversives, because that simply isn't true!

So why not use both, then, someone might ask. Why not practice "balanced" training where you mainly work with rewards but where you also apply some corrections if the dog really does something wrong—or to produce a behavior you want? We don't use aversives for the following reasons:

- Aversives sabotage your training by building in tension and stress and by limiting the dog's freedom to experiment (the opposite of what you're trying to accomplish by clicker training your dog).
- When reward-oriented trainers use even minor aversives, it signals that their reinforcement regimen isn't good enough. If you're contemplating applying an aversive, think through what is lacking in your training. Are you rewarding the correct responses often enough? Skimping on the rewards is probably the most common mistake. Is the situation too difficult for your dog (or for you)? Did you ask for too much too fast? Should you have taken a break several minutes ago? Are the rewards you're offering not good enough? Did you fail to control other potential reinforcers? Is your dog physically and mentally fit to do what you're asking of him?
- The opposite of adding a reward is withholding a reward—not adding an aversive. In reward-based training, withholding the reward tells your dog that he made a bad decision. Your dog will either work to get a reward, or work to avoid an aversive—he can't do both at the same time. Applying an aversive switches the dog's focus from "How can I get the good stuff?" to "How can I avoid the bad stuff?" Stick to adding and removing nice things, and you'll enable your dog to focus all his energy on how to get those rewards.
- Remember Pavlov! Whenever you use aversives in your training, you risk that your dog will make a negative association with you or some aspect of training (classical conditioning). Classical conditioning plays a powerful role in producing frustrated, stressed-out, insecure, or shut-down dogs. Even if you try to override the occasional aversive with lots of rewards, you still take the risk that your dog will make undesired associations.
- Agility is supposed to be fun for both you and your dog. It's just a game. If you feel the need to apply aversives in your training, maybe you're losing perspective. Even if your dog is so eager to work that he can "handle" being treated harshly, that's beside the point.

So if you ever feel the need to add some kind of aversive, consider instead how you can reinforce the times your dog actually gets it right, thus creating that contrast between rewarded responses ("Yes, that was right") and non-rewarded responses ("Nope, that wasn't it").

TAGteach: Clicker training for people

The principles of clicker training make for fun and efficient dog training. But your dog isn't the only one who is learning—you, the human half of the team, are constantly learning as well.

Since we're absolutely convinced about the brilliance of the clicker training approach, naturally we want to apply the same principles to humans.

TAGteach is clicker training for people. The abbreviation "TAG" stands for Teaching with Acoustical Guidance, a method that makes it possible to train yourself (or any other human being) by adhering to the same clever principles as you do when you clicker train your dog.

A TAGTEACH GLOSSARY

TAG   Teaching with Acoustical Guidance

tag point   Your criterion

tagger   Your marking device, for example, a clicker

TAG talk   Phrasing instructions in a positive and clear manner when teaching yourself and others

Learn more about TAGteach at www.tagteach.com.

- The key elements of TAGteach are essentially the same as in clicker training: You focus on behavior. First you define your goal, then you break it down into manageable pieces, known as tag points. When training, you focus on a single tag point at a time. An example: "The tag point is: Give treat with hand nearest to the dog."
- You use a marker (called a "tagger," for example a clicker) to indicate precisely when the tag point is met. If the tag point is "give treat with hand nearest to the dog," for example, a friend can stand beside you during one or two of your dog training sessions and "tag" you (mark) every time you give a treat with the correct hand.
- You reinforce the correct response. The nice feeling of getting it right is often reinforcing enough, but real rewards work even better—for example, 20 tags equals a small bar of chocolate.
- Just as with your dog, you build your behavior step by step, gradually moving on to more complex tasks as your skills increase.
- You avoid the use of aversives. That means that you don't label your mistakes "wrong" or "bad"; you just try again. Catch yourself being right!

Training yourself this way doesn't mean that you have to have a training partner or instructor present, though it does help to have someone tagging you. The mere process of setting clear tag points for yourself, and paying attention to when you get them right, will speed your learning along immensely. Throughout the book you'll find suggested tag points that will help you learn the proper mechanics.

Let's summarize what we know:

- Dogs are dogs.
- In training, behavior is what matters.
- Involuntary, emotional responses are learned through classical conditioning—your job is to make sure your dog gets the desired associations from training.
- Voluntary behavior is learned through operant conditioning— your job is to provide consequences for your dog's behavior.
- Reinforcement strengthens behavior.
- Criteria, timing, rate of reinforcement, reward quality and reward placement are keys to successful training.
- Learning is most efficient and most fun when you teach one increment at a time, building behavior step by step.
- Both you and your dog are constantly learning!

These core principles should come alive in your agility training. To help you accomplish this, we've set up three basic rules that should govern all your training. We refer to these guidelines as *Good Agility Practices,* and we'll go through them in detail in the next chapter.

Good Agility Practices

We strongly believe that everything in and around the training situation should happen in a manner that's appropriate to agility training. We call this concept *Good Agility Practices*. Good Agility Practices should apply from the beginning of your training, far away from the equipment, and throughout your entire agility career.

The rules of Good Agility Practices

The three rules of Good Agility Practices are simply stated:

1. Keep your focus on the exercise and on your dog.

2. Work with high intensity when training.

3. Remain true to your system of handling throughout your training.

We'll discuss each in greater detail below.

1. Keep your focus on the exercise and on your dog.

Why?

- You'll do a better job as a trainer.
- Your dog depends on you; don't abandon him.
- You'll avoid uncertainty, frustration, and unnecessary mistakes.
- If you stay focused, you make it possible for your dog to do the same.

How?

- Make plans so that you know exactly what to do once you bring your dog out.
- Clearly define the start and end of each exercise.
- Keep sessions short.
- Put your dog away when you take breaks.

You and your dog should be in your own private bubble during training—fully concentrated and focused on the task at hand, hardly noticing the outside world. To enable you both to remain focused during training, you should make sure all exercises are well planned, well defined, and sufficiently short.

Make your plan before you bring your dog out.

You need to plan both how to train yourself and how to train your dog. To be able to reinforce at the correct moment, you have to know *what* you're going to reinforce. You have to be organized so that you can do the right thing at the right time. How are you going to begin the exercise? Where will you stand? Where will your dog be? How and where are you going to reinforce? What are you going to do if something goes wrong? How are you going to go about starting over? And so on. That means first go through the exercise yourself (without your dog). You should involve your dog only when you feel absolutely confident in what you're about to do, from the moment you get him until the session is over.

During the actual exercise you're just going to *do,* rather than contemplate about how things are going or plan what you're going to do next. Breaks are for planning and analysis. Every exercise should be short and clear-cut enough that you can remain focused and remember what happened and analyze it afterward. If you're training together with other people or with an instructor, it's extra important that you maintain your focus (even if somebody gives you advice during your training). Take care of your dog first—you can talk afterward!

When you're working with your dog, use a long-lasting reward (treat or tug toy) during short breaks or when moving to another spot. That way both you and your dog can move around or get a moment's rest without him being left out or tempted to focus on something else. We also recommend putting your dog in his crate or on leash when you're not working. Let your dog save his "brain capacity" and focus for training.

2. Work with high intensity when training.

Why?

- It maintains the edge in dog and handler alike.
- You decrease the risk of unwanted behaviors and frustration.
- You make it a habit for yourself and your dog to work with high focus in high-intensity, somewhat stressful situations.

How?

- Reinforce often.
- Keep your exercises simple and clear-cut; avoid "messy" situations.
- Move swiftly through each exercise.
- After each reward, be prepared so that your dog can start working again right away.
- If something goes "wrong," keep working; don't freeze or try to fix "mistakes."

Top intensity—no breaks between reward and work!

Agility is an intense sport that requires split-second reactions from dog and handler alike. No matter whether you have a calm dog or the rocket kind, as a team you need to get used to working intensely from the beginning. What we're looking for is intense training at a brisk pace in all exercises. This makes both dog and handler maintain an edge and reduces the risk of random or "garbage" behaviors and frustration. Training with high intensity also enables you to reinforce your dog many times in quick succession, which means that your training will progress faster.

Make sure that the exercises are simple and straightforward. You should be so well prepared that your dog can offer the desired behavior right away and can resume working right after you've rewarded him. Even if something goes "wrong," we want the dog to keep his intensity and his sense of direction, *so let your dog keep working.* If you ever feel the need to slow down your dog in order for him to "get it right," break down the exercise into smaller steps instead.

Training with high intensity in no way means that your training should be sloppy or stressful. If you've been thorough in thinking through what you're going to work on and remain focused on the exercise and on your dog, you can keep up the speed and intensity without compromising quality. If you find it hard to keep the intensity high during training, you may not be focused enough, perhaps as a result of bad planning.

Some may advise that you should train at a slow pace first, and that the speed and intensity will come as your dog gains confidence. If your dog first learned agility behaviors at a slow pace with calm, quiet training, however, you'd run the risk that those behaviors would fall apart once you picked up speed. Your dog might begin to break his start lines, "forget" about his contacts, or become less responsive to your handling.

A dog that is slow and careful by nature might experience that things go "wrong" when he runs faster and learn to perform slowly, just in case. A fast, energetic dog may become stressed out and frustrated by the mistakes that often follow when you increase speed, so you might have to redo all your training again at the higher speed.

Instead, we recommend that you divide your training into small, simple exercises that allow you to work with high intensity and reasonable speed from the beginning. Don't rush your dog; just make sure that everything around training is conducted with high focus and intensity, and set up your dog for success.

If you keep your sessions short, stay within your private bubble, make sure that your dog really wants the rewards, and that he is successful, you can train with intensity and speed even if the behavior you're working on is miniscule or completely new to your dog.

3. Remain true to your system of handling throughout your training.
Why?
- You make it easier for your dog to learn to follow your handling.
- Your handling will become fluent when you use it all the time.
- You establish good habits for both you and your dog, and avoid rehearsing bad habits.

How?
- Be absolutely clear about the foundations of your handling system.
- Remain consistent in your handling at all times.
- Until you have carefully considered if and how any new moves would fit into your system, don't integrate them into your handling.
- Work through exercises first without your dog, in pantomime (including how to move between exercises and how to reward).

Handling is a special feature in agility. Eventually, you'll use your body language as handling cues on the agility course, telling your dog in which direction to go with split-second precision. To make the handling logical, each dog/handler team needs to follow some basic rules on course. These are what we refer to as a handling system.

Since you can't detach your mind from your body, however, potentially you'll always be "communicating" with your dog through your nonverbal language—even when you're not deliberately directing your dog's path. Throughout all your training (actually, throughout your life…) *you* will build habits of moving in certain ways, and *your dog* will notice and learn what your movements mean (even if you don't intend him to). So you should make sure to build the right habits for both of you from the start—and that's what you accomplish by always following your system of handling.

For us, following our handling systems means that we always face the direction the dog should go, use the nearest arm to signal and reward him, keep the dog on the outside in turns, and avoid switching sides with the dog behind the handler's back. (See "The handling part," page 47, for a further discussion of handling and handling systems.) Whichever handling system you use, it's essential that you follow your system consistently throughout your training.

When you're running sequences and courses, you should constantly follow your system of handling because then your dog completely relies on your handling to know where to go. Your dog will be working in synchrony with your body language all the time. Even if you run into trouble, whether it's you or your dog that made the mistake, you need to stay true to your system of handling and continue to give your dog directions. Never just quit handling; that would leave your dog in limbo.

In all other situations in your agility training, you should also strive to follow your system of handling, not so much to direct your dog but to build good habits and avoid inadvertently teaching your dog (and yourself) to work counter to your handling system.

Being consistent in the way you handle your dog is essential. By making sure to be consistent not only when actually handling sequences and courses but also when rewarding and moving around in agility situations, you'll create good habits in yourself, and your dog will take notice.

Pay attention to your movements and adhere to this third rule of Good Agility Practices when you play with your dog before the session, when you move to the starting point, throughout the exercise, and while you reward— in short: always! Both you and your dog will benefit from your minding your handling system in your everyday life. For example, you can follow your handling system when sending your dog to the car (turning with him on the outside and using the nearest arm) and when you're out walking together (again, turning with him on the outside, not switching sides with him behind your back, and using the nearest hand when giving treats and presenting toys). The more you stay true to your handling system (on and off the agility course), the more automatic it will become (for both you and your dog), which will greatly benefit your agility training.

In the beginning, of course, you'll need to pay a lot of attention to your own movements to get it right all the time, but the effort is definitely worth it. Eventually you'll hardly have to think about how you move about—the right moves will come naturally.

Together with the principles of clicker training, Good Agility Practices guide the way we train and give you our recipe for *how* to train agility. In the next chapter, we'll take a look at *what* to train, describe how *we* think about agility, and set out some specific goals for obstacle performance and handling. If you choose to set your goals differently, that's fine, as long as you follow clicker training principles and Good Agility Practices.

5

Agility basics

Agility is absolutely fascinating! It's like a dance where you're the lead; both teamwork and individual efforts are required, and you and your dog have different responsibilities. *Your dog* needs to learn both to work on his own and to follow your handling, and *you* need to fill the shoes of both the dog trainer and the agility handler.

What agility is all about

Remember the goals that we stated in the beginning of this book? What we want is *a happy and confident dog—a dog that is focused, works intensely, embarks on any given task with great enthusiasm, and enjoys both the exercises and the rewards.* Everything about our agility training strives toward happiness and confidence in both partners of the team. On top of this, our training program also seeks to *build a dog and handler team that is able to get around any course with flow, speed, and precision.* So you need to know not only *how* to teach your dog but *what* to teach your dog, so that you have clear goals of what you're training toward.

List of priorities

To get a happy and confident agility partner, we subscribe to the following priorities in our agility training:

1. **Attitude:** Your dog should always be excited and animated about training. An assertive, enthusiastic attitude is top priority no matter what you're working on, and if that's lacking, you have to fix it before you can do anything else.

2. **Direction:** Your dog needs to have a sense of direction: "I know I'm going that way!" Make sure your dog always has a fair chance to get a feel for which way the exercise goes. For your dog to get that sense of direction you need to pay special attention to what you do when mistakes happen. Never stop short and back up; that will only undermine your dog's understanding of direction, and you can't rewind time anyway.

3. **Precision:** The finer details of how a behavior should be performed are only important once your dog really loves the game and has that sense of direction. Since you split the training into tiny, easy-to-learn pieces, you'll automatically build precision into every step of the training process.

Attitude is always priority No. 1. Here the dog soars confidently and exuberantly over the long jump to get to his beloved toy.

Obstacle performance and handling: different areas of responsibility

Agility can be divided into two major areas: *obstacle performance* and *handling*. The *obstacle* part is about teaching your dog all the behaviors you want him to perform independently on the agility course (his responsibility). *Handling* refers to how you use your body language (and perhaps some verbal cues) to direct where your dog is going (your responsibility).

This separation between areas of responsibility is true at all times; it just looks slightly different at different obstacles.

If you look at the "short" obstacles (such as jumps, short tunnels, and so on, which a dog can perform quickly), there's no marked gap between your dog's job and your job as a handler. You're handling the dog the entire time he's performing the obstacle because of the nature of the obstacle. But it's still your dog's job to perform the obstacle independently. For example, he has to jump over the bar and run through the tunnel.

While there are still poles left, they are your dog's job. Your job is giving him information with your handling about where to go next.

The separation of responsibilities is easier to spot on the "longer" obstacles (the weave poles, teeter, A-frame, dogwalk, and so on, that take more time to complete). What these obstacles "tell" your dog to do overrides your handling cues until the obstacle is completed. Take the example of the weave poles: You might make an abrupt turn while your dog is in the weaves, and then your dog needs to know to focus on his job and finish the poles regardless. He should turn with you as soon as he exits the weaves, but not sooner.

Notice that your handling is merely supposed to tell your dog where to go—not what to do! You shouldn't use your body language to "help" your dog perform the different pieces of equipment correctly. Trying to solve training issues with handling is a very common mistake; examples of this error include knee-blocking or pointing to guide the dog's path in the weave poles, or stopping short right next to the down contact. By "helping" the dog to get it right (by directing him with your body language at obstacles, instead of really teaching him what to do step by step), you actually are invading your dog's area of responsibility. Such so-called "help" sabotages all attempts to teach the dog independent obstacle performance. Use handling to show your dog in which direction to go, and use clicker training to teach him how to perform the obstacles!

The obstacle performance part

On an agility course you'll find various kinds of jumps (such as the winged jump, the wall, the spread jump, and the long jump) for the dog to leap over, a tire to jump through, tunnels to run through, and a table to jump onto. There are also weave poles to zigzag past (entering to the right of the first pole) and contact zone obstacles (A-frame, dogwalk, and teeter) to run over, stepping with at least one paw in the colored zone at each end.

The obstacles—as the rulebook sees them

The rulebook states what each obstacle looks like and how your dog should perform it to avoid being faulted. If you wish to compete, you should study the rulebook of your organization to learn about the obstacle heights and lengths, the different classes and how to qualify, what earns faults, and so on. Then you can put the rulebook aside and start thinking about how to best train your dog. You see, the rulebook isn't of much help for you as a dog trainer. It merely sets the framework; you have to set the specific goals for yourself if you want to train a happy and confident dog with a fast and consistent performance.

The obstacles—as we choose to train them

We believe it's critical to really *teach* the dog the skills he needs to perform obstacles independently on the agility course. Here are some suggested training goals:

Obstacle	Our suggested training goal for the dog:
For all obstacles: independent performance	Aim for the obstacle as soon as directed toward it by your handling and perform it fast and accurately. Once your dog has committed to the obstacle, he should finish it correctly no matter what.
Jump, oxer, wall, and long jump:	Jump over bar(s)/wall/planks, between uprights. Judge the distance and jump efficiently with accurate technique. Adjust his jumping style depending on where you're going next. When turning, jump close to the inside upright to get the shortest path.
Tire:	Perform the same as at the other jumps, plus aim with precision to go through the tire without bumping it.
Open and collapsed tunnel:	Go through the tunnel and push the chute open. Shoot ahead out of the tunnel or shorten his stride and turn tightly at the exit, depending on where you're going next.
Weave poles	Enter to the right side of the first pole, going to the left of the second pole, and so on. Nail the entry regardless of the angle, and rhythmically zigzag through all the poles.
A-frame and dogwalk	*For these you really have to make your own decisions. There are many possible contact performances that can be trained. Here is one possibility:* Aim for the very beginning of the up side, run fast over the entire obstacle, nail front feet to the ground at the end and hold still there, waiting for a start cue. On cue, explode away in the direction given by your body language. (Possible addition for very long-strided dogs: On the way up, stop with front feet on the obstacle and back feet on the ground, wait for cue to start, and on start cue proceed over the obstacle.)
Teeter	*Everything said about the A-frame and the dogwalk goes for the teeter as well. In addition, we want the dog to* Run as far out on the teeter as possible, actively working to get the teeter to move fast and slam to the ground.
Start line (not an obstacle per se, but fits in when we talk about obstacle performance since we want independent performance here as well)	*Here you'll also have to make your own decisions. One possibility:* Freeze in a stand, balanced yet poised for action, with four paws on the ground. Remain still, waiting for a start cue. On cue, explode away in the direction given by your body language.

Independent obstacle performance

Teaching your dog something and directing him to perform a certain behavior are not the same thing. It's quite possible to use lures and some handling to get a dog through an agility course. Most dogs could be taught to follow a handler's directions and lures over and through all the obstacles within a few hours. But there's a big difference between helping and directing the dog over and through the obstacles, and teaching him to do them independently and properly! Training toward independent performance means building skills carefully, step by step, a procedure that does take some time and thoughtfulness but that really pays off both during the process and in the end.

The handling part

Your handling is what tells your dog where to go on the course, and your movements, coordination, and timing are crucial for fluent communication. Your body language is your primary handling tool, and by using it in a consistent handling system you'll be able to give precise directions with split-second timing—way beyond what you could ever do with just words.

Handling systems

There are virtually hundreds of different possible handling signals (directing the body in diverse ways, twists and turns, arm movements, footsteps, finger points, and so on), but each handler and dog team needs to have its own limited repertoire to avoid confusion and contradictions. The goal is for you as a handler to have a smoothly functioning system to follow when deciding how to address different situations. Then your dog will be able to trust that "when my handler does that, I should do this."

INDEPENDENT OBSTACLE PERFORMANCE VS. HANDLER-DEPENDENT OBSTACLE PERFORMANCE

Benefits of teaching independent obstacle performance	Drawbacks of handler-dependent obstacle performance
You'll be happier and more confident since you know you can rely on your dog doing his part of the job.	You would have to babysit your dog and guide his obstacle performance.
Your dog will be happier and more confident since he knows exactly what to do when he encounters each obstacle.	Your dog would risk frustration and uncertainty.
Your dog will have fun and be successful throughout the training process, earning rewards for tiny steps toward the final goal.	Most likely you would lump together too many training steps at the same time, setting up your dog for failure.
Your dog will be safer and at less risk of injuries since he knows how to tackle each obstacle properly.	Your dog would focus on you, not on the obstacles, which might lead him to trip, fall, slip, twist, or hurt himself in some other fashion.
You'll get a competitive edge since your dog will be able to perform the obstacles correctly even at a distance.	You would risk more faults and longer course times since your dog would depend on you to babysit him. He'd take chances in performing obstacles and/or he'd have to wait for you to catch up.

YOUR DOG'S INNATE UNDERSTANDING OF BODY LANGUAGE

As hunters and social pack animals, dogs are highly attuned to reading the body language of others, both of prey and of "pack mates." Their ancestors' very lives depended on it, so it's not surprising that dogs readily coordinate their own movement with others. You'll find that your dog tends to head in the same direction as you, to turn with you, to rush ahead as you pick up speed, and to hit the brakes as you stop since those are all ethologically relevant cues. Likewise your dog is expert at reading your intentional movements (leaning, shifting your weight or your gaze, slightly turning a shoulder, and so on). Your dog's literacy in body language makes agility handling a simple concept for him to grasp: As long as you're consistent with your movements, he'll quickly learn to follow them.

If your handling is well executed, your dog will know *before* each obstacle where he's going *after* performing that piece of equipment. Then he doesn't have to wait and ask you for directions, or take a chance and perhaps choose an off-course obstacle. Instead, your dog can run fast and take the shortest path with tight turns. Agility becomes a lot simpler and more fun for your dog if you can handle him in a clear and consistent manner. Your way of moving on course, in other words, should make your dog's job simpler.

So what then is a system of handling?

- A structure governs when and how you use the different signals.
- A few basic principles apply throughout the system.
- Each handling cue means one thing and one thing only.

You want your handling system to be as clear-cut as possible, limiting the number of options for both you and your dog, and making it easier for him to work independently at top speed. Please note that there isn't one "correct" system of handling. What is important isn't *which* system you follow, but that you actually *have* a system. Make sure you choose or create a system that is consistent, so that your dog can rely on your handling.

WHY IS IT IMPORTANT TO HAVE A WELL-THOUGHT-OUT SYSTEM OF HANDLING?

Benefits of a clear and consistent system of handling	Drawbacks of non-systematic handling
You'll be happier and more confident when you know what you're supposed to do in different situations.	You'd get bewildered and confused and would have to make new decisions all the time on the fly.
Your dog will be happier and more confident when he can rely on your handling. A slow and/or careful dog becomes more self-assured and faster, and a faster and/or high-spirited dog becomes more reliable and "clear-headed."	The dog may get frustrated and disoriented at constantly having to ask for directions, or simply guessing where to go next. Frustration could lead him to slow down, sniff, generally shut down or stress out, spin, bark, or fly ahead willy-nilly.
At the "shorter," "quicker" obstacles (like jumps) your dog will know *before* each obstacle where to go *after* that obstacle, making it possible for him to focus properly on the job at hand.	While the dog is taking an obstacle, he'll be busy trying to figure out where you're going next, risking knocked bars and a less-independent obstacle performance.
Your dog will be safer and at less risk of injury since he'll always know where to go.	The dog may often head in one direction only to suddenly realize he should be going in the other, causing him to make abrupt turns that increase the risk of slipping, tearing a muscle, or spraining a joint.
You'll get a competitive edge since your dog will be able to take the shortest path between obstacles. This will minimize both your course time and the risk of him taking the wrong obstacle.	The dog will often turn wide or head for the wrong obstacle, losing time or going off-course.

The basics of our handling system

These are the handling basics we use ourselves and that we teach in our classes:

- Point your shoulders in the direction your dog should go.
- Use the arm nearest your dog.
- Turn with your dog on your outside.
- Never switch sides with your dog behind your back.

GREG DERRETT'S HANDLING SYSTEM

The system that we base our handling on is one developed by Greg Derrett, a British agility trainer. We were very happy to come upon Greg Derrett's system—it's well thought through and exceptionally clear and consistent. Greg Derrett has made a number of DVDs covering and explaining his system and giving a multitude of handling exercises. We highly recommend that you watch these DVDs (See "Resources," page 435). The handling training presented in this book is our take on the subject, and the explanations stem from us.

Our basics are few and simple, designed to make training easier for both you and your dog from the very beginning, so naturally this is what we recommend and use throughout the rest of this book. But, your handling system is a matter of your choice! If you work within a system whose basics differ from ours, we encourage you to modify the training to make sure it fits *your* system of handling.

Now that we've discussed what a handling system is and the basic principles of the system of handling that we've chosen to follow, let's take a look at some fundamental elements of handling.

Which side? In agility you work with your dog equally on both sides. On course your dog is always on either your left side or your right side—even if he's far behind or far ahead of you. So you have

- Left-side handling (your dog is on your left side)
- Right-side handling (your dog is on your right side)

Your shoulders show the way. The direction of your shoulders is your most critical handling cue. Your dog should head in the direction your shoulders are pointing.

- *Going straight:* You keep your shoulders pointing straight ahead, and your dog keeps moving straight ahead.
- *Regular turn:* You turn away from your dog, and your dog follows the direction of your shoulders and turns with you.

Pointing your shoulders in the direction your dog should go is something your dog will easily understand. Just look at how it works when you're taking a hike in the forest together: If you're walking north, your dog's general direction is also north. If you turn and start walking eastward, your dog will notice your change of direction and head the same way. Pointing your shoulders in the direction your dog should go will also make your job easier on the agility course since it's easier to move quickly if you're facing forward than if you're crabbing sideways. By making a point of *always* pointing your body where you want your dog to go, he'll quickly learn to cue off your body's direction, which means you can guide him with high precision.

Turning with your dog on the outside is a concept that we find extremely helpful for dogs and handlers alike. By making a habit of turning *away* from your dog and letting him take the longer path around you, you'll achieve at least four major benefits:

- Your dog will learn to drive forward to get around you as quickly as he can.

Turning with your dog on the outside and letting your dog run the longer, outside lap will allow you to take the shortest path on course, making it simple to show your dog where he's supposed to go next.

- You'll avoid unnecessary confusion since your dog can see where he's going (because you're not crowding him, as you would be on an inside turn).
- You can take the shortest path on the course while your dog is doing his job, which makes it easy for you to show him where to go next.
- Because your dog probably is faster than you are, by letting him run the longer path you'll gain time.

Which arm? When referring to your own arms (or shoulders/hands/legs/feet) you have

- your nearest arm (the arm nearest to your dog).
- your opposite arm (the arm farthest away from your dog).

Using the arm nearest to your dog to signal and reward him keeps your shoulders pointing in the same direction and is also easiest for your dog to see. But, in fact, you don't have to use your arms at all: Because the direction of your shoulders will tell your dog what he needs to know, you can handle your dog around a course perfectly well with your hands behind your back. Your arms just add clarification.

Switching sides. Sometimes you'll want your dog to be on your left side, and sometimes on your right side. When switching from left-side handling to right-side handling or vice versa, we use

- a *front cross* when you're ahead of your dog, switching sides with him "face to face."
- a *rear cross* when you're behind your dog, switching sides behind his tail as he takes an obstacle.

When running agility, you'll sometimes be farther ahead on the course than your dog when you want to switch sides. In such cases, you'll choose a front cross. Other times, when you're behind your dog, you'll choose a rear cross. When teaching foundation skills, however, your side changes will occur while you reward your dog or while you move your dog to a new starting point. In these situations you'll always use front crosses.

We have ruled out another kind of cross: the *blind cross,* where the handler switches sides by turning her back to the dog, letting the dog slip over to the other side behind the handler's back. We simply don't have room for it in our system of handling, since it would clash with other elements (it's incompatible with our basic tenet of the dog "staying on the outside").

Always follow your handling system

Our third rule of Good Agility Practices says: "Follow your system of handling throughout your training." Your "default behavior"—what you automatically do, if you haven't made a conscious decision to do the opposite—should be to follow your handling basics all the time. With our handling basics, this means:

- You support your dog's path by pointing your shoulders in the direction he's going. For example, if you're moving to a new starting point, leading your dog by his collar, you should aim your shoulders in the direction you're going. And if your dog is running toward a treat bowl, your shoulders should be pointing toward that treat bowl until he has reached it.
- You use your nearest hand to deliver rewards, whether they be treats, tug toys, or thrown toys.
- Whenever you turn, you do so with your dog on your outside. Consciously doing outside turns all the time will greatly add to your handling awareness, so let your dog take the longer path at all times.
- You never switch sides with your dog behind your back. We see many a handler doing unintentional blind crosses—switching hands on the leash as the dog travels from side to side behind her, turning her back to her dog before starting an exercise, or spinning around and losing sight of the dog while rewarding. Even if we had chosen to include blind crosses in our system of handling, they would only occur on cue from the handler—we'd never want the dog to willy-nilly switch sides behind the handler's back nor the handler to willy-nilly switch sides on her dog. Consciously avoiding these blind crosses will greatly improve your handling awareness and will also make it much easier for your dog to understand and follow your movements.

There will be instances when it makes sense to break these rules, but then it should be an educated and considered choice, not something that just happens without your noticing it. For example, you might choose to use both hands when rewarding in a situation where you want to deliver rewards very quickly and from various directions, reasoning that the dog-training benefits outweigh the drawbacks of using your opposite hand. Or, you might choose to do turns with your dog on the inside because you specifically want to teach him to yield when you invade his space (we actually do this as a specific exercise, as preparation for some of the advanced handling maneuvers). But in general, you should follow your handling system throughout your training.

Your understanding of how dogs learn, of how clicker training works, of Good Agility Practices, and of obstacle training and handling will pay off in the subsequent chapters. With clicker and rewards in hand, you're ready to start training. You are the first subject; then we'll move on to your dog. Remember to

- proceed in baby steps.
- reinforce what you want.
- and keep the rewards coming—for both yourself and your dog.

Part II
Foundation skills for you

and your dog

About foundation training

The time has come to make use of your knowledge and start actually training. Agility training is so much fun in all its intensity and complexity! Each "foundation skill" that you teach yourself or your dog is a detail that you will use and benefit from later on in the training process. But don't be mistaken: Foundation training is not just something you do *before* you start training agility "for real." Foundation training *is* agility training! Well executed, foundation training is agility at its best.

What you'll learn in Part II, *Foundation skills for you and your dog*

You may be wondering: Where do I start? What do my dog and I need to learn? The foundation skills presented in this part of the book are *our* suggestions. Please consider your own goals, take a look at yourself and your dog, and try to figure out how you can be a good dog trainer by breaking down skills into manageable pieces and, once trained, putting the pieces all together. This is what foundation training is all about! Maybe your list of basic skills will be the same as ours, maybe it will be different, and maybe it will change over time as you figure out new details that you wish to teach yourself or your dog.

Keep in mind that to change your dog's behavior you first have to change your own. Training is never directly about altering your dog's behavior: training is about creating situations where your dog gets new experiences in an informative and rewarding way so that he learns whatever it is you want him to learn.

These are the foundation skills we'll cover in this part:

Foundation skills for you:

- Coordination and body control: Learn to move purposefully and smoothly.
- Timing: Mark behavior at the exact right moment.
- Setting criteria: Learn the basics of shaping.
- Reward delivery: Present treats and toys quickly and purposefully.
- Remaining neutral: Work with your dog, mark, and give release cues without letting body language reveal more than you intend.
- Varying your own behavior: Help your dog generalize his responses.
- Handling basics: Adhere to the basics of your handling system.

Both you and your dog need to know your jobs. Here the handler's job is to point her shoulders in the direction she wants the dog to go. The dog's job is to go between the two cones and to continue in the direction of the handler's shoulders.

Foundation skills for your dog:

- Rewards: Teach your dog to enjoy different kinds of rewards and build a repertoire of functional reward procedures.
- Transports: Learn different procedures for moving your dog around between exercises.
- Strategies for getting behavior: Understand and learn to teach our core strategies: *Aim for it* and *Race to reward*.
- Going between/around/onto/over/under/through: Teach your dog ways to interact with various objects and materials to prepare him for training on agility obstacles.
- Creating noise and movement: Develop your dog's passion for making a tumult.
- Rear-end control: Build coordination and strength in your dog's rear end.
- Stay and start: Instill the thrill of starting on cue and waiting for that start cue.
- Follow the shoulders: Teach your dog to read your shoulders when running in circles and when racing to you.

You can use a game of tug both as a great reward and a means to move your dog to a new location.

Some old pipes in the backyard make excellent foundation training equipment.

THE ROAD AHEAD: *PUTTING IT ALL TOGETHER*

In the third and final part of the book, *Putting it all together*, we'll describe how to put together all the skills you've learned to build more complex behaviors. Here is a peek ahead at what you and your dog will learn to master in Part III:

1. Handling maneuvers on the flat (without obstacles)
2. Jumps and tunnels (including all kinds of jumps, the long jump, pipe tunnels, the chute tunnel, and the tire)
3. Handling sequences
4. Contact zones and contact obstacles
5. The table
6. The weaves

Some of the skills we've included in *Putting it all together* are taught away from the obstacles; therefore, these skills could be considered foundation skills as well. Examples are handling maneuvers on the flat (teaching the specific handling cues you'll use on course) and contact preparation training (teaching the contact-zone behavior). We've chosen to place them in *Putting it all together*, rather than in this section about foundation skills, because they are quite elaborate and require you to first have a thorough grounding in the more basic foundation skills discussed here..

Once we introduce the obstacles, the dog is very well prepared.

Dog training isn't strictly linear

Many of the skills presented in this book build on each other, so it makes sense to establish the simpler skills before you start working on the more complex ones. But dog training is not linear; the skills also feed each other. You and your dog will often benefit from training many skills in parallel and from moving back and forth in your training. So even though the skills are presented in a logical order, do not feel you must train them strictly in order of appearance.

Dog training is also nonlinear in the sense that you're always going back to earlier exercises to refresh skills. Foundation work is not something that you do once, and then it's over and done with. Instead, foundation skill exercises will make up some of your everyday training, and they are available whenever you need to revise or refine your dog's performance.

The benefits of foundation work

There are many benefits of thorough foundation training:

- Foundation training helps you work on and focus on one thing at a time, building behaviors step by step; it truly teaches you and your dog essential behaviors.
- Training progresses much faster when you train small aspects of behavior.
- Working with tiny details makes it easier to maintain a high success rate.
- Working with tiny details decreases the risk of frustration and disappointment and increases both your own and your dog's happiness and confidence.
- It is easy to put complex behaviors together once you have trained one aspect at a time.
- Foundation training teaches your dog not only specific skills but also to work with focus and intensity.
- While teaching your dog foundation skills, you get to rehearse and use all your mechanical skills and implement Good Agility Practices.
- By working through the foundation skills away from the agility obstacles, you'll achieve success right away once you start working with the obstacles.
- Throughout your agility career, well-established foundation skills will help you avoid snags and give you something to fall back on if you run into problems.
- Since you are training away from the regular agility equipment, you can train anytime, anywhere.

THE DRAWBACKS OF SKIPPING FOUNDATION WORK

1. Trainers who skip foundation work tend to lure, guide, and babysit their dogs to get them to do things instead of actually teaching independent skills.
2. Stepping right out onto the agility course and attempting to start training "the whole thing" right away is incompatible with working on one thing at a time. It's impossible to learn a hundred things simultaneously—trying to do so only builds unfortunate habits and causes lots of frustration for dog and human alike.
3. Without proper foundation behaviors, the dog will often encounter situations for which he isn't prepared. This is unfair to the dog and increases the risk of the handler reverting to aversives to "correct" the dog's mistakes.

Teaching your dog foundation skills

When teaching agility foundation skills, we generally strive to teach the dog to spontaneously offer behaviors. By "spontaneously offer" we mean that, in a training session, your dog enthusiastically performs the behavior as soon as he gets a chance, without any cueing, prompting, guidance, or luring from you other than the direction of your body.

Here are a few examples, just to illustrate what foundation skills look like:

Go between things (for instance, two big buckets): The dog hangs on to a tug toy while the handler turns around so that they both face the buckets. As soon as the handler removes the tug toy, the dog surges forward and dashes ahead between the buckets where his reward appears.

Here the dog first is tugging (left). As soon as the handler removes the tug toy, the dog aims between the buckets (center), and the handler clicks and tosses the toy ahead (right).

Run across an odd surface (for example, a big piece of cardboard): The handler shows the dog a remote reward placed on the opposite side of the cardboard. She holds on to the dog until she feels that he is aiming in the right direction. Then she lets go, and the dog immediately races ahead, runs over the cardboard, and gets to the treats.

Here the dog is spontaneously racing to the treat bowl, running across the cardboard on the way.

Create noise (for example, by knocking over a stack of metal bowls): The handler holds on to the dog's collar with one hand and builds a small tower of metal bowls with the other hand. As soon as she lets go of the collar, the dog enthusiastically smashes the tower with his nose, feet, or body (much as any one-year-old child would).

Here the dog creates noise by smashing the tower as soon as the handler lets go.

LEARNING TO OFFER BEHAVIORS VOLUNTARILY

Your dog needs to learn that he can earn rewards by offering behaviors voluntarily. Dogs that truly understand this concept often are called "clicker-savvy." They know the rules of the game. They try out behaviors to see what works (in other words, what earns rewards), and they strive to repeat behaviors that previously earned rewards. A dog that is used to waiting for lures or prompts won't offer much voluntarily; a clicker-savvy dog, on the other hand, practically throws behaviors at you.

Your dog will learn to offer behaviors voluntarily through-out our training program. But the more often he gets to spontaneously try things out and earn rewards for it, the more clicker-savvy he'll become. So don't limit yourself to agility training; all kinds of clicker training will do the trick. For inspiration and training tips, see, for example, Karen Pryor's *Getting Started: Clicker Training for Dogs*, Melissa Alexander's *Click for Joy*, or Morten Egtvedt and Cecilie Koeste's *Clicker Training: The 4 Secrets of Becoming a Supertrainer.*

We want your dog to offer behavior as soon as he possibly can. There should be no gaps in the reward–behavior–reward sequence other than if you are physically holding on to your dog and then releasing him again. We want your dog to be a bit crazy here! Politeness is not in the picture. By teaching your dog to spontaneously offer behaviors without any prompts and cues, you'll build a creative learner that seeks to take the initiative, experiment, and figure out what to do to earn those precious rewards.

Working with spontaneously offered behaviors builds strong behaviors and confident dogs that learn to drive ahead and work independently, without asking you for permission all the time. On an agility course, you'll want your dog to be drawn to the obstacles like a guided missile (while following your handling directions, thus aiming for the correct obstacle). Teaching your dog to spontaneously offer the foundation skills is an imperative step toward that goal.

Equipment

It's a good idea to begin your dog's agility training far away from the agility obstacles; we always work with other objects and materials first. When you start this way, you can customize your dog's training by working with just the kind of equipment you need. This also allows you to make your preliminary training mistakes away from the actual obstacles (where you can't really ruin anything). By first working through the foundation skills with other kinds of equipment, you can ensure that both you and your dog know your jobs well before you start practicing with real obstacles on an agility course.

For your foundation training, all you need is a variety of objects to work with (such as buckets, chairs, blankets, and so on). We make suggestions of what to use for the various exercises throughout the chapters, but feel free to be inventive and use whatever you have handy. (When we use the term *equipment* in these foundation training chapters, we thus are referring not to actual agility obstacles but to whatever objects you choose to work with.)

A word about verbal cues

We humans tend to be verbal control freaks, craving to put labels on everything under the false belief that naming will facilitate the learning process. But remember that dogs aren't verbal creatures: The words in themselves don't carry any meaning to them and won't help them learn what it is you want them to do. If a verbal cue is added, it should be to a well-established behavior. But cues are superfluous even for well-trained foundation behaviors since the goal is for your dog to learn to offer each behavior "on the fly" as soon as he gets the opportunity. The direction you're facing and your well-timed rewards will do the talking for you, and your dog will learn to read the context and know what to do.

There are a few exceptions to this no-cue recommendation. One verbal cue that you absolutely do need to teach is the start cue (for example, "go") that you will add when training start-line stays. For practical purposes we also suggest you teach a cue for "thank you" (release the toy).

Working equally on your left and right sides

In all agility training you'll work with your dog equally on your left side and your right side. Your agility training will progress more easily if you and your dog do not have a "preferred" side. Moreover, your dog will benefit physically by putting equal strain on both sides of his body.

If you and your dog are already bilateral, that's great. If your dog is glued to either of your sides, you have some work to do. Begin right away! You can accomplish a lot simply by thinking about the left-side/right-side division in your everyday life. Capture and reward the moments when your dog happens to be on the more awkward side, and make a point of having him on that side as often as you can—when you let him out of the door, when you put down his food, when you walk on leash, and so on. When working through the agility foundation skills, have your dog at least as much on the more awkward side as on the familiar, comfortable side.

Throughout the foundation training you should frequently alternate between left-side work and right-side work. To switch sides, turn face to face with your dog in a front cross. In some situations, where your dog is busy (for example, eating from a treat bowl), you can also switch sides with a rear cross, switching sides behind his tail.

A great training session

The spirit of Good Agility Practices should inspire each and every training session. To ensure focus and intensity, your training session might look something like this:

- Pottying and warm-up.
- Preparation: Put your dog away and prepare for the training session.
- Training: Play—brief bout of training—mini-break with play—brief bout of training—play.
- Break: Put dog away, evaluate, and prepare for the next session.
- Training again.
- Cool-down.

Pottying and warm-up: Before you start training, you need to potty your dog. Then you need to make sure he is properly warmed up—both physically and mentally. Getting your dog into training mode is a vital part of the warm up. Start by just walking, tossing in some rewards for nice behaviors as you go along. Then move on to running, playing, doing fun tricks, and so on. Try out different procedures to find your own best physical and mental warm-up routine for your dog.

Preparation: After you potty and warm up your dog, we suggest you put your dog away for a little while. Then you can plan your actions and prepare for the actual training so that you are 100% focused once you get your dog.

Training: When you actually start training, the old clichés hold true: Quality over quantity. Less is more. The best setup for successful learning is to train in brief bouts since you and your dog then stand a good chance of staying in your private bubble, working intensely and focusing on the task at hand.

Begin and end your sessions with play, to build energy and get in the right mood.

Each training session should begin with play. Choose an intense game that pumps up your dog's energy, and make sure you are at the best starting position when you end the play. Follow the play with a brief bout of training (for example, four repetitions of a behavior, or 10 clicks and treats if you're shaping a new behavior). There should be no gaps between behavior–reward–behavior–reward. Always end with some high-energy play: just prolong the final reward and party on.

If you wish—if both you and your dog are up for another go—you can continue with another bout of training. Just make sure you keep your dog fully engaged during the mini-breaks, so you can catch your breath and regroup without leaving your dog in limbo. So one training session might consist of one or several bouts of training, with play first, last, and in-between.

Break: When it's time to take a longer break, you need to make sure that your dog can really relax and recuperate. Put him away in his crate, on his bed, in your car, or go for a relaxing walk. If you like, you can give your dog a light massage or simply toss him some treats for staying calm. Don't allow him to just wander about, and don't keep him hanging around your feet either—you'd be leaving him in limbo between work and rest, and you'd risk him engaging in less desirable behaviors and your nagging him for it. Banish tension and conflicts from your agility training—including during the breaks!

Cool-down: After training, take the time for a proper cool-down. Go for a walk, massage your dog, and just wind down. Physically cooling down is at least as important as warming up, and after an intense training session, you and your dog need the mental cool-down as well.

Checklist for great training sessions

The following checklist is designed to ensure that each training session meets its full potential of fun and success for both you and your dog. To become the best trainer you can be, you need to make a lot of choices. We don't want to limit you by making all the choices for you; this list is meant merely as a starting point to pick and choose from as you form your own, personalized training checklist. In the beginning, it may seem like an awful lot to keep track of, but don't sweat it. After a while, most of it will come automatically if you just get into the right habits.

THINKING, PLANNING, AND RECORD KEEPING

Thinking through your training, making plans before you take action, and then examining what actually happened—these three things really do improve the quality of your training sessions. It is wise to make notes so that you have your thoughts in black and white: then you know how you were thinking and what you and your dog actually did rather than just trusting your memory. Keeping a journal can mean anything from making a few notes once a week to making detailed entries after every training session. Just start keeping a journal at a level that you can maintain, and enjoy seeing your progress as those pages get filled.

Happiness and confidence saturate every training session. Don't analyze while training—just enjoy!

A GREAT TRAINING SESSION: Thinking and planning

Step	Considerations
The big picture	
Know your goals.	Do your goals form a clear picture in your mind so that you know what it is you are aiming to teach your dog? Do you have both major, more distant goals, and minor, more proximate ones?
Make a plan.	Do you have a plan for how to train toward your goal, step by step? Which part are you going to work on during this session?
Break it down.	Have you broken down the behavior into the tiniest pieces you can think of?
Make sure that you know your job.	Do you have the skills needed to train this behavior, or do you need to train yourself first? Are there tag points that you need to work through?
The surrounding features	
Decide where to train.	Is the area safe, and do the distractions match your training level?
Prepare everything you need.	Are all rewards, clicker, equipment, helpers, and so on where you want them?
Decide how long each bout of training is going to last.	6 repetitions? 5 rewards? 30 seconds? And so on.
Determine how to know when to stop training.	Count the repetitions while you train? Have 5 treats in your hand and stop when they are gone? Use a stopwatch?
Decide what to do with your dog during the brief breaks between your bouts of training.	Briefly put your dog in his crate? Play tug? Perhaps do some fun tricks?
Set a maximum time for how long you are going to work before you take a longer break or quit.	3 brief bouts? 5 minutes?
Plan for record keeping.	Are you going to try to just remember it all and make mental notes? If you're going to make written notes, when and how?
The actual training	
Plan for the warm-up.	What are you going to do to get your dog warmed up and in the right mood?
Plan your play and your transports.	What are you going to do right before and right after each brief bout of training? How are you going to get your dog to the perfect starting point to begin each exercise?
Plan your handling.	How will you stay true to your system of handling during the training?
Set your criteria.	Which response are you going to reinforce?
Decide what to do if things go right.	How, where, and with what are you going to reward? How are you going to continue after the reward?
Decide what to do if things go wrong.	How will you continue as swiftly as possible?
Plan for the cool-down.	Where will you go? What will you need to bring?

A GREAT TRAINING SESSION: Thinking and planning (continued)

Step	Considerations
The final preparation	
Prepare your helpers.	Do your helpers know exactly what to do?
Work through the exercise without your dog—in your mind, or in reality.	Do you know your part of the job?

A GREAT TRAINING SESSION: Working with your dog

Step	Considerations
Focus on your dog and the training and have a blast!	Just relax and have fun with your dog! Do not think too much about getting everything right. You have prepared yourself the best you could, and if everything does not go exactly as you planned—and we promise, often it will not—it's no big deal. What's important is that you and your dog enjoy yourselves and the training.

A GREAT TRAINING SESSION: The review

Step	Considerations
Review the rate of reinforcement.	Did your dog get it right and get rewarded most of the time?
Review your timing.	Did you mark and reward at the right moments? Were you neutral while marking?
Review the quality of your rewards.	Were the rewards good enough? Did they suit your training purposes?
Review your reward delivery.	Did you deliver the reward in the manner and place you had planned?
Review your dog's focus and intensity.	Did your dog do anything but work with focus and intensity?
Review your own focus and intensity.	Did you do anything but work with focus and intensity?
Review your handling.	Did you follow your system of handling throughout the session?
Review your criteria and plan the next session.	Should you change anything? Should you make it easier in any way? Is there any more preparation that you or your dog need, any other exercise you should practice beforehand? Or did everything go so well that it's time to make things a bit more complex?

EMPLOY TAGTEACH

We recommend that you take advantage of the opportunities TAGteach offers to speed and refine your learning. In several of the exercises you will find suggested tag points—criteria to set for yourself. Ideally, a helper will observe and tag you (mark the correct response). Anyone can tag "deliver treats with the nearest hand." You don't need an agility trainer or even a trainer. If you are practicing alone, you can "self-tag," saying "tag" to yourself as you accomplish the tag point.

Use a tag point when you feel the need for it. A tag point is—and should be—strictly defined and explicit. If there is one specific detail that you need to practice and that you want precise feedback about, then set a tag point. But if you are just running through an exercise, getting an overall feel for it without looking to perfect any specific aspect, then do not set any tag points: Just run through it and get some feedback afterward.

When you are working with a tag point, only that specific point matters—ignore any off-point errors! The idea is to focus on one thing at a time and to get feedback (like a click, a ping, or a verbal "tag") as you get that one thing right.

The tag points we list throughout the book are merely suggestions. Don't get hung up on them; you can always find other possible tag points for every exercise. If you find any part of an exercise the least bit difficult, then identify the critical part, set a tag point, and focus on getting that right.

Reader's guidelines

For each of the foundation skills we present in the upcoming chapters we aim to answer the following questions, thoroughly and precisely, explaining in detail the hows and whys of our training:

- What should it look like?
- Why do you need it?
- How can you train it?

These questions, and their answers, are valid both when you train yourself and when you train your dog. We provide guidelines for building each skill, with illustrative photos and diagrams complementing the text. We'll note skills you've already learned that you might want to rehearse before tackling the next stage of training, and we'll let you know what you'll require for starting to train a particular skill: a plate? a favorite toy? a helper to hold a treat bowl? three pairs of boots? Often we'll suggest specific, step-by-step exercises and tag points to help you get things right.

In the end, you are in charge of your own training; please don't just do as we say because we say so! Make your own choices and your own decisions. Above all, have fun with your dog!

Not only does foundation training provide a solid foundation for both you and your dog to fall back on. It also gives you the tools to fix problems that might need to be addressed at a later stage, and great exercises to keep you and your dog going off-season. Let's get started!

7

Training yourself

Becoming a great dog trainer and handler is a matter of both mind and body. Knowing what to do and why to do it are critical elements—but if that knowledge stays in your head, it won't help your training. To train and handle your dog the way you want, you need to be able to perform the right actions at the right time. That's what you'll learn in this chapter.

Becoming a trainer and a handler

Your dog's learning goes through you! As your dog's *trainer,* you need to be fast, accurate, and smooth; in other words, you need fluent mechanics. Spot-on timing, clear criteria, and quick and decisive reward deliveries are necessary skills for successful training. Remaining neutral and varying your own behavior will make all the difference when teaching your dog to work independently of you.

The agility dance also calls upon you to clearly and consistently show your dog in which direction to go. As your dog's *handler,* you need to internalize the handling basics so that they become automatic. Then, once you bring your dog out, you'll be able to focus completely on your dog and still manage to stick to your handling system.

The good news about training and handling skills is that you don't have to be "a natural"— you can learn them by practicing them step by step, and your agility training will benefit

You are your dog's trainer, responsible for setting up clever learning situations and reinforcing desired responses. You are also his handler, cueing his direction in a consistent manner.

accordingly. Learning these skills *before* you begin actually training your dog would be ideal, but it's never too late to improve your own skills. You simply have to get to work!

In this chapter we'll give you exercises designed to refine your trainer and handler skills. You'll notice that all the exercises are in some way connected to the five keys of successful training (criteria, timing, reward rate, reward quality, and reward placement) and to Good Agility Practices (maintaining focus and intensity, and following your system of handling).

Get in the mind-set

When you attempt to teach yourself the mechanics of good dog training and handling, remember that the clicker training principles are valid not only when teaching your dog, but also when teaching yourself. Break down each task into tiny parts so you can focus on one detail at a time, and keep your successes (not your mistakes) in mind. Learning will progress *much* faster if you allow yourself to focus on one detail and let go of the others for the time being. Remember, you're not supposed to get everything right from the start!

Your brain is the most prepared for learning when you are relaxed and happy, so make sure to create positive training situations: Practice exercises that you can manage, and focus on what you have at hand.

Many people seem to have an innate aversion against practicing exercises that seem simple. Let go of all such reluctance! Just relax and let your muscles and your nervous system concentrate on the details in each small, seemingly simple task. These are exercises you need to do—just reading about them will not improve your mechanical skills. We advise you to first read the descriptions slowly and to try to "feel" the moves in your body at the same time. Then try working with a friend, so you can help each other and give support and feedback during training.

If you feel awkward, don't give up after one failed attempt: keep at it until you feel fluent! You can always break down an exercise into smaller parts if you feel that you are struggling with some particular aspect. We promise: good training not only builds good behavior in your dog—it builds good behavior in you as well.

Coordination and body control

Being an agility trainer and handler definitely puts some demands on your coordination and body control. Point your body this way, look that way, use this hand, and do something else with your feet—all while you are busy working with your dog.

It's a good idea to engage in some other activities that enhance body awareness, such as aerobics, tai chi, yoga, or dancing. Actually, every time you engage in learning new and unfamiliar movements, you will improve your body awareness.

In our agility classes we often do a short "know-your-body" drill to remind our students of some elementary facts about what the human body can do. Since in part it resembles the safety drill that flight attendants run through before takeoff, we refer to it as the "flight attendant drill."

"Arm down but forward" is what your body does when you deliver a reward a bit ahead of your dog. This placement of reward enhances the dog's forward motion.

You can turn your head and glance at your dog while your shoulders are pointing forward!

Exercise 1: The flight attendant drill

Stand up and try this!

Check how your arms can move: You can move them forward, backward, up, down, out, in, and in a cross in front of your body. Your arms can move simultaneously, or one at a time, or both at the same time doing different moves. The moves can be combined, for example to "out–slightly forward–pointing down." In addition, your arms are jointed at the elbows, so you can bend them.

Check how your body can turn: You can turn your shoulders while your feet are standing still, and your head can turn even if the rest of your body is pointing forward. You can also turn your feet in one direction and your body in another.

Check how you can lean: You can lean forward, backward, and sideways.

The "flight attendant drill" may sound a bit silly, yes, but it is helpful to run through all the different poses and "feel" them. Purposefully going through how your body can move improves your ability to perform desired moves while avoiding others. For example, if you try delivering a treat a little bit ahead of your dog, you are more likely to get it right if you have actually tested the difference between "arm straight down" and "arm down but slightly forward." And if you are aware of what it feels like when your body is pointing straight ahead as compared to when you are twisting to one side, it will be easier for you to maintain your direction when working with your dog.

Timing

"Timing is everything," the saying goes —especially in dog training. The more precise your timing is, the more efficient your training will be.

A clickable moment.

What should precise timing look like?

- In training situations where you use a clicker (or other marker), you click as your dog offers the desired response. After the click, you deliver a tangible reward.
- In training situations where you do not use a marker, you make the reward appear as your dog performs the desired response.

Using a marker will greatly improve your timing, so in situations where you want to reinforce a specific, miniscule response (for example, when shaping your dog to point his nose straight ahead), you should definitely use a marker. At other times, when you want to reinforce more complex behaviors (for example, when rewarding after your dog completes the weave poles, or rewarding in the flow of handling while running a sequence), you might just deliver the reward without marking first. Either way, you get what you reinforce, so stay alert!

Improving your timing: Mark at the right moment

Marking at the exact right moment requires refined eye–brain–hand coordination. In the beginning you might be slow and make lots of mistakes, but practice makes perfect, so we suggest playing some timing games to improve both your observational skills and your timing. Precise timing requires a high level of focus and is tiring, so you need to work in short sessions—no more than a minute at a time—to stay alert.

The following exercises will help you refine the timing of your click. You'll need a helper and a clicker, and sometimes an object. Your assignment is to click precisely when your criterion is met. If you make a mistake, just let it go, move on, and focus on the next clickable moment. These exercises are also great to practice in a group where everyone has a clicker and tries to be as precise as possible. In the beginning the clicks might be quite scattered, but after some practice everyone will develop better timing and eventually you'll hear one synchronous click.

You'll find that if you press the clicker as the criterion is fully met, your click will be late. To click fast enough, you need to anticipate the action and click a bit earlier than you might think at first.

Exercise 2: Clicker practice

Observe, be ready, click!

	What the helper does:	**Your criterion (what you click):**
Bounce	Bounces a tennis ball	Ball touches floor
Wink	Sits across from you looking into your eyes	Helper winking
One or two?	Raises one or two fingers, randomly	One finger in the air
Hit the table	Repeatedly drops a pen on the table	Pen touches table
Ready-Steady-Go	Counts "ready-steady-go" but randomly replaces "go" with other similar words such as "gold," "game," "glad," and so on	Helper says "go" or other "release" word

Helpers are expected to try to fool the trainer any way they can, for example, by varying the time lapse between trials and by making intentional movements without following through. Quickly dropping the pen five times in a row and then just pretending to drop it often causes a premature click and a burst of laughter.

For further variation, here is an exercise that you can practice alone in the comfort of your TV chair. All you need is a TV and DVD/VCR player, a show or movie, and a remote control with a Pause button. You will use your remote control instead of a clicker.

Exercise 3: Press Pause

1. Choose a behavior to look for on the screen (such as somebody standing up, smiling, bending the right knee, or turning his head to the right).
2. Press Play and pay attention!
3. Press Pause at the exact moment the chosen behavior shows up on the screen.

The best aspect of the "Press Pause" exercise is that it provides precise feedback: Since you freeze the frame, you will clearly see if you successfully clicked (pressed "Pause") at just the right moment.

A few tips

- You will find that if you press the clicker as the criterion is fully met, your click will be late; this is because your brain has to register the event and send an impulse to your thumb, which then presses the clicker. To click as something happens you therefore need to anticipate the action and actually click a split second before it happens.
- If you make a mistake, just let it go, move on, and focus on the next clickable moment.
- Practice for no more than a minute at a time to avoid tiring.
- If sometimes you want to use a different marker signal such as the word "yes," make sure to practice this as well.

Setting criteria: the basics of shaping

Shaping—building behavior step by step by rewarding successive approximations of the behavior—is all about setting appropriate criteria and reinforcing the responses that meet criteria.

How do you know if you set your criteria correctly? Look at the behavior—if it's progressing in the direction you want it to, you're on the right way!

What should appropriate criteria look like?

- Criteria are easy enough for the trainee to be successful.
- Criteria are raised in sync with the trainee's performance.
- The rate of reinforcement is high so the trainee gets rewarded often.

If criteria are properly set and raised, the trainee will keep responding, constantly trying to earn clicks and treats, and the behavior will steadily improve toward your goal.

Practicing setting criteria

Working on one's shaping skills with a human as "guinea pig" is a classic exercise you may have encountered before. Playing the Training Game is an excellent way to improve your skill at setting criteria wisely, and wise criteria are what make it possible for you to keep the rate of reinforcement high enough.

In the Training Game, one person (the trainer) picks a behavior for another person (the trainee) to do, for example, sit in a chair, raise her right hand, or open a window. Your job as a trainer is to teach the trainee to perform the desired behavior without prompts, aids, or verbal cues—just through free shaping, by observing and reinforcing the tiniest steps toward the goal. If your goal is for the trainee to sit in a chair, you might begin by clicking and treating the trainee for looking toward the end of the room where the chair is and then reinforcing every movement the trainee makes in the correct direction. You have succeeded when the trainee performs the desired behavior at least five times in a row, without trying any other behaviors in between.

Play the Training Game

For this game you need at least two people: a trainer and a trainee. You also need a clicker and treats that your human trainee wants (for example, chocolate, peanuts, raisins, or, for the party version, a sip of wine). It helps to have a third person who observes and whom the trainer can bounce ideas off and get feedback from during breaks. The rules are simple: The trainer is fully responsible for the training process but is not allowed to do anything but click and reward; the trainee can never do anything wrong. Hop to it and have fun!

Exercise 4: The Training Game

1. Send the trainee out of the room.
2. Choose a goal behavior.
3. Bring the trainee back in.
4. Keep still and quiet.
5. The trainee acts, trying to earn clicks and treats.
6. Click and treat for all tendencies toward the goal behavior.
7. Raise criteria as the training progresses.

To avoid mental exhaustion, take a break every few minutes, sending the trainee out of the room. The game is over when the trainee repeatedly performs the chosen behavior.

Suggested tag point (Remember to phrase as "The tag point is..."):

- Be quiet

Playing the training game. Here, the goal was "arms in the air." First the trainer shaped the trainee to stand up, then to move her arms. These pictures only show some of the responses the trainee offered. Getting up earns a click (left). Raising a foot—no click (center left). The first slight arm movement—click! (center right). Arms up—click! (right).

The Training Game, plush animal version

You also can practice your behavior-shaping skills by using a stuffed toy as "trainee" for the Training Game. There are actually several advantages to shaping a plush giraffe or a teddy bear. As a trainer it can be easier to focus on what the "trainee" really is *doing* when it's a stuffed animal instead of a human.

Since a plush giraffe won't be offering many behaviors on its own, your stuffed toy will need a human assistant to hold it and help it try out different movements. Manipulating a stuffed animal often seems to be easier than being the actual trainee—it's easier to just go with the flow and not think so much when you're holding a plush giraffe.

As before, the trainer chooses a behavior (such as wiggling the right ear, nodding the head, spinning, and so on), sits ready with clicker and treats, and clicks and treats for the slightest tendency to do something that eventually can evolve into the chosen behavior.

The trainer and the assistant are not allowed to talk during the session. Because you (as trainer) have to focus solely on the plush giraffe and what it is doing during this game, this often can be quite a realistic exercise and perfect preparation for future shaping sessions with your dog. What do you do, for example, when the stuffed toy—or your dog—just stands still looking at you, or bounces up and down in frustration? The answer is almost always the same: Find even tinier responses to reward so that the flow of information (the clicks and treats) increases. And don't forget to take breaks. Your trainer skills will get better and better, and your dog will probably send grateful thoughts to the patient, plush giraffe.

In this shaping game with a plush giraffe, the trainer is teaching the giraffe to nod its head.

A few tips

- Never mind what the trainee thinks or believes. Just focus on the behavior. That is what you are affecting with your well-timed clicks.
- Shaping is a creative process: there is no one right way!
- Take a break every few minutes so you and the trainee can rest your brains. During these breaks you can get feedback from others observing the game—just make sure the trainee leaves the room first.
- Do not ask your trainee for too much at one time. It's your responsibility to make sure that the shaping process takes place in steps small enough to allow the trainee to continually get feedback through clicks and treats. The shorter the time lapse between clicks, the more information you'll pass on to the trainee.
- Click every tiny response in the right direction. When the trainee then tries something "wrong" and does not get a click, he or she will notice right away that the effort did not generate a click and try something else.
- Give one treat for every click. Even if a person (in contrast to a dog) can understand intellectually that the click means "correct," getting a tangible reward will make a difference in the training process. The rewards do not necessarily have to be consumed right away; it's OK to put the "treats" in a jar for safe keeping.
- A tip to the trainee: Try to relax and quit thinking! Don't try to use your intellect in this exercise. The designated behavior will build itself without your having to figure out what the trainer wants. The responsibility for getting it right is not yours but the trainer's. So don't think. Just do.

Smooth treat delivery requires training!

Treat delivery

You need to work at becoming quick and purposeful in delivering both treats and toys. Remember, both the *source* and the *placement* of a reward can help—or hinder—your training.

What should effective treat delivery look like?

- You deliver the treat quickly and purposefully.
- Your movements are well coordinated.
- You deliver the treat with the nearest hand.

Practicing treat delivery

Remember Good Agility Practices: Keep your focus, work with intensity, and follow your handling system. Your reward delivery should not only be prompt and deliberate; it should also follow your system of handling. We integrate features of our handling system directly into the mechanics of training. This means we pay special attention to training you to use the hand closest to your dog (the nearest hand) to reward him, and to always point your shoulders in the direction your dog is heading. So the exercises in this section aim to improve your reward delivery (and thus make your training more efficient) *and* to build good handling habits.

Treats to plate

This exercise will help you learn to deliver treats efficiently and at a high rate, using the hand closest to your dog. You'll need a plate set on a table, a handful of treats (small kibble works fine) stored in a plastic bag or a cup, and a stopwatch. The plate functions as the mouth of a hungry dog, and your job is to give treats to that dog as quickly as you possibly can.

Practicing treat delivery to boost speed and accuracy

Exercise 5: Treats to plate, basic version

1. Stand with your left side toward the table.
2. Hold the treats in your right hand, anchored at your tummy.
3. Take one treat at a time with your left hand and put it on the plate.
4. Put as many treats as you can on the plate in 30 seconds.

Then switch sides so you stand with your right side toward the table, hold the treats in you left hand, and deliver with your right hand.

Suggested tag points:

The tag point is...

- Treat-holding hand touches tummy
- Deliver treat with nearest hand

Count your treats: Are you equally fast with both hands, or does either hand need more work?

WHERE TO KEEP THE TREATS AND TOYS

In the exercise described here, you keep the treats in your hand and let that hand rest against your tummy. There's nothing magical about this particular position. We recommend it because it resembles where you *sometimes* might keep your treats, and because it allows you to anchor your hand to your body, making it easier to keep still (thus not revealing your intentions). An alternative for the treat-to-plate exercises is to keep the treats in a treat bag hanging from your belt.

But where should you keep your treats when training? Anywhere! There is no one correct place to keep treats or toy rewards. You might store your treats in a treat pouch on your hip or on your tummy, or in your pockets, or have several treats in one hand (by your tummy as in the treat-to-plate exercise, or behind your back, or by your side, or somewhere else). Sometimes you might keep many treats in one hand and give your dog one treat at a time. Or maybe you'll keep treats in a bowl next to you, or in your mouth and spit them at your dog. You can hold toys in your armpit, hidden up your sleeve, hung around your neck, or dangling from a pocket. The point is there are lots of possibilities. And when you add the potential of helpers that reward, and remotely placed rewards, the possible variations become practically endless. Your strategy concerning where to store treats will depend on the particular circumstances and goals for the training exercise at hand.

You can, for example, hold a toy in your armpit.

For variation, you can try holding several treats in the hand closest to your dog and delivering them one by one. Your other hand holds the clicker and the treat bag/cup (in case you need a refill). When you're holding many treats in the delivery hand, slipping the dog one treat at a time, you can be quick with treat delivery because you don't have to pick up a new treat for every delivery.

Exercise 6: Treats to plate, many treats in the delivery hand

1. Stand with your left side toward the table.
2. Hold treats in both hands, touching your tummy (left hand delivers; right hand is for storage).
3. Deliver one treat at a time with your left hand.
4. Left hand goes back to tummy before delivering the next treat.
5. If left hand runs out of treats, refill from right hand.
6. Keep putting as many treats as you can on the plate in 30 seconds.

Then switch sides so you stand with your right side toward the table, mirroring the exercise.

Suggested tag points:

*   Hold many treats in delivery hand
*   Hand back to tummy between deliveries

Switching hands

Quite often you may pick up or hold a toy or treat with the hand farthest away from your dog (the "wrong" hand), but plan to deliver the reward with the hand closest to him. For these situations you need to practice moving the toy or treat between your hands smoothly and efficiently—which is a simple, yet not always natural, action. We all get the giggles in classes when a student just freezes, looking at the toy in the "wrong" hand and the empty, "correct" hand, pondering how to follow instructions to use the hand nearest her dog when the toy obviously is in the wrong hand.

Switching hands before rewarding (moving the reward from the farthest hand to the nearest).

Practicing switching the reward in advance will forever solve that dilemma, and it only takes a few minutes. Strive to keep the recipient hand (which will be the hand nearest your dog) still, "smuggling" the reward to it.

Exercise 7: Switching hands

1. Hold a toy in your left hand and walk forward, hands by your sides.

2. Smuggle the toy to your right hand by moving only the delivering, left hand.

3. Keep walking, now with the toy in your right hand, hands by your sides.

4. Switch the toy back to the left hand again (moving only the delivering, right hand).

Then try the same thing while running!

Suggested tag point:
• Motionless recipient hand

Precision throwing

When throwing a reward you want it to land in a precise spot. If you intend to place a thrown reward with any precision, you need the mechanical skill to put it where you want and not 15 feet away, straight up in the air, or on your dog's head (believe us, we have been there and done that…). To follow your system of handling you also need to be able to throw with both your left hand and your right hand. Not everyone is a natural thrower—some of us need practice! To get the very best results you should contact a sports coach, but the exercises outlined in this chapter will at least provide you with a start in the right direction.

What should precision throwing look like?

- You throw the reward a set distance in a set direction, so that it lands where you intend it to land.
- You use the nearest hand when throwing (decide which side your imaginary dog is on).
- Usually you'll use underarm throws when rewarding your dog, since that makes your throwing motion less visible—but which technique you use will depend on where you are, where your dog is, and how you want the reward to fly through the air. To make sure you can adapt your technique to the situation, practice both overarm and underarm throws.

The reward should appear along your dog's intended path. Sometimes you want to toss it just a short way (left); other times you want it to land farther away (right).

Practicing precision throwing

Training is most efficient when you focus on one aspect at a time. Therefore we suggest that you start by practicing throwing with both left and right hands, then practice direction and distance separately, and finally put it all together. By varying the thrown object, you prepare for real-life dog rewards: throwing a tennis ball is quite different from throwing a tug-rope or a stuffed toy.

Remember the rule of 80% success rate? This is just as true for you as for your dog. Make sure that you succeed at least 80% of the time before advancing to the next level of difficulty.

First, work with the direction of your throws.

Exercise 8: Throw along a set line

1. Make a middle stripe (for example, with paint, sand, or a plastic ribbon) to aim along. The stripe should start at your feet and extend in front of you a bit longer than you wish to throw.
2. Make a corridor around the middle stripe. The corridor can either be parallel to the middle stripe, or grow wider as the distance increases. The corridor is your criterion—every throw within it counts as a successful throw.
3. Throw the toy along the stripe so that it lands within the corridor.

Vary between right-handed and left-handed throws, and narrow the corridor as your precision increases.

Then, forget about the direction for a while and focus on the distance instead.

Decide where you want the toy to land. Then throw it!

Exercise 9: Throw a certain distance

1. Make a few stripes at different distances in front of you (like the concentric marks for the javelin-throw event at track competitions).
2. Decide which distance (between which stripes) to throw.
3. Throw just that distance.
4. Raise criteria by adding more stripes within the set distance, tightening the space where your toy has to land.

Finally, combine direction and distance, throwing to a specific spot.

Exercise 10: Improve your precision throwing

1. Place a large container (roughly a meter across) close to you.
2. Throw the toy into the container.
3. Gradually increase the distance.
4. Switch to a smaller container at the shorter distance.
5. Gradually increase the distance again.

Eventually you will be able to throw with high precision. Then try the exercises while running!

Suggested tag points:

- Attempt to throw with the non-dominant hand (yes, any attempt counts)
- Tense tummy muscles when throwing
- Look at the desired landing area

Note: The tag point is not "hit the designated area"—that'll be the outcome of your actions.

Remaining neutral

As a dog trainer, you are very aware of what your dog is doing and how he is moving. But you need to be equally aware of your own movements. Dogs are experts at identifying patterns, so if you don't intend for a movement of yours to create a pattern that your dog might respond to, you need to be able to remain neutral. Remaining neutral means that you do not change what you are doing: If you are moving, keep moving; if you are waving an arm, keep waving that arm; and if you are standing still, keep still.

What should "remaining neutral" look like?

- You keep doing whatever it is you are doing.
- Your body movement is disconnected from your dog's behavior.
- Your body movement is disconnected from your verbal cues.
- Your body movement does not reveal any upcoming clicks or rewards.

Why is it so important to remain neutral?

In agility it is especially important that your dog learns to work independently even though you are moving around, since you will be in motion (often running fast) while he is executing obstacles. You do not want to inadvertently prompt or influence your dog's behavior with your movements while he is busy performing a task on his own, so you need to remain neutral while your dog is working.

It is also important that you remain neutral while you mark a behavior before rewarding it, and when you give verbal cues that are meant to be separate from your body movements (for example, your release cue). If your dog can tell from looking at you that a reward is coming or that you are about to give a cue, he will be looking for those signs of body language instead of listening for the marker or cue. Giving away your intentions by making your marker signal or your cues contingent on certain movements or expressions would quickly dilute their meaning—so be careful not to give your intentions away.

"Neutral" doesn't mean "motionless." It simply means that your movements are disconnected from your dog's behavior and from any verbal cues, clicks, or upcoming rewards.

Click for moving ahead (left). Then deliver the reward (right)

Practicing remaining neutral

By becoming aware of your own movements and expressions and making sure that you can remain neutral, you will reduce the risk of confusing your dog and make all your training a lot easier for both of you.

Here are a few exercises that allow you to practice remaining neutral during two common training situations: when marking and when saying your start cue.

Click first, then treat to plate

Whenever you use a marker, your body and your movements have to remain neutral until you have marked the behavior. Otherwise the marker will lose its meaning for your dog, and he will start looking for other signs that say that the reward is coming. Such signs might be moving your hand toward the treat pocket (or, if you already have the treat in your hand, moving your hand toward your dog) *before* you have marked the behavior, or moving your clicker hand toward your dog (like clicking through channels with the remote control). There should be no such signs before the click! Since the marker functions as a precision tool, you have to make sure that marking happens independently of the later reward and that the reward then arrives as quickly as possible. Coordinating the click and treat thus calls for some practicing.

The exercise presented here builds directly on the treat-to-plate exercise, so you need a plate set on a table (functioning as the dog's mouth), a handful of treats stored in a plastic bag or a cup, a stopwatch, and a clicker. Keep the treat bag/cup and the clicker in the same hand (the one farthest from the "dog"), anchored at your tummy. Click, pick up a treat with the hand nearest the "dog," and put it on the plate. Your goal is to remain perfectly neutral while clicking, and start moving to grab and deliver the reward *after* the click.

Exercise 11: Click, then treat to plate

1. Stand with your right side toward the table.
2. Hold the treats and the clicker in your left hand, anchored at your tummy.
3. Stand still.
4. Click the clicker: Remain absolutely still when you click.
5. Take one treat with your right hand and put the treat on the plate.
6. Continue clicking and treating as many times as you can in 30 seconds, constantly making sure you remain still when you click.

Then switch sides so you stand with your left side toward the table, hold the treats in you right hand, and deliver with your left hand.

Suggested tag point:

- Be absolutely still while clicking ("statue tag")

Sometimes you might want to be prepared with a treat in your "delivery hand" before you click, so that you can be even faster in delivering your reward. Then the sequence will be: Pick up a treat, click, and put the treat on the plate. Compared to the former formula (when you *first* clicked and *then* picked up the treat), this routine will shorten the time lapse between the click and the treat. Since we often want to treat immediately after the click, before the dog has time to turn his head, we often recommend this practice.

Exercise 12: Treats to plate, one treat ready in the delivery hand

1. Stand with your right side toward the table.
2. Hold the treats and the clicker in your left hand, anchored at your tummy.
3. Pick up one treat with your right hand.
4. Hold still.
5. Click (remain still).
6. Put the treat on the plate.
7. Continue to pick up a treat, click, and deliver the treat as many times as you can in 30 seconds. Remember to hold still when clicking.

Switch sides and mirror the exercise.

You can also hold many treats in the delivery hand and give them one by one:

Exercise 13: Click, then treat to plate, many treats in the delivery hand

1. Stand with your right side toward the table.
2. Hold the clicker in your left hand, anchored at your tummy.
3. Take a handful of treats with your right hand. Anchor that hand too at your tummy.
4. Click (remain still).
5. Put one treat on the plate.
6. Return the delivery hand with all the treats to your tummy.
7. Keep clicking and treating until you run out of treats.

Switch sides, mirroring the exercise. To avoid running out of treats you can keep more treats in the other hand, refilling whenever the delivery hand runs empty.

Suggested tag point:

- Deliver one treat from a handful

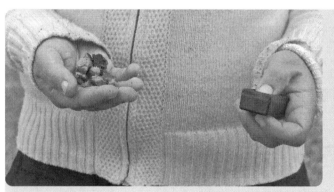

By keeping many treats in the delivery hand, you can deliver treats quickly.

When working with your dog, you'll sometimes be clicking–treating–clicking–treating in very quick succession—you might not even have time to withdraw your hand properly before you click again. That's OK. Just remove the delivery hand quickly and distinctly, and your dog will learn to ignore it and keep working. To further advance reward-delivery training, do the exercises while walking in place (or while walking forward, having a helper follow you with the plate). Your job is still to remain neutral while clicking, thus not revealing your intentions.

If you want to use markers other than the clicker (for example, a tongue click or a verbal "yes"), do the exercises with these markers as well.

Giving a start cue while remaining neutral

You will need a verbal start cue that is not connected to any movement on your part. If you happen to connect your verbal cue with a certain movement, your dog soon would

You need to teach your dog to start on your verbal cue alone: He shouldn't cue off your body language, since then he might start because of some inadvertent move you make. Here the dog waits for the proper start cue off the seesaw (rather than starting just because the handler looks back or begins fiddling with the toy). Teaching your dog to start only on your cue begins with your learning to remain neutral while saying your start cue.

key into that movement and cue off the movement instead. Remember: Dogs are more acute observers of body language than of verbal cues. For example, if you repeatedly accompany your start cue with a lowered shoulder (or a throwing movement, or a step forward), your dog will soon take that shoulder dip (or throwing motion, or step forward) as a cue to go, regardless of the verbal cue. He probably will learn to wait patiently for that body cue rather than starting on the verbal cue alone.

Teaching and maintaining a verbal start cue is easy as long as you can remain neutral while you say the magic word. If you are standing still before the cue, you should remain still until you have given the cue. If you are running, you should keep running while you give the cue. If you intend to throw a ball as a reward when your dog takes off, don't reveal that intention until *after* you have given the cue.

When your start is fully trained, the order of events should be:
- First, while remaining neutral, you give the start cue.
- On your verbal cue, your dog explodes away.
- When your dog has started, you either reward (perhaps with a toy thrown in the direction he is heading) or start handling, directing your dog wherever you have decided to go.

Before you can teach your dog a verbal start cue, you need to make sure that you can say that special word while remaining motionless. Sound simple? For some people it is. Others—unintentionally—get stuck in a "cue + movement" habit that can require some work to eliminate. To ensure that your cue is disconnected from your movement, here is an exercise where you get to practice saying your start cue first, then throw a toy.

For this exercise try to get a helper to stand next to you and give you feedback when you get it right. Your job is to remain absolutely neutral while saying "go" (or any other start cue of your choice), without any intention movement revealing that you are about to throw.

Exercise 14: Say "go," then throw the toy—while standing still

1.	Stand still with the toy in your left hand.
2.	Say "go" (remain still).
3.	Toss the toy forward.

Then practice the same with your right hand.

Suggested tag point:
- Neutral while giving start cue

Now do the exercise while you are moving:

Exercise 15: Say "go," then throw the toy—while moving

1. Walk or run forward with the toy in your left hand.
2. Say "go" while you keep running (remain neutral).
3. Toss the toy forward (keep running!).

And then, of course, repeat with your right hand.

Suggested tag points:

- Neutral while giving start cue
- Running while tossing the toy

Varying your own behavior

Because dogs are masters at identifying patterns, they will look for patterns in your behavior and use these patterns as clues for when to offer which behavior. Your dog's natural tendency is to look to you to figure out what he should do, and this makes teaching your dog to work independently a tricky business. Making sure not reveal intent by remaining neutral when standing still or running is only the first step in training an independent worker. To truly teach your dog that the behavior in question "works" no matter what you do, you also have to become a master at varying your position and movements. By constantly and randomly varying your own behavior in the training situation, you will help your dog discover that it is *his* behavior—not what *you* do—that produces the rewards. He will learn to *generalize* the behavior—that it works in all contexts, no matter what you're doing.

Whenever you are teaching your dog a behavior that you eventually want him to perform on his own (in other words, all equipment-related behaviors), make sure to introduce slight variations in your own behavior from the very beginning. By behaving in slightly different ways all the time, you also lessen the risk of giving your intentions away before marking or rewarding or cueing.

In keeping with Good Agility Practices, however, there are two rules that you need to be consistent about in order to stay true to your system of handling: Always be conscious of which way your shoulders are pointing and which hand (if any) you are using.

Feel free to vary everything else! For example:

- Which side your dog is on: left or right
- Lateral distance (distance from your dog's side)
- Distance behind or in front of your dog
- Standing still, stepping with one or two feet, running in place
- Pace changes: walking, jogging, running
- Finger, hand, and arm movements: wiggling fingers, waving hands, arms behind your back or over your head, and so on
- Head movements: looking at or ahead of your dog, nodding, shaking, making faces

The smallest variations are the most important ones. Simply moving a tiny step back or forth, wiggling your fingers a bit, or tapping one foot makes a huge difference to your dog. Work with your variations as you would work with any other distraction; make sure your dog can still succeed and get rewarded, and increase the difficulty in tiny steps. You don't have to work through every possible variation in every step of your training; just make sure you vary your position, posture, and actions so that you don't look the same all the time.

Varying your behavior is something you'll always need to pay attention to, not just in the early stages of training. After a few years, many a good, independent, contact performance or weave-pole entry has fallen apart and become dependent on a handler's inadvertent body cue because the handler has not been mindful of unconscious habits. It's extremely easy to slip into unintentional patterns when training agility, so make sure to work at avoiding these habits throughout your dog's agility career.

In this section, we have chosen not to give you any specific exercises—we have merely offered some tips and advice for what to vary when you work with your dog. If you wish to transfer these caveats into specific drills to improve your performance (and yes, of course we recommend you do that!), you can add the parameter of varying your own behavior throughout any of the exercises in this chapter. You can test a new variable for each session (for example, stepping in place, waving your arms, or nodding your head) or try varying your behavior within one session (for example, step in place at the start, stand still in the middle, and wave your arms at the end). The trick is to make sure your variations are not contingent on what your dog does or on your marking, rewarding, or cueing. Be random!

A handler (white jacket) and her "dog" (black jacket) in the Oval.

Handling basics in the Oval

The basics of our handling are simple:
- Point your shoulders in the direction your dog should go.
- Use the arm nearest your dog.
- Turn with your dog on your outside.
- Avoid blind crosses.

We have a favorite exercise, the Oval, which is specifically designed to enable you to practice *all* these handling basics in a controlled setting. The Oval is an exercise just for *you*. This exercise allows you to rehearse the handling basics in a clear-cut setting where you can focus on one thing at a time. There is never any point in involving your dog in this exercise; the Oval is strictly designed to help *you* get the mechanics right.

What should performing the Oval look like?
- Two guideposts are set up about 3 meters (10 feet) apart.
- A human acts as your "dog."
- You, the handler, walk or run in an oval around the guideposts, all the while staying consistent with your system of handling.

- Your shoulders face the line of the Oval: straight forward on the straight line, and following the arc as you turn around the guideposts.
- You keep your "dog" on the outside so that you move next to the guideposts.
- You give your "dog" a treat now and then, using the nearest arm.
- After one or two laps you change direction by turning face-to-face with your "dog" and head in the opposite direction. This means you switch sides with him in a front cross.

The dog is on the outside, and the handler's shoulders are pointing in the direction the dog should go.

Why do you need it?

Working on one thing at a time makes learning go faster and smoother. By practicing the Oval you will give yourself a good foundation and help make your handling consistent. After some practice, the correct moves will come more and more automatically. This means you will be more likely to get it right even when your attention is somewhere else—as when you are training your dog.

Practicing the Oval

For the Oval you need a friend who can act as your "dog" (the "dog's" job is to walk beside you following the direction of your shoulders) and two guideposts (chairs, training bags, whatever) that you set up about 3 meters (10 feet apart). If possible, get another friend to stand on the sidelines, observing you and giving you feedback.

The best way to train the Oval is first to find the right path to follow, and then to perfect the details one at a time.

Step 1: Find your path: Walk in an oval around the guideposts with your "dog" on the outside.

Step 2: Switch directions (and switch sides): After a couple of laps, turn 180°, facing your "dog," and keep walking in the other direction. Your "dog" will also turn toward you and end up on your other side.

Step 3: Mind your shoulders: Point your shoulders forward, facing the path you are going to walk. You can imagine a flashlight shining from each shoulder, lighting your way. Pay special attention to where your shoulders are pointing when you come around the curve and enter the straight line—that moment will reveal how truly your shoulders are aligned. If your shoulders are parallel to the guideposts when you come around the corner (at "X" in the diagram), you know you have got it right!

Step 4: Use the nearest hand: As often as you wish, you may give your "dog" a treat— using the nearest hand, of course. Deliver the treats a bit ahead to enhance your "dog's" forward motion. The rest of the time your arms just hang by your sides while you focus on pointing your shoulders in the direction you are heading.

SHOULDERS!

The single most important part of the Oval exercise is to get your shoulders pointing in the right direction. Especially if your "dog" gets a little bit behind you in the turn, you might be tempted to start crabbing sideways instead of facing forward. It is perfectly OK to turn toward your "dog" and "catch" him if he is about to sneak behind your back, but then you must twist back and face the right direction again. So no crabbing around the curves!

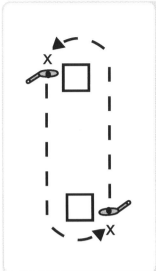

The tag point is: Shoulders parallel when you come around the corner. Note: This diagram—the first of many such in this book—is a convenient way of illustrating, in a bird's eye view, the path you or your dog will take.

With the fundamental mechanics of training and handling under your belt, you are well equipped to teach your dog. Good luck with your training! Your dog is the winner here, because when you get it right, his job is simple.

Reward procedures

Your ultimate job when teaching your dog is to provide consequences for his behavior. In a training program based on positive reinforcement, that means rewards—lots of them and lots of different kinds of rewards. In this chapter, we'll show you the ins and outs of rewards and procedures for rewarding your dog.

The role of rewards in your training

At its best, training is a constant chain of joyous events:

- Your dog does something you want, and that behavior is immediately followed by one of two desirable possibilities:
  - an attractive reward
  - or by the opportunity to perform another behavior

- Each reward procedure, also, is immediately followed by either
  - another reward
  - or by the opportunity to perform another behavior.

So each correct behavior leads either to a reward or to the opportunity to perform a new behavior. And each reward leads either to another reward or to another chance to perform a behavior. The only time you should interrupt this chain is when you take a break, and then your dog should either be involved in some game with you or be put away on leash or in his crate.

To get this chain of events flowing smoothly, you need functional rewards that suit your training purposes. The most important role of a reward, of course, is to reinforce (strengthen) behavior. But to most effectively aid your agility training, your rewards also need to meet a lot of other requirements. For example:

- You want them to appear at the right time and in the right place.
- You want to be able to deliver rewards while you stay true to your system of handling.
- You want rewards that can last while you move around or catch your breath.

Establishing the rewards procedures you need requires some thinking, experimenting, and training. That's why foundation training for your dog starts here.

The most important reward requirement is that your dog must love the reward and be willing to put in some effort to get it!

Reward requirements

In agility training, rewards need to meet many specific requirements. Besides functioning as desired consequences, your rewards should also help you conform to the rules of Good Agility Practices (working with focus and intensity and following your handling system) and to the five keys to successful training (criteria, timing, rate, quality, and placement). By having access to a broad spectrum of reinforcers, you can always choose the reward that is the most suitable for the situation.

You need rewards that
- your dog really loves and is willing to work for.
- can appear at the right time.
- you can withhold or remove in case your dog does not offer the behavior you want.

- can be delivered while you stay true to your system of handling.
- allow your dog to offer a new behavior quickly again after the reward.
- can be given quickly, multiple times, in a specific position.
- are interactive and high-intensity.
- can be placed remotely, in advance.
- can be thrown to a specific spot.
- your dog can chase in a specific direction.
- can last while you move around or take a short break.

You need a reward that you can throw to a specific spot and that can appear at the right moment

You need a remote reward—here a bowl with lovely treats, guarded by a helper.

You need a reward that can be given quickly, multiple times, in a specific position.

You need a reward that can last a while and allows you to move around or take a short break.

To choose the best reward for a specific training situation, we suggest that you ask yourself the following questions:

- Does the reward enhance Good Agility Practices?
  Will it improve focus?
  Will it improve intensity?
  Will it allow you to stay true to your handling system?

- Does the reward make it easy to live up to the keys to successful training?
  Timing: Can it be delivered at the right time?
  Rate: Can it be delivered as often as required?
  Quality: Is it good enough?
  Placement: Can it be delivered where it most benefits your training?

SO YOUR DOG IS GOING CRAZY OVER HIS REWARDS? PERFECT!

Your dog cannot love his treats or toys too much! If he goes crazy when he sees them, that's perfect—it means you have something he'll really work hard to get. Through training, your dog will learn that rewards are contingent on his behavior, not on their access or vicinity—so you shouldn't feel that you have to hide them from him while he is working. Instead, make sure you're in control of the rewards, and set proper criteria so that he learns that he can easily earn the coveted reward. At first, you might need to reinforce anything he does that is not an attempt to steal the treat or toy. If his behavior gets out of line, he simply doesn't get the reward. Your dog will soon grasp the concept that offering behaviors is what will get the ball to come out and play.

VARY REWARD TYPE, SOURCE, AND DELIVERY

When teaching agility skills, vary the reward. Sometimes you see clicker trained dogs that expect only food after the click and show both surprise and disappointment if they get a toy instead. It's also common to see a dog that immediately turns toward his trainer after the click, expecting the treat to appear from that direction. Such expectations hinder agility training, but it's easy to avoid them. Just make it a habit to vary what happens after the click: what the reward is, where it comes from, and where it is delivered. That way you'll be much more likely to choose the most suitable reward for each situation and use rewards to enhance your dog's direction, helping him to work ahead and negotiate the equipment without your help.

Various rewards and reward procedures

Various treats and toys are without a doubt your most useful rewards. To meet all the reward requirements you need many different kinds of treats and toys—experiment to figure out what your dog enjoys, and don't forget that reward procedures can be *taught*. Don't just settle for what you've got: Constantly work with your rewards, building your dog's desire for various treats and toys.

Tasty treats

Treats come in many shapes and flavors. When you're shaping a miniscule behavior you'll find it most useful to use treats that are really small (so you can dole out a lot of them), don't crumble, and don't require lots of chewing (so your dog can eat them quickly and get back to work). Cheese, pancakes, beef, or chicken—all of which are soft and easy to cut into pieces—are perfect. Depending on your training requirements, you can give these treats from your hand, you can toss them and let your dog catch them, or you can throw them on the floor. In other situations you might want larger, longer-duration treats that can function both as a reward and as a means for transporting your dog from one place to another. Food tubes are great, and so is semi-mushy stuff (such as sausage or meatballs) that can be continually nibbled from your hand.

Only your imagination sets the limits when it comes to figuring out which goodies your dog really goes crazy over. The best treats are often right in your own kitchen, but you can also check out the pet store or the Internet; hundreds of recipes for homemade dog treats can be found on the many web sites devoted to dog care and training.

The less obvious treats often make for the greatest success—especially at times when you really want your dog to go "Wow!" Surprise your dog with an ice cream, some leftover meat sauce (in a plastic box), a big bite of a Big Mac, a juicy meat bone, or your turkey sandwich. These treats often take some time to finish but, on the other hand, can be delivered with more social interaction between you and your dog, for example at the end of an exercise or as a special surprise for an extra effort.

If you have a small dog or a dog with a sensitive stomach you might not want to exchange too much of your dog's ordinary food with delicious but less nutritious treats. One way to solve that problem is to flavor your regular kibble: Put kibble and some real tasty treats together in a plastic bag, let it soak for a while, and voilà—you have special-tasting kibble! You can also use a food tube, allowing your dog to lick off just a small amount of the delicious contents.

Which is your dog's favorite toy?

Thrilling toys

Toys are versatile rewards. You can throw them, you can let your dog chase them, you can play tug with them, and while your dog is tugging you can easily move to where you want to go, ponder your next move within an exercise, or just untangle your legs from a twisty handling exercise. We do like our dogs to play tug and to retrieve toys that we throw, but the most critical part is that your dog aims for a toy and enjoys the game. So playing with a toy does not necessarily have to mean mouthing; it can be chasing, pawing, or whatever your dog loves doing.

Different toys fit different kinds of toy games. Test all kinds of toys to figure out what your dog really is wild about. For example, try rabbit skins, deer hoofs, squeaky toys, balls or KONG® toys on a rope, a cap, the dog's leash, a long whip with a toy attached to it—the list is endless!

Treats disguised as toys

If your dog is more into treats than toys, you can disguise your treats as toys to get the benefits of toy games. Treats disguised as toys can also be a fun variation for the dog that loves his toys—an added bonus, so to speak. There are lots of stuffable toys on the market, which use a Velcro or zipper closing, as well as food tubes of different kinds. You can fashion a homemade variety by using old socks, empty toilet-paper rolls (fold in the ends), or small containers with screw caps. Some of these items make tug toys (for example, the Velcro toy or the sock); yet others make it possible to throw treats with more precision and without tossing food all over the place (food tube, old container, toilet-paper roll).

Some edibles work fine as toys without embellishment. You can throw chewies such as rawhide bones and pig's ears quite far or play tug with them, and you can tie larger edibles (such as a meaty bone) to a rope so that you can reel it in after throwing it.

With your clicker, you can mark precise responses. Here the handler clicks for "front foot approaching box."

Introducing the clicker

Before discussing how you can teach your dog to enjoy various reward procedures, we'll show you how to teach your dog the meaning of the clicker so you can start using it to help build and enhance your reward procedures. The clicker will become a hugely significant and valuable reinforcer for your dog, since it signifies that good things are coming. So each time you use your clicker, your dog will get a "double" reinforcement: first the click, then the actual reward.

By using a marker such as the clicker, you're able to pinpoint very specific responses. The marker gives your dog precise information that the behavior he just tried "worked" and will earn him a reward. By using a marker you can reinforce with accurate timing (marking as the behavior happens, and then following up with the actual reward), instead of trying to deliver the actual reward at the exact moment when the correct behavior happens.

You've already worked on timing your click just right (see page 72). What's left is to introduce the clicker to your dog and to put it to clever use in your training.

What should "click and treat" look like?

- Each click is always followed by some kind of treat or toy.
- A click can be followed by either a treat or a toy.
- The treat or toy can be presented in many different ways.
- The treat or toy can appear from any direction.

What should it look like when you use your clicker to mark a behavior?

- Your dog works actively until he hears the click.
- Your dog hears the click, and then a treat or toy appears.
- Your dog readily accepts and enjoys a broad variety of treats and toys after the click.
- Once your dog has swallowed the treat or released the toy, he is ready and eager to work again because he knows that he can earn a new click.

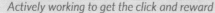

Actively working to get the click and reward

Teaching your dog the meaning of the clicker

To teach your dog the meaning of the clicker, you pair the "click" sound with treats or toys. This pairing is often referred to as "charging" the clicker and is pure classical conditioning. Whether or not you need to do this pairing first, before you start using the clicker in your training, is subject to some debate. Our experience is that you can just begin using the clicker. Making sure that you always follow the click with a desirable toy or a treat will ensure that the pairing occurs, and the dogs seem to catch on straight away.

On the other hand, if you do want to charge the clicker, we suggest that you click and reward randomly, when your dog is least expecting it. Another option is to simply click the clicker and deliver a treat or a toy, many times in a row. The downside to this method is that the dog usually looks at the trainer or at the treat the whole time, thus inadvertently learning to stare at wherever the treat comes from (which is not beneficial for agility training). Therefore we prefer to either condition the clicker by clicking and treating randomly (as described in the following section), or to simply begin using the clicker in actual training where the dog soon learns that clicks equal treats.

Charging the clicker

In an everyday setting, charge the clicker by randomly clicking and following each click with a great reward. While charging the clicker, never mind what your dog is doing when you click. You're not looking to reward any specific behavior—you're just pairing the sound of the clicker with upcoming rewards.

Make sure to remain neutral—don't reveal your intentions! Later, when you use the clicker in your training, you want your dog to stay focused and keep working until he hears the click rather than looking at you to see if you're about to click or if a reward is about to appear. This is why remaining neutral is important. From your dog's perspective, the click should come "out of the blue"!

Since you want to be able to use treats and toys interchangeably in your training, vary what happens after the click. Sometimes it's a delicious treat, sometimes it's a thrilling toy game. Also vary where and from where the reward appears; in your agility training you don't want your dog to look back at you just because he hears a click. You just want him to expect a reward to come his way.

Exercise 16: Charging the clicker

1. Keep an eye on your dog while he just hangs around.

2. Do not reveal your intentions: Act neutral. Hold the clicker behind your back or invisible in your hand (so that you teach the sound and nothing else).

3. Press the clicker.

4. Directly after the sound, give your dog a treat or start a fun game with a toy.

Repeat this pairing randomly 10 to 20 times over a couple of hours (or several days). Vary the reward and the source and placement of the treat or toy: you can toss it ahead, or deliver it from your hand, or even have a helper give it to your dog so he does not always look at you after the click.

Suggested tag point:

• Remain neutral while clicking

To test if your dog is conditioned to the sound, press the clicker and see how your dog reacts. Does he look as if he's expecting a reward? Then he's got it.

Developing a taste for treats

Eating is vital for survival, so all dogs do eat. But some dogs are not all that enthusiastic when it comes to food treats being used as rewards during training. However, you can develop your dog's taste for treats. View *eating treats* as a behavior that you're training; you need to build your dog's eagerness to get his treats before you can use the treats as rewards.

Here are some suggestions:

• Hungry wolves are eager hunters—don't feed your dog right before training! Of course, you shouldn't starve your dog; just make sure he isn't already full. For your agility training, use the tastiest treats you can find and make your training sessions as short as necessary—always try to quit working while your dog is still excited about the treats.

• You can develop your dog's eagerness to eat by having him work for most of his regular dog food (searching for it in the garden, earning it by doing tricks, or simply prying it from your closed fist). Many dogs seem to find it more exciting to eat on the job than to get big portions in a bowl on the kitchen floor—and it seems that the more often your dog gets to work for his edibles, the more eager he'll be to get them.

• If your dog is more into toys than treats, you can use the Premack Principle (using a more likely behavior to reward a less likely behavior) to teach him to enjoy treats. Give a few treats, then play a fun toy game. Eating is rewarded by playing (so if your dog chooses not to eat, then there is no toy game either). If the "eat first, then play" pattern is repeated often enough, he'll get more and more eager to get his treats because they herald toys to come.

• You can employ the Premack Principle in other situations as well: Have your dog eat a treat before going out the door, before being allowed to greet another dog, and so on. The behavior of eating the treat is rewarded by the fun that follows, and your dog will gradually start enjoying treats more.

Remember to practice *eating treats* in various circumstances. Your goal is that your dog will eat anywhere, in any situation. Start easy, with no distractions, and move on gradually.

The treat magnet

Treats are usually "short" rewards: your dog gets a treat, swallows it, and that's it. But it's possible to prolong the ceremony by using a *treat magnet*—treats you hold in your hand that your dog hangs on to and follows around. Along with the game of tug, the treat magnet is our favorite extended reward, excellent for keeping your dog occupied while transporting him to a new starting point or during a mini-break.

What should the treat magnet look like?
- Your dog hangs on to the treats in your hand, keeping his nose in constant contact with your hand.
- You slip him a treat now and then.
- Meanwhile, you can do what you need to do (think, talk, put your toy away, or whatever) or move around to where you need to be next.
- To end the treat magnet, you quickly and distinctly pull your hand away (either slipping your dog a final treat or keeping the remaining treats).

With the treat magnet, your dog's nose should be locked to your hand.

Why do you need the treat magnet?
- It prolongs the treat reward ceremony.
- It helps you stick to Good Agility Practices, working with focus and intensity, since it ensures that your dog stays "within the training bubble."
- It enables you to keep your dog "attached to you" during brief breaks or while transporting him to a new starting point.
- It enables you to easily position your dog exactly where you want him to start the next repetition.

How can you train it?
The goal of the treat magnet training is to get your dog to "glue" his nose to treats in your hand so you can lead him around and keep him occupied. Picture a strong magnet: You can't pull your hand away from your dog's nose, and vice versa. Make sure you feel that wet nose touching your hand throughout the exercise. Naturally you'll be working on this exercise equally with your left and right hands (in other words, with your dog on your left side as well as on your right side).

We teach the treat magnet in three steps:

Step 1: Get the treat magnet behavior: "nose touching hand with treats."

Step 2: Build duration so that your dog's nose sticks to your treat hand like a magnet, hanging on to it when you move the hand.

Step 3: Add distractions to ensure that your dog sticks to the treat magnet no matter what.

The treat magnet should have a distinct start and a distinct finish, and you need to be the one ending the game. To end the treat magnet exercise, either you can slip your dog a final treat and then remove your hand, or you can quickly pull your hand away with a distinctive, fast movement (keeping the remaining treats). Once you start using the treat magnet in your actual training, your dog will move on to offering behaviors when the treat magnet ends, which is why it's vital to end the treat magnet clearly and abruptly.

Step 1: Get the treat magnet behavior

To begin the treat magnet game, present your hand with treats in it next to your dog's nose. Let him succeed in prying little bits of treats out of your hand—voilà, there's your treat magnet.

Exercise 17: Teach the treat magnet

1. Hold a couple of tasty treats in your hand. This is your magnet.
2. Present the "magnet" to your dog's nose (as if you were giving him the treat, but here you hold on to the treat).
3. When your dog's nose touches your hand, slip him a treat.
4. Keep your hand still.
5. Your dog touches his nose to your hand again.
6. Continue slipping him treats while his nose touches your hand.
7. To end the treat magnet, abruptly remove your "magnetic" hand.

Suggested tag point:

• Feel your dog's nose

The use of a marker is optional. If your dog offers the correct behavior right away and simply presses his nose to your hand, you can just slip him the treats without marking the behavior. If, on the other hand, your dog is doing a lot of things with his mouth other than just touching your hand (gaping, biting, and so on), you might want to include "mouth closed" as part of the criteria. Then, using a clicker, you can make it easier to convey to your dog exactly what he needs to do to get the treat. For instance, if you have a dog that will bite (perhaps hard) to get the treat, you hide the treats in your hand, click for "touching without teeth," and then slip him a treat.

As long as your dog is varying his behavior (often doing other things than continuously pressing his nose to your hand), reinforce the correct behavior *as soon as* it happens, *every time*, by slipping him a treat when he gets it right. Your dog needs lots of information about which behavior is correct. When he continuously offers the proper behavior, you can reward less often with the treats—but not until then!

A CUE FOR THE TREAT MAGNET BEHAVIOR?

If you like, you can choose a special hand cue for this exercise. Simply hold your treat hand in a unique way that you use only when it serves as the treat magnet, and your dog will learn that hand cue. This way you eliminate the risk of your dog starting to offer the treat magnet behavior when he is not supposed to.

However, the mere fact that your treat hand remains at your dog's nose after you have delivered one treat will function as a cue for the treat magnet behavior. As long as *you* know when it's treat magnet time and when the treats in your hand are just a distraction, your dog will figure it out.

End the treat magnet by abruptly and distinctly removing your hand. Your dog should be in no doubt that the treat magnet is over! You can either slip a final treat to your dog, or just pull your hand away. When using the treat magnet in your agility training, it's often most efficient to just pull your hand away. This way your dog can start working right away without having to chew down a treat first.

Step 2: Build duration

When your dog's nose continuously touches your hand, start moving your hand around and deliver treat after treat as your dog's nose sticks to your hand like a magnet. Add duration and movement in small doses, making sure your dog's nose is touching your hand all the time. If your dog lets go of the treat magnet sooner than you intended, don't engage in any other activity: let him come back to the magnet and work some more.

You can make a fun game of the treat magnet, moving it in zigzag, up and down, or up your own body. Get your dog working intensely to hang on to it!

Playing around with a treat magnet.

Step 3: Add distractions

Challenge your dog by adding distractions: Can your dog follow the treat magnet even if you're holding a toy in the other hand? Even when you move close to a tempting piece of equipment? Remember: You decide when the treat magnet begins and when it ends.

Developing a joy for toys

Your agility training works best if you can vary between treat and toy rewards. Some dogs are toy maniacs, but others need to learn to enjoy toys and toy games. If you have a dog that is reluctant to play, it's worth every effort to get him excited about toys and interacting with you. The rule is: You need to be enjoying the game as well!

Here are some guidelines for setting off your dog's interest in toys:

- Encourage all kinds of interaction with the toy—grabbing with the mouth isn't the only game in town.
- Making the toy more "alive" is often a hit: Move it along the ground like small prey, or attach it to a rope or whip and make it dance.
- Hiding a yummy treat in "toy clothes" will intrigue the food-motivated dog. In the beginning make it easy for your dog to get to the goodies. You can even open the toy together, helping your dog reach his treats. As your dog gains experience, you can make it harder for him to get that treat out.
- Focus on the toy, making it the center of the universe, and your dog will be intrigued. Don't wave the toy in your dog's face; let your dog come to the toy.
- Try hiding the toy and then whipping it out again.
- Play with the toy by yourself or with somebody else while ignoring your dog—this often triggers the dog's interest.
- Try playing when your dog happily greets you as you arrive home from work, or when he has just had a bath, or whenever he normally acts a bit goofy.
- End the game before your dog does. By ending the game while your dog is still interested, you avoid inadvertently teaching your dog to quit on you.
- The Premack Principle, of course. is viable here as well: for the food-driven but toy-ignorant dog, treats come *after* play.

Put a sheep skin on a long line and make it come alive!

When your dog shows interest in the toys, you can reinforce his interest in many different ways—either by adding extra flavors to the ongoing game or by giving a reward that interrupts the play. When your dog engages in the toy, for example, you can make fun noises, add extra playful body language, push your dog lightly, pretend to chase him, let him steal the toy from you, and so on. You can also use treats or other toy games as rewards for various play behaviors—for example let the yummy treats appear as a result of a good tug session, or throw another ball just as your dog grabs the first one. You'll find more detailed instructions about how to teach "tug and release" and "chase and come back" in later sections of this chapter.

Make sure you're the one ending the game. If you have presented the toy to your dog, do not give up if your dog does not seem to want to play along or if he ends the game before you do. We don't mean that your dog has to all-out play, but if you have invited your dog to play, make sure you get some kind of play response or at least some interest before quitting.

When your dog has started to enjoy your toy games, take his new-found interest "on the road." Your goal is that your dog will play anywhere, under any circumstances. Remember: In situations where your dog will not play, you cannot use toys or games as a reward! Since you want to be able to train—and use the reward most suited to the training—in all kinds of situations, you should invest time and energy in building a desire to play in every possible situation.

Release the toy

As soon as your dog starts to develop an interest in toys, you need a strategy for how to end the game and get the toy back.

What should release the toy look like?

- Your dog keeps playing until he hears your "thank you" cue.
- When you say "thank you," he spits out the toy.
- The release is immediately rewarded with treats or another toy game, or leads to the opportunity to perform a behavior (which, in turn, leads to a reward).

Play, release, eat a treat, and continue the play!

Why do you need it?

- For effective training, you have to be able to end the toy game whenever you wish.
- A toy-crazy dog needs to learn to give the toy back without a hassle.
- The more hesitant dog needs to learn to keep playing until you end the game.
- The release is an integrated part in the games of "tug and release" (see page 106) and "chase and come back" (see page 111).

In your agility training, toy *play* is vital. You really need rewards that you can throw and rewards that enable you to play interactive games with your dog. Therefore we put a lot of effort into teaching the dog to enjoy his toys.

The *release* is more of a practical issue; it'll help your training a lot to have a dog that releases his toy when and where you want him to, but teaching a smooth release is secondary to teaching enthusiastic play.

How can you train it?

First and foremost, recognize that *releasing the toy* is an operant, reinforceable behavior. In other words, you should make it worthwhile for your dog to give up the toy by rewarding him for doing so. The reward might be a delicious treat, another toy, or a new play session with the toy he just let go of. Usually, the most coveted reward is resuming the game with the toy he just released to you!

We'll go through the training in three steps:

Step 1: Get the release behavior, and reward that.

Step 2: Put the behavior on cue: "thank you."

Step 3: Maintain the release.

Step 1: Release the toy

To get the "release the toy" behavior, either you can use a lure (a treat or another toy that your dog wants) or you can simply wait for your dog to drop the toy. Either way, reward immediately as he releases. If you like you can use your clicker to mark the release behavior—or you can simply deliver the reward.

Getting the release by using a treat lure: End the game by offering some tasty treats. You might even put the treats in your dog's mouth—most dogs let go of the toy to swallow the treat. The "lure" treat then transforms into a reward. You can follow the "lure" treat with more treats, or with a new toy game (with the same toy, or with a different toy).

Getting the release by using a toy lure: End the game with one toy by beginning to play with another toy yourself. Preferably use a similar toy (or a different toy of similar value). Make the "lure" toy totally irresistible; as your dog lets go of his toy, he gets rewarded by a thrilling game with the other toy.

Getting the release by turning passive: End the game by simply quitting playing yourself, taking the fun out of the game. This can be done in many ways:

- Hold on to the toy and hold it perfectly still (anchored to your body).
- Hold your dog by his collar without touching the toy.
- Simply become still and ignore your dog and the toy.

Eventually, with the fun gone out of the game, your dog will let go of the toy. Just wait for however long it takes, and reward immediately as he drops the toy. You can reward with a bunch of treats, a different toy, or a new game with the same toy. If your dog is reluctant to give up his toy, often the best reward is to play again with the *same* toy as soon as he lets go.

If your dog is prone to running off with his toy, keep either him or the toy on a leash or a long line to prevent escapes.

Step 2: Add a "thank you" cue

The behavior of releasing the toy is one situation where we do opt to add a verbal cue, so that the dog learns to spit out the toy on a spoken "thank you." Remember the golden rule of adding cues: *First* get the behavior, *then* add the cue. Give the "thank you" cue only when you expect to get the proper behavior. If you're not sure, keep quiet and reward your dog when he (eventually) releases the toy spontaneously.

Teach the cue by saying "thank you" when your dog is about to release the toy, and immediately reward him for doing so. When your dog happily gives up his toy in order to get his reward, start using your "thank you" cue to tell him when to let go. Remember to reward the release!

Once the "thank you" cue is established, we want the dog to keep playing with the toy until he hears the cue—in other words, we normally don't continue to reward spontaneous releases. When you always end the toy game with a "thank you" cue, your dog will learn to continue playing until he hears that cue. This enables you to choose precisely where and when the play should end, which is very practical in your agility training.

If your dog ever "forgets" to release the toy when you say "thank you," simply turn passive. If you need to, hold your dog by the collar to prevent him from continuing the game on his own. Wait until he lets go of the toy, and immediately reward lavishly—preferably with a new game of tug or chase, if that's what he was playing.

Step 3: Maintain the release

To get and maintain a good release it is essential that you keep rewarding it. Follow every release immediately with a reward (like a game of tug or a tasty treat) or the opportunity to perform a behavior to earn another reward.

If your dog repeatedly hesitates about the release, go back to getting and rewarding spontaneous releases (as in Step 1, without a "thank you" cue). Reinforcement builds behavior, and that is just as true for the toy release as for any other behavior.

SKIP THE "THANK YOU" CUE; JUST STEAL THE TOY!

You also have the choice of simply stealing the toy from your dog when you want it back. Some dogs really enjoy the game of you trying to pry the toy from them—sometimes you win it; sometimes your dog manages to keep it. There's nothing like forbidden fruit, so playfully fighting your dog for the toy can bring extra fire and energy into the play. Just make sure it remains a fun game for your dog. You don't want your dog to give up or become hesitant when you win the toy; neither do you want the situation to degenerate into a battle.

Remember: When you "play outside the rules" and steal the toy, your dog is entitled to do the same and put in every effort to keep it! Strictly distinguish between "theft" and proper releases, so that your dog doesn't get confused. We usually alter between the two, sometimes stealing (or at least trying to steal it), sometimes using a release on cue.

Tug

The game of tug-of-war is one of your most valuable reward procedures—not that it's impossible to train an agility dog without it, but it's so much easier to work with a dog that truly enjoys a good game of tug!

What should the game of tug look like?

- Your dog's teeth grasp the toy without touching your hands.
- Both you and your dog are enthusiastically engaged in the game of tug.
- Your dog is so engaged in tugging that you can move to a new location while he hangs on to the toy.
- Your dog keeps tugging until you either give your release cue or get the toy out of his mouth.
- On your release cue your dog immediately drops the tug toy.
- After the release cue your dog instantly goes back to work, trying to earn another reward. (While you teach the tug-and-release, your dog will be occupied with his reward after releasing the toy.)
- For our agility training purposes, the *tug* part is more important than the *release* part. You can use the game of tug as a reward even if the release isn't fully trained yet—the tug behavior, though, is a necessity.

Fully focused on tugging. Playing low saves your dog's neck and back from unnecessary twists and strains.

Why do you need the "tug" part?

- Tugging is an intense, interactive, and fun reward.
- Tugging enhances your dog's interest in playing toy games with you instead of on his own.
- Tugging is a perfect reward for the "chase and come back" game—your dog will come back with the toy to keep tugging.
- Tugging allows for easy transports; while your dog just hangs on to the toy, happily tugging away, you can easily move him around.

Why do you need the "release" part?

- The release enables you to end the game quickly and distinctively, where and when you want it to end. That way your dog can move on to offering behaviors right away.
- When you integrate the release into the game of tug in a continuous cycle, your dog learns to enjoy both the tug and the release.

First, play tug—then release the tug, and go weave.

How can you train it?

Tugging—like all other operant behaviors—is driven by its consequences. If good things happen when your dog tugs, he'll tug more. Teaching your dog to play tug thus is not just about getting him to tug; what's more important is *reinforcing* him for tugging.

In this section we'll discuss how you can reinforce nice behaviors within the tug game, and we explain how you can teach any dog to play tug (even dogs that aren't yet interested in toys).

We'll describe the training in four steps:
Step 1: Get the tug behavior. There are two ways to do this:
- Shape the tug using the toy game itself as a reward.
- Shape the tug using treat rewards.

Step 2: Build duration, so that your dog keeps tugging as long as you want him to.
Step 3: Add distractions, so that your dog grabs and keeps tugging no matter what.
Step 4: If you like, **add the "get it" cue**.

Step 1, version A: Shape tug using the game itself as a reward

Within a tug game, your dog will find some events more exciting than others. By letting the most exciting events happen as a consequence of the more desired behaviors, you can teach your dog to play tug the way you want him to. Remember: Your dog decides what's "fun"! Here are some examples of events your dog might enjoy:

- You making sounds (playful growling, loudly inhaling, squeaking, weird noises, and so on).
- You putting in an extra effort to steal the toy (pulling back, grabbing it closer to your dog's mouth, and so on).
- You "teasing" him with your eyes and your body language.
- You shaking the toy or making it squeak.

- You letting him win the game (either fully letting go of the toy, or almost letting go for a few seconds).
- You saying "thank you" and rewarding the release. (Since the release is highly rewarded, the release cue can function as a reward—especially for dogs that are a bit hesitant to play tug).

Most of the events listed above can also be used to elicit play—but here we want you to use them primarily as *reinforcers* within the tug game, to strengthen desired behaviors. When your dog does something you wish to see more often, reward it by making the toy game even more fun to your dog.

Here are some examples of desired behaviors—behaviors that you might wish to reinforce during the play:

- approaching the toy
- teeth touching the toy
- grabbing the toy without touching your hand (or grabbing the toy far away from your hand)
- pulling back from you, with toy in mouth
- maintaining a clean hold (instead of grabbing over and over)

So, play around with a toy and reinforce any responses that may lead to nice tugging by adding extra fun to the game!

If your dog does something you really don't want (like biting you instead of the toy), do the opposite of what your dog might find fun: in other words, "go boring" (turn passive and/or remove the toy for a while).

Integrate your "thank you" cue into the game, often asking for a release and rewarding that release with a new game of tug. Tug-and-release should be a cyclic chain. When you eventually wish to end the game, reward the release in some other fashion. Later, when you use the game of tug in your agility training, you can follow the release by an opportunity to perform a behavior and earn a new reward.

Step 1, version B: Shape tug using treat rewards

If your dog isn't at all interested in tugging, you can shape the tug from scratch using treats as the reward. Our favorite method is to use a toy (a sock works well) with a treat hidden inside. Reward any attempt to tug by loosening your grip on the toy so that your dog can get to the treat.

In the beginning, use big chunks of a high-value treat (a chicken breast, for example, or half a hamburger) that your dog can pry chunks off, and make your dog's job really easy: Roll up the sock so that the treat is almost visible, and reinforce all attempts to get to the goodies. Reward by letting your dog get to the treats in the sock—either open the sock slightly while still holding on to it, or let go of it. Remember, this is shaping! Your criteria and your timing are crucial; make sure you reward desired responses such as touching, grabbing, and pulling. If you reward by letting go of the sock, you probably don't need a marker—you can easily just loosen your grip on the sock. If you reward by opening the sock for your dog, click to mark the correct response and then open the sock.

Here is a suggested criterion plan (add any in-between steps that you need):

1. dog's nose touching sock
2. teeth touching sock
3. biting on sock
4. pulling ever so slightly
5. pulling hard
6. pulling vigorously, perhaps shaking ("killing") the toy

Exercise 18: Get into that sock

1. Hide a big chunk of a tasty treat in a sock and let your dog investigate.
2. Your dog touches the sock (or even nibbles or grabs it).
3. Open up the sock and let him grab a bite of the treat.
4. Close up the sock again, hiding the remaining goodies.
5. Continue shaping, letting your dog get to the treats in the sock when he nibbles/grabs/bites the sock.

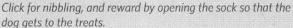

Click for nibbling, and reward by opening the sock so that the dog gets to the treats.   *Step by step shape the tug.*

Play around, get the toy moving, and let your dog chase it and work hard to pull it out of your hand. If your dog ever lets go before you do, play with the sock yourself and let him try to steal it again.

After a while, tugging on the fabulous sock usually becomes highly reinforcing in itself. You can then use the sock (with the treats in it) as any regular toy, only occasionally opening it.

Of course, it's possible to train the same way without hiding the treat in the toy: Click and give a treat for nose touching toy, teeth touching toy, and so on. If you have a dog that sometimes plays, it is a good idea to capture the behavior by clicking and treating. Do not worry if your dog switches to food mode and does not want to play anymore. He'll figure out that treats become available only when he plays tug.

TUG—RELEASE—TUG AGAIN!

It's a good idea to integrate releases into the game of tug—this way, you make it a cyclical game where your dog learns to enjoy both the tug and the release. Intermittently let your dog release the toy, and reward immediately—sometimes by resuming playing, sometimes with another reward. (For a recap of how to teach the release, see page 103.) Remember to use the "thank you" cue only if you're sure the behavior will happen, in other words, that your dog will happily release the toy. If you're not sure he'll release on cue, get a spontaneous release instead (swap with another toy or a treat, or go passive and wait him out) and reward lavishly.

Properly trained, the tug and the release will reinforce each other in a continuous cycle:

The release reinforces the tug: Since great things always follow the release, your "thank you" cue will function as a reinforcer for the tug (it'll have practically the same effect as a click). Especially with a dog that's less interested in the toy, it's important that you cue "thank you" while your dog is tugging nicely, to continually strengthen the tugging behavior. You can even use your release cue when shaping the tug: Instead of using a clicker or other marker, you can simply say "thank you" when your dog touches the toy, and then follow up with a reward. The tugging behavior will increase since it leads to good things (the release cue and the reward).

The tug reinforces the release: For the tug-crazy dog, another game of tug is the best reward for the release. If you often follow the release with another game of tug, your dog will happily let go when you say "thank you."

You can also combine the methods: Start with the hidden treat in a sock and then move on to shaping the tug with any toy, reinforcing by clicking and treating. This way, your dog will soon learn to play tug with all kinds of toys (both the ones with treats in them, and the "clean" ones).

Step 2: Build duration

No matter how you got the tug behavior (using the game itself as a reward, or using treat rewards), build duration so that your dog keeps tugging as long as *you* want him to. The key is to make sure you're the one ending the game. At first, play in brief sessions. Gradually lengthen the duration, always ending the game (with a click or a "thank you" cue followed by some kind of reward) while your dog is hanging on to the tug toy. If your dog lets go prematurely, keep playing until he engages in the game again.

Step 3: Add distractions

You'll want your dog to play tug in the face of various distractions: people, other dogs, interesting equipment, other toys, or delicious treats. Distractions might be present when you begin the game, while your dog is hanging on to his toy, and/or when he releases. Begin easy and gradually introduce more challenging distractions.

Left: Playing tug with a sock in the presence of a distracting sheepskin.
Right: A "thank you," followed by getting the sheepskin, is the best reward for tugging on the sock.

Step 4: Add a "get it" cue

When your dog enthusiastically engages in the game of tug whenever you want him to, you can add a "get it" cue. Having a "get it" cue can be practical since it enables you to tell your dog when to go for the toy.

To teach the "get it" cue, begin by saying the cue as your dog goes for the toy. Eventually, you can use the cue to elicit the game. When you're playing around with your dog, you can also teach him to wait for your "get it" cue and to go for his toys only after that cue. Simply say the "get it" cue when your dog waits for a nanosecond—and remove or cover the toy if he tries to grab it before the cue.

Chase and come back

When training agility, the best placement of a reward is often ahead of your dog so that he keeps aiming forward; this is why throwing a toy often works brilliantly. If your dog knows and enjoys running ahead, grabbing a toy, and coming straight back to you to continue the game, the training session will run a lot more smoothly and efficiently.

What should chase and come back look like?

For our agility training purposes, the *chase* part is more important than the *come back* part. Above all, you want your dog to enjoy running after a toy you have tossed. You can use the chase as a reward even if your dog just runs to the toy and waits for you to come to him, or comes back without the toy. However, it's more practical if your dog brings the toy back to you.

The chase is what's most important.

A perfect "chase and come back" should look like this:

1. Your dog runs straight to the toy and grabs it.
2. After grabbing the toy your dog immediately runs as fast as he can toward you.
3. As he reaches you, he pushes the toy into your hand (this is optional but makes a perfect goal for him to aim for).
4. You respond with either a game of tug or a release cue followed by something fun (a treat, another game of tug, another throw, or a new opportunity to work and earn another reward).

A thrown toy can appear just where you want it, when you want it. Here the toy turns up right in front of the dog as a reward for "leaving the contact on cue."

Coming back with the toy to continue to enjoy the game with the handler.

Why do you need the "chase" part?

- Throwing a toy enables you to choose the best possible placement of the reward. The toy can appear as your dog is moving away from you, landing wherever you like.

Why do you need the "come back" part?

- It is practical and makes your training smoother since your dog comes straight back to you with the toy instead of spending time playing on his own, possibly even disturbing others around you.
- Coming back with the toy means that your dog enjoys playing with you more than playing on his own.
- You reduce the risk of time gaps where your dog doesn't really know what to do. If the chase-and-come-back sequence functions as a chain, your dog will stay focused and intensely engaged throughout the reward procedure.

How can you train it?

Chase and come back form a chain of behaviors: Your dog runs out, grabs the toy, turns, and brings it back to you. Then you play tug or give a release cue, followed by a great reward. One way to train this chain is to simply throw the toy and tempt your dog to chase it, and then work on getting him to grab it and bring it back to you. This informal approach requires figuring out ways to *entice* rather than *teach* your dog to do the behavior. For a dog that naturally loves fetching, this is usually all you need.

To *teach* your dog to chase the toy and bring it right back, we recommend back-chaining, starting with training the final act, the delivery of the toy to your hand. When back-chaining, you want to start at the end—but in this case, the end behavior is "pushing the toy into your hand," and you cannot teach that until your dog is actually holding something in his mouth. And to hold it, he first has to open his mouth to grab it. It is also beneficial to separately teach a hand target behavior, as a preparation for "pushing the toy into your hand."

Once your dog eagerly performs the end of the chain (pushing the toy into your hand), the actual back-chaining can begin. You first add the "coming to you" part, then the "picking up the toy" part, and finally the "chasing the toy" part.

By employing back-chaining, your dog will be eager to chase the toy so he can grab it and deliver it to you, where the *real* fun begins.

We'll describe the training in four steps:

Step 1: Push the toy into your hand.

   Stage 1: Teach a hand target.
   Stage 2: Get your dog to grab and hold the toy. (You can shape the grab and hold using click and treat rewards—or, if your dog enjoys tugging, you can make use of the grab and hold you get within the tug game.)
   Stage 3: Shape the push into your hand.

Step 2: Come back to you with the toy.

Step 3: Pick up the toy.

Step 4: Chase after the toy.

At the end of this section, we'll also give you some advice for enticing the chase and the come back in informal play settings.

Pushing the toy into the hand

Step 1: Push the toy into your hand

Your goal is for your dog to actively push the toy into your hand until you click and treat, give your release cue (and subsequent reward), or start playing tug with him.

Stage 1: Teach a hand target

Separately teaching your dog to target your hand, before introducing it in the toy game, is quite helpful. It's a fun and simple behavior to train, and can be used in many other circumstances as well. The goal is for your dog to press his nose into the palm of your hand.

Present your hand close to your dog's face but a bit to the side. Most likely he'll look at your hand when it appears—capture that! Click for "nose aiming toward hand," and place the reward close to the target hand (either put the reward in the target hand after the click, or have it appear right next to it). Incrementally raise the bar so that your dog has to do more for each reward. Possible criteria are:

1. looking at your hand
2. nose approaching your hand
3. nose touching your hand
4. nose pressing toward your hand
5. nose pressing toward your hand for longer and longer periods (ping-pong back and forth, sometimes rewarding immediately, sometimes waiting a bit longer)

Hand target

Exercise 19: Shape the hand touch

1. Present your hand at the side of your dog's head.
2. Your dog looks briefly at your hand.
3. Click for nose pointing toward hand.
4. Treat close to (or in) the target hand.
5. Remove the target hand and present it again.
6. Continue shaping, clicking, and treating for nose approaching/touching/pressing against the hand.

If your dog doesn't point his nose toward the target hand within three seconds, remove it briefly and present it again.

Stage 2: Get the grab and hold

If your dog enjoys tugging, you already have the "grab and hold"; you'll be able to make use of that when shaping him to push the toy into your hand. Your dog, however, then needs to really enjoy the game of tug—and tugging needs to be an interactive game, so you want to build your dog's desire to play with *you,* not to keep the toy to himself. To give your training a flying start, it might be worthwhile to use all toys for tug games for a while, so that your dog learns that toys equal playing tug with you.

You can also shape a "grab and hold" using clicks and treats. This is definitely the way to go if your dog isn't (yet) that enthusiastic about toys, but we usually practice this exercise with all dogs (parallel to working with the tug). To shape the grab and hold you can use any object—if your dog wants to start playing with the toy, use some more boring object in the beginning.

Here is a sample of criteria for shaping the grab and hold:

1. nose turning toward the toy
2. nose approaching the toy
3. nose touching
4. mouth slightly open
5. teeth touching
6. mouthing
7. teeth gripping the toy
8. holding the toy for a nanosecond
9. holding for longer and longer periods (ping-pong back and forth, sometimes rewarding immediately, sometimes waiting a bit longer).

Early in the training, it usually works best to hold the object in your hand to the side of your dog's head, close enough for him to reach it by just turning his head. Use your clicker to mark the correct response, and reward with treats or some toy game your dog enjoys.

Getting from "teeth touching" to "holding" can sometimes be a bit tricky. Be careful to mark as your dog's nose and teeth *approach* the object. You don't want to click late, since that would mean clicking as his teeth *retreat* from the object. If you miss the perfect opportunity to click, just wait for a new response. To make it easier to get from teeth touching to that first second of the hold, it might help to vary the setting a little bit. Try these suggestions:

- Move the toy away slightly as your dog grabs it (so that he really has to "catch" it).
- Wait for two or three brief grabs, intermittently rewarding consecutive grabs—in this process your dog will probably vary his behavior a little bit, and then you can reinforce all the better holds.
- Get yourself and your dog up and moving, letting him grab the object while moving around.
- Hold the object close to the ground or high up in the air.
- Keep a potential reward in view, giving your dog something to focus on besides the retrieval object. For some reason this sometimes makes the dog "forget" to open his jaws and drop the object.
- Transform the retrieval object into a toy after the click (playing tug with it, or tossing it away). Of course, this works only if your dog enjoys playing with the object.

INTRODUCE YOUR RELEASE CUE

When you use the clicker to mark the correct behavior, it simultaneously ends the grab/hold behavior (since your dog releases the object as you click, in order to get his reward). As soon as you don't feel the need for the split-second precision of the clicker, you can replace the click with your release cue: Say "thank you" as your dog performs the desired behavior, and reward the release immediately.

You then have two possible ways to end the hold; either you can click (meaning that your dog can spit out the object, and that a reward is on its way) or you can cue "thank you" (meaning that your dog should spit out the object, and that a reward is on its way). Through the rest of your chase-and-come-back training, use the clicker if you need precision; otherwise use the "thank you" release cue.

Build the duration gradually, ping-ponging back and forth between shorter and longer holds so that your dog never knows when the click will come.

Stage 3: Push the toy into your hand

For your dog to know exactly where to bring the toy, teach him to touch your hand with it (pushing his nose into your palm with the toy in his mouth). While your dog is holding the toy, present your hand and shape him to push the toy toward your hand.

If your dog enjoys tugging, introduce brief interruptions in the tugging. Let go of the toy mid-tug and move back (or run away). When your dog approaches you, grab the toy and resume tugging—from this, you can gradually shape him to push the toy into your hand.

If your dog doesn't come toward you immediately, run off in the other direction and keep running until your dog catches up with you. Don't play or interact with him as long as he keeps at a distance—just keep moving away. When he comes to you, either resume the tug game, or reward in some other way. To decrease the risk of his running off and enjoying himself, you can put a line on the toy—but you also need to make sure that playing *with you* is a lot more thrilling than playing on his own.

You want your dog to pester you to keep tugging!

If you have been shaping the grab and hold, now present your target hand while your dog holds the toy. Click and reward when his nose approaches your hand while still holding the toy. Gradually advance toward having him actively pushing the toy into your hand, ending with your release cue.

Here is a sample of criteria for shaping "pushing the toy into your hand":

Reward when your dog holds the toy in his mouth and:
1. looks at your hand
2. moves toward your hand
3. touches your hand
4. presses the toy into your hand
5. presses the toy toward your hand for longer and longer periods

The reward can be more tugging, a click and reward, or your release cue and a reward.

If your dog drops the toy prematurely, you can remove the hand that he was supposed to push the toy into and simply pick up the toy yourself. Then start over. You can also wait for a second and see if he spontaneously picks up the toy himself—if so, you should of course let him try to push it into your hand again.

Step 2: Come toward you with the toy

Once the end of the chain is established, the rest (moving toward you with the toy, picking it up, and going out to get it) is simple. Your dog then already knows his goal: delivering the toy to your target hand (either as soon as you let go of the toy during a game of tug, or when you present your hand when shaping a grab/hold).

Begin by moving just your target hand, so that your dog has to follow it a few steps in order to be able to push the toy into it. Then start backing away, letting your dog follow you. Gradually move farther away while sticking to the same criterion; give your release cue when your dog presses the toy into your hand.

Step 3: Pick up the toy

Present the toy farther away from your dog's nose (up, down, or to the side). Let go of the toy just as he grabs it, and present your hand target for him to push the toy into. Then move on to dropping the toy on the ground so that your dog has to pick it up.

Step 4: Chase after the toy

Gradually add distance by throwing the toy farther and farther away. Congratulations! Your dog chases the toy, grabs it, hurries back to you, and presses the toy into your hand to get his reward. To many dogs, the act of chasing and grabbing will become rewarding in itself (even if your dog wasn't really interested in it at the start), but to maintain and continuously strengthen the chain, keep rewarding your dog for pressing the toy into your hand and releasing it on cue.

Informally encouraging your dog to chase and come back

When informally playing around with your dog, encourage and reinforce the behaviors you like. The advice offered here will help you build a chase-and-come-back game. Notice, however, that you can't expect perfection without training for it, so if you feel the need for higher precision, stick to the proper back-chaining procedure presented above.

Racing to the toy—the winner gets the prize!

Chase the toy

- Attach the toy to a rope and employ a helper to bring it to life.
- Use a toy that hides treats that your dog can get by himself.
- Use a toy that hides treats, and run up to your dog to help him open it.
- Run up to your dog when he grabs the toy and play with him and the toy.
- Race your dog to the toy. The first one to reach it gets it!
- Avoid verbal coaxing since it tends to reinforce hesitation.

Come back

- Use two similar toys. As your dog grabs one toy, start playing by yourself with the other one or throw it in the opposite direction, past you. Your dog will probably drop the first toy and go for the second. Whip out the first toy again and have a great time by yourself: Your dog will want to join in and he might bring the toy he got with him as he comes back to you. Either way you teach him to turn toward you when he grabs a toy, anticipating amazing things will happen where you are.
- Put the toy on a line and reel in both the toy and your dog. Play tug or throw the toy again.
- Reward your dog lavishly for coming back, with or without the toy. Eventually he may bring the toy with him, and either way you do get him back quickly after each throw.
- Run in the other direction. If your dog runs past you, turn and run again. Keep running until your dog reaches you.
- Wait to interact until your dog is coming back to you. Avoid giving your dog lots of attention when he is at a distance with the toy (calling and coaxing, trying to catch the toy as he runs past you, and so on). The more you interact with your dog at a distance, the stronger that behavior will get.

You've now made sure to create rewards and reward procedures that meet the specific requirements for your agility training. In the next chapter you'll learn how to use the treat magnet and the game of tug (along with some other procedures) for a purpose that you might not have considered: to cover gaps in time and space while keeping your dog's focus and intensity strong.

Transports

It's important that you always keep your dog in the training bubble so that you never leave him hanging. In this chapter we'll show you how to keep your dog occupied when you need to move him around, take a quick break to collect yourself, or briefly prepare in some way. We refer to these periods, when your dog is "in transit," as *transports*.

Staying in the training bubble

Moving your dog around while keeping him happy and occupied may be a skill you haven't thought of, but smoothly "transporting" your dog from one spot to another is essential for your agility training. Any productive training session starts with getting your dog to the right starting position and, as the session progresses, often requires repositioning him for a new start. At the end of a session you'll want to move him away from whatever equipment you have been working on. Sometimes you also need to keep your dog occupied for a brief time while you take a break and catch your breath, move some treats from one pocket to the other, or just think for a second.

A treat magnet can keep your dog occupied while you think for a second.

If we could teleport the dog from one spot to another, making him vanish and reappear when and where we wanted to (without him noticing the lapses), we would! But since that isn't possible, we do the next best thing and make sure the dog is occupied whenever we need to bridge gaps in time and/or space. It all boils down to Good Agility Practices: To build and maintain your dog's focus and intensity and to avoid "gaps" in your training session, you need to help your dog stay "in the bubble" the whole time.

We use the term *transport* as a collective name for all the different activities we use to bridge such gaps in time and/or space.

Transport requirements

Your methods for transport should

- be easy to use.
- be something your dog enjoys.
- prevent your dog from engaging in other activities (such as wandering off, running around, or starting to work prematurely).
- enable you to place your dog precisely where you want to, facing the direction you want.
- end clearly and distinctly so that your dog can start working.

Different means of transport

There are many possible ways to move your dog from point A to point B. Here are some possibilities:

- Treat magnet
- Tug
- By collar (or leash)
- Lift and carry
- Recall
- Hand target

What we really don't want to see is the handler moving around with the dog just plodding along next to her. We want transports that keep the dog occupied and that begin and end distinctly, so he can learn to aim ahead and start working whenever the transport ends.

Treat magnet and tug transports

The treat magnet and tug are our absolute favorite transports. They are fun, they keep your dog engaged, and, especially with the treat magnet, you can position your dog precisely. The treat magnet and tug are particularly useful when you have rewarded one behavior and wish to move your dog to a new starting point to continue working: Just let the reward last longer, and move your dog around while you're rewarding.

With a treat magnet or a tug toy, you can transport your dog to precisely the starting point you want.

But we also use these transports (especially the treat magnet) at other times. Sometimes when your dog has made an attempt but not met criteria, you need to get him to a new starting point so that he can try again. You can still use the treat magnet for transport, even though you do not wish to reward the previous behavior. Just make sure there is a substantial difference in quality between the actual reward (which follows the desired behavior) and the means for transport (which follows a "wrong" behavior).

When you use a treat magnet or a game of tug to transport your dog, make sure that your behavior is distinct: it should be crystal clear to your dog when he is "in transport" and when he is not. The treat magnet must be just that, a magnet, with your dog's nose touching your hand. When your dog is where you want him, swiftly remove your hand (with what is left of the treat), and your dog can start working right away. The same goes for tugging; make sure your dog keeps tugging throughout the transport, and when he is where you want him to be, cue him to let go and remove the toy. By ending the transport distinctly, you'll enable your dog to learn when to focus on the treat or toy (during the transport) and when to ignore the treat or toy (when the transport has ended).

USING TRANSPORTS AFTER A MISTAKE

Some will ask, will the transport function as a reward for the wrong behavior if you use it after your dog has made a mistake? People question particularly the use of the treat magnet and the tug toy for transports, because they perceive them as rewards and do not feel comfortable using them after a behavior that has not met criteria (though any method of transport that you have trained your dog to enjoy also can function as a reward). So how can we use these transport rewards after a behavior that we do not wish to reinforce?

Just as you should continue to work even if your dog makes a mistake, sometimes you simply need to transport your dog to a new starting point after a mistake, and then you should do so in a fashion that keeps you and your dog in the training bubble. You have two choices: possibly rewarding a mistake (by adding a pleasant transport after the mistake), or sacrificing your Good Agility Practices and undermining your dog's happiness and confidence (by disconnecting from your dog or not giving him a proper chance to keep working). Obviously we choose the first alternative.

Instead of worrying about potentially rewarding the wrong behavior, make sure to lavishly reward the right one! That means adding even nicer things when your dog gets it right, so that the contrast is between a pleasant transport (a mildly reinforcing event after a mistake) and a thrilling reward (tasty treats and plenty of enthusiasm after the desired behavior).

Remember: Look at the behavior! If the behavior you're working on is improving, then you know your training is on the right track and your transport treats have not served as rewards for the wrong behavior. If the behavior is not improving, look at other aspects (such as the keys for success: criteria, timing, rate, quality, and placement). In our experience, the transport treat is rarely the problem.

Collar transports and lift-and-carry

Holding and leading your dog by the collar or harness is a useful means for transport. With a reasonably small dog, you also have the option of lifting him up and carrying him. If you do this, we recommend either cueing the dog to jump into your arms, or using a verbal cue for "lift" to alert the dog that he is about to lose contact with the ground. These hands-on transports need training, though, so that your dog learns to enjoy your grabbing his collar or lifting him up. Your dog should *want* these interactions! This is easy to accomplish using classical conditioning: Simply pair the collar grab (or your lifting your dog) with fun events. For example: Touch the collar and give your dog a treat; lead your dog a few steps and end by running away, letting him chase you; or lift him just off the ground and whip out a tug toy as you let him down.

Using a collar transport, you can release your dog when you feel him aiming correctly.

Classically condition the collar grab to mean "tasty treat is on its way." The order of events is important: First grab the collar (left); then present the treat (right).

With a reasonably small dog, lift-and-carry can be an excellent way of "teleporting" him to where you want him.

You can use a leash, too, but holding the collar or harness gives you more precision: It simply is easier to move your dog exactly where you want him to be. It is also more obvious to your dog that you're restraining him, which reduces the risk that he'll start trying to work before the transport is over and get accidental yanks on the leash.

Using a recall

A recall is another way to move your dog from one spot to another: Cue him to stay or have someone hold him, move to wherever you need to be, and call your dog to you. For the recall to work as a transport you must make sure you end the recall properly (for example, with a game of tug or a treat magnet), never leaving your dog in limbo.

Hand target transports

Another possible way to move your dog that we wish to mention, even though we don't use it much ourselves, is a hand target behavior. First you need to teach your dog to press his nose against your hand continuously until you reward. Once your dog targets your hand eagerly, you can use the hand target to position your dog's nose wherever you want it to be. We give a brief description of hand-target training on page 113 in Chapter 8, "Rewards."

Practice getting to a good starting point

Your transport should keep your dog occupied while you move around. The transport should also enable you to position your dog exactly where you want him, to set up for a smooth start. Transporting your dog to a chosen spot calls for some practice, so here's an exercise designed solely for that purpose.

Exercise 20: Get to the starting point

1. Choose a method for your transport.
2. Draw a line on the ground. This is your start line.
3. Play with your dog.
4. Transport your dog to the start line so that his front feet are on (or close to) the line.
5. Reward, and play again!

Practice your transports! Treat magnet to the "start line" and stop with the front feet close to the line.

Collar transport to the "start line" and end with some play.

Try this exercise with different transport methods, and remember to work your dog on both your left side and your right side. Note that your dog isn't really supposed to do anything except just hang along for the transport and get rewarded for staying in the game while you figure out how to maneuver him to the spot of your choice.

Congratulations! Now that you've got all the reward and transport procedures trained, you can put them to use as your dog actually "does" agility. The next chapter presents the two strategies that you'll use most often to train specific agility skills: *Aim for it* and *Race to reward*.

Getting behavior: two favorite strategies

In our agility training, we have two favorite strategies for getting behavior; we call them *Aim for it* and *Race to reward*. These strategies form the core of our agility training, and you'll find innumerable references to them throughout the rest of the book. In this chapter, we present *Aim for it* and *Race to reward* in detail; you'll learn how to teach your dog to work ahead without prompts and to drive with speed and intensity to a remote reward. Both of these strategies are critical in developing the confident, independent obstacle performance you need from your agility partner.

Our favorite teaching strategies

As an agility trainer, you want to teach your dog many specific skills (like going between, over, or under various pieces of equipment). You also want to develop a dog that focuses ahead, drives forward, and works independently of you on the equipment while aiming in the direction given by your handling. The strategies you choose for getting behaviors when teaching specific skills will have a profound effect on how your dog works in relation to you, the equipment, and the rewards—which is why we're very particular about which teaching strategies we use. Our two favorite strategies—*Aim for it* and *Race to reward*—fill these double purposes: They are excellent for teaching many different skills, and simultaneously they'll teach your dog to aim ahead and think for himself while constantly working in accordance with your handling. We make use of these strategies from the earliest foundation stages all the way through teaching obstacle performance and handling maneuvers.

In Aim for it *the dog aims ahead on his own, expecting a click and a reward.*

Aim for it is a fast-paced shaping procedure that's initially measured in milliseconds of behavior—it'll sharpen your observational and mechanical skills. Reward placement is critical to keep your dog headed forward; each reward should promote your dog's forward motion. *Aim for it* teaches your dog to be creative and to offer behaviors on his own. It also teaches him the invaluable—and, sadly, often ignored—skill of working ahead without prompts. *Aim for it* closely resembles a real agility run in that your dog cues off your direction, aims ahead, and works independently with whatever piece of equipment he encounters in his path. Since there is no lure or prompt involved, your dog learns that his job is to *drive ahead* to the equipment, an essential ingredient in creating a great agility dog.

You'll learn the details of how to get behavior using the *Aim for it* procedure in the upcoming section. We also describe how you can work with *Aim for it* in a continuous loop, dubbed "the Bermuda Triangle."

In *Race to reward* your dog runs to a remotely placed reward, eventually performing various behaviors on the way. *Race to reward* builds the intensity and speed you want from your agility dog and teaches him to race ahead in full drive. With *Race to reward* your dog eventually will also learn to really work for whatever reward is out there, cueing off your handling and completing every task along the way. Just running straight to the beloved treat bowl or tennis ball won't always do the trick. However, racing to the reward is the vital first step, and in the last section of this chapter you'll learn how to train it.

In Race to reward *the dog races to a remote reward. In this setup, he first dashes between the jump wings, then turns toward the reward.*

PRACTICE WITHOUT YOUR DOG FIRST!

Practicing exercises first without your dog makes excellent sense and should become a habit, especially for our two favorite strategies, *Aim for it* and *Race to reward*. *Aim for it* puts some demands on your mechanical skills, and *Race to reward* might seem deceptively easy but is a fast-paced exercise during which you need to follow Good Agility Practices.

Before they get their dogs, our students work in groups of three people (one is the handler, one is the "dog," and one is an observer/helper) to rehearse the exercises first so they'll stand a better chance at executing their part of the job flawlessly when working later with their dogs.

Here the group is practicing Race to reward.

When training agility we rotate between these two strategies since we find them both valuable and since they supplement each other nicely. If we had to choose to use just one strategy to get behavior in agility training, without a doubt we would choose *Aim for it*. But since we don't have to choose, we use both!

Shaping *Aim for it*

We love the art of free shaping! It's fun, your dog learns to think for himself and to really work to get his rewards, and you don't get stuck with any prompts or lures that you later have to work to get rid of.

In training agility foundation skills, almost all free-shaping sessions involve teaching your dog to aim and work *away* from you and *toward or with* some piece of equipment. The goal might be to teach your dog to go between two buckets, through a hula-hoop, or under a draped cloth. All these skills eventually will transfer to the different agility obstacles such as jumps, weave poles, tires, and collapsed tunnels. To get independent and reliable obstacle performance, you need to teach your dog to focus ahead and work away from you from the beginning. To accomplish this, we rely on shaping *tiny steps* and making the best possible use of *reward placement*.

What should *Aim for it* look like?

- Your dog spontaneously focuses and works ahead as soon as he gets a chance.
- He aims in the direction you're facing and gathers information from your clicks and rewards, thus performing whichever behavior it is that you're working on at the moment.
- You place each reward *ahead* of your dog, in the direction you want him to work.

As soon as the reward is over, you should feel that your dog is being "pulled" forward by some unseen force toward whichever piece of equipment you're working with.

The clicks and rewards tell the dog what to do.

Why do you need *Aim for it*?

Aim for it lays the foundation for future obstacle training and thus helps build and refine many more complex behaviors.

Aim for it teaches your dog to
- offer behaviors spontaneously.
- look ahead and move forward.
- drive toward equipment.
- work independently of you.
- start working again directly after each reward.

Aim for it offers you, the trainer, the opportunity to
- practice resisting the temptation to prompt your dog forward.
- practice the art of setting criteria and raising them wisely. Set your criteria extremely low at first, so that you can manage to click after the reward is over but before your dog has time to turn his head the wrong way.
- practice swiftly placing the reward in the correct position (in the direction your dog is working).
- practice working intensely with no gaps in the sequence of behavior–click–reward–behavior–click–reward.
- practice using extended rewards to transport your dog to new starting positions.

MAKING USE OF *AIM FOR IT*

We employ *Aim for it* in many areas of our training. Here are some examples:

Between, around, over, onto, under, through, page 159.
Creating noise and movement, pages 178, 181.
Rear-end control, page 190.
Handling maneuvers on the flat, page 240.
Jumps and tunnels, page 264.
Handling sequences, pages 300 (box), 324.
The contact obstacles, pages 357, 360.
The weave poles, pages 410, 412.

Aim for it *will teach your dog to look ahead and drive toward equipment.*

How can you train it?

Arrange a piece of equipment for your dog to work toward, and free-shape him to look at it, move toward it, and perform some behavior when he reaches it (stepping onto it, for example).

The shaping procedure we find most useful follows this pattern:

1. Get yourself and your dog to a good starting position using a treat magnet or a game of tug.
2. Remove the toy or treat.
3. Immediately click for the first possible, tiny response that eventually might develop into the behavior you're looking for. Usually that will be "nose pointing forward, toward the piece of equipment."
4. Quickly deliver the reward (give a treat, throw a toy, deliver a tug toy, or whatever) ahead of your dog's nose, in the direction your dog should be working—either just a step ahead, or farther ahead. The reward should appear before your dog has time to turn his head toward you.
5. You have two choices for this final step
   a. Start over at Step 2: Stay where you are, dog facing the equipment, remove the treat or toy, and click and treat again for the first possible desired response.
   b. Start over at Step 1: Play and transport your dog around to a new starting point.

Keep the sessions brief and intense (30 seconds is usually plenty enough).

Shaping the dog to go under a plank:
Left: First, transport to a good starting point. Center: Forward motion earns a click!
Right: The reward appears ahead, before the dog has the chance to turn toward the handler.

As your dog starts to get the picture, you follow the same procedure but raise criteria so that he has to look ahead longer, move forward, and eventually perform whatever behavior it is that you're looking for to get his click and reward.

PLACE THE REWARD AHEAD OF YOUR DOG!

When training *Aim for it*, there are many benefits in placing the reward ahead of your dog, in the direction you want him to work. Your placement of reward will enhance your dog's forward motion, get him moving during the reward, and give you a new starting point.

To get the placement of reward correct, picture the path you want your dog to move along. Each reward should appear ahead of your dog, somewhere along this imaginary path.

You can deliver the treats just a little bit ahead of your dog so that he can keep working forward after each treat, each time starting from a slightly different position. This way you get to reward several times in quick succession, and your dog gets lots of reinforcement for "facing forward."

You can also place the reward farther away (by throwing a toy, for example). Your dog then will get all the way to the mat (or whatever you're working toward) in just one reward. This option leads to fewer rewards in a session (since you throw a toy once, instead of clicking and treating five or six times), but it does build high expectations for cool stuff happening farther ahead.

Varying between the two options is a good idea; that way your dog will get both the information from many clicks and treats when he moves toward the mat, and great expectations and intensity from the cool rewards that appear at the mat. You can also structure your training so that you start out with a few quick treats for looking in the right direction and then throw a toy. Use the reward that you think will benefit your training the most at the moment.

Notice the difference between a lure and a reward: What we're talking about here are rewards, appearing *after* the click. Yes, your placement of reward might bring your dog all the way to or past the equipment—that's perfectly OK! We urge you to take advantage of clever reward placement, since that will propel your training forward. What you click for (the behavior you're reinforcing) is still "looking ahead" or "moving ahead."

TRAIN YOUR DOG; DON'T HIDE THE REWARD

When playing the game *Aim for it*, at the earlier stages you're going to need to keep the treats in your hand to reward your dog quickly enough. If your dog glues his eyes on that treat-holding hand, that's not a signal for you to put the treats elsewhere. Your dog needs to learn that rewards are contingent on his behavior—not on their mere presence. If he goes for the reward when you're hoping to work with *Aim for it*, your first criterion needs to be "nose moving away from the potential reward in your hand." From there you can advance to clicking and treating for the nose pointing in the desired direction. Make sure you stick to your criteria, and your dog soon will grasp the concept.

NOT A "GO TO YOUR PLACE" EXERCISE

Aim for the mat is not an exercise about shaping your dog to "go to bed" (to go to a place and spin around to look at you, and/or lie down). Here we're only interested in shaping the dog from the handler to the object (here the mat), nose continually pointing forward. How you advance from there (working with different skills and different objects) is described in "Teaching between/around/over/onto/under/through using *Aim for it*" (page 159).

Shaping *Aim for the mat*

The shaping process you use in training *Aim for it* teaches your dog the essential agility behaviors of continuously looking ahead and driving forward. Shaping *Aim for it* is so fundamental to our whole program that we want to give you a basic exercise for practicing this procedure. *Aim for the mat* teaches your dog to spontaneously run ahead to the mat as soon as he has finished the previous reward. We'll go through the shaping process in four steps that mirror the criteria we reward:

Step 1: Nose pointing toward the mat for a millisecond.
Step 2: Actively point the nose forward.
Step 3: Step forward, toward the mat.
Step 4: Dash all the way to the mat.

A clicker-savvy dog/trainer team can reach Step 4 within one brief session; a newbie team might require some practice to get there. Remember, the process is invaluable in itself—you and your dog will gain lots of valuable skills through the *Aim for it* training, and once your dog gets the hang of it, future training will be much easier.

Step 1: Nose pointing toward the mat for a millisecond

In the earliest phase of training *Aim for it, you* become accustomed to intense, fast-paced training and get your mechanics in order. *Your dog* begins to learn that rewards will appear ahead of him when he keeps his nose pointing forward toward the mat.

First, practice the *Aim for it* procedure with many clicks and treats, each reward delivered just a step ahead of your dog. Prepare so that you have your mechanics in order and a mat, your clicker, and several treats ready.

Exercise 21: Begin shaping **Aim for the mat,** *delivering many rewards on the way to the mat*

1. Use a treat magnet to get your dog to a good starting point less than a meter away from the mat, facing the mat.
2. While your dog is still moving, end the transport by removing your hand with the treat.
3. Immediately—while your dog's nose is still pointing toward the mat—click for "nose toward mat."
4. Quickly reward with a treat ahead of your dog, so that he has to take at least one step toward the mat to reach it.
5. As you remove your hand, click again while your dog's nose is still facing the mat.
6. Quickly reward again, one step in front of your dog so he must continue to move toward the mat.
7. Continue this process until your dog puts one foot on the mat. Click for "foot on mat," and this time rev up the reward!
8. Use a treat magnet to move in a circle (dog on the outside) back to the starting point, and start over again.

Treat one step ahead of your dog, so that he needs to move to get the treat. Use the hand nearest to your dog.

Also, practice the *Aim for it* procedure using just one reward per repetition, placing the reward far ahead of the dog (in this case, on the mat). Here we usually find it most efficient to use a thrown toy.

Exercise 22: Begin shaping Aim for the mat, *delivering just one reward far ahead (on the mat)*

1. Use a treat magnet or a game of tug to get your dog to a good starting point half a meter away from the mat, facing the mat.
2. While your dog is still moving, end the transport by removing your hand with the treat.
3. Immediately—while your dog's nose is still pointing toward the mat—click for "nose toward mat."
4. Quickly reward with a thrown toy that lands on the mat, so that your dog rushes forward to get it.
5. Play with your dog while moving in a circle (dog on the outside) back to the starting point, and start over again.

When using *Aim for it* you'll benefit from varying the placement of reward: sometimes just a step ahead, sometimes far ahead, but always along the path you intend your dog to move along.

Here, the click is for the dog moving toward the mat. The toy is thrown so that it lands on the mat.

Preferably your dog shouldn't have time to look anywhere but ahead. But if he starts looking at you (or at the reward in your hand), just wait him out. Eventually he'll glance ahead (or at least glance away from you)—click for that, reward ahead, and now try to click before he has time to look at you.

GUIDELINES FOR SHAPING *AIM FOR IT*

What's important?	Why?
Start training close to your chosen piece of equipment.	To get the behavior as quickly as possible, closer is better. We usually start no more than a meter away (often much closer). Never begin adding more distance until your dog reliably offers the desired behavior.
Remove the transport treat or toy distinctly so your dog realizes the opportunity to earn another reward has arrived.	By making a sharp contrast between reward/transport (dog's mouth attached to treat or toy) and independent work (treat/toy removed), it is much easier for the dog to learn when to start working independently.
Click for "nose pointing toward mat" before your dog has a chance to turn away.	"Nose pointing toward mat" is the first rewardable moment, whether or not your dog consciously chose to point his nose that way. When his nose points forward, you click and reward, and that will strengthen the behavior.
Be quick to click!	In the beginning, the transitions between behavior–click–reward–behavior–click–reward should be so fast that your dog doesn't have time to turn toward you.
If you miss the clickable moment, wait for the next one.	Timing is everything! Don't click late, since that'd mean clicking for the nose pointing elsewhere. If you miss the magic moment, just be patient and wait for the next possible opportunity to click.
Click first, then reward. Do not start getting or presenting the reward prematurely.	Your dog will cue on the first thing announcing that the reward is coming. If the click comes first, he'll learn to work until he hears the click (which is what you want). If your movement comes first, he'll start looking for the reward prematurely (and you don't want that).
Be quick to reward!	Be prepared to deliver the reward immediately after the click. Your dog shouldn't have time to turn his head toward you between the click and the reward. That means you need to keep the reward ready in your hand or employ a helper that can make the reward appear ahead of your dog just after your click.
Reward with the nearest hand.	Always follow your handling system! Using the nearest hand will keep your shoulders pointing forward.
Face in the direction your dog is heading (no crabbing).	Always follow your handling system! You want your dog to move ahead, so that's the direction your shoulders should be pointing.

GUIDELINES FOR SHAPING *AIM FOR IT* (continued)

What's important?	Why?
Place the reward a bit ahead of your dog, so he has to take at least one step toward the mat to get it.	By placing the reward ahead you will **1.** enhance forward motion **2.** give your dog a new starting position **3.** get him up on his feet if he sits down
Let your dog offer behaviors on his own. Do not prompt or point, and resist the temptation to use words or gestures to get your dog to work ahead.	If you're silent and neutral, your dog will soon figure out that his own actions cause the click and reward to happen. Prompting, pointing, urging, or luring your dog to move forward would teach him only to wait for your help, reinforce his passivity, and make it harder for him to focus and figure out what you want.
When your dog has stepped onto the mat, use an extended reward to transport him back to the starting point.	When your dog reaches the mat, his job is done. By using the last reward to transport your dog back to the starting point, you avoid attention gaps, and your dog can start working again as soon as the reward is over.
Make sure the transports are distinct. When starting over, your dog must be on a treat magnet or tug toy all the way to the next starting point.	If the dog follows the treat or toy around without hanging on to it, he'll learn to walk next to the handler and look at the hand with the treat or toy. Then, when it is time to work ahead, he most likely will keep staring at that hand because the picture will look almost the same to him. Since you want your dog to work ahead when the transport ends, he needs the difference between "hanging on to a transport" and "working ahead on his own" to be obvious.
Turn with your dog on the outside when transporting him to a new starting point.	Always follow your handling system! Turning with your dog on the outside will make it easy for you to get him to the desired starting point, facing in the direction he should work.
If something goes totally wrong and you need to take a second's break or get to a new starting point, use a treat magnet or a tug toy transport.	Never ever leave your dog in limbo; whenever he cannot earn clicks and treats by aiming ahead, he should be occupied in a transport.

Step 2: Actively point the nose forward

Look at your dog: Is he beginning to focus forward as you remove the transport treat/toy? Then click as he *actively points his nose forward*. Practically, this means building a tiny bit of duration (going from a millisecond to perhaps half a second). If he happens to look at you, just wait and let him figure out that it's "nose pointing forward" that produces clicks and treats. Remember to use your placement of reward to get your dog moving after the click. Deliver the reward along your dog's intended path, and often use exciting rewards that your dog gets to chase to develop maximum focus ahead. As soon as your dog starts to offer "nose forward," move on to Step 3: The goal is to teach your dog to *move toward* the mat (not to stand still and stare at it).

Tips for Step 2:
- Click for "pointing the nose toward the mat."
- Place each reward at least one step forward, toward the mat.
- End the trial when your dog reaches the mat, using the final reward to transport him away for a new repetition.
- Move on to Step 3 as soon as possible!

Step 3: Step forward, toward the mat

Since you constantly have clicked for "nose pointing forward" and placed your reward a bit farther ahead so that your dog has had to take at least one step forward to reach the reward, most likely he'll start heading forward more and more. Now withhold your click a little bit and shape "stepping forward" (perhaps beginning with "leaning forward" and/ or "lifting a foot") rather than just "nose pointing forward."

Move on to Step 4 when your dog confidently and without hesitation moves ahead toward the mat as soon as you end the transport.

High-intensity rewards will boost your dog's enthusiasm.

Step 4: Dash all the way to the mat

Finally, click and treat only when your dog actually reaches the mat, not on his way toward it. This means there will be only one reward per repetition: for stepping on the mat. To get maximum speed and enthusiasm, use intense rewards like a game of chase or tug. You can also expect your dog's speed to increase spontaneously as he becomes sure of his job and reliably and confidently takes off for the mat.

WHAT IS "TROUBLESHOOTING"?

"Training" and "troubleshooting" really refer to the same thing. It's all about teaching your dog what you want and avoiding teaching him what you don't want. When troubleshooting, typically you're trying to get rid of a behavior—but your focus still needs to be on what it is you want and teaching that instead.

If your dog makes an occasional mistake (happens to perform the wrong behavior once or twice), you can simply extinguish the wrong behavior by not reinforcing it. Let your dog try again, and reward him handsomely when he gets it right.

If your dog continues to make the same mistake (and/or if his confidence and happy attitude ebb), you need to take further action: You need to change something so that your dog gets it right. Then gradually increase the difficulty again—either within the same session, or at a later (sometimes much later) stage. You want to keep up a high rate of reinforcement, so make sure most of your dog's attempts are successful!

Troubleshooting

Treats, toy, clicker: I have too many things and too few hands. Help!

Refining your own mechanics without your dog (preferably employing a friend to be your "dog") is always a great idea. Practice first without your dog, and you'll be better equipped to progress without feeling the need to grow a few more arms.

You can start and finish the exercise with a treat magnet, so that you need only treats and no toys. Alternatively, you can do the whole exercise with just a toy and no treats.

You can employ a helper who takes care of some of your duties. For example, the helper can be in charge of the clicker; it actually may be easier to see your dog from the sidelines. Or the helper can deliver the rewards.

You can also opt to use a verbal marker instead of your clicker. The pro for this choice is that it unclutters your hands; the con is that a verbal marker is less precise than a clicker.

Remember that as soon as your dog starts to get the behavior, the mechanics become much easier since you don't have to be quite as fast in catching his nose pointing forward. You'll also become more proficient as you keep practicing. It's OK to feel a bit clumsy: keep trying and it will get better!

My dog never looks forward, he just stares at me!

The keys to success are extremely relevant in training *Aim for it*: criteria, timing, rate of reinforcement, quality of reward, and placement of reward.

Criteria: If your dog just stares at you, that means you're at Step 1 and that you have missed the second of "looking forward" that happened as you removed the previous reward. Since you're rewarding in a forward direction, your dog will at least have his nose pointing forward at that point. Click before your dog has time to turn his head. If you miss the opportunity and your dog starts looking at you, click for the tiniest tendency to look away from you. Reward ahead and now click while the nose points ahead.

Timing: If your dog begins staring at you, you know you weren't fast enough (because when you ended the transport, there was a millisecond where your dog's nose *was* aiming forward…). If that happens, just wait and click for the smallest desired response, such as "head turning slightly in the right direction." Your dog eventually will take his eyes off you, and then you have a clickable moment. Timing also relates to the delivery of the reward: Make sure the reward appears right after the click so that your dog doesn't have time to look back at you between the click and the reward.

Rate: After each click, reward—and then click again as soon as the reward is over, while your dog's head is still facing forward. In the beginning the rate of reinforcement should be *extremely* high, essentially as fast as you can click and treat.

Quality: Use really attractive rewards. Your dog will learn faster if the reward that appears after the click is something he really desires. Yes, the best rewards might make your dog more prone to stare at your hand or your pocket, but since you're not reinforcing staring, the staring behavior eventually will disappear.

Placement: Place the reward in the direction you want your dog's nose to point. That means forward and down, toward the mat. You can also use a helper who delivers the reward (or you can take turns rewarding, so that your dog never knows where the reward will come from).

What not to do: Do *not* try to prompt your dog forward by pointing or body cueing! Such "help" will only make your dog focus on you even more. Before the click, it's your dog that must be active. After the click, you must be active and place the reward.

A couple of tricks: If your dog, like many seasoned obedience dogs, gets glued to your left side, it may prove easier to start this exercise with your dog on your right. To avoid your dog getting stuck next to you (a familiar position where he might be inclined to stay for a long time before trying anything else), you can keep moving in tiny baby steps all through the exercise instead of standing still. Remain neutral and just move your feet forward half a step at a time. Yes, this will be a prompt forward, but a silent one that does not disturb the training.

For an extreme case of a dog glued to the trainer's side or staring at the trainer, there is one more thing you can do: Forget the clicker and the behavior, simply break off the transport and hurl the reward forward. All you're really after is getting your dog to expect good stuff happening ahead of him. Repeat a few times, and see what it gives you. Does your dog keep his nose pointed forward for a millisecond or perhaps move ahead after you've ended the transport? Great! Get back into training mode, get your clicker out, and get to work shaping the behavior you're after.

It feels as if I'm just luring and clicking!

In the beginning you'll hardly have time to remove the reward before you click and reward again, so that feeling is probably correct. That's OK. The goal, of course, is to click for looking/moving ahead *after* you have removed the hand you just rewarded with. So just get on with the training, making sure that you deliver treats and toys distinctly, that you remove your treat hand or toy equally distinctly (even if you don't move it far away), and that your dog's nose is pointing forward as you click. Keep in mind that your goal is to get your dog's nose pointing forward. Soon you'll have progressed beyond this initial stage.

I'm getting the behavior but my dog moves very slowly!

In the beginning it's OK if your dog moves a bit slowly; you're rewarding tiny movements, and your dog is trying to figure out what the game is about. Once your dog has gotten the picture, however, you should see his speed increasing. Make sure you use really cool rewards that your dog dashes ahead to get—a thrown toy that flies ahead, for example, or a tug toy that your dog gets to chase and grab. Also remember to stay a short distance from the mat—there is no point in adding distance until your dog is happily rushing ahead.

Shaping *Aim for it* using the Bermuda Triangle

The setup we call "the Bermuda Triangle" is one of our favorites—it's "where all problems disappear." The Bermuda Triangle is an infinite *Aim for it* loop. By placing a series of identical pieces of equipment in a circular or a triangular pattern, you create a setup where you can always continue ahead to the next piece of equipment. Thus you can always work ahead instead of having to reverse direction or spin around to get to a new starting position. The Bermuda Triangle is useful throughout your agility career—from foundation training where your dog learns to aim ahead and go between/over/under objects, to fine-tuning your competition dog's obstacle performance. The concept remains the same, so you and your dog will feel right at home even if the task at hand varies.

Most of the time we use three pieces of equipment or obstacles—that is why we call it the Bermuda *Triangle*. It's quite possible, however, to work in the same way with a different number of objects. You can use just one or two pieces of equipment and work in a circle going round and round, but it's a lot simpler to use at least three in formation since then you automatically always arrive at a new piece of equipment with less transit time.

We use the Bermuda Triangle to shorten the transports and to make sure it's always possible to keep working ahead. Here you can see two examples: Teaching the dog to Aim for the mat (left) and practicing the weaves (right).

What should *Aim for it* look like in the Bermuda Triangle?

- Whenever you're working in the Bermuda Triangle, you're on the inside and your dog revolves around you, working the outside lap, spontaneously aiming for the equipment.
- When you reward, you do so along your dog's intended path.
- You constantly continue ahead to the next piece of equipment.

Left: Click for aiming toward the mat.
Center: Reward on the mat (while refilling with treats from the pocket).
Right: The reward continues while the dog is transported a couple of steps forward to a good starting position for the next mat.

Why do you need the Bermuda Triangle?

The Bermuda Triangle makes it easy to

- get to a new starting point (since the next piece of equipment is just a little bit ahead).
- deal with mistakes in the best fashion by continuing to work ahead (since there is always a new piece of equipment ahead).

Later on in your training, the Bermuda Triangle also makes it possible to

- let your dog perform several pieces of equipment for one reward (since if you withhold the reward at one piece of equipment, he can simply continue to the next one).

How can you train it?

The Bermuda Triangle is just an alternate setup for working with *Aim for it,* so the training process is the same. The difference is that you don't have to transport your dog all the way back to the same starting point. Instead, you can simply continue ahead to the next piece of equipment a shorter distance away. You can use the triangular setup from the very beginning in your training. The Bermuda Triangle is designed to make training easier, so we use it whenever we can.

When shaping *Aim for the mat* (or whatever equipment you're working with) in the Bermuda Triangle, you just follow the *Aim for it* protocol:

  Step 1: Nose pointing toward the mat for a millisecond.
  Step 2: Actively point the nose forward.
  Step 3: Step forward, toward the mat.
  Step 4: Dash all the way to the mat.

What's special about the Bermuda Triangle is that it shortens the distance to a new starting point. For example, if you're working with three mats set three meters apart, you might want to start one meter from one mat. Transport your dog to your chosen starting point, shape him to the mat, and prolong the final reward so that it continues while you transport your dog toward the *next* mat. A meter from that next mat you end the transport, shape your dog to that mat, and reward—and so the loop continues.

ANOTHER BONUS OF THE BERMUDA TRIANGLE

Later on in your training—especially when teaching jumps and tunnels (see Chapter 18), you'll be able to make even more use of the continuous loop of the Bermuda Triangle.

Once you've taught your dog to drive to the equipment from some distance away, the Bermuda Triangle will make it possible for you to skip the transport altogether. You'll simply reward after the equipment, and when you end the reward your dog will drive directly to the next piece of equipment in the triangle.

Eventually, when your dog is really skilled at his job and fluently performs a single piece of equipment, you can let him perform several pieces of equipment in a row for each reward, which will build his persistence and teach him to continue working ahead until the reward appears.

A few Bermuda Triangle tips

- When you build your triangle, all three pieces of equipment should look the same so that the dog's job is the same throughout the lap.
- You should be on the inside of the triangle, so that your dog is working the outside lap.
- When a reward procedure ends, make sure you and your dog are facing in the direction of the next piece of equipment and that your dog is at a suitable starting point (not too far away).
- If something goes wrong, just transport your dog to a new starting point by the next piece of equipment.
- Remember the possibility of alternating between many clicks and treats along the path to one piece of equipment, and using just one reward placed farther ahead.

Race to reward

Our other favorite teaching strategy is *Race to reward*. Enthusiastically running to a treat or toy as fast as he can without any help from you is a vital behavior for your agility dog, and mastering this behavior is a first step toward conquering many other agility skills.

For the *Race to reward* behavior to be useful in future training, you must first teach it separately. For a dog that lacks focus or is shy or hesitant, it obviously is important to build an expectation and a desire to run to the reward, but even the eager dog's training has to begin here.

What should *Race to reward* look like?

1. Show your dog the remote reward and transport him to your chosen starting point.
2. When you let go of your dog, your shoulders are pointing in the direction your dog should run.
3. Your dog spontaneously explodes away as soon as he gets a chance.
4. He runs as fast as he can to the remote reward (a treat bowl or toy).

The behavior should be voluntary and spontaneous. You don't "send" your dog ahead—he runs ahead by himself.

Later in your training you'll be able to vary between spontaneous starts (where your dog starts directly after the transport ends) and start-line stays (where your dog starts on your cue)—see Chapter 14, "Starts and stays," but at this foundation stage there is no start cue involved.

What you're looking for is top speed and intensity.

Why do you need *Race to reward*?

You can use *Race to reward* to

- prompt or lure your dog to run in a certain direction.
- proof performance by setting criteria that your dog must accomplish on the way to the treat or toy.
- proof your ability to adhere to your handling system.
- teach a start cue, and teach your dog to hold a stay until he hears that start cue.

Your dog needs to be skilled at racing to remote rewards before you can use them in your training. Remotely placed rewards can add speed, intensity, and explosivity to even the simplest foundation skill. You'll find that these remote treat bowls or toys often serve multiple functions: They can build intensity and desire to dash in a certain direction, they can function as distractions (when you want your dog to head in another direction), and they can function as rewards when your dog actually gets to run all the way to them.

When working with various pieces of equipment, you'll alternate between Aim for it *and* Race to reward.

Race to reward *will come into use when you practice handling on the flat.*

Race to reward *is a key ingredient in teaching start-line stays (left) and starts on cue (right).*

MAKING USE OF *RACE TO REWARD*

In the earliest training, the remote reward can function as a lure: You place a piece of equipment between your dog and the treat or toy, and your dog goes between, onto, over, under, or through the equipment on his way to the reward. Later in your training, you'll add criteria for what your dog must do on his way to the reward. For example, your dog will learn to race to the equipment (even if that isn't the shortest route to his treat or toy), to perform specific behaviors when he reaches the equipment, to stay at the start line or contact and wait for your cue to go, and to follow your handling until you send him to the reward. Here are some examples where we employ *Race to reward*

Between, around, over, onto, under, through, page 165.

Starts and stays, page 203.

Handling maneuvers on the flat, pages 240, 243.

Jumps and tunnels, page 264.

Handling sequences, pages 300, 322.

The contact obstacles, pages 357, 364 (see box).

The weave poles, pages 410, 420.

How can you train it?

The idea behind *Race to reward* is simple: Show your dog the remote reward, transport him away, turn toward the reward, and let go of him, letting him race to the reward. The remote reward should be totally irresistible, so in the beginning employ a helper who can make the reward come alive.

When moving your dog around while teaching *Race to reward,* you should use a transport where you physically hold him. This means using a collar (leash optional) or harness or lifting and carrying your dog. At this early stage you want to build the most intense desire possible in your dog to get to the treat bowl/toy. That means he should "leave his brain in the treat bowl" and really strive to get back there as soon as he can, so politely walking or running back with you for another repetition is not an option. Even if he isn't that crazy (yet), act as if he'd bolt away instantly if you let go of him. You can combine the collar transport with a treat magnet if you need to (to avoid dragging your dog with you), but don't let go of that collar until you want your dog to dash off!

Following Good Agility Practices requires you to be on top of your game: When your dog has reached his reward, run up and meet him there. Then swiftly transport him back to the starting place for another repetition. Make sure to point your shoulders in the direction your dog should go (both during the transport and while he races to his reward). Use your nearest hand to hold his collar (if you need to give treats or use a treat magnet as well, you're allowed to use both hands). And make sure that you turn with your dog on the outside (both when retrieving him at the treat bowl, and when turning at the start point to face the reward again).

The basics of *Race to reward* training are:

> **Step 1: Get the behavior: Teach your dog to race to the reward.**
> **Step 2: Reduce the helper's actions; introduce variations and distractions.**

At the end of this section, we present some troubleshooting advice to help you perfect your *Race to reward* training.

Step 1: Get the behavior: Teach your dog to race to the reward

First and foremost: Get the behavior! Since the remote reward is a lure in itself we're not afraid at first to use *a lot* of prompting, coaxing, and luring—but all that cheerleading comes from *where the treat or toy is,* never from the handler. Let a helper manage the reward—the helper becomes part of the reward and thus is allowed to do whatever she can to make the reward irresistible. When your dog has learned the procedure, you fade those helping aids. Resist the temptation to use any kind of cue; this part of the training is all about getting the behavior.

Use the best stuff to motivate your dog: hamburger, hot dogs, chicken, a tug toy, a tennis ball, a rabbit skin. You want your dog to be really crazy to dash to his prize. If you're thinking, "Oh, I can't use the tennis ball because my dog loses his mind," then get out the tennis ball. We so want your dog to lose his mind! If your dog is super-eager to run to whatever reward you have placed at a distance, this training (and all its variations) will be simple. No marker is needed for this training—your dog simply sees his reward and races toward it.

Exercise 23: Teach your dog to race to his reward

To describe this exercise as clearly as possible, we have divided it into instructions for the handler and instructions for the helper. Here a bowl of tasty treats serves as your dog's reward.

Instructions for the handler:

1. Bring your dog (by the collar or on leash) up to the helper with the remote reward; let your dog see the treats and perhaps have a taste from the bowl.

2. Take your dog's collar (or keep him on a short leash), turn away with your dog on your outside, and quickly transport him 2 to 20 steps away. (You know your dog: You choose the distance!)

3. Hold your dog's collar (with your nearest hand) and turn toward the treat bowl (dog on the outside of the turn). As you turn, your helper will do whatever necessary to make your dog eager to run to the treat bowl.

4. As soon as you feel your dog is eager to go, open your hand and let go of his collar— no verbal cues, no cheering, no pointing forward, no pushing your dog, no nothing except just opening that hand!

5. Stand still while your dog runs to the bowl.

6. While your dog is eating from the bowl, go up to him and cross behind so that you come up on his other side (in other words, do a rear cross). Gently take his collar and/ or attach the leash. (If he was on your left side when you released his collar, he should be on your right side as you take the collar again.)

7. Turn away from the treat bowl (dog on the outside).

8. Quickly return to your release point (or a bit farther away, or closer—your choice).

9. Hold your dog's collar with your nearest hand, turn toward the treat bowl (dog on the outside of the turn), and repeat from #4 again.

Repeat four times in succession, each time switching sides as you retrieve your dog from the treat bowl.

Show your dog the wonderful treats in the bowl (left). Take him with you (here the trainer is using a collar transport), making sure to turn with him on your outside (center). When you feel him eager to run to the bowl, let go (right)!

Instructions for the helper:

1. Make sure that you have more treats available.
2. Let the dog have a look at the bowl and perhaps a taste to thoroughly spark his interest.
3. As the handler and the dog move away, make some enticing noises to keep the dog's mind on the treat bowl.
4. When the handler turns toward you and gets ready to release her dog, do whatever you need to make the dog eager to race to the treat bowl. Rattle the bowl, make noises, wave the bowl around, move closer to the dog, or run farther away—whatever works!
5. When the dog is eating, keep adding more treats one by one until the handler has taken the collar.

THREE WAYS TO SWITCH SIDES

Actually, there are three possible ways to switch sides in the *Race to reward* exercise:

1. Rear cross while your dog is engaged in his reward: In the example given in "Instructions for the handler," you switch sides by crossing behind your dog as you walk up to him while he is busy at the reward. If your dog was on your left side when you let go of him at the starting point, he should be on your right side when you retrieve him at the reward.
2. Front cross as you retrieve your dog: You get your dog, start turning away from the bowl with your dog on the outside, and, in the middle of the turn, execute a front cross (in other words, turn face to face with your dog so that he ends up on your other side), then continue to your release point where you turn with your dog on the outside.
3. Front cross at the starting point: You can also retrieve your dog on the same side as you just released him, turn with him on your outside, hurry back to the release point, and do a front cross there (instead of the outside turn).

We strongly suggest that you choose one method of switching sides for each session. If you start varying crosses within a session, you may lose track of what you've done, continually releasing your dog on the same side. Of course, you could also work one whole session with your dog on your left and then one session with your dog on your right—but this exercise offers great practice in smooth side changes. Take advantage of it.

Step 2: Reduce helper's actions; add variations and distractions

As your dog's speed and intensity grow and he eagerly runs straight to the treat or toy as soon as you release him, it's time to reduce the helper's actions and bring in variations and distractions. Eventually you want your dog to immediately race to a treat/toy anywhere, no matter the distractions and without a helper present.

Notice that the *handler's* job remains the same: just open your hand and let go of your dog. So, while the helper is still responsible for doing whatever is necessary to get your dog to the treat or toy, she shouldn't do more than is required to keep your dog running at full speed. Eventually the helper should be able to step out of the picture altogether.

You should also introduce variations and distractions, to ensure that your dog can explode away and run to his treat or toy in many different situations. In other words, you need to generalize the behavior. For example, you can

- vary who the helper is.
- vary where the helper stands.
- vary the distance to the reward.
- vary the reward.
- vary the location and environment.
- slightly vary your own behavior (take a step, wiggle your fingers, put a hand in your pocket, and so on).
- add all kinds of distractions, such as other dogs working nearby, people moving around, and so on.

When you add new challenges, if necessary, increase the helper's actions for a while to make it easier for your dog.

Troubleshooting

But it feels as if my dog is just trying to get away from me!

Well, that means that you have done a great job at building his desire for that treat bowl. For the moment, that is perfectly OK. Let him act crazy!

If your dog is very reluctant to leave the treat bowl, you can begin by transporting him just a very short distance away before turning around and releasing him again. Your dog soon will realize that being transported to the starting point is a vital part of the process, since it leads to that fun part of running fast to the treats. If you need to, you can use a treat magnet to get your dog to come with you away from the remote reward. Hold on to his collar as well, though.

If your dog avoids you when you come to retrieve him, make sure the reward procedure continues for a while even after you take his collar. Your dog needs to be busy eating! Your helper should continue to add treats to the bowl even after you've reached your dog, and you should give him some yourself, too, so that you're not the "party pooper." You can also let your helper gently take his collar before you arrive. In addition, practice collar grabs separately: Grab the collar. Give your dog a tasty treat. And repeat 100 times for the next couple of days. Your dog needs to learn that you grabbing his collar is a good thing.

What should I do if my dog is hesitant and asking for permission to go?

First of all, remain silent and neutral. Your objective is to teach him to *spontaneously* race to the reward. No cues, no cheerleading, no pointing, no trying to "bowl" your dog toward the treats. Attempts to "help" your dog actually make it harder for him to figure out what his job is—in this case, exploding away without any prompts from you.

Make sure the rewards are the coolest possible and that your helper is working hard to make them enticing. If your dog has previously learned to wait for a cue from you (and therefore politely resists the temptation), begin just a very short distance away. Your dog literally should just have to reach forward to stick his nose in the bowl and take his treat—your helper can even stick the bowl right under your dog's nose. This ploy often makes even the politest dog forget his manners!

A helper playing up the reward, getting ready to run off!

Stay in motion as you turn toward the helper and just let the collar slip out of your hand as you turn. Many dogs "park themselves" when the handler stops, so if you're already standing still, turn in a small circle with your dog on the outside and let go while you're still moving.

Sometimes it can be easier to get the behavior going if you use a treat magnet transport instead of a collar transport. When working at an extremely short distance, you can even end the treat magnet transport by dropping the treat magnet treat into the bowl. Once you've got the first ounce of spontaneous *Race to reward* behavior (even if it's just taking one step to reach the treat bowl), you have something to build on.

What do I do if my dog is reluctant to run to the helper?

Make sure the helper does not look threatening in any way—she can turn her back to the dog and look away. If your dog is shy, having the helper make noises and run around will be counterproductive. Instead, the helper should tone herself down while "toning up" the reward.

Start from a short distance—at first, your dog should just have to reach forward to get his nose into the treat bowl.

With very shy dogs it's possible to work without a helper; just start a short distance away from the treat bowl, and make sure you set up the situation so that you can remain neutral and just release your dog. But as your training advances, you'll want to use helpers from time to time, so you might as well start working through that challenge as soon as possible. In the beginning the helper might be more of a distraction than a help, though. It's your helper's job to make sure your dog runs to the treat bowl, so if your dog hesitates, do nothing. The helper will find a way to get your dog to come to the bowl: If nothing else, she can come all the way to your dog so that he just has to lean forward to get his treats or his toy.

THE SPONTANEOUS STARTS ARE IMPORTANT

Eventually, you'll also teach your dog a start-line stay where he holds still, waiting for your cue to start. You'll still need the spontaneous starts as well, though, so it's worth every effort to get your dog racing to that reward without any prompts or cues from you.

For a detailed discussion of spontaneous starts versus starts on cue, peek ahead to Chapter 14, "Starts and stays."

Won't this exercise create rude and crazy dogs that run around wildly and stick their noses into anything that catches their fancy?

No. This exercise forms a special context, which signals to your dog that, "In this situation do not ask for permission—just run!" You're teaching just the behavior of running to treats and toys.

Make the ritual obvious to your dog: show the remote reward, transport your dog away, turn around, and let go. Your dog will recognize the contextual cues for the exercise.

Eventually, in other exercises, your dog will learn that he can get the remote reward only if your handling directs him to it, and only if he performs the indicated tasks along the way.

Now that you and your dog are familiar with the *Aim for it* and *Race to reward* procedures, introducing equipment will be a walk in the park. In the next chapter you'll employ both training strategies when teaching your dog the skills of going *between, around, over, onto, under* and *through*.

11

Between, around, over, onto, under, and through

Performing agility obstacles requires your dog to aim toward and then pass between/around/over/onto/under/through various pieces of equipment. We teach this array of behaviors away from the obstacles, using lots of different "equipment." The *Aim for it* and *Race to reward* strategies make it easy for you to teach your dog to go between, around, over, onto, under, and through things. At the same time, your dog will learn to work independently with equipment from the very beginning, and you'll both get accustomed to a way of working.

FOUNDATION SKILLS

Going between *a pair of boots*

Balancing on *a wall*

Going under *a picnic table*

Going under *and slightly pushing* through *a blanket.*

Stepping over *a pair of boots on the ground.*

Stepping onto *an upside-down bowl*

Going around *a bucket*

OBSTACLES

Running on the dogwalk.

Jumping onto the table

Going between the wings, over the bar

Going around the jump wing

Jumping through the tire (over the bottom, under the top, between the sides)

Going between the two poles in the weaves, wrapping around each pole.

Going through the tunnel (onto the bottom, under the ceiling, between the walls)

Working with various pieces of equipment

In this chapter your dog will learn an array of equipment-related skills:

Between: Your dog goes between two objects placed on the ground, wide enough for him to easily pass through.

Around: A version of *between,* where your dog wraps around a single object.

Over: Your dog steps or jumps over something.

Onto: Your dog steps onto different objects and materials that are either lying on the ground or that your dog has to climb or jump up on.

Under: Your dog goes (or crawls) under something.

Through: Your dog pushes or squeezes himself through something.

The training strategies of our choice are *Aim for it* and *Race to reward,* which we introduced in the previous chapter. With *Aim for it,* you've already practiced shaping your dog onto a mat. You'll use the same strategy to teach all the skills in this chapter—all that varies is the equipment and the path you'll be shaping your dog to take. With *Race to reward,* you'll expand the procedure a bit by adding equipment along your dog's path, and by adding angles so that your dog doesn't always have a straight path to his reward.

Whether you're teaching going between, stepping onto, or crawling under, the training procedures are practically the same, which is why we have lumped this training into one chapter. Through this training your dog will learn to aim ahead and to make correct choices, performing various pieces of equipment on his own. At the same time you'll get to internalize both your training mechanics and your handling system, practicing the procedures you'll later use to teach and refine your dog's obstacle performance.

When your dog performs the various pieces of equipment, ultimately it should look like this:

- As soon as the previous reward or transport is finished, your dog aims ahead (in the direction you're facing) toward the next piece of equipment.
- As soon as your dog gets the opportunity, he goes between/around/over/onto/under/through "on the fly," without any gaps in the reward–behavior–reward flow other than if you're physically holding on to him and then releasing him.
- Your dog works totally independently of you throughout these exercises, but your handling supports his path, your shoulders pointing first toward the equipment, then toward where the reward is or will show up.

Left: Transport to a good starting point
Center: When the transport ends the handler's shoulders are pointing ahead, and the dog aims ahead.
Right: The dog goes around *the tree while the handler supports the path with her shoulders.*

AVOID LURING

Luring with a treat or toy in your hand, or prompting with your voice and body language (the most typical choices for most novice trainers), are common but poor strategies for teaching your dog agility behaviors. Luring is especially tempting when you're trying to get your dog to "do something" with "equipment." Luring is deceptive since it might seem as though your dog is performing a lot of behavior at once. But what your dog actually is learning is to pay close attention to you and to follow the lure, and not much else.

Remember the division of responsibilities: On the agility course, your dog's job will be to perform all the obstacles without help from you, and your job will be to tell him where to go. You should choose training strategies that bring you closer to your goals! If your goal is to teach independent obstacle performance, then make sure to focus on getting your dog to work on his own from the very beginning.

Also remember that the between/around/onto/over/under/through behaviors are only part of the goal. Even more important is teaching your dog to offer behaviors voluntarily, to make choices, to work independently, and to aim ahead on his own. Your dog misses out on these aspects of training if he simply follows a lure. With luring there's also a significant risk that you'll coax your dog into situations that he is not comfortable with.

Our favorite strategies avoid these pitfalls. *Aim for it* is free shaping: there are no prompts or lures involved, which means your dog really learns to work independently. *Race to reward* does include an element of luring (the remote reward is an obvious lure in the beginning), but the benefits override the drawbacks, especially since the training process advances rapidly to the point where your dog will choose an indirect path to the reward, offering behaviors on the way.

The equipment

You don't need any special equipment when training between/around/over/onto/under/through. Just use your imagination and whatever you have nearby. Got two buckets lying around? Perfect. Use them to practice running *between*. Washing your car? Get out the mats and use them to work on stepping *onto*. Commercial on TV? Use the time to get the mat off the couch, drape it over a couple of chairs, and train going *under* it and then advance to pushing *through* it. The training possibilities are endless!

You can even use the same equipment for several different behaviors: The same cardboard box might be for crawling *through* one week and for going *around* the next week. Your rewards will tell your dog which behavior you're working on at the moment.

Your handling while your dog is working

When teaching your dog to go between/around/over/onto/under/through equipment, the setup and the rewards are what tell your dog where to go. He only needs you to provide him with a good starting point and to make sure that rewards appear at appropriate times and places. To make sure he is really working on his own (not just following you), you'll be slightly behind him most of the time. That way he'll learn to aim ahead, away from you and toward the equipment.

At this stage you aren't using your handling to send your dog to the equipment. He'll learn to aim for the equipment because that is how he earns rewards, but you should still follow your handling system! Point your shoulders in the direction of your dog's intended path, *as if* your handling was telling him where to go. By supporting his path with your handling, you form good habits for both him and you, internalizing the basics of handling. Even though your dog might not seem to notice your handling, pointing your shoulders in the "wrong" direction inadvertently would teach him to ignore your handling. So by remaining consistent in your handling while your dog is working, you'll actually teach him a lot about the concept of working in the direction your shoulders are pointing.

Teaching the skills with both strategies

Both *Aim for it* and *Race to reward* help your dog learn to work the equipment without prompts and lures from you and make it easy for you to follow Good Agility Practices. *Aim for it* teaches your dog to focus ahead and offer behaviors voluntarily; *Race to reward* creates speed and explosivity while teaching your dog to aim for the equipment in the face of a distracting and attractive reward.

With Aim for it *(left), you'll begin with just a fraction of the behavior (performed totally independently), while with* Race to reward *(right), you'll get the whole thing right away (using the remote reward as a lure). We apply both strategies when teaching the skills of* between, around, onto, over, under, *and* through.

You'll find that you quickly get big chunks of behavior using *Race to reward,* while the progression of *Aim for it* may seem slow, especially for a novice clicker team. Just keep working on both—each strengthens the other. Especially in the beginning, the two strategies will seem very different to your dog. Taking the first voluntary step in *Aim for it,* however, is just as great a success as sprinting 50 yards in *Race to reward.* We recommend moving back and forth between these two strategies since each teaches your dog valuable lessons, and since you'll later use both when training the actual obstacles.

It doesn't really matter which skill you begin teaching, and we usually work with between, around, over, onto, under and through concurrently. Just start with easy versions of the equipment, and gradually increase the difficulty. We use *Aim for it* for all the skills, and *Race to reward* for most of them. If your dog is the least bit hesitant about the equipment you're working with (if it's a weird surface to step onto, for example), or if you don't want your dog racing at full speed (when climbing or balancing on something high off the ground, for example), you should work *only* with *Aim for it. Race to reward is* a form of luring, and we don't want to lure the dog into doing something he isn't really keen about, or where he might risk injury. With *Aim for it* your dog gets to work at his own pace and can earn plenty of rewards along the way.

TEACHING EQUIPMENT-RELATED SKILLS using *Aim for it* and *Race to Reward*

The chart below summarizes how we apply the two core strategies to teach the various equipment-related skills. In the upcoming sections we'll go through exactly how you should work with each strategy.

	Aim for it	*Race to reward*
Between transfers perfectly to the work you'll do with jump wings later on (see page 266). We work with between a lot. What's most important isn't the material or object but your dog's aiming ahead and driving along the intended path.	Here, the procedure of the training is just as important as the end result. This is an excellent exercise for *you*, where you truly get to practice setting criteria and placing rewards wisely. As a result, *your dog* will learn to aim toward and between the equipment. *Placement of reward:* To get your dog driving *between* (not stopping at the equipment), use exciting rewards that often appear far ahead, on the opposite side of the equipment.	Work through all steps thoroughly! Especially, work with all angles so that your dog learns to aim correctly.
Around is just a version of between, simulating "the nearest wing of a jump." Trees, fence posts, and garbage bins all make excellent *around* equipment.	Here we usually have the dog exit in the direction of the handler (just wrapping around and coming back to you). *Placement of reward:* Use thrilling rewards that appear a bit ahead of your dog, letting him chase the reward along the intended path. Since your dog's intended path goes back to you (just wrapping around), you can deliver the final reward from your hand.	Work with *around* as a variation of *between* training, practicing various angles and distances.
Over is the least important of the skills presented in this chapter—it's merely another variation of what you can do with equipment. We don't practice *jumping* here, merely passing over. (For details on jumping, see Chapter 18, "Jumps and tunnels.")	Use low objects, shaping your dog to pass over the equipment with his front feet (or with all four feet). *Placement of reward:* To enhance forward movement, often use exciting rewards that appear quite far ahead of your dog.	Don't practice *Race to reward* at all (at least not at longer distances). We don't want jumping here, and if the dog approaches at speed (as he does in *Race to reward*) even a low bar triggers a jump.

TEACHING EQUIPMENT-RELATED SKILLS using *Aim for it* and *Race to Reward* (continued)

	Aim for it	*Race to reward*
Onto is a vital skill. Your dog needs to learn the concept of stepping onto an object (both with just his front feet, and with all four feet) and moving around on it. We practice *onto* with all kinds of objects and materials—big, small, wide, thin, high, low, and made of wood, plastic, metal, cloth, stone, and whatever else we can think of.	Use all kinds of objects and materials. Using *Aim for it* you can teach your dog to step onto and move on practically anything. Notice that you can end the session whenever you want and transport your dog away for a break—you don't always have to shape him all the way up on the object! *Placement of reward:* At flat pieces of equipment (like mats or boards), you can reward far ahead if you like, letting your dog fly off the equipment after the reward. At equipment that requires balancing or climbing (rocks, planks, chairs), deliver the rewards close to the dog. Use the final reward to transport him off the equipment (or lift him off).	Use *Race to reward* only at simple, stable objects where you want your dog to race, and where your dog is confident about the surface.
Under requires your dog to duck down and pass under equipment (like a table or a log with some space under it).	Using *Aim for it* you can teach your dog to go or crawl under practically anything. As with *onto,* you can end the session whenever you like and simply transport your dog away before he goes all the way under. *Placement of reward:* Since you want your dog to go *under* the object, deliver all rewards low. To get your dog to *pass* under the object and exit on the other side, end with vivid rewards that appear quite far ahead.	Begin with spacious passages and gradually move on to lower spaces. Since your dog will be in a hurry racing to his reward, make sure the "ceiling" has a soft edge so that he doesn't risk hurting his back.
Through is a variation of *under.* We teach dogs to *push through* materials like cloth or tarps and to *go through* various openings like a hula-hoop, an open box, or a bottomless barrel.	Work just as with *under.*	Work with *through* as an expansion of the *under* training, gradually lowering, tightening and/or lengthening the passage.

Teaching between/around/over/onto/under/through using *Aim for it*

When fully trained, the *Aim for it* procedure looks exactly like perfect agility on course: Your dog runs in the direction your handling tells him and correctly performs the equipment he encounters on his way.

What should it look like?

1. You transport your dog to your chosen starting point where both you and your dog are facing the equipment.
2. As soon as you end the transport, your dog spontaneously aims ahead toward the equipment.
3. He drives to the equipment and executes it correctly.
4. He leaves the equipment and continues in the direction your shoulders are pointing—where a reward or another piece of equipment appears.

The dog aims ahead, balancing on the planks.

Rewards appear ahead of the dog, along his intended path. A reward can appear at any of the following times:

- While your dog heads for the equipment
- As your dog performs the equipment correctly
- As your dog leaves the equipment

Your handling supports your dog's path:

1. While your dog is heading toward the equipment, you point your shoulders in that direction.
2. As your dog moves ahead you can either stand still or move slightly forward. You should remain behind your dog, however, as he aims toward the equipment.
3. As he leaves the equipment, either the reward appears immediately (in which case your shoulders are pointing in the direction of the reward) or you turn your shoulders in the direction he should go, handling him to where a reward or another piece of equipment will show up.

Why do you need it?

- Your dog learns to spontaneously head for the equipment, away from you, without any lures or prompts.
- Your dog learns to anticipate that rewards are likely to appear along his path, even though they are not placed there in advance.
- You get the opportunity to selectively choose exactly what to reinforce, since you decide when to reward.
- You learn to differentiate between your dog's job (to work ahead toward the equipment and perform it correctly) and your job (to point your shoulders in the right direction, and to reward your dog as he makes good choices).
- Later you'll use this procedure again, for precision training and problem solving.

Aiming for the tire.

How can you train it?

Use the procedures described in "Shaping *Aim for it*" (page 129) and "Shaping *Aim for it* using the Bermuda Triangle" (page 140), replacing the mat with whatever equipment you want to work with. Even though your dog is already familiar with the *Aim for it* procedure, he can't know what it is that you want him to do with each piece of equipment, so you have to start from scratch. In the beginning you need to be *very fast,* clicking and treating for him pointing his nose in the right direction and staying on track. Catch him before he has a chance to turn his head. Remember, this is free shaping that offers your dog little choice! Guide your dog through the process with loads of reinforcements for keeping his nose in the right direction, and strategically place the rewards farther ahead along the path you want him to take; this will allow your dog to get it right without having time to make mistakes or to stop and hesitate. Successively you'll let him do more and more for each reward. Moreover, the many clicks and treats make the dog aware of the equipment he is working toward (and classically conditions him to love it).

Left: Stepping onto with a front foot.
Center: The reward appears ahead of the dog.
Right: Stepping onto with a rear foot as well.

For each piece of equipment you have to decide where your dog's job should end. Sometimes you might just want him to get *to* and interact *with* the equipment; in other situations you'll want him to *pass* the equipment, exiting on the other side. Picture the path you intend your dog to take, shape him to move along that path, and reward in a way that serves your purposes.

Here are some examples of what the *Aim for it* procedure might look like in various situations:

- **Merely passing the equipment:** When working with *between, around,* and *over* you'll merely want your dog to pass between, around, or over the equipment. Shape him to follow an imaginary path on the ground, leading between/around/over the equipment. Strive to get your dog moving as much as possible as early as possible; otherwise he may get stuck at the equipment instead of just passing by it. The easiest way to avoid your dog getting stuck is to always click and reward before the dog has time to stop, and to use a toy reward that appears a bit ahead and dances forward, so that your dog can chase it (for instance a tug toy on a string, bumping along the ground)—this creates lots of anticipation ahead. Rewarding this way means fewer rewards per repetition (often just one), but you get a dog that focuses forward and never stands still.

In extremely simple versions of *onto, under,* and *through* (for example, walking onto and over a mat, going under a hanging blanket with lots of space under it, or going through a big hula-hoop secured on the ground) the dog is also merely "passing" the equipment, and you can use this strategy there as well.

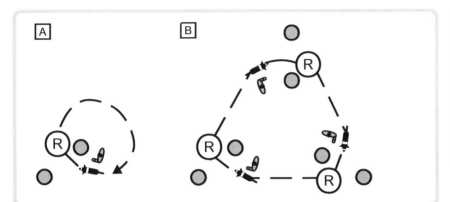

Here you can see how to get to a new starting point after the final reward.

A. If you use only one piece of equipment, transport your dog in a circle around you to start over.

B. If you use a Bermuda Triangle setup, simply transport your dog a few steps ahead toward the next piece of equipment.

Dotted path = transport

Dog/handler = starting point (where the transport ends and the dog starts working)

White "R" circle = where the reward appears.

Pairs of shaded circles = equipment you're working with

To teach your dog to pass between the buckets, click for moving along the intended path and toss a fun reward ahead to further encourage the forward momentum.

The last reward appears farther ahead, to encourage the dog to exit and avoid getting stuck in the equipment.

- **Aiming for and interacting with the equipment:** With most versions of *onto, under,* and *through* your dog first needs to learn to aim for and interact with the equipment. Begin with clicking and rewarding many times in quick succession to get your dog aiming in the right direction (nose forward, nose downward and under, or whatever the equipment requires). Place the reward where you want your dog's nose to be (usually low, close to the equipment).

- Then, if you want to teach your dog to actually pass onto, under, or through the equipment and exit on the other side, make sure to reward *while your dog is moving,* and let the rewards appear farther ahead. A thrown toy adds gusto and builds anticipation at the exit.

- **Climbing onto or balancing on the equipment:** When teaching your dog to climb or jump up onto something high (like a rock or a fallen log) you don't want him to fly on and off, you merely want to shape him to get up there. So click and reward for working in the right direction, deliver the final reward while he's still on the chosen object, and then transport him off with a treat magnet or simply lift him off.

Remember that you never have to get the whole behavior within any given session—you can always end whenever you like and just transport your dog away.

Balancing on the cement pipe (left) of course earns a reward (center)! The session ends with a treat magnet transport back to the ground (right), to avoid a fly-off.

THE DIFFERENCE BETWEEN A THRILLING, MOVING REWARD AND A LURE

When reinforcing only once for "looking ahead" and placing the reward so that the dog completes the equipment while chasing the toy, you might feel as though you're just luring the whole behavior. But you're not: the reward is appearing as a consequence of the behavior of looking ahead. This is an important distinction to make. Your dog has to do something to make the reward appear. And since it's a shaping process, he'll eventually have to do more and more on his own before he gets his reward.

The reward is what happens after the behavior. Your click marks the division: Before the click, your dog is actively working. After the click, you are rewarding, and your dog is enjoying his reward.

The reward shouldn't require any elaborate performance or "new" behavior from your dog. For example, if you click for "looking ahead between two boots," you may perfectly well reward by throwing a toy between the boots for your dog to chase. If your dog is a bit uncomfortable about climbing stairs, however, and you click for "one foot up on a stair," it isn't fair to then place the reward higher up so that your dog has to climb farther to get it. That would require further performance and thus doesn't constitute placement of reward.

With each skill and each new object you're using, you can work through the following steps:

> **Step 1: Get the behavior:** Shape your dog to go all the way between/around/over/onto/under/through.
> **Step 2: Vary the angle** (when applicable).
> **Step 3: Add variations and distractions** (generalizing the behavior so that your dog will aim for the object or equipment anytime, anywhere).
> **Step 4: Increase the distance**.

Once your dog is stepping all the way between/around/over/onto/under/through as soon as he gets a chance, you can move on in many different ways. You can start over and shape the same behavior with a different piece of equipment, you can vary the angle (if that makes sense on that piece of equipment), or you can generalize the behavior by varying your own behavior slightly or by adding various distractions. It doesn't really matter in which order you advance as long as you work on one feature at a time, easing up on the rest as you raise the bar for one aspect. Finally, you can add distance—but distance challenges should always wait until last, when you've built a solid behavior, and often there's no point in adding distance at all. It's the work *with* the equipment that's important.

Step 1: Get the behavior

We recommend you start with either *onto, over* (barely off the ground), or *under* since these are simple barriers that are easy for both you and your dog to recognize. In the previous chapter we used "step onto a mat" as an example, so for variation we'll describe "go under a chair" here. With every new skill and every new piece of equipment, go back to kindergarten and shape the behavior from scratch.

"OK, going under it is!"

Exercise 24: *Go* under *a chair using* Aim for it

1. Use a treat magnet (or a game of tug) to transport your dog to a good starting position (within half a meter from the chair).
2. While your dog is still moving, end the transport.
3. Immediately—while your dog's nose is still pointing toward the chair—click for "nose toward chair."
4. Quickly reward a bit ahead, quite low (along your dog's intended path).
5. Continue shaping your dog to go under the chair, clicking and treating for movement along the intended path.
6. As your dog's nose pokes out on the other side of the chair, rev up the reward and play for a while.

If you wish to take a break or end the session before your dog has passed all the way under the chair (and you should take a break after about 5–15 clicks and treats), simply use the final reward as a transport to get away from the chair.

Gradually let your dog work more and more for each click. Here is a suggested training plan to get the full behavior (add in-between steps as needed):

1. Nose pointing in the correct direction for a millisecond
2. Keep the nose pointing forward
3. Step forward
4. Nose under chair
5. Head under chair
6. Step forward under chair
7. Nose appears on the other side of the chair
8. Pass all the way under the chair

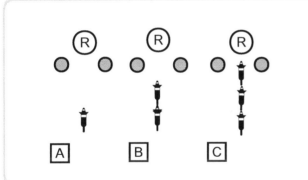

Gradually let your dog work more and more for each click and reward. In this example the dog gets one high-energy reward per repetition, and that reward is delivered quite far ahead (the white "R" circle).

A. The dog looks ahead. Click and reward

B. The dog takes a step ahead. Click and reward

C. The dog's nose passes between the equipment. Click and reward.

Vary the angle and shape your dog along the new path. The white "R" shows the final reward. You might click and treat several times along the way, or you might choose to deliver just one reward that flies ahead.

Continually vary the context! Even small variations count, as in this example:

Left: Left-side handling, sitting down, parallel to the equipment

Right: Right-side handling, standing up, behind the equipment.

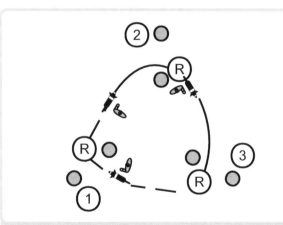

Increase the distance by simply ending the transport sooner. In this Bermuda Triangle illustration, the starting point (where the dog is) is close to the equipment at #1, a bit farther away at #2, and at quite a distance at #3.

Step 2: Vary the angle (when applicable)

When working with *between*, angles are definitely relevant since the equipment looks a bit different to your dog, depending on which angle he approaches from. You can also play around with angles when working with other skills in settings that include an element of going between (like going under a blanket between two chairs, or going through a cardboard box).

When you vary the angle, your dog's intended path changes. So you simply shape him to move along the new path. Notice that when your dog's path is curved, you should be on the inside of that curve.

Step 3: Add variations and distractions

To further strengthen the behavior, add variations and distractions and make sure your dog can perform the task even if the context changes. To generalize the behavior you can vary your own behavior slightly while your dog is working (wiggle your fingers, nod your head, and so on). You can vary the environment, training the same behavior in many different places. You can also add distractions—like a person standing nearby, or another dog within eyesight, or a toy lying on the ground behind you, or anything else that is a bit challenging but still within your dog's capacity.

Step 4: Increase the distance

Until now you have always started just a short distance away from the equipment. When your dog is really skilled at performing the equipment, always doing it correctly and with top intensity, you can add some distance. Generally, we only find it meaningful to add distance to *between* and *around*—with all the other skills, performing the equipment (not going to it) is the challenge.

When adding distance, ping-pong back and forth so that you gradually stretch the number of steps your dog has to take before reaching the equipment: Sometimes end the transport just a step from the equipment, sometimes a meter away, sometimes more. Monitor your dog's performance: If he ever hesitates, the distance is too long and must be reduced immediately.

We humans have an unfortunate tendency to go for distance too early and too often—but that limits the number of repetitions you can make (since each repetition takes a longer time) and thus limits the number of rewards your dog can earn. Shorter distance equals more reinforcement, which equals stronger performance, which in turn makes it easy to add distance once you really need to. Going for distance before the behavior is really solid also risks making the dog tentative, slow, and handler dependent. You get the point—work mostly at short distances!

TO MARK OR NOT TO MARK WHEN TRAINING *AIM FOR IT?*

Your marker is invaluable during the early steps of *Aim for it,* enabling you to pinpoint specific responses. As soon as your dog reliably aims ahead and offers the behavior you want you can—and should—quit marking every attempt. You can vary using a marker:

1. Sometimes click early (for aiming) and reward.
2. Sometimes click for completion and then reward.
3. Sometimes just reward without marking first.

If you always click for completion, your dog will start anticipating the click at that point and may stop to search for the click. When training *between/around/over/onto/under/through* we want the dog to keep moving away from the equipment, so continually marking the completion would be counterproductive.

When you work with *Aim for it,* you'll find that it's simple to add new dimensions, since you and your dog always can go back to "click for nose pointing in the right direction" and continue from there. To help you make good decisions in your training, always keep the goal in mind: that your dog voluntarily, without any help from you, aims ahead toward the equipment to get his reward.

Racing under the blanket toward the remote reward

Teaching between/around/over/onto/under/through using *Race to reward*

What should it look like?
1. You place a remote reward somewhere on the opposite side of the chosen equipment.
2. You hold your dog by his collar, show him the reward, and transport him to your starting point with both you and your dog facing the equipment.
3. As soon as you end the transport, your dog spontaneously explodes away toward the equipment.
4. He executes the equipment correctly on his way to the treat or toy.

Your handling supports your dog's path (but doesn't prompt his forward motion):
1. While your dog is heading toward the equipment, you point your shoulders in that direction. After your dog has started, you can also move forward.
2. As your dog "performs" the equipment, you turn your shoulders toward the reward. You can also move in that direction.

Why do you need it?
- Your dog learns to head away from you, toward the equipment, at full speed.
- Your dog learns to tackle different pieces of equipment correctly—even when attractive rewards lie farther ahead.
- Your dog learns to approach, execute, and leave the equipment in flow, without hesitation.

Weaving toward a remote reward

- You learn to observe and judge your dog's intentions and release him with proper timing.
- *Race to reward* provides easy success, which builds confidence in both you and your dog.
- You'll use *Race to reward* again later, when working with actual agility obstacles.

How can you train it?

Your dog already knows how to race to a remotely placed treat bowl or toy. Now you'll add equipment along your dog's path that he "accidentally" performs on his way to the reward (for example, dashing between two buckets or pushing under a piece of cloth).

Then the rules change a bit: Next your dog will learn that not only must he run like the wind to get to his beloved treat or toy but that he also has to actively *choose* to do something on his way to the reward. It becomes *his* responsibility to dash between two buckets rather than running around them. Precisely what your dog needs to do to earn his reward depends on what you're training and how far he has progressed. Using *Race to reward* allows you to proof performance by setting criteria for what your dog has to do on the way to the toy or treat bowl.

USE *RACE TO REWARD* ONLY WHEN YOU WANT YOUR DOG TO ACTUALLY RACE!

Race to reward is excellent for working with *between* and *around*, where the equipment merely requires your dog to *choose the correct path*. Especially with *between*, we strongly recommend that you work through all the steps in this chapter—this will greatly benefit your work on the actual agility obstacles.

Race to reward also works nicely when training your dog to go *under* and *through* rather wide spaces where he can rush ahead (for example, under a piece of cloth hanging down, or through a big cardboard box rigged so that it stands firmly)—but if you're working with a narrower or less secure space (for example, under a chair turned upside down), stick to *Aim for it*.

With *onto* you can use *Race to reward* as long as you're using low, simple, and safe pieces of equipment that you simply want your dog to step onto (for example, onto a big mat). Whenever you're working with higher, smaller, or less stable objects that require your dog to climb or balance, you should stick to the *Aim for it* procedure.

Over in *Race to reward* means jumping—please wait before tackling that! The act of jumping is so much more than just passing over something, so we'll give you detailed instructions about how to introduce jumps in Chapter 18, "Jumps and tunnels".

The training follows these steps:

> **Step 1: First, get the behavior: Add equipment in *Race to reward*.**
> **Step 2: Add angles, requiring that your dog choose the right path.**
> **Step 3: Vary the distance.**
> **Step 4: Increase the difficulty of the equipment.**
> **Step 5: Add variations and distractions**.

The order of these steps is not strictly set—you can ping-pong around with angles, distances, the difficulty of the equipment, and variations/distractions. Just make sure to add only one new aspect at a time, and to ease up on the other features when you make one more difficult. Throughout the training

- remember to use your best treats or your dog's favorite toy for this exercise. We're looking for speed and enthusiasm here!
- pay careful attention to Good Agility Practices: Set up your dog for success by keeping your focus sharp and your intensity high, and make sure you know how to follow your system of handling throughout.
- begin by going up to the remote reward and showing it to your dog. That'll form a familiar procedure, telling your dog that it's *Race to reward* time.

- be scrupulous about your transports. We recommend using a collar transport or lift-and-carry, so that you hold on to your dog while moving together from the remote reward. This way he can rush back to his treat bowl or toy as soon as you don't physically restrain him, which helps build maximum intensity and speed. Furthermore, by holding him you can feel where he is aiming to go and release him only when you feel him aiming in the right direction.
- release your dog as soon as he aims in the correct direction, without saying or doing anything. You should not be in focus here—the remote reward should be the only thing your dog cares about.
- do not stop your dog if he chooses the wrong path. It's his choice, and you want him to drive ahead and try things out! Just let the reward disappear, and go get him for another try.
- plan on using a helper in all situations where it might be necessary—to spice up the lure/reward and/or to remove it if your dog makes the wrong choice.

"Wow, this is simple—I'm just racing to my reward as usual!"

Step 1: Add equipment in *Race to reward*

Before you add any equipment, you need to make sure your dog is fluent at running to his treat or toy. (For a full description, see *"Race to reward,"* page 142 .

1. *Is your dog fast and reliable?* On the "flat," does your dog run as fast as he can to the remote reward?
2. *Have you faded the helper?* Have you reduced your helper's actions so that your dog runs like the wind on his own?
3. *Have you generalized the behavior?* Have you varied the distance, the reward, your helper, your behavior, the environment, and so on?

When adding equipment, you simply repeat the reward exercise but add equipment in your dog's path, so that he runs between/over/onto/under/through something in a straight line on his way to the reward. (*Around* doesn't apply when just running straight).

At this stage, *your dog's* job is to run to the treat or toy; *your job* is to set up the exercise so that he automatically passes—and "performs"—the equipment in the way you have intended. This exercise will train *you* to make the exercise easy enough so that your dog *cannot* make a mistake. If he makes a mistake and, for example, runs *around* instead of *between* the equipment, reward anyway! You don't want to punish your dog for your bad decision: you didn't make the exercise easy enough. Your dog is still doing his part of the job; he's running to the remote reward.

To ensure success, start close to the equipment, place the remote reward close to the equipment, and make the task easy (make the *between* space wide, the *under* space roomy, and so on). Don't let go of your dog until you feel him aiming for the equipment, straight toward the remote reward.

WHAT IF MY DOG HESITATES?

If your dog for some reason hesitates at a piece of equipment, immediately make it easier so that he performs it without any hesitation. The equipment should not be a challenge—it's just something that your dog passes on his way to the reward. Never use the *Race to reward* procedure to cheer or coax your dog into doing something that he is reluctant about.

If you can't make it easy enough—for example, if your dog hesitates to step onto a certain material—switch to using the *Aim for it* procedure. In *Aim for it* you'll be able to reinforce much smaller steps, and your dog will get to choose for himself and get rewarded for the tiniest tendency in the right direction. With the *Aim for it* procedure you run less risk of getting more behavior than your dog is really ready to offer, which decreases the risk of setbacks.

When you add angles, your dog will learn to perform the equipment first, and not just take the shortest path to the remote reward.

Exercise 25: Race to reward, *equipment added*

1. Bring your dog up to the remote reward and show it to him.
2. Hold your dog by the collar, turn away from the remote reward with your dog on the outside, and quickly transport him to the other side of the equipment.
3. Turn toward the equipment (dog on the outside).
4. Your dog aims for the equipment, toward the reward.
5. Let go!
6. Your dog races to his reward, executing the equipment correctly on his way.
7. While your dog is engaged in his reward, walk up and retrieve him for another rehearsal.

Switch sides sometimes so that your dog gets to do the exercise on both your left side and your right side. You can switch sides with a rear cross as you walk up to your dog (while he is engaged in his reward), with a front cross as you turn him away from the reward, or with a front cross at the starting point (just before you release him again). Add different pieces of equipment so that your dog gets to go between, around, onto, over, under, and through various things.

Here is a reminder for Step 1:

- Criterion: Race to the remote reward.
- Responsibility: You're responsible for setting up for success. Your dog gets the reward even if he runs outside or around the equipment.
- Mistakes: No matter what happens, your dog gets his reward when he gets to the treat or toy. Move on to Step 2 after a few successful repetitions.

Step 2: Add angles, requiring that your dog choose the right path

By making the path to the equipment a slight "detour" from the treat or toy reward, you introduce a whole new dimension to the exercise. Now your dog doesn't just *accidentally* perform the equipment on his way to the treat or toy. Instead, he has to actively *choose* to steer off the straight path to the treat or toy to get to the equipment. This means shifting criteria, from merely *Race to reward* to *take the correct path to the treat/toy*. This also means you do need a helper to scoop up the reward if your dog makes a mistake. Adding angles will greatly improve your dog's understanding of the exercise and is a critical step in the process of teaching him to perform obstacles on his own.

We normally work angles only with equipment that has some kind of "side barriers" so that you can judge whether your dog is choosing the correct path or not. In *between* and *around* it's a given (*around is* what is left if you remove the farthest object in a *between* pair), but when working with *onto, over, under,* or *through* you might need to add some kind of sides to frame the equipment.

When you add angles you need to pay extra attention to your handling. When you set up the equipment at an angle, your dog's path will be a regular turn on your outside: first going toward the equipment, then turning to get to the reward (if he is on your right side, he'll turn left: see diagram). In the beginning your dog will turn ever so slightly—he'll probably not even notice you turning since he's focusing on the remote reward—but you should still support his path with your handling so that you don't inadvertently teach him to ignore your shoulder cues. Make sure your dog is on your outside, and make sure you point your shoulders in the direction he should go (first toward the equipment, then toward the reward).

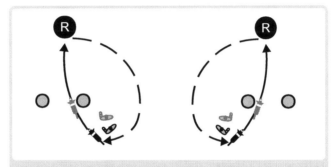

Make sure your dog is on the outside and that you are pointing your shoulders in the direction he should go.

Dotted path = transport

The first dog/handler (black) = at the starting point (where the transport ends and the dog starts working) the handler points her shoulders toward the equipment.

The second dog/handler (gray) = as the dog performs the equipment, the handler points her shoulders toward the remote reward

Black "R" circle = remote reward.

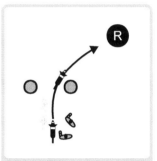

For variation you can move the remote reward off to the side, creating an angle that way.

Make it easy in the beginning: Start close to the equipment but slightly off to the side, so that your dog has almost a straight line to his reward. This way he has to make a choice: to aim to go *between* or *around* the equipment. Release him as you feel him aiming correctly. If your dog happens to take the wrong path, your helper simply removes the reward.

Here is a reminder for step 2:
- Criterion: Go between/over/onto/under/through on the way to the treat/toy.
- Responsibility: Your dog now is responsible for taking the desired path toward the treat/toy and only gets his reward if he takes the correct path.
- Mistakes: If your dog misses the equipment, your helper removes the treat or toy, and you retrieve your dog for a new start.

Exercise 26: Go between *at an angle*

1. Show your dog the remote reward.
2. Turn away and quickly transport your dog to a good starting point close to the equipment, slightly off to the side, dog on the outside. Point your shoulders toward the equipment.
3. Hold on to your dog's collar and feel where he's aiming to go.
4. Your dog aims in the correct direction, toward the equipment.
5. Let go!
6. Your dog passes the equipment correctly and races to his reward.
7. As he goes between the equipment, turn your shoulders toward the reward.

If your dog isn't aiming in the correct direction, don't release him yet. If necessary, move him slightly sideways so that his intended path becomes almost straight, but do not prompt him in any way—let him choose.

By starting close to the equipment, it's easy to feel when the dog is aiming correctly.

Left: Hold on to the collar until you feel your dog aiming correctly. If he aims in the wrong direction, just don't let go!

Center: Here the handler has simply moved the dog a little bit toward the middle, to increase his chances of choosing the right path

Right:When the dog aims in the correct direction, let go!

If you happen to misjudge and release your dog prematurely so that he runs *around* the *between* objects, it's no big deal: your helper will remove the reward as soon as she sees that your dog is choosing the wrong path, and you can retrieve your dog for another try.

Step 3: Vary the distance

As long as you keep your dog on your outside and point your shoulders where you want him to go, you can progress gradually both to steeper angles and to longer distances. You can move a bit with your dog if you like (you don't have to stand still), but it's the exercise—the context—that sets his path; your handling supports it.

Build angles and distances until you can release your dog from practically anywhere, and he promptly will run to the equipment and complete it on his way to the treat or toy. When working with *Race to reward* we don't have that many precautions about distance (since the remote reward draws the dog ahead). But, of course, if your dog starts making mistakes or seems the least bit hesitant, immediately revert to a shorter distance.

Ping-pong the distance, gradually progressing to longer distances at all angles.

HOW TO DEAL WITH MISTAKES

Always let your dog keep going—even if he makes a mistake. Never try to stop your dog—no verbals, no trying to catch him or block his way. Let him choose! Your helper will remove the treat/toy. You want your dog to be eager to go and feel as if he can take on the world. If you try to stop him in any way, most likely you'll make him feel uncomfortable and will trigger him to look to you for information. That's counterproductive if you want to create a happy and confident dog that knows his responsibility and can work on his own without your help.

By removing the treat/toy (preferably the instant that your dog makes the wrong decision rather than snatching it away from him when he reaches it), you're more likely to get a "Darn!" reaction from your dog and make him revise his choice the next time around. Remember, though, that it's the *rewards for the successful attempts* that will build the desired behavior.

If a mistake occurs, quickly go and get your dog. You can praise him or give him a tiny treat for staying in the game as you grab his collar, then simply go back to your starting position and give him another chance. The main reason for getting your dog (instead of calling him back to you) is that you want your dog to remain focused on that reward—in essence, to keep focusing ahead. If he anticipates that you're going to call him back, he's likely to run hesitantly, stop aiming ahead, and curl toward you (since you might turn him around). Moreover, if your dog's recall is not solid, you may end up nagging him, which could confuse him or make him reluctant, causing a break in the flow of training.

If your dog happens to take the wrong path, do not try to stop him! Let your helper remove the remote reward—or, if you took a chance and used a remote reward without a helper, simply live with your decision and let your dog have his reward! What's most important is that you don't dampen your dog's confidence or his forward drive!

TO MARK OR NOT TO MARK WHEN *RACING TO REWARD*?

Just as in first teaching the *Race to reward* procedure, we typically do not use a marker in these exercises. Your release will function as a well-timed reward for your dog's aiming correctly, and getting the remote reward will reinforce his whole performance. If you choose to use a marker (for example, to highlight the correct choice when sending at an angle), watch that your dog does not become dependent on the click: You don't want him to start hesitating and waiting for the click before he continues to the reward. So if you choose to mark sometimes, vary with easy repetitions without any marker and eventually drop the marker altogether.

Step 4: Increase the difficulty of the equipment

Vary the equipment, and gradually increase the difficulty. For example, narrow the "go *between*," lower the "go *under*," and change the surface of the "go *onto*." To ensure success when you increase the difficulty of the task, go back to the straight line and gradually add angles again as your dog gains proficiency. Your goal is a fast and reliable performance on more challenging equipment.

Step 5: Add variations and distractions

Adding variations and distractions will ensure that your dog can perform equipment on the way to his treat or toy under any circumstances.

Now that your dog knows to go between, around, over, onto, under, and through various pieces of equipment, both in the *Aim for it* and the *Race to reward* settings, he is well prepared to start working with most of the actual agility obstacles. But you also need to prepare your dog for equipment that moves and makes noise. In the next chapter you'll learn how you can teach your dog to love making a racket!

12 Noise and movement

Besides being lots of fun, teaching your dog to like, create, and demand noise and movement "inoculates" him against feeling afraid amidst all the commotion you'll most likely encounter at agility trials. It's also an essential ingredient in teaching a blazing teeter performance.

Bombproofing your dog

On an agility course there are lots of things that can be noisy and unstable. Tunnels and dogwalks can move under your dog's feet, weave poles can wiggle as your dog zigzags through them, speakers can boom, and jump bars (or even jump wings and other obstacle parts) can fall. All kinds of sudden noises and movements are common on and around the agility field.

There is even one obstacle that is characterized by noise and movement: the teeter. When you start training the teeter, it will be your dog's job to get the plank moving and make it slam to the ground. A confident and secure teeter performance relies (among other things) on your dog being trained to enjoy creating noise and movement on his own so that he actively seeks to smash the teeter plank to the ground.

On the teeter your dog should "demand" both movement and noise, really striving to make the plank move and go boom!

So we want your agility dog to *like* noise and movement: he should consider all kinds of hullabaloo good news. We also want your agility dog to actively *create* noise and movement, striving to make things go crash and kaboom—and even to *demand* noise and movement, working hard to get the commotion going. Training your dog to love noise and movement gives you a great opportunity to teach him that things that could be considered scary and uncomfortable can be positive and worth working to achieve.

We'll describe the training of noise separately from the training of movement, but the process is much the same for both:

> **Step 1: Teach your dog to like it (classical conditioning).**
> **Step 2: Teach your dog that he can create it on his own (operant conditioning).**
> **Step 3: Teach your dog to demand it (operant conditioning).**

Making use of classical and operant conditioning

Step 1: Teach your dog to like it (classical conditioning): To teach your dog to *like* noise and movement, you simply pair the noise or the movement with something that your dog enjoys, which eventually makes the noise or movement itself enjoyable. Classical conditioning is an involuntary process. Your dog does not *do* anything; you just expose him to the pairing of the stimuli.

Step 2: Teach your dog that he can create it on his own (operant conditioning):
To teach your dog to *create* noise and movement, there are two different approaches.

a. A: *You* still make the noise or movement (just as in the teach-him-to-like-it step), but you set criteria for what your dog must do to get you to act. In other words, your dog will be creating noise or movement *through you*.

b. B: Shape *your dog* to perform some behavior that actually causes noise or movement (for example, knocking over a stack of cans to create noise, or stepping on a wobbly surface to create movement).

Step 3: Teach your dog to demand it (operant conditioning): Teaching your dog to *demand* noise or movement is simply a matter of requiring that he work harder to make it happen, so that he really has to go out of his way to cause it. This final stage will prove his eagerness to produce noise or movement and is a real confidence booster.

In Steps 2 and 3, where reinforcement builds your dog's behavior, the noise or movement eventually will function as the first part of the reward: Your dog acts, which causes noise/movement, which leads to a great reward. And—did you notice?—there will be continuous classical conditioning going on as well because the "real" reward follows the noise or movement. This pairing of stimuli happens every time you practice. So throughout the training your dog will form more and more positive associations with noise and movement (classical conditioning), and he'll become more and more skilled at making it happen (operant conditioning).

In the following chapters we show you how we train noise and movement, but our way is not the only way. Please don't limit your training to our suggestions! What's important is that your dog learns to like, create, and demand noise and movement. How you reach that goal is up to you. Be creative, use your imagination, and have fun!

> ### A NOTE ON DIFFERENT KINDS OF DOGS
>
> The benefits of the noise/movement training are obvious if you have a sensitive dog. But even if your dog is one of those cool guys that couldn't care less if the sky fell down, he'll benefit from this training when you start working on the teeter. What we are looking for is a high level of participation, where your dog becomes aware that his job is to create that noise or movement.
>
> For the sensitive dog it is critical to progress in small steps, never pushing beyond your dog's limits. Watch your dog's behavior: Is he keen to stay in the game? Is he eager to start over after a break? If so, you're in the clear and can move on. If not, you probably have been pushing your luck and immediately must return to a much easier level. Remember, you're working on building positive and pleasant feelings. Keep it that way!

Teaching your dog to like, create, and demand noise

What should it look like when your dog likes, creates, and demands noise?
We want your dog to

- prick his ears and look expectant when he hears a sudden noise.
- work actively and intensely to create as much noise as he can.

Imagine your dog, with anticipation and joy shining in his eyes, knocking over a large set of tin cans on a baking tray!

Let's make some noise!

Why do you need it?

- Enjoying making noise is a necessary skill for teeter training.
- A dog that loves making noise is more confident around all kinds of noises that may occur on or around an agility course or at a trial.

How can you train it?

We suggest a four-step training process for teaching your dog to like, create, and demand noise:

Step 1: Teach your dog to like noise.
Step 2: Teach your dog to create noise (through you).
Step 3: Teach your dog to create noise (on his own).
Step 4: Teach your dog to demand noise.

A bold and careless dog might go through all four steps in just a couple of sessions, but a noise-sensitive dog might require much more extensive training with small approximations.

Step 1: Teach your dog to like noise

Conditioning your dog to react positively to noises requires no action from your dog; he just hears the noise and eats treats (or plays with a toy, or with you). Your goal is for him to look expectant and happy when he hears a sudden noise.

Exercise 27: Classically condition your dog to enjoy noise

1. Make a noise.
2. Give your dog a tasty treat.
3. Wait for several seconds or more.
4. Make a noise again.
5. Give another treat.
6. Repeat until your dog pricks his ears and looks expectant when he hears the noise.

Suggested tag points:

- Noise first
- Treat after noise

Start with a soft sound (for example, lightly slapping the table) so that your dog does not get scared or uncomfortable. Give your dog a yummy treat right after the sound. Take a break, and then repeat. Taking a break after each repetition helps avoid the risk of inadvertently teaching your dog that getting a treat predicts weird noises, which might make him wary of treats. If during the training process your dog shows any signs of stress or calming signals such as looking away, licking, or gasping, you have gone too far, too fast.

Since your dog cannot control what happens, it is essential that you pursue this training in small steps; it is your responsibility to make sure your dog is comfortable and to tell his brain that noise is a good thing.

When your dog starts looking expectant when he hears the noise, move on to something that creates more of a racket, like a shoe dropped on the floor. It is a good idea to train in short sessions (perhaps just one repetition) several times a day and in different places. Make sure your dog is relaxed and confident at each level before taking the training further.

How far should you take the classical conditioning? How loud should the noises be before you start teaching him to create noise himself? It's your choice. Many sound-sensitive dogs actually progress faster with operant conditioning than with classical conditioning (probably because the dog is in control of the noise), so it might be a good idea to start teaching "create noise" as soon as your dog starts anticipating treats when he hears relatively soft sounds. On the other hand, the louder the noises your dog has learned to enjoy, the faster you can proceed when training him to create noise himself.

Teaching your dog how to *create* noise means switching to operant conditioning, where your dog learns by the consequences of his actions that creating noise is a sure way to earn reinforcement.

Step 2: Teach your dog to create noise (through you)

Teaching your dog to create noise *through you* is an elegant way to start teaching your dog to make noise happen.

NO AVERSIVE NOISE

Sometimes people use noise on purpose to scare a dog (a hard stomp on the ground, throwing things at or near a dog, and so on). Needless to say, such practices will have the opposite effect from what you're trying to accomplish. We want your dog to look happy and expectant when he hears a sudden noise!

Use a behavior that your dog readily offers when given the opportunity (for example, a hand touch, putting a paw on a target, or simply eye contact). As your dog performs this easy behavior, make a noise and follow it with a fabulous treat or toy game. Here the noise actually functions as a marker just as the clicker does, so your dog will learn quickly to work to get you to make that sound, which leads to the "real" reward.

Exercise 28: Teach your dog to create noise through you—hand touch version

1. Hold out your hand.
2. Your dog offers a hand touch.
3. Make a noise (such as slapping the table, or banging a pot).
4. Deliver a fabulous reward.

Suggested tag points:

- Make noise after the behavior
- Deliver reward after the noise

Equipment for making noise

The dog offers a hand touch (left), which leads to a rattle in the kettle (center), which is followed by a yummy treat (right).

One advantage to this approach is that you can control the *level* of the noise, while your dog controls the *timing* of the noise. If the noise is stressful, he'll start hesitating to perform the behavior that triggers it. You must not cue, coax, or prompt your dog: he has to be free to choose.

Another advantage is that the timing of the noise can be precise: you can make the noise just as your dog performs the required behavior. In contrast, when your dog knocks things over himself, there always is a delay between the behavior and the noise.

Step 3: Teach your dog to create noise (on his own)

Teaching your dog to create noise on his own is straightforward shaping, using the *Aim for it* formula to train him to topple a construction.

Exercise 29: Teach your dog to create noise on his own

Criterion: Shifts from "nose pointing toward construction" toward "knocking down the construction."

1. Arrange a construction that your dog can knock down easily.
2. Play with your dog while transporting him to a starting position close to the construction.
3. End the transport.
4. Immediately click for nose pointing toward the construction.
5. Reward ahead, in the direction you want your dog to work.
6. Continue shaping, clicking, and treating for looking at, moving toward, and interacting with the construction.
7. If your dog actually knocks down the construction, click the toppling.
8. Reward generously while the construction is falling down and making noise.
9. When you wish to end the session (or when your dog has knocked the construction over), use the final reward as a transport to move your dog away from the construction or to keep him occupied until you've rebuilt it and are ready to have another go.

Suggested tag point:

• Reward toward equipment

Start with quieter "bangs" from objects that are easy to tip over, such as a book on a carpet or a pile of lightweight plastic bowls. Reinforce looking at, moving toward, and interacting with the object. Reinforce all kinds of interaction—with nose, paws, and body. Sooner or later your dog will accidentally knock over your construction. Jackpot!

Shape the behavior step by step until your dog actually knocks over the construction. At the moment, you're reinforcing the act of knocking over, so this is the order of events:
1. Your dog interacts with the construction and earns clicks and treats.
2. Your dog knocks the construction (with his nose, paw, or body).
3. Click as he hits the construction.
4. Treat while the construction is falling down and making noise.

You can let the treat emerge from the pile of stuff your dog just knocked down by placing your hand with the treat in the pile or by dropping goodies for your dog to search for. You also can use the reward procedure to keep your dog away and busy while you rebuild the construction, for example, by letting him nibble treats out of your fist.

It is time to move on when your dog confidently knocks over your arrangement as soon as he gets a chance. Now make the noise your criterion for reinforcement, rewarding the *sound* rather than the act of knocking down the arrangement. Switching criteria will cause your dog to strive for the noise. Now the order of events will be:
1. Your dog knocks the construction.
2. The construction falls down and makes noise.
3. Click for the noise (optional).
4. Treat.

The click is no longer strictly necessary—the noise itself will function as a marker, telling your dog that a reward is on its way. Gradually move on to greater noise and racket. A pile of metal bowls on a corrugated metal sheet makes quite a clatter! If your dog creates the noise, but then flinches or jumps backward, he is still not comfortable. Make sure that you're not asking him to create more noise than he is happy with. Use cool rewards, deliver the reward in the middle of the noise-making objects, and do not go for too much commotion at once.

Step 4: Teach your dog to demand noise
Once your dog is skilled at creating noise, it's time to get him into "demand mode." Make your constructions more and more difficult to knock over so your dog has to work harder to get a result. The more furiously your dog attacks your constructions, the better! The demand stage of training is a true confidence booster. Challenging your dog's wrecking skills is also hilarious fun for both dog and human: you have to playfully fight to keep him off your construction until you have it built, and then he'll confidently destroy it with the vigor of any one-year-old child. Remember: You *want*

your dog to throw himself at your constructions, so between repetitions hold him by the collar or use an extended reward. Do not verbally stop him if he tries to get back to work; it is your responsibility to plan the training session so that your dog is busy all the time.

Hold on to your dog while you're building (left) because the minute you let go, he'll throw himself at your construction (right)!

For your teeter training, the demand part of your noise training is vital. When working with the teeter, you'll want your dog to really push the plank down—in essence demanding that it crash to the ground. A dog that is willing to work hard for that bang will be confident and truly enjoy teeter training.

Playing on a wobbly board

Teaching your dog to like, create, and demand movement

What should it look like when your dog likes, creates, and demands movement?

We want your dog to

- step onto and ride moving or unstable surfaces without hesitation and with a happy attitude.
- work actively and intensely to create as much movement as he can.

Picture your dog jumping onto a wobbly board and moving about or shifting his weight around to make the board flip back and forth.

Why do you need it?

- Just as with making noise, enjoying making things move is a necessary skill for teeter training.
- A-frames, dogwalks, tunnels, and weave poles are also surfaces that can move, so your dog needs to be comfortable with suddenly shifting equipment.
- These exercises also are great for building confidence, body awareness, and body control.

How can you train it?

Teaching your dog to like, create, and demand movement follows the same pattern as the noise training. The only difference is that your dog actually has to be on a specific surface (one that can move) when the training starts, which means he needs a bit of preparation training.

Choose a surface that you can easily control, for example a wobbly board (a board with a block or hemisphere underneath the middle so that it can rotate in every direction).

The training proceeds through five steps:
Step 1: Preparation: Teach your dog to stand on the board.
Step 2: Teach your dog to like movement.
Step 3: Teach your dog to create movement (you move the board).
Step 4: Teach your dog to create movement (your dog moves the board on his own).
Step 5: Teach your dog to demand movement.

Step 1: Preparation: Teach your dog to stand on the board

Since you eventually want your dog to make the board move, it is crucial that he first learns to enthusiastically get onto the wobbly board. Use the *Aim for it* procedure to shape your dog to step onto and stay on a secured wobbly board.

Shape your dog to step onto the stationary board

Exercise 30: Teach your dog to mount a stable board

1. Hold on to the board so that it cannot move, or build it up to make it steady.
2. Transport your dog to a starting point close to the board.
3. End the transport.
4. Immediately click for nose pointing toward the board.
5. Reward ahead, in the direction of the board.
6. Continue the shaping, clicking, and treating for aiming for the board, moving toward it, putting front feet on it, and eventually standing on it.
7. When you wish to end the session, use the last reward to transport your dog away from the board.

Place the rewards wisely, in the direction you want your dog to work, and keep your focus and intensity high. To get him to stay on the board, simply deliver many treats in quick succession so your dog doesn't have time to step off. Then use the final reward to move him off the board. When you end that reward he should be drawn back to the board like a magnet—reward that! When you want to take a break, hold on to your dog or move the equipment away.

Step 2: Teach your dog to like movement

When your dog enthusiastically gets on the board as soon as he gets a chance, it's time to introduce some movement. You want your dog to look expectant and happy when the board moves. The idea is to employ classical conditioning (movement equals treats or toys) so your dog will get his treats on the board when the board moves no matter what he does. That means that you must reward your dog when he chooses to jump off the board right after it moves, even if it makes subsequent training lengthier and more difficult. The trick is to make sure that initially you move the board so slightly that your dog barely notices it, so he stays on the board when he gets his treat. Should he get off the board, reward anyway, placing your reward toward the board. And make a mental note to move the board even more gently and be quicker with the reward next time, so that your dog doesn't have time to hop off!

You can either let your dog place just his front feet on the wobbly board, or let him get on it completely. Rock the board ever so slightly and instantly deliver a tasty treat (or a fun game of tug) while your dog is still on the board.

Exercise 31: Introduce your dog to movement on the board

1. Hold the board steady.
2. Transport your dog to a starting point close to the board.
3. End the transport.
4. Your dog gets on the board (front feet only, or all four).
5. Rock the board ever so slightly.
6. Immediately deliver a fabulous reward.
7. Repeat the pairing of rock-reward a few times.
8. Use the final reward to transport your dog off the board.
9. Let him offer to repeat the exercise.

If your dog stays on the board the whole time, and happily returns after you've transported him off, you have done a good job and can proceed to rock the board a bit harder. If he hops off and/or hesitates to get back on, he is telling you that the last time was a bit difficult and that you need to make the challenge easier.

The board moves a bit, and the tastiest treat magically appears!

Where you place the goody will make a difference to your dog: It should appear as though it grows out of the moving board. Quickly deliver the treat or toy so that your dog gets it while he is still on the board; and keep the good stuff coming, so that he associates the movement with staying on the board and eating or playing. If he has already bounced off, place the treat/toy close to the board so that he comes back to get it.

Immediately follow the movement of the board with a reward. You do not need your clicker here; just deliver the reward. The movement itself will take on the role of the clicker, signaling that a reward is on its way.

Step 3: Teach your dog to create movement (you move the board)

Next you want to teach your dog to act to get the board moving. You'll hold the board steady and rock it a bit when your dog acts, so that he is creating the movement through you. The sequence will be: Dog acts—you move the board—dog gets treat or toy.

So what should your dog do to make you start moving the board? We usually choose to correlate criteria with your dog's signs of anticipation, for example, "pricked ears" or "looking forward/downward," but you can also choose to shape, for example, a foot movement. What's important is that your dog learns that he can act to get the board moving. To help your dog keep his balance, his center of gravity should be quite low—so it's a good idea to choose some downward motion as your criterion. After rocking the board, remember to reward low!

The dog looks for the board to move, and it moves (guided by the trainer).

Exercise 32: Teach your dog to trigger you to move the board

1. Hold the board steady.
2. Transport your dog to a starting point close to the board.
3. End the transport.
4. Your dog gets on the board.
5. Wait and observe your dog for signs of anticipation.
6. Your dog "looks expectant" (perhaps pricks his ears, or looks downward).
7. Rock the board.
8. Reward!

Step 4: Teach your dog to create movement (your dog moves the board on his own)

Now you want your dog's action to physically get the board to move. Don't hold on to the board—just let him get on it and make it move by himself. You'll immediately reward the movement he creates. The sequence now is: Dog gets on board—board moves—dog gets treat or toy.

Exercise 33: Teach your dog to move the board himself

1. Transport your dog to a starting point close to the board.
2. End the transport.
3. Your dog gets on the board.
4. Your dog makes the board move.
5. Reward!
6. After each reward, either wait and let him figure out how to make the board move again, or transport him off and let him start over.

Step 5: Teach your dog to demand movement

To get your dog into demand mode, make the board a bit more difficult to "start" so that your dog will have to work hard to get the board to move. Hold on to the board so your dog has to apply pressure to make it move. Play with your dog, so that you both have a blast while he works as hard as he can to get that board moving. Reward his creativity, enthusiasm, and persistence well.

Left: "Come on, move!" Right: "Hah! Treats for me!"

Noise and movement in your everyday life

If your dog tends to react to noises in the environment, try to make all sudden noises predict the appearance of good things. Just as in your formal training, by pairing noises with what your dog likes, you'll classically condition your dog to become more relaxed and even begin to like the noises. The same goes for movement. If you and your dog happen to find yourselves on uneven, unstable surfaces such as jetties, metal staircases, or any other surface that moves in any way, try to make the sudden movement indicate that good things will follow.

SOCIAL FACILITATION

Social facilitation comes in handy in the process of teaching your dog to like movement. Just watching others having a great time on a moving surface will contribute to the association that "movement = fun."

Some dogs get excited when their handlers act silly, so you can play on the board yourself, letting your dog join in on his own terms. You can also let your dog interact with other, motion-proof dogs, or just watch them playing with their humans while the surface moves underneath them.

Since dogs are so sensitive to social cues, you want your dog to experience that you, and other people and dogs around him, find moving surfaces entertaining. So if your dog seems worried, act cavalier. And if your dog gets to see other dogs move on moving surfaces, make sure those dogs are enjoying themselves!

Should your dog happen to create noise or movement on his own, by returning to an unstable surface, rocking a hammock, overturning something on purpose, and so on, make sure to reward him. Formal training time is great, but don't forget to think of what you want your dog to enjoy and be happy around when you're out and about in the real world.

And don't forget trick training! There are loads of tricks that you can train that will facilitate teaching your dog to like, create, and demand things to go boom and move. Train your dog to jump into your arms, sit on your lap, stand on your back as you walk on all fours, stand between your legs and walk with his front feet on yours (hitching a ride on your feet as many kids like to do), correctly put blocks into a children's toy (the blocks make noise as they drop into place), pull on a bag with empty cans, and so on. You'll both have a good time and learn more about training. The fact that you can incorporate noise and movement training into it all is just a bonus.

Amusement park training—the more turmoil there is, the more fun it is!

Liking, creating, and demanding noise and movement are important skills, not just for the sake of creating a happy and confident agility dog, but also for making your dog's life in the society we live in a calm and happy existence. There are a lot of things and situations out there that will both rock your dog's world and go kaboom!

13

Rear-end control

Agility requires acceleration and deceleration, turns and jumps, weight shifts and balancing acts. To perform these movements safely and with precision at top speed, your dog depends on his strength, flexibility, body awareness, and coordination. So that your dog can use his body efficiently on course, he needs to learn how to work with his core and his hindquarters. Some dogs actually seem totally unaware that their body continues behind their shoulders. Exercises in this chapter will build your dog's body awareness and coordination.

Developing rear-end control

A dog that has developed good rear-end control will

- have the strength and coordination to handle most situations that he finds himself in.
- use his rear end efficiently (not pull himself by the front).
- be less prone to injuries since he uses his body skillfully.
- be able to jump, weave, and handle the contact obstacles in the best possible fashion.

One of the best ways to engage those rear-end muscles is simply to take one step at a time. In this chapter we describe how you can train step-by-step walking, backing up, and side-stepping. But please, don't stop there! Every time you teach your dog to manipulate his body in novel ways, he gains more knowledge about how to use his body. All kinds of trick training are great for building body awareness and fine-tuning your dog's motor skills.

To get the best rear-end work, go for deliberate and controlled movements that engage your dog's core muscles and/or his hind legs, and work both sides and all directions (forward, backward, and sideways). Start off easy to build muscle stamina and coordination. Have fun!

Taking a step at a time, with full control of the body: forward (left), backward (center), and sideways (right).

Step by step: forward, backward, and sideways

Walking *step by step* in various directions (forward, backward, and sideways) might seem remarkably simple, but appearances can be deceiving! Slowly walking forward step by step requires much more muscle work than trotting or bouncing around since your dog has to use pure muscle strength to lift one leg at a time. By training your dog to walk straight forward as well as in circles and serpentines, you'll strengthen his back and increase his body control. Backing up (walking step by step backward) makes your dog further aware of what his hind legs are doing; backing up is an exercise that you can vary infinitely for additional challenge. Sidestepping (walking step by step sideways) engages less-used neural pathways, increasing your dog's coordination and rear-end control. Moving step by step is also a superb warm-up for other activities.

Stepping over bars, one foot at a time, with the head low

What should step by step look like?

When working with *step by step* your dog should

- move slowly and deliberately, step by step, lifting one leg at a time.
- keep his head relatively low, since his back and his hind legs then will work most freely.
- use both sides of his body equally.

Why do you need it?

Step-by-step exercises

- activate the tiny muscles in your dog's back and hind legs.
- build new neural connections.
- increase coordination and body awareness.
- increase strength and mobility.
- increase your dog's ability to excel in agility.

Agility puts high demands on the dog's ability to push off from the rear end.

How can you train it?

Rear-end control is an odd bird among the foundation skills, since it is a skill that you'll incorporate into your agility training only indirectly. Your dog will never be required to walk step by step on an agility course, so how you choose to get the behavior is not that important. What we're after here is that your dog learns to use his body in a certain way: Independent performance and following your handling system are not the goals, but, as always, you should work with focus and intensity. The golden rule is: The slower, the better. The idea is to allow new muscles to work and to enable your dog to coordinate his movements in novel ways. If your dog moves too fast, his body will switch to autopilot and will work the usual old muscles in the usual old way. So aim for slow motion. Start easy and give your dog time to build the necessary muscles and neural connections, stamina, coordination, and understanding for the exercises.

Keep a close eye on your dog during rear-end training: The slow and deliberate movements it requires may reveal issues that you hadn't noticed before. If you find that your dog uses his body unevenly and/or struggles a lot with some exercises, have him checked by a vet, a trained physiotherapist, or other health professional.

Put out some bars for your dog to step over. Begin low.

Walking forward

Walking slowly and stepping over things with deliberate, controlled leg movements gives your dog a great physical workout, engaging all the tiny muscles in the back and hind legs. It also increases body awareness since your dog must take one step at a time and has to consider carefully where he can place each foot.

To get the first slow and conscious steps, you can simply try going for a slow walk. You can also guide your dog with a target or a lure, or you can use free shaping (our favorite). You can practice step-by-step walking almost anywhere: on grass, in rich vegetation, over bars, or between the rungs of a ladder you have placed on the ground. You can vary the height your dog has to step, from just above the ground in the beginning to above knee-high for an experienced dog. Vary between walking straight and walking in arcs and between having your dog on your left side and on your right side.

Take a walk in the woods with your dog. Walk slowly, off the beaten track, with your dog on a rather short (but not tight) leash. Some dogs get the idea right away and start stepping properly by themselves. Yet others prefer to bounce or trot and need more information from you in the form of well-timed clicks and treats—and then you should switch to guiding or free shaping, rewarding every proper step.

Guide your dog with a treat lure in your hand, or use a target stick (a stick that you have taught your dog to target with his nose so that he nudges the stick's near end). Move your hand or target stick slowly, and click and treat when your dog follows and steps over whatever is on the ground. This is an easy way to get the behavior; the drawback is that your dog may focus more on what is in front of his nose than on what his feet are doing and thus may largely miss the point of the exercise. In that respect the target stick usually works better than the treat lure. Feel free to experiment and switch between different methods. Since new, untrained muscles tire quickly, start with brief sessions (perhaps just 30 seconds).

Free-shape the behavior. Work your dog by your side (so that you're slowly moving forward with him) and start by clicking and treating for any attempt to step forward. The advantages of free shaping are that it allows your dog to move freely and that it often makes him more conscious of what he is doing.

Here an experienced dog is working with randomly set bars. The handler is free shaping-forward steps, clicking for left hind foot over bar and delivering the treat ahead, in the direction the dog is working.

Tips for getting the first steps forward:

- At first, reinforce every single step or, even better, several positions of every step.
- Maintaining a high rate of reinforcement will keep your dog focused and enable him to discover quickly what the exercise is all about.
- Focus especially on the hind feet. Your criteria can be "leaning forward," "lifting left rear foot," "holding left rear foot in the air," "left rear foot touching ground," or whatever response you feel needs reinforcement.
- Marking and reinforcing all kinds of weight shifting and foot and leg movement will increase your dog's awareness of what his body is doing.
- Whichever method you choose to get the behavior, make sure you place the reward where you want your dog's head to be, typically straight ahead of your dog's body and relatively low to the ground so that your dog does not have to twist his neck or jump up to reach it.
- When walking forward, watch that your dog
    - lifts his legs straight (in other words, doesn't angle his knees outward, swinging or rotating the legs outside his body).
    - keeps his rear in line with his front end (in other words, doesn't pop his rear end out to either side).

If your dog moves improperly, the exercise is probably too difficult and/or the rate of reinforcement is too low. Lower the "obstacles," and click and treat for standing still, for lifting one foot, and so on. If your dog still moves oddly, he needs a checkup by a professional.

When your dog readily steps with one leg at a time, let him take several consecutive steps before you click and treat. If you have been using any lures or targets, begin fading them. When your dog offers correct stepping most of the time, you can stretch the sessions bit by bit. As your dog's strength increases, you can take up to 15- to 20-minute-long, slow walks. Vary the surface, walk up hill, down hill, along slopes, and so on. Also, vary between walking straight forward and moving in circles and serpentines.

Backing up

Backing up is a great way to increase rear-end control, and you can vary and escalate the exercise infinitely. When your dog is skilled in backing up, you can teach him to back uphill, downhill, over small obstacles, or up stairs. When backing up, your dog should walk straight backward, moving one leg at a time. To get the first back-up steps it is easiest to start from "front position," with your dog standing facing you (yes, we know, the opposite of all the rest of your agility training). If this is a new position for your dog, you should start by teaching him to stand facing you. Just back away from him and click and treat for his approaching you head on, and he'll quickly learn to offer a front position. Then you can start training the back-up:

- Start by looking at your dog in everyday settings. Does he ever step backward? Try to capture those steps by marking and rewarding them.
- You can free-shape the behavior, which makes your dog keenly aware of what he is doing and gives you an excellent chance to practice your observational and timing skills.
- To get that first back-up step, you can try putting a treat on the floor between your feet. Encourage your dog to take the treat. Most likely after your dog takes the treat, you'll get one or two steps of backing away. Capture that.

To get the first back-up steps using free shaping, look for the following reinforceable responses:

1. Your dog stands up.
2. Your dog moves his center of gravity backward without sitting down.
3. Your dog leans backward and starts to lift a foot.
4. Your dog takes his first step backward: "jackpot" with a big serving of special treats.

Click for backward movement, and deliver the treat in a fashion that enhances the backward motion.

Deliver rewards to your dog in a fashion that promotes backward movement—toss them to him, or deliver them under his chin, between his front legs. If you want your dog to learn to offer backing up without body cues from you (which is a good idea since he then becomes even more aware of his own movements), then make sure that you're keeping perfectly still or moving randomly. When your dog readily offers backward movement, it's time to increase the number of steps. The key to getting your dog

When backing up over bars, your dog truly has to be in control of his rear end.

to keep backing up (instead of settling on a pattern, for example "back up two steps and stop") is to vary when the click comes: sometimes just when your dog starts to back up, sometimes in the middle of Step 4, sometimes at the beginning of Step 2, and so on. Randomize the variation so your dog never knows which step will be reinforced. Timing is important: Make sure that you mark and reinforce backward motion, not stopping or standing still. When your dog promptly offers straight backward steps on the flat, you can develop the behavior further, letting him back up over uneven surfaces such as carpets or bars on the ground. You can even teach him to back up and down slopes and stairs or over obstacles, if you wish. Give your dog a starting position very close to (or in the middle of) whatever you want him to back over, so that he knows it's there. When increasing the difficulty, remember to lower criteria and reward the tiniest steps, such as weight shifting and foot lifting.

Sidestepping

Most dogs rarely sidestep by themselves, so this exercise will need some training. The process of shaping sidestepping will teach your dog a lot about what he actually can do with his hind legs, and it offers you an exercise you can expand and vary infinitely.

When sidestepping, your dog should pivot to the side with his hind legs, one step at a time. He'll move first one hind foot out from his body sideways and then follow with the other hind foot.

There are two standard variations of sidestepping:
- Walking sideways with both front and rear end
- Pivoting with the rear around a stationary front end (with the front feet up on something)

To get the first steps to the side, you can use a combination of capturing, free shaping, and prompting. The easiest method is for your dog to start in front position.

Walking sideways with both front and rear end: Start with your dog facing you. Try taking tiny steps to the side and let your dog figure out how to get back to the front position. In the beginning, reward him for all movement, even if he just walks with you: the more behavior he offers, the greater the chance that he eventually will happen to take a step out to the side with a hind leg. Pay close attention to his rear end. Click and jackpot for any tiny tendency to sidestep, but do not worry if your dog does not sidestep right away—sorting out that rear end can be quite tricky for him!

Front end still: Start by shaping your dog to stand with his front feet up on something (like a phonebook, or an upended wooden box). Then start reinforcing all hind leg movement. If you like, you can stand facing your dog and step to the side so that he has to sidestep to

Front feet on the box—click for right hind foot moving!

get back into front position. The advantage of this approach is that since his front feet are "stuck," the only way to move is to step to the side with the rear end. In the beginning, remember to reward all hind leg motion. If your dog just starts moving those hind feet, the sidestep will come.

Tips for getting the first sidesteps:
- Your observational skills and your timing are vital.
- Look for the slightest movement of a hind leg.
- Make sure at first to reward all hind leg action.

Have faith: As long as your dog keeps offering movement, he will sidestep sooner or later. When your dog readily offers steps to the side, it's time to increase the number of steps. Just as with backing up, you may want your dog to just keep going, so vary when the reward comes.

You can also let your dog work on a different surface or to sidestep over something. See if your dog will sidestep on a blanket or on a slightly slippery surface. That will change the way he needs to work with his body. You can also set up objects that he needs to step over. Start low at first, but then raise them ever so slightly. Remember that when increasing the difficulty, ease up on your criteria and reward the tiniest tendency to sidestep.

Advanced sidestepping over bars

OTHER REAR-END AND BODY CONTROL TRAINING

Trick training is excellent for increasing your dog's rear-end control and overall body control. Especially tricks where he gets to move slowly and deliberately will benefit your agility dog (and actually, your dog's overall health, both physical and mental). For example, you can teach your dog to balance on various objects, to lift a foot at a time, to bow, to touch his tail with his nose, and a zillion other tricks. The process of learning new physical skills is the point here. As a bonus, your neighbors will be impressed by all the cool stuff your dog knows, and both you and your dog will become experts at shaping new behaviors.

In your everyday life, you can do many little things that will help along your dog's body control training. For example: When walking your dog, get off the path and forge your own trail. When serving your dog's dinner, spread it out in some high grass so that he gets to step around while eating. Give your dog ample opportunities to use his whole body! Every little something counts and will help your dog find his feet and build his strength.

Massage, Tellington Touch™, and other kinds of body work are also great for increasing your dog's body awareness (along with all the other benefits of such practices).

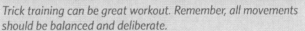

Trick training can be great workout. Remember, all movements should be balanced and deliberate.

Both puppies and adults should be given lots of opportunities to use their bodies in various ways.

Rear-end control work is needed throughout your dog's life, to help him use his body correctly and to its full extent. It's entertaining to come up with all the possible tricks you can teach your dog—and not only will it help keep your dog in excellent health, it also will stretch both your minds and give you an opportunity to work on your skills as a trainer. As always, have fun!

14

Starts and stays

Every agility course, and every exercise during training, begins with a start. Each time your dog resumes working after a reward, it's a kind of start. This means that every agility team executes thousands of starts in its career, and these starts often set the tone for what follows. This chapter is all about starts—discussing spontaneous and cued starts, and explaining in detail how you can teach a reliable start-line stay and start on cue.

Spontaneous or on cue?

There are two possible ways to start: the *spontaneous start* and the *start on cue.*

- In a spontaneous start your dog starts ahead and offers behaviors as soon as a reward or transport ends.
- In a start on cue your dog stays put on the start line, starting only on your verbal cue.

For training purposes you need them both!

The spontaneous start

Spontaneous starts are what you've practiced throughout the previous chapters. To us, the spontaneous start is the top priority. As clicker trainers we want our dogs to offer behaviors voluntarily, without waiting for cues from the handler. The spontaneous starts also give you ample opportunities to let your dog work ahead on his own, in the direction given by your shoulders.

The spontaneous start is our "default behavior": If your dog doesn't get any other information, he should enthusiastically aim ahead and offer behaviors "on the fly" as soon as he gets a chance. His "cues" to go will be nonverbal: The facts that a reward or transport has just ended and that he is not "parked" in a stay tell him that he should start working right away.

Here are some examples where the dog starts spontaneously:

- **Aim for it training, going under a chair:** You transport your dog to a suitable starting point using a treat magnet. You remove your treat hand, and when your dog glances forward, you click and give your dog a treat. Your dog swallows the treat, aims ahead, and you reward him yet again. So, your dog spontaneously resumes working after each reward.
- **Racing to a treat bowl:** You show your dog the bowl, grab his collar, lead him to your chosen start point, turn so that your shoulders and your dog's nose are facing the bowl, and let go of him (without stopping first). Your dog starts when you let go of his collar, and flies like the wind toward his treat bowl.
- **Practicing the weave poles:** During ongoing play with a toy, you move to a suitable starting point (at the distance and angle you wish to work). When your dog is in the right spot, turned in the correct direction, you cue "thank you." Your dog lets go of the toy and starts working right away—he looks ahead, spots the weave poles, and runs ahead toward them.

Here, the dogs start spontaneously as the transport ends: from a treat magnet (top), from a collar transport (middle), and from a toy transport (bottom).

Start on cue

A start on cue means that your dog waits for your verbal start cue and explodes ahead as you give the cue. We use a start cue only in specific situations where we want the dog to keep still until released:

- from start-line stays
- from contact zones
- from the table

In start-line stays, we end the transport when the dog is standing still. The fact that you hold on to your dog until he has positioned himself in a stay (or cue a stationary position, such as sit or stand—but we prefer to let the dog offer his position spontaneously) will tell your dog that he should wait for his start cue.

On the contacts and the table we teach the dog to offer the correct behavior (put his front feet on the ground at the contact's downzone, and lie down on the table). Then we use the start cue to end that behavior. That way, the dog learns to hold his position until he hears the start cue.

Here, the dogs start on cue from a stationary position: from a start line (top); from a contact (bottom left), and from the table (bottom right).

Use both spontaneous starts and start-line stays

When teaching new behaviors, we usually want the dog to start spontaneously, offering the behavior without any start cue. Later you'll want to vary—sometimes using spontaneous starts, sometimes using a stay and start on cue. Your dog will easily learn which start to do in which situation as long as you're clear about the rules. The contrast we make is:

When using spontaneous starts you just end the transport (remove the tug toy or treat magnet or let go of the collar) *while your dog is on the move,* without him coming to a perfectly balanced stay first. Then his job is to move ahead spontaneously.

When training start-line stays you hold on to your dog *until he has positioned himself in a stay*—"parked himself." Then, when you let go, his job is to keep still until he hears your start cue.

Make sure you maintain your spontaneous starts, so that your dog continues to aim ahead whenever you end a transport while he is moving.

For the rest of this chapter we'll discuss *start-line stays* and *starts,* first teaching your dog to start on cue and then to stay put until he hears the start cue.

The secrets of a perfectly reliable start-line stay

Teaching a perfect start-line stay and start means putting together two apparently contradictory behaviors:

- Be still and wait for a cue to start
- On the handler's cue, start with full speed and intensity

Waiting for the start cue (left) and dashing off on cue (right).

As a handler you want your dog to be eager to go, but at the same time you want to control *when* he takes off.

Teaching a perfectly reliable start-line stay is a simple and straightforward process. Success depends on three elements:

1. **Your dog starts on cue.** First and foremost, you must teach the start behavior and put it on cue. If you're ever going to get reliable stays, your dog has to explode away on your start cue, without any other prompts.

2. **You vary everything but the start cue.** When you vary everything but the cue, your dog will become expert at differentiating the start cue, and you'll thereby gain stimulus control. Your dog will start on cue, and only on cue.

3. **You stick to your criteria for the stay behavior.** If you're consistent with your stay criteria, your dog will learn quickly. If you're inconsistent, it's impossible for him to figure out what to do. If you give the start cue only when criteria are met, your dog will start on cue, and only on cue.

Teaching the start, teaching the stay

Teaching the start on cue is our first priority. "But," someone might say, "*Starting* is not the problem. My dog starts all the time. It's the *stay* part that we're struggling with." That may well be true: *Starting* might not be the issue per se, but *starting on cue* definitely is. If the dog isn't sure of when to start, he'll be taking chances all the time, and start-line trouble is sure to follow. Likewise, for the less explosive dog, wanting to run and knowing to do so on cue are essential for a good start-line behavior (and set the tone for the rest of the run as well).

So first and foremost, your dog needs to learn to start on cue. Once he knows to start on cue, your start cue will serve three functions:

- The start cue releases your dog from the previous behavior ("You're free to leave your stand/sit/contact/table").
- The start cue reinforces the previous behavior. (Remember: Cues trained with positive reinforcement function as rewards.)
- The start cue tells your dog to explode away in the direction you indicate by your handling.

Once you have taught your dog to start on cue, you can teach him to stay put and wait for that magic cue. Our favorite strategy for shaping the *stay* behavior is by using the start cue as the reward, but it's also possible to shape the stay behavior separately by rewarding your dog in position. We prefer to use the start cue as a reward since it puts your dog in control. You'll truly be working with his own initiative: He learns that by staying, he can make you give that magic start cue. Also, it enables you to reward your start-line stays 100% of the time, since your start cue will always be present. You're simply using the Premack Principle to get those lovely reliable start-line stays: For keeping still, your dog is rewarded by something he really wants, which is hearing that start cue and getting to dash off.

We view *start on cue* as one foundation skill, and *stay* as another. Since our stay training always includes a start cue, *start on cue* is a prerequisite for *stay*.

The whole process looks like this:

1. Get the start behavior. (You've already done this by teaching your dog *Race to reward*.)
2. Add the cue for the start behavior.
3. Shape the stay behavior.
4. If you like, add a cue for the stay behavior.

In the following sections we explain how you can teach the start cue and how you can shape the stay (both by solely using your start cue as reward and by rewarding in position).

Start on cue

To get reliable starts, first and foremost, you must teach the start behavior and put it on cue.

THE START CUE

Your start cue should be verbal and distinct, standing out from everything else you might say during training. In our examples we use "go" as our start cue, but, of course, you can choose another cue. Just watch out for words you might use a lot when talking to your dog or to people around you. For instance, "OK" is probably not the best choice.

The reason that the cue should be verbal is that you want to be able to move around freely (going as far as you want, as fast as you want, even tripping if that should happen, and so on) and your dog should still stay put and wait for his cue to start. If your start cue had anything to do with body movement, motion, or speed, it would be less black and white for your dog. Also remember that you'll be using your start cue to release your dog from his contact position and the table. A verbal cue will allow for a completely independent obstacle performance. If the cue were to be linked to you and your body, your dog would have to watch you for it and his independent performance likely would suffer.

What should *start on cue* look like?

- You remain neutral and say your verbal start cue.
- When you dog hears the start cue, he explodes away in the direction your shoulders are pointing.

Why do you need it?

- The cue to start will release your dog from stationary behavior (such as start-line stays, contacts, and tables).
- The cue to start will function as a reward for the stationary behavior.
- Your dog will start only when you want him to and not at any other time.
- If your dog excels at exploding away on cue, teaching your dog to wait for the cue will be a walk in the park. You will just need to set criteria and stick to them while you add various variations and distractions to proof your dog's understanding of when to stay and when to start.

How can you train it?

We begin teaching the start on cue by using the *Race to reward* procedure. If your dog knows how to explode away and race to his reward, you have an excellent start behavior to put on cue.

Parallel to the *Race to reward* procedure, we also teach the start on cue by using a thrown toy (as a lure in the beginning, and then purely as a reward) to ensure that your dog can start even if he doesn't have a remote reward ahead. Below we describe teaching the start cue using both the *Race to reward* and the *"Go" and throw* procedures.

Teaching the start cue using *Race to reward*

First rehearse *Race to reward* (see page 142). Before adding the start cue, you need to make certain that your dog dashes away at top speed toward his reward when you release him. You want his start to be as explosive as possible, so get your helper to really rev up the remote reward!

Then rehearse *remaining neutral* (see page 81 in "Training yourself"). Before saying the start cue to your dog, you have to make sure that you're able to say your cue without any accompanying body movements! Your start cue should be verbal, distinct, and disconnected from all body movement.

Now, "name" the start behavior by adding the start cue as your dog explodes away. Work through the exact same procedure as in the earlier *Race to reward* training, but say "go" (or whatever cue you choose), *as* you let go—in other words, immediately *before* the behavior happens—so that your dog will start associating the word with the start behavior. This way the cue will become a "green light" telling your dog that now he can race ahead.

When the dog is ready to explode away, say "go," and let go.

Exercise 34: Add the "go" cue

1. Show your dog the remote reward.
2. Transport him away.
3. Turn, stop, and stand still (simultaneously, the helper revs up the reward).
4. Your dog looks ahead, and you feel he's ready to dash away.
5. Say "go" and let go.
6. Your dog blasts away and races to his remote reward.

Suggested tag points:

- Hold on to dog in transport
- Be neutral while saying "go"
- Say "go" as you open your hand (tag for saying the word)
- Open your hand as you say "go" (tag for opening the hand)

Feel free to start introducing all kinds of minor variations right away; remaining neutral doesn't have to mean freezing! While you're holding your dog by the collar, saying the start cue, and letting go, you can wiggle your fingers, move your feet, and so on. Just make sure there's no fixed pattern between your movements and the start cue: if you're wiggling your fingers, keep wiggling your fingers while you give the cue, if you're jogging in place, keep doing so while giving the cue.

Teach *"Go"* and throw

"Go" and throw teaches your dog to respond with intensity and purpose to your start cue without having a remote reward ahead. We're not looking for your dog to run 20 meters on his own; what we're looking for is simply a start, showing that your dog releases on your verbal start cue. You'll reward his forward motion with a thrown toy.

At first the thrown toy will function as a lure, but soon it will transform into a reward that appears after the desired behavior. You can introduce *"Go"* and throw as soon as you have established the start cue in *Race to reward* training.

YES, THIS TRAINING PROCEDURE CONTRADICTS WHAT WE NORMALLY ADVOCATE

Normally we add cues only to solid behaviors—we don't usually give cues and then lure to get the behavior. The *"Go"* and throw procedure is an exception. Use this procedure only in tandem with *Race to reward* training once you've added the start cue, so your dog has at least some understanding of the cue. In the *"Go"* and throw procedure, your dog will learn to start ahead on your "go" cue in anticipation of a reward flying ahead of him.

There's an everyday parallel to this training procedure. It's the same as when your throw a tennis ball 10 times and then fake a throw: Your dog starts off anyway, anticipating that the ball will appear. In *"Go"* and throw training, once your dog has learned the drill, instead of seeing you throw, he'll hear your start cue. Since your start cue reliably predicts that a toy is about to come flying, he'll start off as he hears the cue. Then the toy no longer will be a lure but a reward, since it actually appears *after* the behavior has occurred.

From your dog's perspective, the *"Go"* and throw procedure at first will look like this:
- Stands by your side
- Hears the start cue
- Sees a favorite toy or treat magically appear midair, straight ahead
- Dashes to get the reward

Soon, you can delay the toy throw slightly so that your dog starts on your start cue and is rewarded by the toy. Then it will look like this to your dog:
- Stands by your side
- Hears the start cue
- Responds to the start cue by moving forward
- Sees a favorite toy or treat magically appear midair, straight ahead
- Dashes to get the reward

To begin practicing *"Go"* and throw we recommend having a helper stand behind you, invisible to your dog, who throws the toy so that it appears "out of nowhere" in front of your dog immediately after you give your start cue. You could simply say "go" and then throw the toy yourself, but then your dog might come to rely on your arm throwing as the cue rather than your verbal cue alone. Therefore it's better to use a helper in the beginning.

Since it's vital that your dog learns to listen for the cue rather than looking for the throw, you and your helper need to prepare yourselves carefully for this one. You need to be so in sync that the toy comes soaring from behind at precisely the right moment, right after your "go" cue. Ask your helper to throw the toy right *before* you give the cue so that when you say "go," the toy then appears in your dog's line of vision. Figure out a signaling system (such as your helper putting her hand on your shoulder) so that you can coordinate. Timing is everything!

Ideally your dog will start moving ever so slightly as you give the cue, and the toy will appear as a reward. But if your dog doesn't respond immediately to your cue, the flying toy will appear anyway, functioning as a lure that triggers your dog to start. By repeatedly combining the "go" cue with the flying toy, your dog will learn to anticipate the toy and start on your "go" cue.

Left: Everybody's ready!
Center: The handler gives the start cue just before the toy appears ahead of the dog.
Right: The dog hears the start cue, sees the toy, and dashes off!

Exercise 35: "Go" and throw: *Say "go" just before the toy appears*

1. Stand with your dog at your side or slightly ahead of you, lightly holding on to him.
2. Your helper stands behind you, ready to throw the toy over your shoulder.
3. Your helper pats your shoulder as she throws the toy.
4. Cue "go" just before your dog sees the toy.
5. Best-case scenario, your dog starts moving ahead.
6. The toy appears in front of your dog.
7. Your dog dashes to get his reward.

Suggested tag points:

- Say "go" at pat
- Remain neutral while saying "go"

If your dog is twisting and turning to see the toy in your helper's hand, simply wait. Throw and say "go" as he looks elsewhere, step by step shaping him to look ahead in order to get his "go" cue.

"Start cue? I'm off! My toy will come."

Keep repeating the *"Go" and throw* procedure, making the toy appear quickly after the cue until your dog reliably anticipates the throw and starts before he can see the toy. When you're 99% certain that your dog will start moving on your cue before the toy appears, say "go" first and throw the toy as your dog starts. The toy now will function purely as a reward. This exercise will teach your dog to reliably dash ahead whenever he hears the "go" cue.

Exercise 36: "Go" and throw: *Say "go" and throw the toy as your dog starts*

1. Stand with your dog at your side or slightly ahead of you.
2. Say "go."
3. Your dog starts.
4. Your helper (or you) throws the toy as a reward.

Suggested tag points:

- Remain neutral when saying "go"
- Throw as your dog starts

Stay

Now that your dog knows how to start on a specific verbal cue, you can teach him to stay put until you give that start cue.

What should *Stay and start* look like?

The start-line behavior is a chain:

- You position your dog at the start line.
- Your dog stays still, looking ahead.
- You give the verbal cue for the start behavior (for example, "go").
- Your dog starts with full speed and intensity.

Standing still, looking ahead is rewarded by the start cue.

Why do you need the stay?

- Start-line stays enable you to position yourself wherever you want.
- Start-line stays make it easier for you to give your dog the best possible line into the course or exercise.
- Start-line stays can later transfer to contacts and to the table.

Which position should I teach my dog?

Which starting position you choose is up to you and your dog. You should take into consideration:

- Which starting position do you think your dog will like, and offer reliably?
- Which starting position will enable your dog to use his body in the best way?
- Are your criteria clear for your dog?
- Are your criteria easy for you to observe, even from a distance?

Perhaps you'll need to make a compromise; decide which factors are more important for you at the moment, and choose your dog's starting position accordingly. Note that arguments like "this position might be harder to break" or "this position feels most different from running ahead" are not valid reasons for choosing a position. Your clever training is what will make your dog stay put.

The start position we usually train—and the one we'll use in our examples—is standing still, four feet on the ground, and looking ahead. Our prime reason for choosing a standing position is that most dogs readily offer a stand to get their start cue. Since the stand is also a position that is easy to observe, it's easy for you to stick to your criteria ("four feet touching ground" in a stand, for example, is much easier to check than "bottom touching ground" in a sit, particularly from a distance). We also suggest you teach your dog to look ahead to get his "go" cue. Looking ahead will transfer nicely to looking at the first obstacle, which coincides with your dog's overall aiming ahead on course.

YOU CAN TEACH MORE THAN ONE START POSITION IF YOU WISH

If you want to have several start positions to choose from, you can teach one position as your default behavior (the one your dog offers on his own) and then teach other positions that you cue. For example, if you say nothing, your dog stands, but if you say "sit," he sits. Just note that every cue you use has to be trained so that your dog happily, quickly, and reliably offers the correct behavior every time you ask for it. Any hassle getting your dog into the desired position will interrupt the flow of your training and might interfere with the rest of the start-line behavior.

How can you train it?

Our favorite strategy when training *Stay and start* is to shape the *stay* behavior using the start cue as reward. This means that, instead of returning to reward the dog for staying at the start line, we teach him that standing perfectly still will lead to that desirable start cue. This is the Premack Principle at work: Your dog gets a chance to do something that he loves to do (dashing away) after doing something that you want him to do (staying put at the start line).

Your start cue is the perfect reward for the stay behavior because

- your dog learns for himself that it's rewarding to be still.
- your dog will build and keep maximum intensity at the start.
- the eager dog learns that it pays to be still, and the more timid dog avoids becoming passive.
- you'll reward your start-line stays 100% of the time—even at trials.

We'll go through how you can back-chain the stay in four steps using *Race to reward* as your sole reward:

> **Step 1: Get the first hint of a stay.**
> **Step 2: Shape a longer stay.**
> **Step 3: Introduce variations and distractions.**
> **Step 4: Let go of your dog.**

When you shape a stay using *Race to reward,* you'll also teach your dog to look ahead (since he'll be focusing on his remote reward). Make sure you always give your "go" cue while your dog is looking ahead.

We'll also give you some advice for contrasting training, alternating between start-line stays and spontaneous starts. By constantly varying which kind of start you do, your dog (and you) will keep up to par on both and avoid any in-the-middle, gray areas. Note that the contrast work should start right away, *parallel to* shaping the stay—that way your dog gets a chance to grasp the rules of the game from the very beginning.

Finally, we'll describe how you can teach the stay separately by machine-gunning rewards to your dog as he stands still. We usually don't do this for the start-line stays, but it will be useful for you to become familiar with the process; it comes in handy for future contact and table training.

Step 1: Use *Race to reward* to get the first hint of a stay

Use the familiar *Race to reward* setting and, if possible, employ a helper who can make the reward come alive if needed. This time, hold on to your dog and wait until you feel him balancing himself for a split second (for instance, he ceases pushing forward, settles ever so slightly, or even leans backward). Leaning backward is excellent; by putting his weight back, your dog will push off nicely from his rear end when he starts.

Reward the first instance of balance by saying "go" and let go. Congratulations! You're now well on your way toward your goal: a dog that's frozen in position, yet poised to go.

Exercise 37: Get the first ounce of balance

1. Show your dog the remote reward.
2. Transport him away.
3. Turn, stop, and stand still, holding on to your dog's collar.
4. Your dog balances himself for a split second.
5. Cue "go" and let go.
6. Your dog starts and races to the remote reward.

Suggested tag points:

- Hold on to your dog
- Say "go" as you feel balance
- Let go right after saying "go"

If your dog is a crazy, all-over-the-place type of dog, you might have to start with easier criteria. If he is jumping up and down, then reward him for approaching the ground by cueing "go" on the way down. You can always find some miniscule response to reward to get the shaping process started as in the suggested progression below. Remain silent and neutral; just reward with the "go" cue when your dog meets criteria.

To continue, simply use shaping to prolong this split-second of stillness and balance. Your goal is for your dog to learn that to earn the "go" cue, he needs to "park himself" in a balanced position, frozen but poised for action. The road from the first little signs of balance to the perfect frozen-but-ready stand depends on

- setting and maintaining clear criteria so that your dog can learn exactly what to do.
- keeping the rate of reinforcement high by moving ahead in baby steps, continually giving the start cue while your dog keeps still yet poised for action.
- your dog really being eager to hear his start cue and to get to go.

Step 2: Shape a longer stay

While holding on to your dog, start shaping a longer stay by varying the time before you give your start cue.

Here are some possible steps for shaping a longer stay:
- Feel your dog balance himself for a nanosecond with all feet on the ground.
- Wait for a quarter of a second of stillness.
- Wait for one second.
- Wait for two seconds.
- Ping-pong back and forth to build longer and longer duration.

You can ease your hold so that your dog is truly standing by himself, but don't let go. Since you're holding on to your dog, there won't be any major mistakes. If he tries to start before the cue, you simply don't let go. If he happens to look away, wait for him to look ahead before you say the start cue (if necessary, have your helper rev up the reward to make it really interesting). Strive to get it perfectly right on each attempt, though.

To instantly reward the dog for balancing himself in a stay, we often choose to give the start cue right away. We vary the duration, of course, but it's even more important to do the quick repetitions than to work on the longer durations. It all boils down to getting your dog to stay on edge, ready to explode ahead, yet frozen in position.

Step 3: Introduce variations and distractions

In the earliest stay training you remain quiet and silent while your dog stays still. The only stimulus that appears is the start cue. But as soon as your dog can hold still for a couple of seconds, you should add some minor variations and distractions. This will proof your dog to really listen for your start cue and only start when he hears the cue.

While holding your dog by the collar, saying the start cue, and letting go, you can wiggle your fingers, wave your arms, make some noise, move your feet, and so on. Make sure your variations in no way are connected to your start cue! That means that you continue doing whatever you're doing while you give your start cue, so if you're waving your arms, keep waving them when you say "go." You're working toward having your dog hold his stay and only taking off when you give him your start cue no matter what else is going on.

Exercise 38: Add variations and distractions while your dog stands still and starts on cue

1. Show your dog the remote reward.
2. Transport him away.
3. Turn, stop, and stand still.
4. Wait for your dog to balance himself and stand still.
5. Keep holding on to his collar lightly, and wave your arm.
6. While you keep waving your arm, say "go" and let go.
7. Your dog starts and races to the remote reward.

Suggested tag points:

- Hold on to your dog
- Say "go" while waving
- Say "go" while your dog looks ahead
- Keep waving while your dog starts

The waving arm is by no means connected to the start cue.

Step 4: Let go of your dog

When your dog keeps still yet poised for action for several seconds and in the face of various distractions, you can start letting go of his collar before saying his start cue.

From now on, if he chooses to start before your cue, he is free to do so. Do *not* try to stop him—that'd be a quick way to ruin his confidence! The only consequence should be that he misses out on his remote reward. If he starts without your start cue, simply go get him, transport him back, and try again.

You can phase out your hold on the collar gradually:

- Hold the collar with just one finger.
- Let go of the collar but keep touching your dog lightly.
- Let go completely.
- Take a step sideways or backward.

Exercise 39: Start-line stay, hands off collar

1. Show your dog the remote reward.

2. Transport him away.

3. Turn, stop, and stand still.

4. Keep holding on to your dog's collar.

5. Your dog balances himself and stands still.

6. Let go of your dog's collar.

7. Your dog remains still and looks at the remote reward.

8. Cue "go."

9. Your dog starts and races to the remote reward.

The dog stands still (left), the handler lets go (center), and the perfect start-line stay is rewarded by the "go" cue (right).

BROKEN CRITERIA

If your dog breaks criteria while you're still holding on to his collar (for example, lifts a foot or hangs forward on the collar), just hold your ground and wait for him to balance himself again. But if you've taken your hand off the collar, your dog is free to choose. Do *not* try to catch or stop him in any way whether he dashes off or just moves a foot. Your helper will simply remove the reward, and you'll cheerfully take your dog by the collar or leash back to the starting point for a new attempt. Even if your dog has just lifted a foot, spin around (dog on the outside) so that he comes into the situation anew and gets to try again.

Your dog gets his start cue only if he looks ahead. If he looks in another direction, simply wait for him to look ahead again. You don't have to start over from the beginning just because your dog has turned his head, as long as he keeps his feet still—but if he seems to lose focus, it's a good idea to give him a fresh start.

"HELPING" DOES NOT HELP!

Don't inhibit or "help" your dog by using your voice or body language to keep him still. As elsewhere in your training, when teaching the start-line stay it's important to keep handler responsibilities separate from dog responsibilities. You want your dog to be responsible for keeping absolutely still, and that is much easier for him to learn if you make the picture black and white: Maintaining the stay criteria generates a start cue, while breaking the stay criteria leads to turning around and starting over from the beginning.

So keep your cool and let your dog make his choice without your help. Your job is to set up a situation that is easy enough (for example, by holding on to his collar, or by just leaving him a very short distance), and your dog's job is to keep still and to listen for your start cue.

YOUR POSITION AND MOVEMENT WHEN PRACTICING *RACE TO REWARD* FROM A START-LINE STAY

Once you begin starting your dog from a stay, you have to pay special attention to your own position and movement to be consistent in your handling. As long as you're standing right next to your dog it's no problem: you can either stand still or move ahead as long as your shoulders are pointing in the direction of the remote reward.

But when you start leaving your dog on the start line, there are a few more things to think about. Here's a summary that will help you stay consistent in your handling and avoid ruining future handling cues when practicing start-line stays and starts:

- **You can be parallel to your dog or a bit behind him,** at any lateral distance. Here you can either stand still facing forward, or move forward.

- **You can be parallel to the remote reward or a bit ahead of it,** at any lateral distance. Here you can also either stand still facing forward, or move forward.

- **You can be somewhere between your dog and the remote reward,** at any lateral distance. Here you must be moving forward when your dog approaches you, and keep moving forward until he reaches the remote reward. That's because here your dog is supposed to blast past you. If you stand still or stop between your dog and the remote reward, he should actually stop with you and not race past you. You'll learn all about this in Chapter 17, "Handling maneuvers on the flat." For your start-line stay training, all you need to do is to *avoid standing still in situations where your dog will fly past you.*

If you are between your dog and the remote reward, make sure you move forward when your dog blasts past you!

When you're able to carefully let go of the collar and take a few steps to the side while your dog stands frozen, looking ahead, and ready for the "go" cue, you've managed to make your dog understand that by staying completely still, on his own, he can make you say the magic word. And this without once asking your dog to "stay"!

Gradually move farther away. Notice, however, that when you move forward so that you end up between your dog and the remote reward, you have to keep moving ahead while he races past you—you don't want to inadvertently teach him to fly past you when you stand still. Always remember to give the start cue only when your dog is looking in the direction of the remote reward—if he looks at you, just wait until he looks ahead before you give your start cue.

Continually vary when you give your start cue. The duration of the stay shouldn't be related to how far you leave your dog: You can stand next to him for 10 seconds; you can run 10 meters ahead and release him while running.

CUE TO LOOK AHEAD?

If you like, you can add a cue—for example, a hand signal in the form of a raised hand—to the behavior "look ahead" while your dog is holding his stay at the start line. Especially when you're leaving your dog for a longer distance, you might want it to be OK for him to look at you as you walk away, but then you want to be able to tell him "now look ahead, and I'll give your start cue." A "look ahead" cue is not a necessity— you can simply let your dog learn from the situation when to look ahead—but it can be a nice tool to have.

To teach the "look ahead" cue, first give the new cue as the behavior happens: While your dog is looking at the remote reward from his start-line stay, raise your hand. Give your start cue while he is still looking ahead. Your hand signal will be built into the "stand still, look ahead" training.

Then teach your dog to actively turn his eyes from you to the remote reward as you give the "look ahead" cue. Leave him in a stay with the remote reward ahead, and wait until he looks at you. As he glances at you, raise your hand and wait for him to look ahead again—and immediately reward him for looking ahead by giving the start cue. (Yes, this also will teach him to glance at you when your hand is not up.) Build the duration of "looking ahead on cue" step by step, varying the time before you give your start cue—but strive to give your start cue while your dog is looking ahead, before he looks back at you again.

Once you've taught the "look ahead" cue, you can choose to keep your hand up while you walk away from your dog— then he should look ahead the whole time, and your start cue can happen at any time—or you can wait until you have reached your chosen position before raising your hand. Either way, your start cue will function as a reward for your dog's looking ahead on cue.

We don't go for total stimulus control here—the dog is free to look ahead even without the cue, and we frequently reward that by giving the start cue as the dog looks ahead. The "look ahead" cue is merely an extra tool in the toolbox.

IT'S ALL ABOUT STIMULUS CONTROL

Once your dog has learned to explode away when he hears the start cue, you need to establish solid stimulus control. When positioned in a start-line stay, your dog needs to learn to start on cue, only on the start cue, and not on any other cue. The lack of stimulus control is the reason why there are so many agility dogs that start when the handler stops walking or starts running, or after exactly two seconds, or when the handler's arm moves slightly, and so on. The problem is not that your dog is "too eager to go" or "disobedient"; the problem is that the start behavior isn't under complete stimulus control.

If stimulus control is lacking, the start behavior will occur on cues other than those the handler had intended. Usually the handler inadvertently has taught the dog to start on a wide variety of cues. To develop reliable stimulus control you must make sure your start cue stands out from everything else that happens. Your start cue should be the only thing that is consistent—not how far you walk, when you call your dog, or whether you begin to run or not. Make sure your cue "go" is disconnected from your movements, and make sure you vary time, distance, and distractions. Dogs discriminate well and will pick up on patterns whether they are intentionally established ones or not, so varying everything but the start cue is an absolute must.

POSSIBLY ADD A "READY, STEADY" CUE

Are you sure that your dog will choose to remain still until he hears your start cue? If you like, you can then add a verbal cue to the behavior "stand still and be ready to go." You don't *have* to add a verbal cue for the stay: You can simply hold on to your dog until he has "parked" himself. When he's parked, he "can't" break his start-line stay without his verbal release cue from you, so that procedure in itself functions as a cue to stay.

But if you want to have a verbal cue for the stay behavior, simply add the cue right before the stay behavior happens: Hold on to the collar, say "ready, steady" (or whatever cue you prefer), carefully let go, and reward your dog for standing still by giving the "go" cue.

We prefer using a cue like "ready, steady" over more traditional cues like "stay" or "wait," since "ready, steady" expresses the spirit we're looking for at the start line. We want a dog that is "on his toes," ready, eager, and willing to go—not a dog that waits passively.

Contrast training: Varying between spontaneous starts and start-line stays

Contrasting your start-line stay training with spontaneous starts is vital, not only to keep the spontaneous starts in your dog's repertoire, but also to ensure perfect understanding of the start-line stay behavior. The contrast will help make it crystal clear to your dog:

- If you let go of him while he is moving, he should just start ahead.
- If you wait to let go until he is still, he should stay frozen and wait for the start cue.

The discrimination between the two kinds of starts calls for constant practice. You can begin varying between them as soon as you have gotten the first fragment of a stay in the "starts on cue" behavior. Actually, the sooner you begin contrasting the spontaneous start and the on-cue start, the easier it will be for your dog to learn and maintain both behaviors.

Exercise 40: Contrasting between spontaneous starts and starts on cue

1. Arrange a really tempting remote reward, show it to your dog, and use a collar transport to get to the starting point.
2. First do a spontaneous start:
   a. Turn around and let go of your dog (without stopping first).
   b. Your dog races directly to his reward.
3. Then do a stay + start on cue:
   a. Turn around and stop (still holding your dog's collar).
   b. Your dog balances himself.
   c. Say your start cue and let go.
   d. Your dog races to his reward.
4. Vary randomly between the two kinds of starts!

Your dog will quickly learn the difference between the two kinds of starts. Repeat most the version your dog seems to need the most practice in, and add all kinds of variations and distractions to ensure that your dog really knows his job.

When you release your dog "on the move" he should start spontaneously...   *...but when you hold on to him until he has "parked" himself, he should wait for your start cue.*

Separately training the stay behavior

Of course it's possible to teach a stay by rewarding in position, delivering rewards directly to your dog while he is staying still. We don't use this approach much, though—we find it more efficient to use the start cue as the sole reward. Sometimes, however, we use rewards in position when working with contacts and tables, and, for that reason, it's a good idea to be familiar with the procedure.

THE STAY CONTINUES AFTER EACH REWARD

Whenever you give your dog a treat while he's maintaining his stay, you're actually including the behavior "eating a treat" into your stay-and-start-on-cue chain. The stay continues during and after each treat and ends only with a verbal cue from you.

The chain might look like this:

1. Planting four feet.
2. Eat treat (or possibly click—treat comes—eat treat).
3. Keep still.
4. Eat another treat.
5. Keep still.
6. Cue to break the stay (for example a "go" or a "get it").
7. Move.
8. Get treat or toy.

Whenever you deliver a reward to your dog while he's keeping still, you must also be cautious about what happens during and after that reward. You want your dog to move out of the stay only after your verbal cue, so make sure you don't inadvertently cause him to move before that cue.

If you choose to use the clicker to mark the stay behavior, you have to make a choice: Do you want your click to function as a release cue (so that your dog moves after the click) or do you want the click, too, to be an integrated part of the chain? Our suggestion is this:

After the click, your dog is free to do what he likes—but if you hurry to give him his reward before he has time to move, he'll have no reason to leave his stay. After you have given him his reward, his job directly starts again. So in theory, he could move after the click—but practically, since you're so quick to reward in position, he'll remain in his stay. Or you can simply skip the clicker and just deliver the treats. Then your dog's mission is always to remain still, waiting for the magical start cue.

To get the stand:

- You can capture the behavior of four feet on the ground. Watch your dog carefully, click as all four feet touch the ground, and then quickly deliver a treat straight in front of your dog.
- If your dog doesn't offer four feet on the ground, you can shape the behavior by clicking and treating for standing up (even if he moves around a bit) and gradually tightening your criteria.
- Another way to get the behavior is to start from a transport (for example, a treat magnet or a collar transport), come to a halt in the transport, remove the treat or toy, and quickly click and treat while your dog is standing still.

To keep your dog in a stand:

- Keep machine-gunning him treats while he stands still. Each treat is a reward for the behavior of keeping still, and the treats appear so fast that your dog does not have time to move. You don't need to keep clicking; it's enough that you just give him treat by treat in quick succession.
- As your dog gets more skilled at keeping still, deliver the treats less frequently but often enough to keep him still. Your treats are distractions until they enter your dog's mouth! If he moves a foot to get the treat, he is per definition not standing still and thus will not get that treat.

To end the stay you *always* need a cue that tells your dog to move. This is true from the very first training session! To end the stay behavior you can use your start cue, sending your dog ahead to a remote reward or throwing a toy for him as he starts on your cue. If you ever wish to end a stay without using your start cue, you need one or more other release cues (for example, your everyday recall cue, or some kind of "get it" cue that tells your dog he can move to get his reward). What's vital is that you *always* use a verbal cue to end the stay, and that you and your dog both know exactly which cues are "stay-breakers." He will not "be able" to break the stay without a cue!

Here is an exercise that exemplifies how you can capture four feet on the ground, nailing your dog in a stand by machine-gunning treats to him, and ending with your start cue and a thrown toy (combining the stand-stay with the *"Go" and throw* procedure).

Exercise 41: Nailing your dog in a stand

1. Play with your dog.
2. Remove the toy.
3. Click for four feet on the ground.
4. Quickly deliver a treat.
5. Keep delivering treats so rapidly that your dog doesn't have time to move.
6. While delivering treats, move yourself so that you're standing to the side of your dog, facing the same direction (if you're not already in that position).
7. Say your start cue to end the stay.
8. Your dog starts.
9. Throw a toy ahead as a reward for his starting ahead.

Top left: First, some play.

Top center: The play ends. Click for four feet on the ground.

Top right: Delivering treats to the dog.

Bottom left: While machine-gunning treats, the handler moves herself so that she and the dog are facing in the same direction.

Bottom center: Start cue.

Bottom right: Reward!

The cue to end the stay is absolutely vital to maintain the chain. If your dog is doing his job and keeping still, you always, always have to give a verbal cue to end the stay.

If your dog breaks the stay before your cue, just withhold the reward and start over from the beginning. If you captured the stay in the first place, just wait until your dog stands still again; if you shaped the stand, start another shaping process; and if you began from a transport, then simply transport him to a new stay.

Generalization, thy name is variation

Continue to add slight variations whenever you do a stay-start. By varying everything but the start cue, you'll help your dog focus on the verbal cue alone. This will proof his stay, making sure he stays put in the face of all kinds of distractions. It will also proof his start on cue, making sure he starts on cue no matter what happens around him.

Besides varying the location where you practice stays and the basic practice setup (*Race to reward* or *"Go" and throw),* here are some examples of variations you can use to bulletproof your dog's stay. If you combine these variables, you'll have almost infinite variations.

Vary your own behavior and position:
- Right or left side
- Position behind, beside, or ahead of your dog
- Lateral distance: right next to your dog, or farther away
- Standing still or moving
- Moving your body in different ways (nodding your head, waving your arms, jumping up and down, and so on)
- Making noise, saying other words (Begin with soft nonsense noise, and ramp it up as much as you like.)

Use potential rewards as distractions:
- Slowly bring a treat toward your dog. If he moves to get it, the treat disappears. If he stays still, the treat ends up in his mouth.
- Throw a toy past your dog while he is standing still. If he moves, have your helper remove the toy. If he stays still, reward—either by sending him to the toy, or in some other fashion.
- While your dog is maintaining his stay, have your helper work the remote reward, making it extremely tempting.
- Practice start-line stays in situations where you can start your dog toward something or someone he really loves (exchanging the remote reward with a lake to go swimming in, dogs to play with, favorite person to greet, and so on).

Throughout stay training you also need to vary when and how you reward. You've already seen most of these variations in the exercises, but a summary might help you keep your variations varied and frequent:

Vary when and how you reward:

(We usually stick to using only the start cue as reward, but since adding rewarding in position is a possibility, we mention it here, as a variation.)

- Give your start cue after 0, 0.5, 1, 2, 5, or 8 seconds.
- Give your start cue as the sole reward, or deliver 1, 2, 3, 7, or 10 rewards in position first.
- When delivering rewards in position, vary when you do it.
- After the start cue, vary between letting your dog race to a remote reward and using a thrown toy.
- After the start cue, vary the distance to the remote reward.
- If you're straight ahead of your dog, you can also deliver the reward from your hand as he catches up with you.

Vary the location and add other potential distractions:

- Practice start-line stays everywhere you can think of.
- Welcome people and dogs into your training (walking, running, and playing—first quietly and far away, gradually closer and more intensely).

Having both options (spontaneous starts and start-line stays with cued starts) makes it possible for you to always use the kind of start that fits your current purpose. Remember that your dog is constantly learning—every time he starts, he learns something about starting. Make sure you always know whether you're looking for a spontaneous start or a start-line stay and start on cue. Whenever you want a spontaneous start, end the transport on the move and reward your dog for working ahead. Whenever you want a start-line stay, hold on to your dog until he has "parked" himself, and give your start cue while he keeps still. No gray areas!

15

Follow me

Since you're always working within your system of handling, your dog automatically is learning to read your shoulders, work in the direction you're facing, and move and remain on your outside. In addition, you can set up specific exercises that don't involve any equipment, teaching your dog the details of how to follow you. Specifically, your dog needs to know how to stay on your outside and how to race to you, which are the subjects of this chapter.

Circle work, dog on the outside. Here your dog will be aiming for you.

Teaching your dog to follow your shoulders

That your dog will follow the direction of your shoulders while staying on your outside—running the outer lap while you run the inner lap—is a core assumption in our handling. Having your dog truly understand the concepts of following your shoulders while getting to, turning on, and staying on your outside will make both your lives easier; it allows you to move more freely, knowing that your dog will stay on the side you intend no matter what. He'll not try to sneak behind your back, and he'll not suddenly veer away from you. That means you'll know where your dog is, and he'll know where to go.

We teach two specific skills to build your dog's understanding of following your shoulders while sticking to your outside: *Outside circles* and *Race to me*. When practicing these skills, your dog will learn to aim *for you*—which will be a contrast from the other skills we've been through so far, where the main focus has been teaching your dog to aim ahead *from you*. Your agility dog needs both types of skills!

Racing to catch up with the handler!

In the *Outside circles* you'll teach your dog to stick by your side and remain on your outside while you walk or run in circles of various sizes. The circle work is a critical foundation skill; it teaches your dog to stick to your outside while reading your shoulders and striving to catch up as you turn away from him.

HANDLING REMINDER

Teaching your dog to follow your shoulders when running circles with you and when racing to you is a vital step in developing his understanding of your handling.

Here is a quick reminder of our handling basics:

1. Point your shoulders in the direction your dog should go.
2. Use the arm nearest your dog.
3. Turn with your dog on your outside.
4. Never switch sides with your dog behind your back. (When you want to switch sides, use a front cross, turning face to face with your dog.)

For a handling recap, look back at "The handling part," page 47. We present further handling training in Chapter 17, "Handling maneuvers on the flat," page 238.

Race to me—as in a recall—is a skill your dog needs for all the times you want him to drive toward you at top speed. By training your dog to race to you, you'll also help him to better understand the skill of staying on the side he's on, even when catching up with you from a distance.

Outside circles

For you to be able to turn with your dog on the outside, your dog needs to learn to stay on your outside when you turn—not something that comes naturally to most dogs. When a handler turns away from a dog that isn't trained for outside turns, typically the dog spontaneously starts to fall behind the handler, trying to take the shortest path by sneaking behind the handler's back. Some dogs, especially the herding breeds, also tend to drift away and

When practicing outside circles, you walk, run, or sprint in a circle. Stay on track while delivering the reward!

In the follow me training, your dog should work very close to you. Once there are obstacles involved, your dog will aim for them and consequently often work at a greater distance while still following your shoulders and keeping to your outside.

flank (herd) the handler instead of sticking to the side and turning tight when the handler turns. So outside turns are something you need to teach your dog.

When moving your dog around and during rewards, making a habit of turning with your dog on the outside helps ingrain this pattern for both of you. But you also need to train the outside turn as a behavior in its own right, setting clear criteria and lavishly reinforcing correct performance. For this, we use outside circle work.

What should outside circles look like?

When working on outside circles, you walk or run in circles of various sizes with your dog on your outside.

Your dog
- follows you as in informal heelwork.
- strives to keep his head ahead of your outside shoulder (so if you turn away from him, he speeds up).
- works equally on your left side and on your right side.

Notice that the circle work is an exercise designed solely to teach your dog to follow your shoulders and stick to your outside: Running with your dog glued to your side is not what it will look like on the agility course! When you practice your circles there's nothing ahead for your dog to aim for—he should simply stick by you and follow your shoulders. On course, where there are obstacles to aim for, he'll work farther away from you.

Why do you need it?

Teaching your dog to stay on your outside is vital for the following reasons:
- His taking the outside path in turns will enable you to take the shortest path on course and let your dog maximize his speed.
- It simplifies your dog's choices—he'll know to always remain on the side he's on.
- It prepares your dog for following your shoulders in regular turns, without veering away from you or trying to sneak behind your back.
- The concept of staying on your outside helps your dog understand the front cross (since executing a front cross will cue your dog to quickly turn toward you and come to your "new" outside).

How can you train it?

To teach the circle work, you simply start moving in a circle with your dog on your outside, continually rewarding him for sticking by you. At first you reward every step he takes; eventually you let him work more for each reward and also begin varying your speed and the size of the circles.

There are many possible responses to reward in the circle work—for example:

- being by your side
- looking at you
- moving forward
- closing the distance (catching up, getting closer to you)

We usually use the clicker here, to mark the response we wish to reinforce. Actually, the training resembles *Aim for it*—only that here, what you want your dog to "aim for" is *you*. We describe the circle training in two steps: first how to get the behavior of staying on your outside, and then how to expand his understanding by varying the exercise.

Before you start moving in circles with your dog, consider your part of the job. First and foremost, keep your shoulders pointing in the direction you want your dog to head. By doing so, your dog will learn to drive past your turning shoulder on the outside. There's only one exception to the shoulder rule: If your dog tries to cut behind your back, it's perfectly all right to "catch" him by turning into him, preventing him from switching sides behind your back. Then quickly turn forward again—without crabbing—and continue on, reinforcing your dog for staying on the outside. Remember that lavish rewards for staying on your outside are key to your dog's success. If he repeatedly tries to cut behind your back, review your training and make sure to reward while he's doing it right, before he has time to sneak behind you.

Step 1: Teach your dog to stay on your outside when moving in a circle

The goal is for you to be able to walk in a circle with your dog on either your right or your left side, without him cutting in behind your back, lagging behind you, or drifting away.

In the first stage it's clever to use treat rewards—preferably soft ones that are easy to swallow—so that you can keep a high rate of reinforcement without breaking the flow of the exercise. Click for moving along on your outside, and deliver your reward with the hand nearest to your dog and a bit forward to help your dog with the understanding that you want him to drive forward.

Point your shoulders ahead and reward your dog for sticking to your outside by delivering treats ahead along the path.

To help keep you on a reasonable circular pattern, you can set out some guideposts to form a circle (we suggest beginning at about 5 meters' width) or put just one object in the middle for you to move around.

Ultimately you want to be able to pick any pace you feel like, from running as fast as you can to walking at a snail's pace—but in the beginning just walk. What is important is that you manage to reward your dog often enough to inform him about what you're up to.

Keep your training sessions short and intense. It's a good idea to decide beforehand how long you're going to train—perhaps set a timer at 30 seconds, or count to 15 rewards. Work equally with your dog on your right and left sides, but practice one side at a time.

Exercise 42: Walk the first circles with your dog on the outside

1. Play a fun game with your dog somewhere in the middle of the circle.
2. Quit the game and turn away from your dog so that he ends up on your outside.
3. Click for him being by your side, on the outside of the turn.
4. Reward with your nearest hand, a bit ahead.
5. Keep moving along the circle with your dog on the outside, continuously rewarding.
6. Take a short break where you play and rev up your dog.
7. Repeat the circle work on your other side.

INSIDE CIRCLES

Actually, there's one more aspect of circle work training. We also practice inside circles, where you move in the same fashion as in the outside circles, but with your dog on the inside. Yes, in other words you're running the outer lap, making this an exception to the "dog on the outside" rule. The idea of inside circles is to teach your dog to yield a little but not turn away from you—which is useful for future rear cross training (see "Rear cross", page 320), and also in the serpentine handling maneuver (see page 338).

We usually do little inside circle work—just enough to check that the dog follows nicely. Invest most of your energy in the outside circles, since striving to keep up with you on your outside is the most critical skill to teach your dog! To teach inside circles, simply repeat the training process from the outside circles, but with the dog on the inner lap.

In the inside circle, the dog has to stick to the handler's side and yield a bit. Here the handler has a distracting toy in her opposite hand.

Suggested tag points:

*   Shoulders facing the circle path
*   Treat with nearest hand
*   Treat slightly ahead of dog

Step 2: Introduce more intermittent rewards, increase the speed, and vary the size of the circle

When your dog happily tags along on your outside while you continuously reward him, begin varying the time between the rewards. Sometimes reward often; sometimes wait for several steps between the rewards. Eventually you'll be able to carry on for quite some time between the rewards—just remember to never go longer between rewards than your dog's behavior allows. He must be on top of the game, every step! As you begin walking for longer periods between rewards, it's a good idea to switch to a toy reward—a game of tug will build even more energy into the exercise. A good place to keep the tug toy while working is in the armpit farthest from your dog; it's easy to whip the toy out from there. Remember to keep your shoulders facing forward and to use the hand nearest your dog when presenting the toy. Your dog may swing around so that he faces you while you're then tugging, but you shouldn't turn into him.

Now you're also ready to pick up the pace to a brisk walk, then a jog, and so on. Continually vary your speed: run, walk, tip-toe, sprint! Also vary the tightness of the circle: run in big circles, small ones, then medium ones. Keep varying your circles while rewarding your dog for sticking with you.

Troubleshooting

If your dog lags behind you during circle work,

- make sure that you're directing your body the way you both should be going. Don't turn toward your dog—if your shoulders start pointing toward him, he can't drive forward and, instead, will lag.
- raise your reinforcement rate and the quality of your rewards: Make it worthwhile for your dog!
- reinforce all forward movement.
- avoid cheerleading—instead, reward the tiniest tendency toward the correct behavior. You can cheer all you like while rewarding, adding social flavor to the reward, but don't use cheering to cover up for a cheap rate of rewards.
- be sure that you're delivering all rewards ahead of your dog, so that he always drives forward to get them.
- experiment with the exact placement of the reward—for example, you can throw a toy forward along the circle, or deliver rewards in front of you so that your dog has to curl around you a bit to get it (this might even call for occasional rewards delivered by the opposite hand).
- get your dog more jazzed up before your start training (raise his level of arousal).
- work in shorter sessions.

If your dog drifts away, "herds" you, or just runs ahead, you can

- raise your rate of reinforcement, so that you reward before he has time to take off.
- turn tightly whenever he moves off, so he has to hurry to catch up with you.
- do a front cross and head in the opposite direction whenever he moves off. Keep doing front crosses until he sticks with you, then reward generously.

If you get dizzy or don't know where you're going:

- get those guideposts out there!
- raise your eyes off the ground.
- work in shorter sessions.

Race to me

Race to me teaches your dog to come straight to you at top speed—following the direction of your shoulders and coming up on the intended side without trying to switch sides behind your back. *Race to me* is also a fun and intense game that will make you very entertaining for your dog.

In Race to me, *your dog sprints to you at top speed.*

The dog has to hurry to catch up.

What should *Race to me* look like?

1. A helper holds on to your dog. (Eventually, you can sometimes leave your dog in a stay.)
2. You move ahead, your shoulders pointing in the direction your dog should go (so you'll have your back toward your dog) but looking at him over the nearest shoulder.
3. You either stand still, or walk or run forward.
4. When you give your start cue, your dog runs straight to you at full speed.
5. He comes up on the side you intended—the shoulder you looked over.
6. You either reward right away, or turn away from your dog (rewarding after a few steps, or continuing in an outside circle before rewarding).

When practicing *Race to me,* you'll reward immediately as your dog catches up with you. Later, when you practice handling on the flat and in obstacle sequences, he'll learn to race by you in the direction given by your shoulders and your movement.

Why do you need it?

Having a dog that will race toward you at top speed is valuable whenever you're ahead of him on course—he should then constantly try to catch up with you. In particular, *Race to me* will help you get tight turns toward you (both for regular turns where you turn away from your dog, and for front crosses where you turn face to face with him).

How can you train it?

Since *Race to me* and *Race to reward* both involve your dog running at top speed toward something, the training for each is basically the same. Just as with *Race to reward* training, start with getting the behavior and then add a cue to it.

Step 1: Teach your dog to race straight to you

Since restraint builds intensity and drive, get a helper to hold on to your dog (around his chest, thighs, or collar) while you run off. When the helper lets go, your dog will explode away and run straight to you (this is a "restrained recall"). When he reaches you, reward bountifully—a game of tug is perfect, but anything your dog loves will work as long as it's intense and interactive, building your dog's desire to race right up to you.

While you reward it's a good idea to turn slightly away from your dog, letting him chase the reward while driving around you on your outside. This further encourages him to hurry to catch up with you and enhances his outside turns.

Exercise 43: **Race to me:** *Get the behavior, no cue*

1. Play with your dog to build up his energy and give him a taste of all the great stuff to come.

2. Grab your dog's collar and let your helper get hold of your dog.

3. From beside your dog, take off running straight ahead while glancing at your dog over your shoulder. If necessary, make enticing noises or wave the treats or toys around on the chosen side, but don't use any verbal cue.

4. As soon as your helper feels that your dog wants to run after you, she lets go of your dog. Ideally, that is just as you take off running.

5. Your dog races straight to you.

6. When your dog reaches you, present the reward with the hand nearest your dog. Party time!

7. Use a treat magnet or a game of tug to play your way back to your helper (turning with your dog on the outside)—or, let the helper come to you.

8. Do the same exercise one more time, this time on the other side.

Suggested tag points:

- Present reward with nearest hand
- Glance at your dog over your shoulder
- Let the reward last for at least 10 seconds

Once your dog has caught on to the game, keep your reward hidden until he catches up with you instead of always showing it in advance. That way you'll know he's chasing you, not just the treat or toy.

Left: The helper gently grabs the dog's collar. Center Left: The helper restrains the dog, and the handler takes off. Center Right: The helper lets go, and the dog races to catch up with the handler. Right: During the reward, the handler turns slightly away from the dog.

Step 2: Add your start cue

When you feel confident your dog will reliably race to you, it's time to add your start cue. In the restrained recall, your start cue will tell your helper exactly when to let go—and when you later practice *Race to me* from a stay, you obviously need a start cue. To add the cue you use the same restrained recall procedure, but this time the helper does not release your dog until you say the cue. Remain neutral when you call—add no extra body cues!

TEACHING AN ATTENTION/ COME-TO-ME CUE

You can also use *Race to me* to teach your dog an attention/come-to-me cue, which you can use, for example, to tell your dog to turn toward you after a tunnel (since he cannot see your handling well while he's in there). Just set up the *Race to me* exercise, but instead of using your start cue, give your attention/come-to-me cue (we suggest your dog's name).

The start cue means "explode away and follow my handling" while the attention/come-to-me cue means "come toward me now"—but in the restrained recall that is the same thing, which explains why you can use both cues interchangeably.

Exercise 44: Race to me: *Add the cue*

1. Play with your dog.
2. Have your helper hold your dog.
3. Start from beside your dog and take off running straight ahead while glancing at your dog over your shoulder.
4. After a few steps and while still running, say your start cue. Remain neutral when you call—don't add any extra body movements to the cue!
5. As you call, your helper lets go of your dog.
6. Your dog races straight to you.
7. When your dog reaches you, reward!

Suggested tag point:
- Remain neutral when giving cue

Step 3: Add variations and start-line stays to *Race to me*

You can take *Race to me* training further; try these variations:

- Vary the distance before you call your dog.
- Vary among running, walking, and standing still, or combinations of them. For instance, you can run a distance, then stop and call your dog (stationary), or you can run a distance, stop, then run again and call your dog (in motion). If you stand still when giving your start cue, make sure there's no fixed pattern between your start cue and you moving ahead (sometimes start moving right away, sometimes after .5 seconds, sometimes after 4 seconds, and so on).
- Add start-line stays (eventually, adding variations and distractions will help proof that your dog keeps still yet ready to dash toward you once you call).
- From time to time, use a helper to restrain your dog, even if your dog has a solid stay. The restraint increases the speed, the intensity, and the fun!

Congratulations! Now that you've got your foundation skills under your belt, and your dog has his, you'll put all these skills to use, building more elaborate agility behaviors and teamwork in Part III, *Putting it all together.*

Part III
Putting it all together

About handling and obstacle training

Now it's time to put together all the general foundation skills you've built. Throughout this last part of the book you'll use, combine, and transform your foundation skills into obstacle skills and handling maneuvers. This will get you on course!

What you'll learn in Part III,

What you'll learn in Part III, *Putting it all together*

Putting it all together covers seven topics:

1. **"Handling maneuvers on the flat"** (Chapter 17) introduces various handling maneuvers away from the obstacles. Your dog will learn to respond to your handling when you go straight, when you turn, when you switch sides with front and rear crosses, and in the special case when you stop or stand still. You and your dog will practice working in synchrony even in the face of tempting distractions, so once you've taught the actual obstacles, you'll be well prepared for handling all kinds of sequences.

As always, first and foremost: Have fun!

2. **"Jumps and tunnels"** (Chapter 18) uses the *Aim for it* and *Race to reward* procedures to teach your dog to perform all the different kinds of jumps, long jumps, pipe tunnels, the collapsed tunnel, and the tire. We have lumped these obstacles together since we teach them basically the same way, building your dog's skills step by step, all the way to fluently negotiating the obstacles in very simple sequences.

3. **"Handling sequences"** (Chapter 19) presents how to use the various handling maneuvers (previously taught on the flat) with the actual obstacles. We have placed this chapter right after the chapter on jumps and tunnels because as soon as your dog is confident on an obstacle (or a certain version of that obstacle) you can start using that obstacle in sequences. This chapter offers lots of exercises for practicing moving straight ahead, regular turns, front crosses, rear crosses, and wraps back to you. It also introduces two more advanced maneuvers: threadles and serpentines.

4. **"The contact obstacles"** (Chapter 20) begins with contact preparation training, teaching your dog a blazing contact zone performance away from the obstacles, and progresses to training a complete dogwalk, A-frame, and teeter performance.

5. **"The table"** (Chapter 21) shows how to produce a fast, reliable table performance.

6. **"The weave poles"** (Chapter 22) discusses how you can teach an independent, fast, and precise weave-pole performance.

7. **"Parting thoughts"** (Chapter 23) offers what we want to leave you with.

When presenting the exercises in this section, we presume that you and your dog have learned all the general foundation skills described in Part II, *Foundation skills for you and your dog.* You don't have to have them all down to perfection, but you should continually evaluate your dog's skills and immediately work on them more when needed. Remember that dog training is not linear: You can, and should, work simultaneously on many skills and revisit earlier stages of training whenever you feel the need.

As always, remember these training basics:

- Adhere to Good Agility Practices! Engage in every training session with total focus and intensity, and always follow your system of handling.
- Stick to clicker training principles: Strive to reinforce the behaviors you want, ignore the behaviors you don't want, and set your dog up for success.
- Keep attitude as your top priority, followed by direction, and then precision.
- Keep your eye on the ball: Remember what you've done so far and why, what your goals are, and how you're planning to get there. Continuously evaluate your training, and dare to push it!
- Have fun! The ultimate goal is for both you and your dog to be happy and confident.

Handling maneuvers on the flat

On the agility course, your job will be to perform the right maneuver at the right moment so that your dog gets correct information about where to go in a timely fashion. But first you need to teach him precisely what your different maneuvers mean, and to respond to your handling cues promptly and accurately. We do this teaching "on the flat," away from the obstacles.

About handling

Every agility handler, no matter which handling system she is following (be it custom-made or the application of some guru's handling principles), should be able to list the functions of her handling cues. Here's our list:

The obstacles and rewards:

- Your dog takes all obstacles and rewards that show up along his path—in other words, that your handling directs him to—and ignores all other obstacles and potential rewards.

The direction of your shoulders is your most important handling tool.

The direction of your shoulders:

- Your dog keeps heading in the direction that your shoulders are pointing, constantly striving to get (and stay) ahead of you. He doesn't flip away from you and he doesn't sneak across your feet in front of you.
- In regular turns (where you simply rotate your shoulders away from your dog), he keeps to your outside and turns with you. He does not take a shortcut by crossing behind your back.
- When you start a front cross (rotating toward your dog and perhaps raising your outer arm), he immediately turns toward you.
- When you perform a rear cross (crossing your dog's path behind his tail, your shoulders pointing in the direction you're going), he loses sight of you for a millisecond, then he turns with you in the new direction. He doesn't turn away from you before you've crossed his path, and he doesn't spin the wrong way as you cross behind him.

- Using your arms is optional—you can direct your dog with your hands behind your back, simply using your shoulders. When you use your arms and hands to direct your dog, always use the nearest arm and point in the direction he should go—that way your arms support the message your shoulders are giving.

Your moving ahead or stopping/standing still:

- As long as you're moving ahead, your dog keeps driving toward where your shoulders are pointing—whether he's behind you or ahead of you.

- If you stand still or stop, it cues your dog to come to you:
  - If he's behind you (at any lateral distance), he first negotiates any obstacles that are between him and the plane of your shoulders—then comes to you.
  - If he's ahead of you and you stop, he turns back to you.
  - If he's approaching an obstacle and you stand still or stop right before that obstacle (close enough to touch the obstacle), he first takes that obstacle—then comes back to you. Your standing still/stopping in that position as he approaches the obstacle cues him to shorten his stride in preparation for a tight turn, and then to wrap back to you after the obstacle.
  - On course, once your dog has turned toward you when you stop/stand still, you'll normally start moving again and direct him wherever he should go next. If you remain still, however, your dog should come all the way to you (where you reward).

DEFINING "AHEAD OF YOU"

Imagine a line going through your shoulders, straight out to the sides. That's the plane of your shoulders. When your dog is behind this plane, he is, per our definition, "behind you"—and, consequently, when he's ahead of the plane of your shoulders, he's "ahead of you." We want the dog to constantly strive to get ahead of the handler—in other words, to get ahead of the plane of your shoulders.

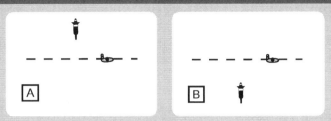

A. Here the dog is ahead of the handler (ahead of the shoulder plane)
B. Here the dog is behind the handler (behind the shoulder plane)

DOG-STRIDE GLOSSARY

Your dog uses his body differently depending on where he's aiming to go. The better he is at altering his stride, the faster and more smoothly he'll be able to get around the course. When your handling is clear and consistent and taught in small steps detail by detail, your dog will learn how to adjust his stride to suit where he is going. This glossary explains some common terms that refer to your dog's stride:

Right or left lead

When your dog is galloping and jumping, either foreleg will lead (advance more). When turning right your dog should be on a right lead, and vice versa. As long as he knows where he is going he'll normally sort this out by himself. But when handling confusions occur, you'll notice that dogs land on the wrong lead.

Collection or extension

When your dog shortens his stride length, he collects. This is something he has to do when preparing for a stop or a tight turn—it's impossible to turn tightly from full steam ahead. Proper collection requires weight transfer: Your dog shifts his weight back (picture a cow pony sliding into a stop—that's extreme weight transfer).

When your dog lengthens his stride, covering as much ground as possible, he extends. This is what he does when blasting ahead. Shifting between collection and extension is quite challenging, calling upon rear-end strength and good body control. When your dog learns how to follow your handling, he'll also learn when to collect and when to extend.

Jumping with a round or flat arc

A jump is simply a stride with a higher arc. If your dog needs to turn tight after a jump, he should jump short with a rounded arc—taking off and landing close to the jump. This requires collection before the jump: Your dog has to shorten his stride and shift his weight back before takeoff. On the other hand, if his path continues straight ahead after the jump, he should jump longer, with a flatter arc, taking off and landing farther from the jump. The trajectory of the jump will be set by the approach (your dog can't alter his trajectory midair), so your dog needs to know before each jump where he's going after the jump, something he'll learn through consistent handling.

Left: Collection: To turn tightly around the jump wing, the dog needs to collect and jump with a short, rounded arc. The dog is on a right lead.

Right: Extension: The dog is flying ahead, jumping with a "long," flat arc.

STOPPING

When we say that you "stop," we mean that you hit the brakes, aiming for a complete halt. Sometimes you'll stop and actually stand still, other times you'll merely decelerate and then move on (for example, turning and taking off in another direction) before you actually come to a complete standstill. Either way, if your dog is fully trained, he'll read your "hitting the brakes" as an intention to stop and respond by coming toward you.

CONSTANTS IN YOUR HANDLING TRAINING

When training handling, of course you'll need to deal with transports, starts, rewards—and mistakes. Here is a review of what these surrounding features should look like:

Transports

- Vary which method or combinations of transport you use (for example, start with a tug toy, grab the collar while your dog is tugging, remove the toy while holding on to the collar, and finally let go of the collar when your dog aims in the right direction).
- Plan your transports so that you can follow your system of handling throughout.
- Always end the transport very distinctly.
- Make sure you decide when the transport ends.
- Make sure that your dog can start working immediately (either he's positioned in a start-line stay where his job is to keep still until he hears your start cue, or the transport ends and his job is to start ahead spontaneously).

Starts

- Vary between spontaneous starts (where your dog starts off the transport, without a start cue) and start-line stays (with starts on cue).
- Every time you leave your dog in a start-line stay you're practicing staying and starting on cue, whether this is your intention or not. Your start cue should reinforce the stay behavior, so only give the start cue when your criteria are met. If your dog breaks your criteria, go back and transport him around for a new try (and make a mental note to immediately resume separate training of your start-line stays and starts on cue).
- If your dog's start-line stay isn't rock solid yet, you can use a helper to hold your dog at the start line. That way both you and your dog can focus completely on the handling task without having to think about start-line criteria.

Rewards

- For your handling training you need remote rewards, throwable rewards, and rewards that you deliver close to you. Tug toys are preferable since they add to the excitement and keep your dog's drive high.
- Rewards can appear anywhere along the path you direct, and by any obstacle that appears along that path—and nowhere else. Be especially careful not to throw the toy so that your dog has to turn away from you to get it.
- All potential rewards are distractions (dummies to be ignored) if your handling doesn't lead your dog to them.
- Vary where the rewards come from. When you can, use helpers to throw rewards and to "guard" remote rewards.

Mistakes

- Always reward your dog for following your handling: If you make a handling mistake and inadvertently direct him to the wrong obstacle, of course he should follow your handling and be properly rewarded for it.
- If something goes wrong, keep working! You must always give your dog information about where to go. Keep handling (giving directions with your body cues) until he is occupied either with a reward or in a transport. Never, ever leave him in limbo!
- Whenever possible, follow through your handling maneuvers. For example, if you're performing a front cross and your dog doesn't immediately turn toward you, keep insisting on that front cross until he responds.

Handling training

Since you've worked through the foundation skills, your dog already knows a lot about how to read your handling.

- During transports and rewards, every time you've turned with your dog on your outside, you've done a regular turn.
- Every time you've switched sides face to face with your dog, you've performed a front cross.
- In all your *Race to reward* and *Aim for it* training, you've supported your dog's path with the direction of your shoulders.
- When you practiced outside circles and *Race to me*, you taught your dog to read your shoulders, turn with you, and hurry to keep up if you tightened your turn away from him.

CUSTOMIZE EXERCISES TO YOUR HANDLING SYSTEM

Obviously the handling maneuvers described here are the ones we use in our system of handling. Remember: That does not mean that other maneuvers, or other ways of doing the maneuvers, are "wrong" per se. They might be absolutely right—within another system! In this and later chapters, we give detailed descriptions of handling training, but we urge you to constantly think principle over method here. If you're working within a handling system that differs from ours, you have to build exercises that fit *your* system.

Even if your handling goals differ from ours, we hope to provide you with lots of ideas and insights about *how* to go about training handling. The following chapters will give you inspiration for how to structure the training, how to split tasks into tiny pieces, and how to focus on consistency when working through *your* handling maneuvers.

- You've also taught your dog to aim ahead, both toward a remote reward (in the *Race to reward* procedure) and toward equipment (using both *Race to reward* and *Aim for it*).
- Last but not least, your dog knows both how to start spontaneously and how to start on cue from a start-line stay, always taking off in the direction your shoulders imply.

In this chapter you'll learn how to teach your dog a solid understanding for each of the following handling maneuvers:

- Straight ahead
- Regular turn
- Front cross
- Stopping/standing still
- Rear cross

You'll also get to work with contrasts between different maneuvers, making sure your dog really follows your handling—for example, going straight ahead when you go straight ahead but turning when you turn.

USING REMOTE REWARDS/DISTRACTIONS TO TRAIN RELIABLE HANDLING RESPONSES

On the agility course you want your dog to follow your handling with split-second precision, confidently relying on you to direct his path. By following your handling, your dog will get to the best places: Either he'll arrive at a spot where a reward turns up, or he'll get to an obstacle that represents the opportunity to earn a reward. So you want to teach your dog to

- take any obstacle or reward that appears along the path you direct.
- ignore any obstacles or potential rewards that appear elsewhere.

We often use remote treats or toys as both rewards (that you handle your dog toward) and distractions (that you handle your dog away from, in another direction):

- Sometimes you'll send your dog all the way to a remote reward.
- Sometimes you'll first send your dog toward a remote reward, and then turn him in a different direction before he reaches it.
- Sometimes remote rewards will merely serve as dummies, set out as distractions.

Using remote rewards this way teaches your dog to cue solely off your handling: The reward is his if you handle him toward it—but he should also key into your handling even when it tells him to go in a different direction. Practicing this distinction will prepare your dog for his actual work on the agility course, where great opportunities (in the form of different obstacles) are omnipresent but where he should go only for the obstacles your handling sends him toward.

If your dog makes a mistake and ignores your handling, he simply doesn't get his reward—your helper will remove it. If you don't have regular access to helpers, use them when you can and skip the remote rewards when you work alone. You can also try using a treat bowl with a lid (naturally you then need to help your dog get to his reward), or some toy that only becomes fun if you join in the game.

Straight ahead

Straight ahead training teaches your dog to both look ahead from the start line and follow your handling straight ahead when running.

What should straight ahead look like?

When your dog is positioned in a start-line stay,

- you point your shoulders ahead.
- your dog looks ahead (eventually he'll look at the first obstacle; while working on the flat, he'll look at the remote reward).

When your dog is running,

- you point your shoulders ahead.
- you move ahead (in situations where your dog will race past you).
- your dog drives straight ahead as fast as he can.

If you stand still ahead of your dog, or if you stop or turn, your dog should not blast by you straight ahead; but those are different training drills that we'll get to later in this chapter.

Racing straight ahead—first on the flat (left), and later on obstacles (right)

How can you train it?

From the *Race to reward* and start-line stay training, your dog is already familiar with the concept of looking ahead and racing ahead. In this section you'll get to expand his knowledge even further.

Using a remote reward, you'll help your dog practice looking ahead and racing straight ahead from a start-line stay, with you in various positions. The remote reward gives your dog a direction to work in, which is a must whenever you add any lateral distance. Later there will be obstacles for your dog to aim for, but here we use the remote reward.

When working with other handling maneuvers it's vital that you contrast with straight ahead so that your dog learns to differentiate between the various maneuvers. Therefore straight ahead is a vital section in this "Handling maneuvers on the flat" chapter. We'll focus especially on practicing racing straight ahead past you as you move ahead.

YOUR POSITION AND MOVEMENT WHEN PRACTICING STRAIGHT AHEAD TO A REMOTE REWARD

Here's a brief reminder of what to think about in order to stay consistent with your handling when practicing straight ahead:

- Point your shoulders in the direction of the remote reward.
- If you're anywhere between your dog and the remote reward, you have to be moving forward as your dog runs straight ahead. If you stand still in that position, your dog should stop by you and not blast past you to the remote reward, and if you hit the brakes before he reaches the remote reward he should turn back to you (see "Stopping/standing still," page 257). In the exercises in this chapter we instruct you to move forward while you give the start cue,

and to continue moving until your dog reaches his reward. That way you're sure to get it right. Another option is to walk out, stop, give your start cue, and then start moving—but this is a bit trickier since you have to be moving when your dog approaches you, and you need to avoid patterning the start cue with your movement (otherwise you risk ruining your start cue).

- If you're parallel to or behind your dog, or if you're parallel to or ahead of the remote reward, you can either stand still or move forward as your dog runs straight ahead.

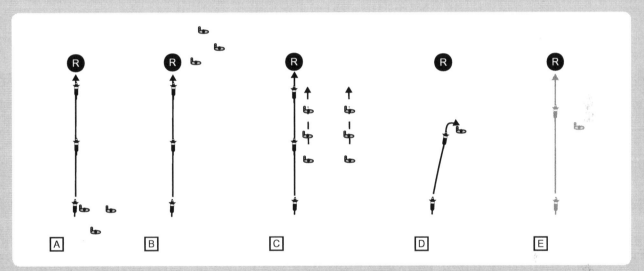

To further clarify the dos and don'ts in your Race to reward *training, here are some examples.*

A. *The handler is parallel to or behind the dog as he starts and can stand still while the dog races to his reward.*

B. *The handler is parallel to or ahead of the reward as the dog starts and can stand still as the dog races to his reward.*

C. *The handler has led out a bit and therefore must move ahead as the dog flies by to his reward.*

D. *If the handler is between the dog and the reward, standing still, the dog should stop with the handler. (You'll teach him this when practicing* Stopping/standing still.)

E. *Never do this! Don't lead out, stand still, and have the dog fly by you. In this situation the dog should stop with the handler.*

Racing straight past you

When you're ahead of your dog and moving forward, you want your dog to keep running straight past you (as opposed to "going Velcro" and getting stuck by you). To teach this, set up a simple *Race to reward* exercise where you start ahead of your dog and where he gets to fly past you to the remote reward. Your forward motion is what should cue your dog to continue ahead as he races past you, so you have to keep moving forward until your dog has reached his reward.

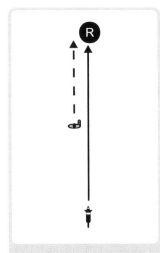

*Keep going straight until
your dog reaches the reward!*

Exercise 45: Run straight past the handler to a remote reward

1. Set out a remote reward.
2. Leave your dog in a start-line stay, facing the remote reward.
3. Walk straight out a bit ahead of your dog.
4. Give your start cue while your dog is looking at the remote reward and while you're moving forward.
5. Your dog starts and races straight ahead.
6. You keep moving forward.
7. Your dog powers by you to his reward.

Suggested tag points:

- Shoulders pointing straight ahead
- Keep moving

You move straight ahead; your dog flies straight ahead past you.

Vary between walking and running (no strolling though: You're in "handling mode," sending your dog ahead); as long as you're moving ahead, it's a cue to your dog to keep going straight to his remote reward. Also vary your lateral distance—and, of course, vary between left-side handling and right-side handling.

To really proof your dog's understanding of straight ahead you can also practice going straight ahead without the remote reward—instead, reward with a thrown toy. This makes the exercise a bit trickier, since your dog doesn't have the remote reward to aim for—instead, you'll teach him to fly past you in anticipation of his toy. As in the *"Go" and throw* training (see page 205), at first the thrown toy may function as a lure (appearing before the behavior has happened) and later purely as a reward (appearing as your dog sprints by you). The toy should appear straight ahead of your dog, "out of the blue," so be sneaky about throwing (helpers often come in handy).

Since your dog doesn't have a specific spot to aim for, don't add any lateral distance in this exercise. Just let your dog race past you, and throw the toy ahead.

Exercise 46: Run straight past the handler to a thrown toy (no remote reward)

1. Leave your dog in a start-line stay.
2. Walk out a bit.
3. Give your start cue while moving.
4. Your dog starts and races straight ahead.
5. Keep moving forward.
6. Your dog races by you.
7. As your dog passes you, throw the toy straight ahead.

Regular turn

What should a regular turn look like?

- You rotate your shoulders away from your dog and move ahead in the new direction.
- Since you rotate your shoulders away from your dog, he'll find himself behind the plane of your shoulders—thus he really has to hurry to catch up!
- Your dog turns with you, following the direction of your shoulders and keeping on your outside.
- A regular turn always means that your dog turns *in your direction*—so when your dog is on your left, he'll make a right turn.

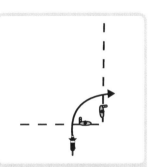

In this diagram you can see how the plane of your shoulder moves away from your dog in the regular turn. Regular turn training teaches him to hurry to catch up while remaining on your outside.

The handler rotates her shoulder away from the dog, and the dog hurries to catch up!

How can you train it?

Teaching your dog regular turns is about teaching him both to promptly respond to your shoulder rotation and to never sneak behind your back as you turn. To accomplish this we use outside circles (where you suddenly turn tightly), *Race to me* setups (where you turn as your dog approaches), and *Race to reward* settings (where you can vary between sending ahead and turning, proofing your handling by contrasting between different handling maneuvers).

Regular turn in the outside circle

When you work in an outside circle, your dog is constantly turning with you while sticking to your outside. By abruptly turning tighter in the circle, you'll teach him to keep track of your shoulders, turn with you, and hurry to keep up with your shoulders.

Exercise 47: Turn tight in the outside circle

1. Run in an outside circle.

2. Abruptly tighten your turn into a much smaller circle.

3. Your dog turns with you and hurries to catch up with you, keeping to your outside.

4. Reward as your dog catches up.

Suggested tag points:

• Turn your shoulders

• Lead with the shoulder closest to your dog (push the closest shoulder forward)

Keep your shoulders pointing in the direction you're going so that you don't start to turn back and look for your dog: Trust him to catch up! But if he really tries to sneak behind you, rotate back toward him and "pick him up."

Run in a circle and abruptly make a tight turn, almost spinning in place.

Race to me and turn

By ending *Race to me* with a regular turn, you'll teach your dog to turn when you turn while sticking to your outside, even if he's tempted to cut behind your back. Except for the turn at the end, this regular turn exercise closely resembles straight-ahead training: You leave your dog in a start-line stay, move ahead, give your start cue, and keep moving forward—but here you rotate your shoulders away from him as he approaches you, which cues him to turn with you instead of continuing straight ahead. Your dog will have to pay close attention to the direction of your shoulders!

To teach your dog to really turn with you while you're moving, make sure you're moving ahead when your dog approaches you (see "Your position and movement when practicing straight ahead to a remote reward," page 243).

Exercise 48: **Race to me *and turn, reward immediately***

1. Leave your dog in a start-line stay.
2. Walk out a bit.
3. Give your start cue while moving.
4. Your dog starts and races toward you.
5. Keep moving forward and, as your dog approaches you, turn away from him (making a regular turn).
6. Your dog turns with you and hurries to catch up with you, keeping to your outside.
7. Reward as your dog catches up.

Turn away as your dog approaches, and reward when he catches up.

The first few times you practice this exercise you might show the toy in advance, luring your dog to chase it and turn with you. Quickly move on to presenting the toy as a reward when you see your dog turning with you. You can vary between delivering the reward directly from your hand and throwing it ahead in the new direction.

At the start of training, make it easy for your dog and begin turning right before he reaches you. When he catches on, you can start turning earlier on his approach toward you to test his understanding of staying on your outside. If your dog sneaks behind your back as you turn, just transport yourselves to a new starting position and try again. Your dog should never switch sides behind your back; no matter how early you turn your shoulders, he should always stick to your outside.

Vary the sharpness of the turn from just turning slightly to turning a full 180°, but do decide in advance how sharp you want your turn to be. On course, you can expect to encounter all variations.

You can also use a remote reward for this exercise, sending your dog to the reward after the turn. With a remote reward your dog has to really work to keep on your outside rather than crossing behind your back to get straight to the reward. Use a helper who can pick up the toy in case your dog goes for it behind your back.

Exercise 49: **Race to me *and turn,* then Race to reward**

1. Set out a remote reward (in your dog's intended path after the turn).
2. Leave your dog in a start-line stay.
3. Walk out a bit.
4. Give your start cue while moving.
5. Your dog starts and races toward you.
6. Keep moving forward and, as your dog approaches you, turn away from him (making a regular turn).
7. Your dog turns with you on your outside.
8. As your dog turns with you, move ahead toward the remote reward.
9. Your dog powers ahead to his reward.

Suggested tag points:

- Point your shoulders straight ahead
- Point your shoulders toward the reward
- Move toward the reward until your dog reaches it

"I follow the shoulders, I stick to the outside. Yeehaa! Now I get my reward!"

Contrast training: straight ahead or turning?

In your handling training, you want your handling maneuvers to become the salient cues that your dog relies on. Your dog should not just repeat what he did last time, or run to the reward just because it's out there; he should keep an eye on what you do and head in the direction your handling guides him. Therefore you should work with contrasts, altering between straight ahead and regular turns within the same setup.

The first session of contrast training might look like this:

1. First do a few repetitions of *straight ahead* to a remote reward.
2. Remove the remote reward (but keep working in the same spot) and do one or two repetitions of *Race to me—regular turn.*
3. Then set out the remote reward straight ahead again, and do a *regular turn* (your dog will now have to break off his path toward the remote reward and turn with you). Use a helper to remove the remote reward if your dog goes for it—and reward lavishly when your dog responds to your regular turn!
4. Repeat until you get one (one!) good repetition where your dog turns with you immediately as you turn, even in the face of the distracting remote reward ahead. This might happen right away, or it might take several repetitions.
5. Once you have gotten one nice turn, do a *straight ahead* repetition, checking that your dog really flies by you to the remote reward when you move straight.

If your dog doesn't get it right after a few attempts, go back and work more on your regular turns without the distracting reward straight ahead. Once he starts to get the picture, vary between straight ahead and regular turns. If your dog hesitates or otherwise doesn't respond correctly to one of the maneuvers, that tells you he needs to practice that maneuver the most. When your dog understands the regular turn, you'll most likely find that you then need to put in a lot of straight-ahead repetitions. You should also look at the quality of your rewards, making sure that your dog gets a big payoff when he makes the correct choice.

Here two remote rewards are set out, and the dog's job is to follow the handling to the correct one. In the first attempt, the handler turns, but the dog continues ahead. The handler sticks to her turn, and the dog eventually turns and ends up by the correct reward. If the dog had carried on all the way to the dummy reward, the helper would have hidden it under her foot so that the dog couldn't get it.

In the next attempt, the dog turns right away. Party time!

Whenever you have a remote reward straight ahead for your dog to aim for, you can also add *lateral distance,* placing yourself farther out to the side. Make sure your dog is looking at the remote reward when you give the start cue, and move ahead as he starts (since your forward motion is what tells him to head for the remote reward). Then you can either keep moving forward (sending him straight to the remote reward) or abruptly do a regular turn (turning him with you, away from the remote reward).

Cheerfully play around with the contrasting exercises. Your dog will occasionally make mistakes. That's perfectly OK: he's trying to figure out the rules of the game. Keep up your intensity, and just give it another go. Remember to frequently send your dog straight ahead since that often becomes the most difficult challenge!

Here are some other possible contrast setups:
- Set up two remote rewards (one for going straight and one for turning) and vary between them.
- Work without remote rewards and vary between sending straight ahead (reward with a thrown toy) and turning (reward from your hand or with a thrown toy).
- Place a remote reward off to the side. Vary between turning (to the remote reward) and sending straight ahead (rewarding with a thrown toy). Continuing straight ahead toward nothing is hard, especially when your dog is hoping to turn toward the remote reward: If your dog can do this, he's truly skilled at following your handling straight ahead!

Front cross

What should the front cross look like?

When executing a front cross you rotate your shoulders toward your dog, briefly facing him, while your feet move in the direction you're going next. Your front cross takes only three steps; then you're off in the new direction. Your dog turns toward you and comes up on your new outside.

As you can see, both the regular turn and the front cross will make your dog turn in your direction (if he's on your left side, both maneuvers will cue him to turn right). In the regular turn he stays on the same side, but in the front cross he ends up on your other side.

The front cross turns your dog toward you, and you switch sides.

Front-cross footwork

Throughout the foundation training you've been doing lots of front crosses while rewarding or transporting your dog, so you're already accustomed to switching sides face to face with him. This is a good first step for your front-cross maneuver on course. Performing an efficient front cross on course while both you and your dog are moving fast, however, requires some more elaborate footwork. So before we go into the details of teaching your dog to respond to your front cross, *you* need some special training on your own.

Remember the Oval exercise from "Training yourself" (page 87)? Our favorite exercise for learning how to execute a front cross is a version of the Oval that we call the "Figure Eight." We teach it in three steps:

> **Step 1: Find your path in the Figure Eight**
> **Step 2: Practice the toes-in, toes-out footwork separately.**
> **Step 3: Polish the perfect three-step front-cross** footwork in the Figure Eight.

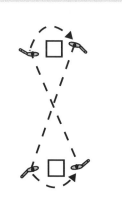

This diagram shows your figure-eight path. It also shows where you'll be right before and right after your front crosses. The crosses happen along the diagonal, while your every step lands on the diagonal line. Note: Just like the Oval, the Figure Eight is an exercise designed just for you, to get your footsteps right. Don't do it with your dog—that'd serve no purpose.

Step 1: Find your path in the Figure Eight

When teaching front-cross footwork in our classes, we begin by setting up two guideposts, about 3 meters (10 feet) apart, just as in the Oval. We divide our students into groups, appoint them either handlers or human "dogs" and tell them:

"Stick to all the basics of the handling system, just as you did in the Oval, with both you and your "dog" still heading around the guideposts, but this time direct your "dog" in a figure-eight pattern."

Then we let our students try it out for themselves. Perhaps you want to try before continuing reading!

Here's how it's done:

1. You start by going around a guidepost with your dog on your outside.
2. As you come around the guidepost you face your dog and turn toward him, while your feet keep going along the diagonal in the middle of the figure-eight pattern.
3. Keep rotating until you're facing forward again—when you come to the next guidepost your dog will be on your new outside.

The front cross thus will happen along the diagonal in the middle of the figure eight—you'll be spinning along the diagonal, continually moving toward the next guidepost. Each step you take should land along that diagonal line. Don't worry if the footwork feels odd and clumsy at first. Just focus on finding the right path to follow while sticking to your handling basics.

ILLUSTRATING THE FRONT CROSS

Drawing front-cross diagrams is a bit tricky—illustrating the actual cross, step for step, would make for very crowded drawings. In other publications, front crosses are often illustrated with a loop.

However, since we don't want the handler's path to be "all over the place" (as it'd be if you followed the loop to the letter), we opt not to draw our front crosses that way. Instead, we draw the handler's path exactly where we want the handler to go, mark the front cross with an [FC] box, and leave it to your imagination to see how the handler twirls along her path.

This front cross is drawn with a loop (which we've opted not to do).

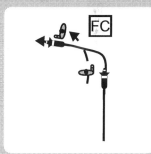

This is how we draw front crosses throughout this book.

To practice the Figure Eight, get a friend to act as your "dog." It's much easier to get it right when you have a "dog" with you, but since you don't want your real canine companion involved yet, employ a human one.

Exercise 50: Find your path in the Figure Eight

1. Draw (or imagine) a figure eight on the ground. The diagonal lines crossing in the center should be straight.

2. Start by going around one of the guideposts with your "dog" on the outside.

3. As you come around the corner your shoulders should be parallel to the guidepost, just as in the Oval.

4. Briefly glance along the diagonal line (so that you know in which direction to go).

5. As you step down the diagonal line, turn toward your "dog" so that you switch sides with him. You'll actually be stepping backward for a moment.

6. When you come out of the front cross, you'll be close to the next guidepost, with your "dog" on your new outside.

7. Go around the guidepost and continue following the figure-eight pattern.

Suggested tag points:

- Shoulders parallel as you come around the guidepost
- Turn face to face
- Feet on diagonal line ("tag" for each foot that hits the line)
- Face forward at the end (dog on new outside)
- Treat with nearest hand (before and after the front cross)

Practicing the figure eight ("handler" in dark vest and "dog" in white jacket):
Left: The shoulders are parallel to the guidepost as the handler comes around the corner.
Center left and center right: Switch sides with a front cross along the diagonal line.
Right: Keep going around the next guidepost.

Step 2: Practice the toes-in, toes-out footwork separately

Did you find it difficult to hit the diagonal line with every step? So do most people! It's like a ballerina drill where you twirl along the line. Here's an exercise that'll help you practice that toe-in–toe-out ballerina motion: *Note:* This exercise requires some speed! If you go slow, you'll probably trip over your own feet.

Exercise 51: Twirl to the right

1. Draw a straight line on the ground.

2. Stand still, facing the direction of the line.

3. Step forward on the line with your left foot, "toeing in" as much as you can.

4. Now lift your right foot and twirl backward, "toeing out" as much as you can. In the best-case scenario, your right foot will hit the ground farther down the line.

5. Keep twirling: Toe-in with your left foot, and toe-out with your right one.

6. Twirling to the right forms the basis for your footwork when performing a front cross that takes you from right-side handling to left-side handling. Now do the mirror image, twirling to the left (as you'll do for a front cross that takes you from left-side handling to right-side handling): Toe-in with the right foot, toe-out with the left one.

Suggested tag points:

- Toes in

- Toes out

- Place foot on line (tag for each foot on line)

Twirl along the line: toes in, toes out. In these pictures the feet are next to the line (because the line is a board, for the sake of illustration). Draw a line in the dirt and step on it!
Left: Ready to start   Center left: Left foot toes in...   Center right: ...and...   Right: ... right foot toes out.

Just get a feel for the toe-in–toe-out motion (don't worry if you don't get it perfectly right) and then you're ready to carry on with your Figure Eight.

Step 3: Polish the perfect three-step front cross

Now let's put it all together in the Figure Eight. You've already found your path in the figure-eight pattern, stepping along the diagonal line while performing a front cross, and you've also learned the toe-in–toe-out pirouette. All that's left is to get your feet planted in the right spots!

Exercise 52: Three-step footwork in the Figure Eight

1. Set up the Figure Eight.

2. Start with your "dog" on your left side.

3. As you come around the guidepost with your shoulders parallel to it: Stop.

4. Put your weight on the foot closest to your "dog" (in this case, your left foot) and stand on one leg. (Yes, we know it feels silly but it helps! From here you can smoothly start your front cross.) You're standing on foot No. 0, the preparation foot.

5. Toe-in along the diagonal line with the foot farthest from your "dog" (your right foot). This is foot No. 1, the first step in the front cross.

6. Toe-out along the diagonal line with your left foot (foot No. 2).

7. The foot that now is nearest to your "dog" (your right foot—foot No. 3) steps in the new direction. Stamp the ground to mark the new direction. (The stamp is optional, but it really does help you put your weight on foot No. 3).

8. When you complete the front cross, you'll be close to the next guidepost, with your "dog" on your outside.

Suggested tag points:

- Stand on foot No. 0
- Toe-in on foot No. 1
- New arm up at foot No. 1
- Toe-out on foot No. 2
- Stamp on foot No. 3

In these pictures you can see just the handler, doing the front cross in the Figure Eight.
Left: Preparing for the front cross: Standing on foot No. 0, the foot closest to the dog.
Center left: Starting the front cross: New arm, rotate toward the dog, and step "toe-in" with foot No. 1.
Center right: Foot No. 2 goes "toe-out."
Right: Ending the front cross: Foot No. 3, which is nearest the dog, steps in the new direction. Stomp!

Continue around the guidepost and do the mirror-image front cross, from right-side handling to left-side handling, along the next diagonal.

Finally, you should also pay some attention to your arms. Remember, when directing your dog you can use either your shoulders alone, or your shoulders along with your nearest hand. In situations where you complement the direction of your shoulders with your arms, you'll switch arms in the front cross. Raise your opposite arm (which is about to become the nearest arm) as you begin the front cross with foot No. 1; you'll start the toe-in and raise the new arm at the same time. Since you never raise your opposite arm in other situations, the change of arms will become a salient cue for the front cross, accentuating your shoulders and signaling your dog to turn toward you.

When you perform front crosses with your dog, your footwork should always follow the three-step pattern. The direction will differ, depending on where you're going after the front cross, but you'll still move your feet in the same way.

How can you teach your dog to respond to your front cross?

Now that you have the front-cross footwork under your belt, it's time to start working on it with your dog. You can practice your front cross in the same types of setups as you practiced regular turns. Begin by doing front crosses in outside circles, and then move on to contrasting the front cross with going straight ahead or doing regular turns.

For each new setup, however, rehearse without your dog first so that you know where you're going, which way you're supposed to rotate, and how to do the footwork. If you can, employ a helper to act as your dog as you practice.

You want your dog to drive hard out of the front cross, so make sure to deliver the reward in the direction you're going after the front cross.

When you perform a front cross, you want your dog to turn as fast as he can, hurrying toward you to get ahead of you again. To ensure that your dog really drives out of the front cross, reward ahead: throw your reward or deliver it from your hand but in the direction you're aiming after the front cross. In some exercises you'll also be able to send your dog to a remote reward.

Front cross in the outside circle

The outside circle is perfect for practicing front crosses. Either you can face your dog and turn 180°, continuing along the circle in the opposite direction, or you can turn into the middle of the circle. Decide in advance where your path will go and "walk the course" properly so you know where to aim with your three-step front-cross footwork.

Exercise 53: Front cross in the outside circle

1. Walk or run in an outside circle.

2. Change direction with a front cross.

3. Your dog turns toward you and ends up on your other side (your new outside).

4. Reward as your dog gets to your new outside.

Suggested tag points:

• Plan your path

• Walk your path

• Point your shoulders in the new direction as you reward

• Reward with nearest hand

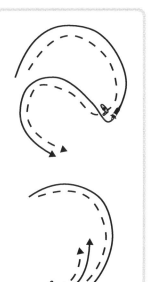

Flat front cross circle: These diagrams show the dog's and the handler's paths as well as their positions just before the handler begins the front cross.

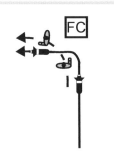

As your dog approaches, rotate toward him and do your three-step front cross. During the front cross you'll be moving in the new direction, so your dog has to hurry to catch up with you.

Race to me and turn with a front cross

You can use the same setups when practicing front crosses as when practicing regular turns: Do front crosses in outside circles, in *Race to me* settings, and in *Race to reward* setups. As with the regular turns, move ahead as your dog approaches you so that your dog really learns to cue off your front cross while you're moving.

Exercise 54: **Race to me** *and front cross, reward immediately*

1. Leave your dog in a start-line stay.
2. Walk out a bit.
3. Give your start cue while moving forward.
4. Your dog starts and races toward you.
5. Keep moving straight forward and, as your dog approaches you, do a front cross.
6. Your dog turns toward you and ends up on your new outside, hurrying to catch up.
7. Reward your dog as he catches up with you.

Contrasts: straight ahead, regular turn, or front cross?

You can add front crosses in the contrasting exercise setup you used when practicing *straight ahead* and *regular turns* (pages 242 and 245), testing whether your dog can discriminate between your handling cues for moving straight, executing a regular turn, and performing a front cross.

- Vary between straight ahead, regular turns, and front crosses.
- Vary where you place remote rewards, and whether they are mere dummies or actual rewards. You can place one or several remote rewards ahead and/or to the side, and either handle your dog to a remote reward, or handle toward a point where there's no remote reward (rewarding from your hand or with a thrown toy).
- When there's a remote reward straight ahead for your dog to aim for when starting, vary your lateral distance to make sure he reads your handling cues properly from a distance.
- When doing front crosses or regular turns, you can vary how sharp the turn is—for example, vary between 90° turns and 180° turns.

Here two remote rewards are set out—one straight ahead, the other off to the left. This time the handler chooses to turn the dog left with a front cross.

The handler stands still, and the dog races right to her.

Stopping/standing still

What should stopping/standing still look like?

- You either stand still, or hit the brakes and stop.
- Your dog turns toward you and races straight to you.

You can think of the front of your knees as your dog's target. When you stop or stand still, it's a cue for your dog to aim for your knees.

When working on the flat, your dog will *immediately* come straight to you when you stop. He'll also come straight to you when you stand still ahead of him. At obstacles, your standing still/stopping can translate into a "wrap," where your dog prepares for a tight turn as he approaches an obstacle, takes the obstacle, and turns tightly back to you. Your standing still/stopping on the takeoff side as he approaches the obstacle will cue the "wrap."

STOPPING/STANDING STILL, CUEING A WRAP

This example will help you envision how you can use standing still and stopping on the agility course. (You'll find further applications and discussions of training on obstacles on page 328.)

In this sequence, the dog is supposed to turn tightly after jump #3. As the dog approaches jump #3, he sees his handler standing still by the wing. In essence, he is getting two pieces of information at once:

- Shoulders pointing forward = get ahead of those shoulders (in other words, take jumps #1 through #3)
- Handler standing still = come straight to handler

So he does both: He takes the three jumps, but when approaching jump #3 he prepares for a tight turn by collecting his stride. He jumps short, with a rounded arc, wrapping around the wing while aiming for his stationary handler. As the dog takes off, the handler can turn her shoulders to where she's going next on course, for example, doing a regular turn toward jump #4.

If this were a sequence in the middle of a course, the handler probably wouldn't have time to get to jump #3 and stand still. Instead she would put the brakes on as the dog approached jump #3, using "stopping" as a cue for the dog to collect, add extra strides, jump tightly, and hurry back to her.

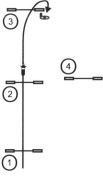

On course, if the handler stops or stands still, the dog wraps tight around the wing.

SOME CAUTIONS

Having your dog run straight to you when you stop short or stand still forms an exception to the golden rule "go where my shoulders are pointing." If your dog currently tends to "go Velcro" and get stuck to you in situations where he should aim ahead, it's much more important to work on his drive and his responsiveness to the direction of your shoulders than to teach him to come to you when you stop or stand still.

You can always wait and teach the stopping/standing still cue later, when and if you feel that you need it. Or, you can teach it but use it only sparingly, focusing mostly on training your dog to aim ahead and follow the direction of your shoulders.

But when you have a dog that flies ahead like a missile, you'll really benefit from teaching him to break off his forward flight and head for your knees when you stop or stand still.

How can you train it?

Use *Race to me* to introduce the concept of stopping with you when you stand still or stop. Then add a remote reward farther ahead, and work on the contrast between stopping with you when you stop/stand still, and racing past you when you move ahead.

It's essential that you practice lots of contrast exercises so that your dog learns to differentiate between continuing on ahead if you keep moving forward and coming straight to you when you stop/stand still. As long as you're moving he should keep driving forward, without any hesitation, in the direction your shoulders are pointing.

When stopping or standing still, deliver the reward right by your knees—that's where you want your dog to aim.

Race to me and stop with me

Set up a *Race to me* exercise where you start moving and stop right before your dog reaches you. Your stopping will be very obvious for your dog, so he'll check in with you to see what's happening. Then, reward!

Exercise 55: Stop with me!

1. Leave your dog in a start-line stay.
2. Walk out a bit.
3. Give your start cue while moving.
4. Your dog starts and races toward you.
5. You keep moving forward and, as your dog approaches, you stop short.
6. Your dog stops with you.
7. Reward by your knees.

Suggested tag point

• Reward by your knees

Next, stand still from the beginning and remain still until your dog has stopped with you.

Exercise 56: Come to me when I stand still

1. Leave your dog in a start-line stay.
2. Walk out a bit.
3. Stop.
4. Give your start cue and remain still.
5. Your dog runs toward you and stops with you.
6. Reward by your knees.

Immediately reward your dog for coming to you!

Contrasts: stop or keep going straight ahead?

To proof your dog's understanding of your stopping/standing still, place a remote reward straight ahead as a distraction. Your dog's job continues to be to stop with you when you stop/stand still. Use a helper to remove the reward if your dog should make the incorrect choice.

Contrast your stop/stand still training with a lot of straight-ahead repetitions, where you keep moving forward and your dog flies by you. You can use a remote reward (which will function as a reward when going straight ahead but as a distraction when you stop/stand still), or you can work without it (which means throwing a toy as a reward when going straight ahead).

When using a remote reward you can add lateral distance (don't do that without the remote reward, though—your dog needs something to aim for when starting). Move forward when you give your start cue so that your dog starts heading straight for the remote reward. Then either keep going straight (which cues him to go straight for the remote reward) or stop (which cues him to turn toward you and come right to you).

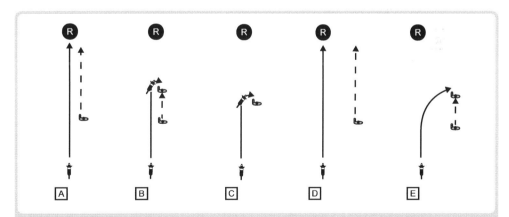

Contrasts between stopping/going straight. As long as there is no lateral distance (as in A, B, and C), the remote reward is optional, but when you add lateral distance (as in D and E) you need the remote reward to set your dog's path.

A. Send your dog straight ahead by moving straight forward (either send to a remote reward, or reward with a thrown toy).
B. Move forward and stop. Reward by your knees.
C. Stand still. Reward by your knees.
D. At a lateral distance, send your dog straight ahead to the remote reward by moving forward.
E. At a lateral distance, move forward and stop. Reward by your knees.

In the rear cross, you switch sides behind your dog's tail.

Rear cross

What should the rear cross look like?

* Your dog is ahead of you.
* As you cross behind his tail he turns his head in the new direction (losing sight of you for a millisecond).

On the flat, we practice rear crosses when the dog is sitting or standing still—so all he'll do is turn his head in the correct direction.

When working with obstacles, we always do the rear cross as the dog is taking off at an obstacle. That way the actual change of sides takes place when the dog is committed to the obstacle, so all the rear cross really cues him to do is to turn his head as the handler switches sides behind him.

How can you train it?

Unlike with front crosses and regular turns, we don't run rear crosses on the flat (on the ground between obstacles). Most of our rear-cross training is done on obstacles—but we do start with some preparatory work away from the obstacles. In this initial training you teach your dog to turn his head in the right direction as you step behind his tail. Start with your dog sitting or standing still; then cross behind him as he remains in that stationary position.

Rear-cross exercise: step behind your dog

This exercise requires that your dog can hold his stay no matter what you do: He shouldn't move his feet at all, only his head. Usually you conduct this exercise while standing beside and slightly behind your dog; another possibility is to sit in a chair with your dog between your knees.

To begin, position your dog in a sit or stand. At first, deliver a couple of treats with your nearest hand to reward your dog for keeping still and to remind both you and him of which side he is on. (Remember, he's always either on your left side or your right side.) Move back, so that you're slightly behind your dog on whichever side you're on. Then step behind him—or, if you're sitting, lean behind him—so that you end up on his other side. When you step behind him you should step across with the foot farthest from your dog (it'll become the nearest foot as you cross behind). Your rear cross should happen with one prompt movement, so that you swiftly end up on his other side and reward him with the now nearest hand.

Exercise 57: Rear cross, step behind

1. Place your dog in a stay.
2. Get beside your dog, but slightly behind him, facing forward.
3. Your dog remains still.
4. Reward with nearest hand (for keeping still).
5. Step across behind him, pointing your shoulders in the direction you're going.
6. Your dog turns his head but remains still with his feet.
7. Reward (for turning his head while keeping still) with the hand that is now nearest your dog.

Suggested tag points:

- Reward with nearest hand
- Step across with farthest foot

Watch that your dog doesn't turn his head too early (before you've crossed behind him). If he begins to anticipate your cross, do lots of "almost" rear crosses and reward him for *not* turning his head if you move toward him *without* crossing behind.

Left: Get beside your dog but slightly behind him.
Center left: Reward with the nearest hand for staying in position.
Center right: Step across.
Right: Reward with your "new" nearest hand

You'll make use of all these handling maneuvers when working with obstacles in handling sequences. But first your dog needs to learn some obstacles—so in the next chapter we start introducing the agility obstacles, beginning with the various jumps and tunnels, and the tire.

18

Jumps and tunnels

The jump, the long jump, the pipe tunnel, the collapsed tunnel, and the tire—though different in appearance—are actually similar in their execution. They all require the dog to approach, perform, and exit the obstacle in one smooth movement. Because we teach all these obstacles in roughly the same way, we've gathered them together in this one chapter.

Teaching jumps and tunnels

Through the *between/around/over/onto/under/through* foundation training, your dog has learned to aim and drive ahead, work independently of you, and make the correct choices, interacting with all sorts of "equipment." Now you will put all these skills to use on the actual agility obstacles:

- **Jumps and the long jump:** He will go *between* the uprights, *over* the bar (or bars, wall, or planks).
- **Tunnels:** He will go *between* the sides, *onto* and across the bottom, *under* the top, in other words, *through* the tunnel. In the collapsed tunnel, the dog will also push *through* the fabric.
- **Tire:** He will go *between* the sides, *over* the bottom, *under* the top, in other words, *through* the tire.

Jumps, tunnels and tire all require your dog to pass between/onto/over/under and/or through! Here, a long jump (left), a round tunnel (center) and a tire (right).

You and your dog are already familiar with these skills and the training procedures we use: *Aim for it* and *Race to reward.* To teach the jumps and tunnels, you'll be practicing basically the same exercises as you did in foundation training; this time, though, both you and your dog come "fully equipped," and your dog will perform actual agility obstacles.

Teaching the obstacles in four steps

We work with each obstacle in four steps. The first three steps—featured in this chapter—focus on teaching your dog to perform jumps, tunnels, and tires fluently:

Step 1: Get the behavior.
- Present each new obstacle (or new feature of the same obstacle) in a simple *Race to reward* and/or *Aim for it* procedure.

Step 2: Expand the understanding.

- Vary the setting until your dog eagerly aims for and masters the obstacle from various angles and distances, both when working toward a remote reward (*Race to reward*) and when working totally independently, with the reward showing up after the performance (*Aim for it*).
- Vary between spontaneous starts and start-line stays (starting your dog on cue).

Step 3: Get the flow.

- Combine several obstacles into simple, smoothly flowing combinations that allow your dog to aim ahead and constantly drive to the next obstacle.

You'll learn the details of how to work through these three steps for each type of obstacle in the sections that follow. Throughout these steps the setups will be simple: We want the dog to be able to focus completely on how to execute the obstacles, so there is hardly any "handling" involved (even though, naturally, you will be following your handling system).

In the fourth step—presented in the next chapter, "Handling sequences"—you teach your dog to truly cue off your handling while working with the obstacles:

Step 4: Handle sequences.

- Implement various handling maneuvers while performing obstacles.

"Jumps and tunnels" is inherently linked with "Handling sequences," since performing obstacles correctly in various sequences is a vital part of obstacle training. We view handling sequences as continued training of each obstacle: As soon as you have worked through the jump-wings section, you can move on to practicing various handling maneuvers with the jump wings. Once your dog is fluent with blasting through short, straight tunnels, you can start practicing handling maneuvers with short, straight tunnels, and so on.

Order of events

Jump wings are perfect for starting your obstacle training. They are simple for you to teach, they are simple for your dog to perform, and you've already been through much of the process in teaching your dog to go *between*. Jump-wing training prepares you for all the other obstacles, and jump wings are excellent to use when working with handling sequences. When teaching jump wings, you'll be working in parallel with the *Aim for it* and *Race to reward* procedures, at first with spontaneous starts only, and eventually adding stays and starts on cue.

Tunnel training exactly replicates jump-wing training, so you can follow the same procedures in the same order, just exchanging the jump wings with various tunnels. The only thing that's new is that the tunnel itself can vary (it can be short or long, straight or bent, or collapsed).

The various jumps (including the long jump) require actual jumping (rather than just running through jump wings). To help your dog learn good jumping habits from the very beginning, we introduce jumps with the *Race to reward* procedure from a start-line stay—that way he is balanced from the start and knows exactly where to go after each jump. Later on, we add the *Aim for it* procedure and the spontaneous starts.

The tire is like a cross between a tunnel and a jump, requiring your dog to jump with high precision. For the tire we prefer to get the behavior with the *Aim for it* procedure, since that enables you to reward many times for just looking at or moving toward the opening in the tire. This way you can highly reinforce your dog for aiming at the right spot from the very beginning. Once your dog is skilled at aiming properly for the tire, you can move on to using *Race to reward* as well. We don't work with the tire on any kind of height until the dog's jumping skills are in place.

Jump wings

Jump wings are just another piece of equipment for your dog to go *between*. If you have access to freestanding jump wings, we suggest you use only the wings (no bar between them) so your dog can just run between the wings without having to pay extra attention to where he puts his feet. If you have jump wings that are connected along the ground (by a plastic or metal bar, for example), add an extremely low, thick, sturdy bar or a "speed bump" (a thick pipe cut in half) that your dog readily notices and doesn't accidentally step or trip on.

What should it look like when your dog performs the jump wings?
- Your dog aims for the "jump" as soon as you direct him toward it.
- He quickly races between the wings and exits in the direction your handling implies.
- When turning, he runs close to the inner upright to take the shortest path.

"OK, between it is!"

Why do you need jump-wing training?

- Jump wings are the simplest version of jumps and tunnels.
- Jump wings are physically easy for your dog to "do."
- Jump wings are excellent for introducing new setups and varieties of handling.

How can you train it?

When training jump wings, we suggest that you work parallel with the *Race to reward* and *Aim for it* procedures. Simply follow these three steps:

Step 1: First get the behavior.
Step 2: Then expand your dog's understanding.
Step 3: Finally, get the flow in smooth sequences.

Step 1: Get the behavior

With jump wings, getting the behavior is simple: Just use *Race to reward* and *Aim for it* to get your dog to spontaneously run between the wings.

Below is a quick review of the *Aim for it* and *Race to reward* procedures (for further details, revisit Chapter 10, "Two strategies" and Chapter 11, "Between, around," etc.) You'll be using these procedures here with the jump wings and then again when working with tunnels, actual jumps (of various types, including the long jump), and the tire.

Boost your dog's speed and enthusiasm by always adhering to Good Agility Practices: Keep your sessions short, sweet, and intense! This is especially important when you're working with Aim for it—*you'll be quite passive for the few seconds your dog is working independently, but his work should be surrounded with high-energy play!*

JUMP WINGS: Get the behavior

GOAL: Your dog spontaneously runs between the wings.
You can begin with either procedure—just make sure you do both eventually.

Aim for it:

Free-shape your dog to go between the wings, starting just a few steps from the wings. You can start straight or at an angle, whichever feels easiest.

Suggested shaping plan (add intermediate steps as needed):

1. Nose toward the wing for a millisecond.
2. Nose toward wing for a longer period.
3. Step toward the wing.
4. Go all the way between the wings.
5. Increase the distance to the wing.

Rewarding with a thrown toy works well, since it builds your dog's anticipation and keeps him heading forward. On the other hand, using treats will give you more rewards per repetition. Always use your nearest hand, and let the reward appear ahead of your dog so that he has to move ahead to get it.

Tips:

You can begin either with just one pair of wings, or in the Bermuda Triangle using three pairs. Either way, deliver the final reward just as your dog passes the wings and then transport your dog to a new starting point.

Race to reward:

Place a remote reward a couple of meters beyond the wings and let your dog race straight to it. He should start spontaneously, racing between the wings to his reward as soon as you let go of him.

In the beginning it's easiest to release your dog from a collar transport, since then you can feel where he is aiming to go. Then you can let him go when you feel he is aiming correctly.

To set up for another repetition, go get your dog at the reward and quickly transport him back to the starting point.

Tips:

When switching sides you can either perform a front cross (as you get your dog at the reward, or at the starting point before you let him go) or sneak behind his back in a rear cross while he is busy with his reward.

Aim for it at jump wings: Click for aiming and moving along the intended path (left), and deliver the reward ahead (right).

Race to reward between jump wings: This is really simple, so move on to angles after just one or two repetitions.

Always remember:

- Either your dog is busy with a reward or transport, or he is off working on his own. No gray areas!
- Point your shoulders in the direction your dog is going.
- Vary between left-side and right-side handling.
- Keep your dog on your outside—especially when you're working with angles.

Step 2: Expand the understanding

Work through both the *Race to reward* and *Aim for it* procedures, making sure that your dog keeps offering the correct behavior, dashing between the jump wings at various angles and various distances. Remember to constantly generalize the behavior while adding minor variations and distractions—for example, work in different places, use different kinds of jump wings, and vary your own movements a bit.

JUMP WINGS: Expand the understanding

GOAL: Your dog dashes through the wings in all the various *Aim for it* and *Race to reward* setups. Work both procedures in parallel—each will enhance the other.

Aim for it:

1. Let your dog spontaneously run between the wings.
2. Vary the angle.
3. Increase the distance.
4. Vary the spontaneous starts with start-line stays.

Tips:

In the *Aim for it* procedure, varying the angle is usually simple—often it actually can be easier to start from an angle than to start straight. Keep building to really severe angles!

Increase distance in small increments so that your dog continues to confidently dash through the wings.

Reward immediately as your dog passes between the wings, and make sure that your shoulders are pointing in the direction where the reward appears.

Race to reward:

1. Let your dog spontaneously run between the wings to his remote reward.
2. Vary the angle (creating a turn to the remote reward).
3. Increase the distance.
4. Vary the spontaneous starts with start-line stays.

Tips:

Employ a helper to guard the remote reward, removing it if your dog runs by rather than through the wings.

Add angles quickly, to ensure that your dog really aims for the wings. When you work with angles, make sure your dog is always on your outside (taking the longer path).

In the beginning use collar transports, so that you can wait to release your dog until you see and feel him aiming correctly.

Keep building to really severe angles!

Race to reward training is often rewarding for the handler: You'll make progress quickly, getting lots of behavior at once. But remember that a remote reward is a very persuasive lure, so don't forget to work with *Aim for it* as well. When your dog takes two steps spontaneously in the *Aim for it* procedure, it can demonstrate as much learning, or more, as his running a long way in a *Race to reward* setting.

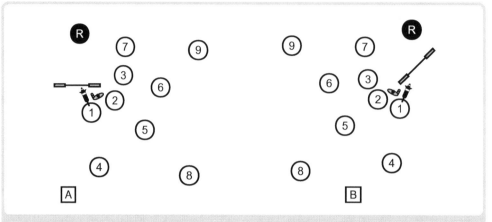

A. Teach your dog to race to the jump wings from all angles, and from various distances. The first diagram shows you nine different starting points in left-side handling, with a remote reward set out (the black circle with "R").

B. For further variation, vary the angle of the "jump." This alters the relation between the "jump" and the reward. You can achieve the same effect by keeping the "jump" straight and moving the reward off to the side. And remember to vary between left-side and right-side handling.

Note: In the sketches in this section we use jumps to illustrate the jump wings. Just disregard the bar and use only the wings!

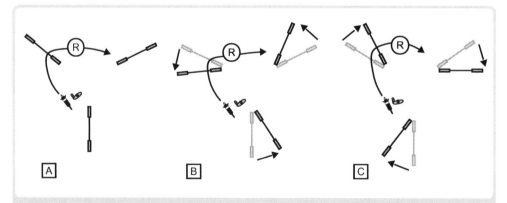

A. With Aim for it we usually work in the Bermuda Triangle, where it's easy to start over by continuing to the next "jump" after each reward.

B. Of course you can vary the setup—for example, if you pivot the outer wings forward, you'll get a more direct approach...

C. ...and if you pivot the outer wings backward, the approach angle becomes more severe.

YOUR HANDLING AT SEVERE ANGLES

At steeper angles, your dog needs to go the long way around the wing. Since he knows to keep to your outside, this is simple!

To make sure you get your handling right, you can imagine there is a line extending straight out from the jump wing (as in the figure below) marking the plane of the jump. You can even draw the line on the ground if you like. At a steep angle your dog first has to pass that line, to get to the correct side of the "jump."

1. First you point your shoulders at the wing—since your dog is on your outside he'll go past the wing, passing the plane and getting to the correct side of the "jump."
2. Then you point your shoulders at the "jump" and your dog aims between the wings.
3. Finally, you point your shoulders toward where the reward will show up.

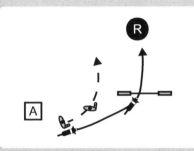
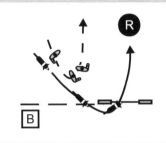
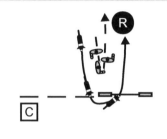

In these examples we use a remote reward (black circle with "R").

A. At a less steep angle, you just point your shoulders first at the "jump," then at the reward.

B and C. When the angle gets steeper, requiring your dog to take the obstacle "from behind," first you need to send him past the plane of the "jump" before he turns to "jump" it.

Here the dog aims for the wings from a steep angle. The reward appears immediately after the "jump."

When you introduce the start-line stay (starting your dog on cue), begin by positioning your dog at your chosen starting point, stay right next to him, and give your start cue when he looks at the jump wings. Gradually move farther away (starting a bit ahead, farther to the side, or even a bit behind your dog). Continually vary between spontaneous starts (directly from a transport) and starts on cue (from a stay), making sure that your dog continues to perform both flawlessly.

AVOID REWARDING AWAY FROM YOUR DOG'S PATH

When rewarding your dog with a thrown toy, make sure you throw the reward along the path directed by your shoulders. If you were to throw the reward so that your dog has to turn away from the intended path (and you) to get it, you'll inadvertently be countering the handling system you've worked so hard to teach your dog. If you're going to throw in any direction other than along your dog's line, throw a bit toward yourself so that your dog has to turn toward you to get his toy. Then just turn your shoulders toward where the toy lands. Turning toward you (a regular turn) is an existing feature in our handling system; turning away from you is not.

Step 3: Get the flow

Combining several obstacles into simple, smoothly flowing sequences, with only minimal handling involved, teaches your dog to aim ahead and constantly drive to the next obstacle. This is a vital aspect of obstacle training. You don't necessarily have to work through every possible aspect in "Step 2: Expand the understanding" before trying out these sequences, but you have to make sure your dog knows enough to get it right, and you have to remember to go back and do the rest of the work so that you don't skip any parts.

JUMP WINGS: Get the flow

GOAL: Your dog keeps working ahead, constantly aiming for the next pair of jump wings. Work both procedures in parallel—each will enhance the other.

Aim for it:

Begin by letting your dog do several obstacles for one reward in the Bermuda Triangle.

Then do variations along that theme, setting up "never-ending" sequences like circles or ovals and randomly rewarding your dog for working ahead.

Also set up sequences that have an obvious end (like a straight line or a horseshoe) and employ back-chaining, beginning at the end and adding one obstacle at a time, always rewarding as your dog takes the last obstacle in the sequence.

Race to reward:

Set up straight or bent paths with a remote reward at the end.

Employ back-chaining, beginning with the last obstacle and gradually adding one obstacle at a time (or, when necessary, one step at a time) to the sequence.

In these simple sequences you can easily vary your own position and movement (for example, being ahead of or behind your dog, being closer or farther out to the side, moving fast or slow), while solidifying your dog's obstacle performance.

Here are four examples of exercises designed to get the flow:

- The Bermuda Triangle (using *Aim for it,* starting wherever you like and rewarding whenever you like)
- The speed circle (which is just an extension of the Bermuda Triangle)
- The straight line (using either *Aim for it* or *Race to reward,* always rewarding after the last obstacle)
- The horseshoe (using either *Aim for it* or *Race to reward,* always rewarding after the last obstacle)

The Bermuda Triangle makes it easy for you to let your dog do several obstacles for one reward, using the *Aim for it* procedure. You can vary the angles of the "jumps" endlessly: Just make sure that you first point your shoulders toward the obstacle and then (when your dog reaches the "jump") direct your dog toward the next jump by pointing your shoulders toward that one.

- At first, reward after every one or two obstacles. Ping-pong the number of obstacles your dog gets to take before each reward until eventually he can do lap after lap.
- Vary your own position and movement: Sometimes hang back a bit so that you're behind your dog, sometimes try to stay ahead of your dog, vary your lateral distance, and vary your speed.
- Keep track of your shoulders, so that they always point in the direction your dog should go, and reward with your nearest hand along the triangle's path.
- When you're behind your dog, always throw the reward so that it appears ahead of him.
- When you're ahead of your dog, either you can throw the reward ahead (which encourages your dog to speed up and hurry past you), or you can deliver the reward directly from your hand.
- A couple of helpers that randomly throw in surprise rewards along the path can help you time and place your rewards perfectly. Preferably they should throw the reward from behind your dog so that the reward appears "out of nowhere" in his path.
- If your dog misses a pair of wings, just keep working ahead. Reward for an obstacle that he actually takes, and next time toss in your reward while he is still on track (before he makes a mistake).

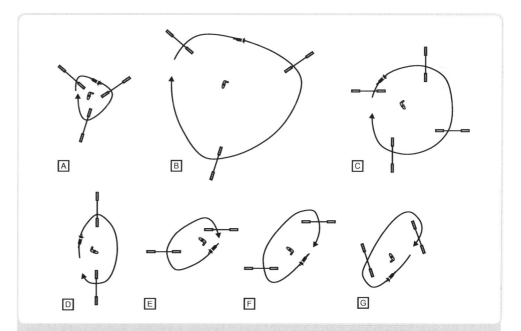

The idea of the Bermuda Triangle setup is that it's a symmetrical figure that allows you get to "the same" obstacle, from "the same" angle, again and again. Vary the design so it fits your training! For example, you can make a very small triangle (A), a big one (B), you can use four pairs of wings (C), or only two pairs (D). With two pairs, you can play around even further with various angles (E, F and G).

THIS IS MY DANCE SPACE, THIS IS YOUR DANCE SPACE...

Sometimes you'll be close to your dog, other times farther away, sometimes ahead, sometimes behind—but throughout, you should stay out of the path that belongs to your dog. By sticking to the shortest route, constantly aiming for the next obstacle, you make it easy for your dog to see where he is going. You also make it possible for him to take the shortest route—saving time and reducing the risk of his aiming for the wrong obstacle.

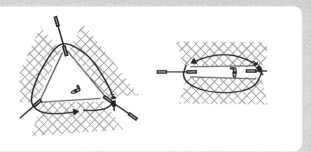

In these sketches, your dog's "dance space" is colored gray. The absolutely shortest path is a straight line, closest to the inner wings. Even though your dog will go wider than that (due to stride length, speed, and some centrifugal effect), you should give him the opportunity to take the tightest path by avoiding stepping into that space.

USING HELPERS TO THROW REWARDS

Employing helpers to throw rewards to your dog really helps. Preferably each reward should just appear ahead of your dog, without him being able to predict where it'll come from next time:

- You can position several helpers who take turns in rewarding, so that your dog doesn't begin to anticipate that helpers equal upcoming reward.

- You can vary between letting your helper reward and rewarding yourself (preferably letting the reward appear from where your dog least expects it).
- You can let your helper "shadow" you, throwing the reward ahead from behind your back.

Use your rewards to build excitement and drive! Here, the handler throws the reward just as the dog runs between the wings (left) quite far ahead to entice the chase (right).

The speed circle is simply an extended version of a Bermuda Triangle, so the same advice applies—but since you can make the speed circle larger than the Bermuda Triangle, you have even more opportunities to vary your own position, movement, and speed so that you actually get to run fast. Remember to reward after every few obstacles—it's your rewards that build your dog's forward drive!

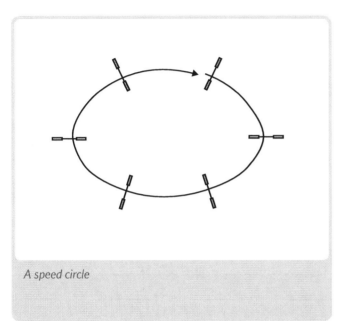

A speed circle

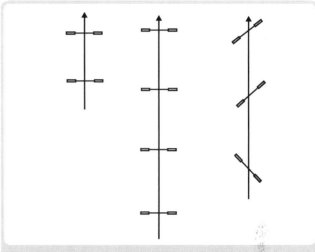

Your dog should run straight all the way until he reaches his reward (whether it's thrown by you or a helper, or set out in advance).

The straight line is a perfect setup to practice back-chaining, using either *Race to reward* or *Aim for it*. The reward always happens at the end, but the starting point varies.

- Set up a straight line of jump wings and start by having your dog "jump" the last "jump"; reward straight ahead. Then do the last two "jumps." Gradually add more jump wings while ping-ponging back and forth the degree of difficulty (for example, doing one–two–three–two–three–four–one jump[s]), so that the sequence doesn't steadily get more difficult for your dog. If you need to, you can add distance even more incrementally, backing up just one step at a time.
- Do practice both procedures. Even though *Race to reward* is easiest, you always need *Aim for it* as well to ensure that your dog truly understands to aim ahead without any remote reward to run toward.
- When you use *Aim for it,* make sure the reward always appears ahead of your dog, along the straight line, before he has time to look back at you after the last "jump."
- If you're standing parallel to your dog when he starts, you can either stand still until he reaches his reward or start moving ahead as he dashes forward. If you're standing farther ahead when your dog starts, you have to move ahead to signal to him that he should continue straight ahead (see Chapter 17, "Handling maneuvers on the flat," for further discussion).
- If your dog ever hesitates or misses a "jump" in the straight line, go back to a much shorter distance and add distance in smaller increments.

DON'T GET STUCK BEHIND THE WING!

If you start from a position behind the middle of the "jump," it's impossible for you to move straight ahead since you will bump straight into the wing. And if your dog is supposed to move straight ahead, you cannot turn laterally to get around the wing since that would be a handling cue telling your dog to turn with you in a regular turn. So if your dog is supposed to go straight ahead, you have two options:

- Stay where you are until your dog has reached his reward (whether it's a remote reward or a thrown toy).
- Begin farther out to the side, so that you can clear the jump wing and move straight forward.
- If your dog is supposed to turn, you're off the hook: your turning will be consistent with your dog's path.

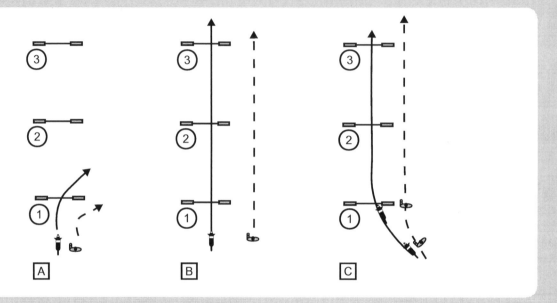

A. If you turn at jump #1, your dog should turn with you!
B. By positioning yourself farther to the side of the jump wings, you can get a straight path.
C. Here the dog approaches from an angle and turns right between jumps #1 and #2. This is a perfectly OK way to handle this situation. Just note that your dog no longer has a straight line from #1 to #3. You'll learn more about straight lines versus regular turns on page 303.

The horseshoe is another back-chaining exercise set in the shape of a horseshoe. As in the straight line, the reward always happens at the end, but the starting point can vary, and you can use either *Race to reward* or *Aim for it*.

- Work as you did with the straight line: start by doing just the last "jump" and then add one "jump" at a time. As with the straight line, ping-pong the distance back and forth while gradually building it.
- The horseshoe is more advanced than the straight line since your dog can't just run straight ahead—he'll have to focus on doing all the obstacles on his way toward the end.
- When you get to the curve you might need to add distance in smaller increments, but since your dog already is skilled at working at angles, this should be easy. If he tends to run by "jumps," heading directly for the end, you probably need to go back and work more with angles at one jump.
- Make sure your shoulders support your dog's path through the horseshoe.

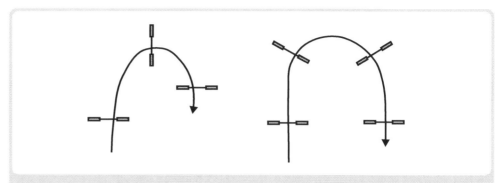

Horseshoes can come in many shapes! As always, play around with your setups, and design the exercises you want for yourself and your dog.

Tunnels

Tunnels are very much like jump wings: they merely require your dog to run through a limited space involving no physical challenge (unless your dog is very tall and has to duck under to crawl through). The only difference between tunnels and jump wings is that there is a bit more plastic or fabric in the tunnels, and that your dog will lose sight of you for a while.

What should it look like when your dog performs a tunnel?
- Your dog aims for the tunnel and runs through it.
- Depending on where he is going next, he either shoots ahead out of the tunnel or turns tightly at the exit.

How can you train it?
The training procedure you used for the jump wings fits perfectly for tunnels, too. Switch back and forth between *Race to reward* and *Aim for it,* and work through the three steps (get the behavior, expand the understanding, get the flow) with both procedures. In this section we'll discuss the special aspects of tunnel training.

Step 1: Get the behavior
Begin with a short, straight tunnel (perhaps scrunched together a bit, to make it even shorter) or a collapsed tunnel with the chute held wide open. For the first repetitions you can choose either the *Aim for it* or the *Race to reward* procedure.

Heading for the tunnel (left). Shooting ahead out of the collapsed tunnel (center, right)

TUNNELS: Get the behavior

GOAL: Your dog spontaneously runs through the tunnel.
You can begin with either procedure—just make sure you do both at some point.

Aim for it:

With *Aim for it*, you can click and treat for looking toward the tunnel, nose inside tunnel, head inside tunnel, and front paws inside tunnel.

Since you have been working with the foundation skills *onto*, *under*, and *through* using *Aim for it*, your dog will probably catch on right away and try going through the tunnel.

The tricky part can be delivering the reward. As usual you should present the reward in front of your dog. For the first clicks you can reach into the tunnel to deliver the reward. After a little while, you won't be able to reach anymore, since the tunnel is much longer than your arm. Then you can do one of three things:

- After the click, throw the reward past your dog and through the tunnel.
- After the click, a helper can deliver the reward at the exit of the tunnel (or even reach into the tunnel from the other end).
- Simply withhold the click and see if your dog figures out that he can continue ahead. If he does, click as he moves forward and treat as he leaves the tunnel (you hope this happens at the exit, but it's OK if he backs out after the click as well).

Race to reward:

With *Race to reward*, simply place the remote reward at the tunnel exit and use a collar transport to move your dog to the beginning of the tunnel.

Get close to the tunnel entrance, so that your dog can put his head into the tunnel before you release him. Then let him go when you feel him aiming to go through the tunnel.

Yes, we know, the *Race to reward* procedure seems so much easier, but don't overuse it. You don't want your dog to become dependent on that remote reward. If you really prefer to work with *Race to reward,* it's a signal that you need to practice *Aim for it* more!

Getting the behavior using Aim for it: *Click for aiming correctly, and deliver the reward ahead. Here you can see three different versions of reward deliveries: A treat just a little bit ahead (left), a toy thrown past the dog into the tunnel (center), and a toy that appears after the exit (right).*

Getting the behavior using Race to Reward: *Prepare the remote reward (left) and release the dog when he aims for it through the tunnel (right).*

When your dog offers running through the short pipe tunnel, you can either start *expanding his understanding* with that tunnel, or you can *get the behavior* with a new kind of tunnel.

There are different tunnel types and formats:
- Pipe tunnels can appear in various configurations: long and short, straight, curved, or S-shaped.
- The collapsed tunnel has a fabric chute for your dog to push through.
- The chute of the collapsed tunnel can be lightweight and flexible, or quite stiff and heavy.
- When you train the chute of the collapsed tunnel, a helper can hold it open or partially lower it.
- Materials and colors can differ (and running into a black tunnel is completely different from running into a light-colored one).
- Tunnel entrances can sport various decorations.

Use a helper to lift the chute so that your dog always flies through.

When teaching the collapsed tunnel, always reward straight ahead so that your dog learns to shoot out of it rather than trying to turn inside the chute and perhaps getting tangled up in it. At first have a helper hold the chute open, and then gradually lower the chute.

When you lengthen and curve the pipe tunnel and lower the chute of the collapsed tunnel, do so incrementally to ensure that your dog always flies through the tunnel. Have a helper continue to lift the chute a bit for as long as you need it. If your dog ever hesitates, you need to make the next repetition easier and increase the quality of the reward. You don't want to end up with a dog that stops and waits for someone to lift the chute up.

STAY CONSISTENT

Even though your dog usually cannot see you when he is in the middle of the tunnel, you should handle as if he could. Otherwise you will contradict your handling system and confuse your dog (and possibly yourself, too). He can see you at the beginning and at the end, he can hear your footsteps, and he notices your position as he exits.

To stay consistent:
• Imagine that the tunnel is translucent, so that your dog can see you all the time.
• Imagine you have exchanged the tunnel with two jumps—one at the entrance, and one at the exit.

Don't stop and stand still, "pondering the view," while your dog is in the tunnel, and don't try blind crosses with the argument "my dog can't see me anyway." He knows where you were when he entered, and he has an idea of where you should be as he exits—so if you aren't where you should be, he will be bewildered.

Be consistent with your handling while your dog is in the tunnel.

Step 2: Expand the understanding

Practice tunnels through all the steps of both *Race to reward* and *Aim for it*.

TUNNELS: Expand the understanding

GOAL: Your dog dashes through the tunnel in all the various *Aim for it* and *Race to reward* setups.
Work both procedures in parallel—each will enhance the other.

Aim for it:	*Race to reward:*
1. Let your dog spontaneously run through the tunnel from a few steps' distance.	**1.** Let your dog spontaneously run through the tunnel to the reward from a few steps' distance.
2. Vary the angle.	**2.** Vary the angle.
3. Increase the distance.	**3.** Increase the distance.
4. Vary the spontaneous starts with start-line stays.	**4.** Vary the spontaneous starts with start-line stays.

Step 3: Get the flow

TUNNELS: Get the flow

GOAL: Your dog keeps working ahead, constantly aiming for the next piece of equipment.
Work both procedures in parallel—each will enhance the other.

Aim for it:	*Race to reward:*
Using *Aim for it*, you can do speed circles, straight lines, and horseshoes.	Using *Race to reward,* you can do straight lines and horseshoes.

You can do sequences with only tunnels, or you can include both jump wings and tunnels in your setups.

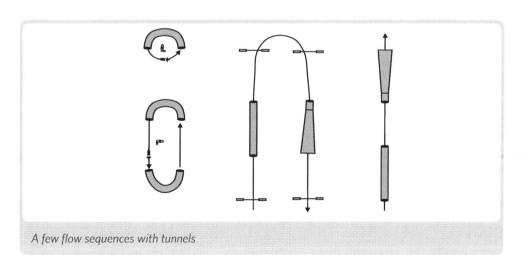

A few flow sequences with tunnels

Different kinds of jumps

What should it look like when your dog performs a jump?

- He jumps over the bar(s)/walls/planks, between the uprights.
- He happily clears jumps of any design.
- He judges the distance and jumps efficiently with accurate technique depending on the height and length of the jump.
- He adjusts his jumping style depending on where he's going next (long, flat, and aiming ahead—or short, round, and turning tight).
- When turning, he jumps close to the inner upright to get the shortest path.

Jumps can be of various designs—here, a wall.

In turns, the shortest path hugs the inner upright.

How can you train it?

When introducing different kinds of jumps we prefer to begin with *Race to reward.* Jumping is not only about learning to go over the bar, between the wings; it is also a technical endeavor requiring your dog to learn a good jumping style from the beginning. In the *Race to reward* procedure, your dog always knows exactly where he is going and can focus totally on the task at hand, which will increase his ability to use his body correctly.

When taking off at a jump, your dog has to know where he is going next. Once airborne, his landing point is set. Left pair: Going straight ahead. Right pair: Turning

To get the best jumping technique it's also a good idea to begin with your dog in a start-line stay. That way he is well balanced and in control of his body when he takes off for the jump. You may even want to start from a sit, since your dog then is likely to use his rear end properly (but only use the sit if your dog happily offers it). If you like, you can hold on to your dog, giving the start cue when he is well balanced and looks ahead.

To further enhance a good jumping technique, position your dog just *one stride from the jump*. That way you increase the likelihood that he will use the power from his rear end rather than using his front to pull himself forward and upward. At low jumps, the distance might be about 1.2 meters (4 feet) for a big dog, and less for a smaller dog. As the jump height increases, your dog will need more distance since he then has to take off earlier.

Some dogs, however, actually have a more balanced jump style when starting spontaneously from a transport from a bit longer distance—especially at the lower jumps. See what works best for your dog.

JUMPING DEMANDS

Jumping requires more from your dog than you might realize. Susan Salo, a former horse trainer who has applied her knowledge and skills to teaching dogs how to jump, lists six aspects of jumping that your dog must learn to evaluate and master, here described in our words:

1. *Path:* knowing which jump to take and where to go after that jump
2. *Distance:* evaluating how far it is to the jump, and adjusting stride length and the number of strides accordingly
3. *Appropriate takeoff spot:* deciding where to take off, and managing to hit that spot
4. *Weight transfer:* shifting and using the power from the rear end properly
5. *Angle of elevation:* jumping flat and long, or steeper with a higher, rounder arc
6. *Height:* evaluating the height, and jumping as high as needed

As you can see, a jump isn't just skipping over a bar. Even if it's just a 10-cm (4") jump, your dog still has to assess all of these aspects. To us, this list is an important reminder of how complex a jump really is.

To make the best possible jumps and turns after jumping, your dog not only needs to understand the exercise—he also needs to have the physical strength and technique to master that kind of jump. The fine details of jumping really do constitute an entire science in itself! For further information about specific jump-technique training, we recommend Susan Salo's articles and DVDs (see "Resources" on page 435 for more information).

Jump grids are great for building jumping skills! Your dog gets to collect and bounce the jumps (taking off directly after landing, without taking any strides in between). Keep the jumps very low and place them quite tight—up to 6 feet for a big dog, and down to 3 feet for a small one.

For jumps, the first three training steps are similar to those used in the previous sections for jump wings and tunnels:

Step 1: First get the behavior using *Race to reward.*

Step 2: Then add new variations such as angles and flow sequences continuing to use *Race to reward.*

Step 3: Finally, introduce *Aim for it*, where the toy shows up as a reward after the behavior. Start varying between working with the remote reward and without it.

GLOSSARY OF JUMP TYPES

Jump designs can vary among organizations, and this glossary is meant merely to give you an idea of what's out there.

- A regular jump is normally one bar between two uprights. The uprights can have wings (more or less imaginatively designed), or the jump can be wingless.
- The bars can be of various thicknesses and color, and there can be several bars or just one.
- Jumps can also be spread jumps (sometimes referred to as oxers, double jumps, or triple jumps), extending the length of the vertical jump, so the dog has to jump "longer" than over a regular jump. In some spread jumps, the bars are parallel; in other jump types, the bars are ascending so the front bars are lower than the rear ones.

- There can also be a wall or a vertical plank jump (light enough for the dog to knock down).
- Last but not least there is the long (or broad) jump, which is almost flat but that requires the dog to jump longer. The long jump is framed by four upright poles, and the dog has to clear the length of the jump.

Step 1: Get the behavior

JUMPS: Get the behavior

GOAL: Your dog jumps in a balanced style, aiming ahead after the jump.
Use *Race to reward* to get the behavior.

Aim for it:	*Race to reward:*
Wait to work with *Aim for it* until later.	With *Race to reward*, start with a *very low* jump (about your dog's wrist height). Place the remote reward some distance away from the jump, at least 4m (13 ft) for a large dog, so that your dog has space enough to land properly and regain his balance before he reaches his reward. Preferably start your dog from a stay, one stride from the jump (so that he's balanced when he begins and pushes off with his rear end).

When introducing jumps, we use remote rewards to make it easier for the dog to develop good jumping habits right away.

As soon as your dog happily skips over the first small jump, either you can move on to *expand his understanding* with that jump, or you can *get the behavior* with a different kind of jump. Here are some ways you can vary the jump:

- Vary the bar (different thickness, length, color/striping/other decorations, slant the bar, use one or several bars).
- Vary the wings (from thin, plain uprights to various more-or-less artistically designed wings, decorative flowers, and so on).
- Vary between a single jump and a spread jump.
- Vary the angle of the jump (keeping your dog's path straight).
- Introduce walls and long-jump planks.
- Vary the spread of long jumps (increase incrementally).
- Vary the height (increase incrementally).

Don't limit yourself to the varieties of jumps you can find on a competition course. The more variations you can come up with, the better. By constantly varying the design of the jump, you ensure that your dog actually notices the jump (and doesn't just jump out of habit). Whenever you come up with a new setup or jump design, remember to make other aspects easier to ensure your dog's success.

Height is your least important variation—keep the height below elbow height until your dog has developed a good, balanced technique, and then add in higher jumps from time to time.

For the rest of your dog's agility career you should constantly vary jumps. Change the design, the height, the width, the decorations—everything you can think of! That way you can make sure that your dog really takes a look at each jump, assesses it, and makes the necessary adjustments in his movements.

"Slicing" an angled jump: Note that the dog's path over the jump and to the reward is straight.

Looking ahead, waiting for the start cue, at a spread jump

Step 2: Add new variations using *Race to reward*

Work through all kinds of *Race to reward* setups, including back-chaining flow sequences with several jumps. You can also begin varying with spontaneous starts.

JUMPS: Expand the understanding and get the flow, using *Race to reward*

GOAL: Your dog jumps confidently in all the various *Race to reward* settings.

Aim for it:	*Race to reward:*
Wait to work with *Aim for it* until later.	1. Your dog starts on cue from a start-line stay, and jumps over the bar to the reward.
	2. Vary the angle, (creating a turn to the remote reward).
	3. Vary the distance.
	4. Vary with spontaneous starts.
	5. Get the flow (in straight lines and horseshoe patterns)

Build up to sharp angles! Spontaneous starts can be helpful here, since you can move toward the jump and release your dog as soon as you feel him aiming correctly. Here the dog needs to go behind the jump and make a sharp turn to take it and to get the reward.

When working straight lines and horseshoe patterns with various jumps, you can use different kinds of jumps and also add tunnels to the mix if you like. Use your knowledge about your dog and your previous training to decide which obstacles you should put in the flow sequences and which you should continue to work in isolation for a while longer.

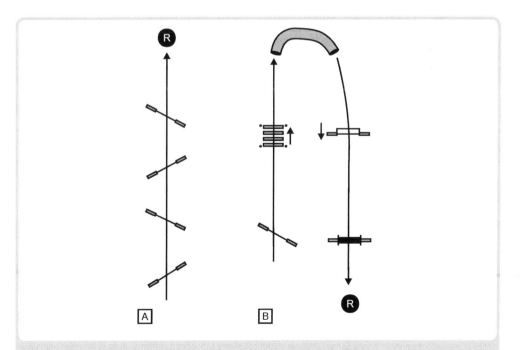

You can vary your flow sequences endlessly! Here are a couple of examples:
A. A straight line with angled jumps
B. A horseshoe pattern with various jumps (inclucing a long jump, an oxer, and a wall) and a tunnel

A backpack by the first jump, a slanted bar at the second one, and some sand bags under the third one contribute some variation.

When introducing new types of obstacles in a *Race to reward* flow sequence, we often choose to put the "new" obstacle either first or last. Taking the first obstacle is similar to taking just one obstacle, so it can be easier to start with the least familiar obstacle. Moreover, by putting the "new" obstacle first, you can give your start cue when you see or feel your dog aiming correctly. On the other hand, if you put the least familiar obstacle last, your dog will get instant reinforcement for taking it. Either way, putting it in the middle of the sequence is a bit trickier—so that's something you should do at a later stage, as a way to up the ante.

JUMP-TRAINING SETUPS

Here is an example of a typical jump-training practice. Each trial uses *Race to reward* from a start-line stay and varies only one aspect at a time. Whenever there are two repetitions, one is in left-side and one in right-side handling.

Session 1: Varying the angle. Winged 20 cm (8") jump
  2 reps from a slight angle
  2 reps from steep angles
  2 reps from the slight angle again

Session 2: Varying the height. Straight line to the reward, one jump
  2 reps at 20 cm (8")
  2 reps at 30 cm (12")
  2 reps at 15 cm (6")

Session 3: Varying your movement. Straight line to the reward, 20 cm (8") wall
  2 reps with you walking past the jump
  2 reps with you jogging past the jump
  2 reps with you remaining standing where your dog started from

Session 4: Several jumps in a straight line. Three jumps in a straight line
  1 rep with only the last jump
  2 reps with two jumps
  2 reps with three jumps
  1 rep with only the last jump

Session 5: Varying your own position. Three jumps in a straight line
  2 reps with only the last jump, with you starting beyond the last jump
  2 reps with two jumps, with you starting between the jumps
  2 reps with two jumps, with you starting next to your dog

... and so on.

Your training doesn't have to be this strictly structured; you just need to make sure that you work all the various jump aspects while your dog builds his skills step by step. But we do recommend that you work on one aspect at a time, since that will make it easier for you to assess your dog's skills and understanding of the exercises, which in turn makes it easier for you to design new exercises that fit your dog.

Beware of the unfortunate human tendency to always go for higher jumps and longer sequences. Your dog will learn much more from ping-ponging back and forth between simple and more difficult challenges.

Step 3: Introducing *Aim for it*

When your dog has developed a good, balanced jumping technique in several different *Race to reward* setups, you can start varying the task with the *Aim for it* procedure. When you introduce *Aim for it* for jumps, you can skip the shaping procedure. Your dog already knows to aim between jump wings, and he is familiar with the jumps from all the *Race to reward* training, so you can put it together right away and position him in a stay, giving your start cue as he looks ahead at the jump. Starting from a stay makes him more likely to jump in good balance. Begin with low, simple jumps (at just above wrist height).

JUMPS: Introduce *Aim for it*, expand the understanding, and get the flow

GOAL: Your dog aims ahead and performs jumps with a balanced technique in all the various *Aim for it* settings.

Aim for it:

When you begin working with *Aim for it* with the jumps, your dog needs to know where the reward will show up (so that he can prepare properly and use his body correctly when jumping). We suggest you use a Bermuda Triangle setup and constantly deliver the rewards along the path toward the next jump. This means you'll be doing a regular turn at each jump, pointing your shoulders toward the next jump as your dog takes off, and then rewarding in that direction.

In the Bermuda Triangle, work through these steps:
1. Your dog spontaneously aims for and jumps over the jump from a few steps' distance.
2. Vary the angle (see "Jump wings," page 273, for a review of how you can vary the angles in the Bermuda Triangle).
3. Increase the distance.
4. Vary with spontaneous starts.

Then get the flow:
5. Do several jumps in the Bermuda Triangle, speed circles, straight lines, and horseshoes using *Aim for it*. Remember to constantly reward along your dog's intended path!

When you reward, try to disturb your dog's jumping as little as possible. Throw the toy low to the ground, and preferably from behind him so that it just appears "out of nowhere" along his path. Helpers often come in handy here. If you're ahead of your dog, you can also deliver the reward from your hand.

Race to reward:

You've already done *Race to reward*.

KNOCKED BARS

If your dog knocks a bar, make a mental note that it happened, but don't reveal it to your dog—just keep working! Dogs knock bars for many reasons, for example:

- misjudging the height or the angle of elevation needed
- misjudging the distance, taking off from the wrong spot
- getting distracted in flight (for example by sudden, unexpected handler movements)
- trying to change the path in the act of jumping (in response to unclear direction)
- poor jumping technique
- physical issues (tripping or stumbling before takeoff, stiff muscles, pain)

You can minimize the frequency of knocked bars by devising sensible jump training that enables your dog to build his skills gradually, by varying the jump design, by clear and consistent handling, and by keeping your dog fit and agile. *Never* punish your dog for knocking a bar (not even by withholding a reward that you otherwise would have delivered). The knocked bar is always merely a *symptom of something else that needs fixing*.

ACTUALLY JUMPING IS KEY

If your dog goes under the bar, around the jump, or steps on the long-jump boards, it might be his way of telling you the jump is too big in that given situation, that he can't find the correct takeoff spot, that he has misjudged your handling—or, perhaps, that he simply hasn't understood that *jumping over* is what earns the reward.

In any case, go back to kindergarten and do simple exercises where success is guaranteed, and where you reward each jump bountifully. Some well-timed clicks for taking off and aiming to go *over* can be of great help. Gradually build step by step. You can make the jumps more inviting by putting two bars in a cross, by setting several bars, by turning over the long-jump boards, or by making the jump a small spread jump where the first bar is a bit lower than the second.

If you work with *Aim for it* at only one jump (without the Bermuda Triangle setup to rely on), it's important that you signal clearly where you want your dog to go after the jump. Your dog will jump very differently depending on where he thinks he is going next, so make sure your handling is clear and that the reward appears in accordance with your handling. For further details, see chapter 19, "Handling sequences."

The reward "magically" appears ahead of the dog, in accordance with the handling.

The tire

The tire is like a cross between a jump and a tunnel. The tire requires good jumping skills: Not only does your dog have to jump a certain height, he must also jump with delicate precision. The tire also requires that your dog truly understands that he needs to aim for that round hole, just as in the tunnels.

What should it look like when your dog performs the tire?

- He aims with precision.
- He jumps through the tire.
- He judges the distance and jumps efficiently with accurate technique.

How can you train it?

With the tire we start with teaching the dog to aim properly for the hole using the *Aim for it* procedure. Our reason for starting with *Aim for it* is that we want to be able to reward multiple times just for looking in the correct direction, richly reinforcing the act of aiming at the tire.

Dashing through the tire.

Step 1: First get the behavior using *Aim for it* from a spontaneous start.

Step 2: Then expand your dog's understanding by working through all the steps of both *Aim for it* and *Race to reward*. Also begin adding start-line stays, and vary your own pace and position.

Step 3: Finally, get the flow in speed circles, straight lines, and horseshoes, mixing jumps and tunnels into the setup so your dog will learn to perform the tire correctly when it appears before and after other types of obstacles.

Step 1: Get the behavior

Teaching the tire using *Aim for it* requires repeatedly rewarding your dog for pointing his nose in the right direction. If possible, begin with a frameless tire low to the ground, and then add the frame and the height.

In the very beginning, 20 clicks and rewards for your dog's looking at and putting his head through the tire without any lure or prompt is worth far more than just one reward for going through it. So for the first few sessions, get in as many rewards as you can. Then you can rapidly shift to just one reward that appears after your dog completes the tire.

Left: Click for nose toward tire; Center left: ... and reward ahead, toward the middle of the tire. Center right: Click for foot through tire; Right: ... and reward ahead.

TIRE: Get the behavior

GOAL: Your dog spontaneously aims at and goes through the tire.
Start with *Aim for it*.

Aim for it:	*Race to reward:*
With *Aim for it*, click and treat for looking toward the tire, nose toward the tire, head through the tire, and going through the tire.	Wait to work with *Race to reward* until later.

Aim for it:

With *Aim for it*, click and treat for looking toward the tire, nose toward the tire, head through the tire, and going through the tire.

We prefer to begin the first sessions with many quick clicks and treats for merely looking in the right direction—this way your dog's nose "gets stuck" pointing toward the tire, which is exactly what you want.

Then shape your dog all the way through the tire just as you did with the tunnel. You can quit the session before your dog has actually gone through the tire by simply transforming a reward into a treat magnet, and leading him away.

Race to reward:

Wait to work with *Race to reward* until later.

Some dogs step on the bottom of the tire instead of jumping through it. This usually sorts itself out once the dog starts working at some speed. If your dog continues to step on the bottom sometimes, start with a thinner tire (perhaps a hula-hoop) and click and reward your dog for jumping rather than stepping.

When your dog spontaneously goes through the tire as soon as he gets the chance, either you can *expand his understanding* of that type of tire, or you can *get the behavior* with a different type of tire:

- Generalize by simply using a different tire (perhaps a different size or color).
- Raise the height (gradually if possible).
- Add the frame (if you have begun with a frameless tire).

Here, the handler clicks for aiming at the tire (left), and the helper delivers the reward ahead of the dog (right).

Step 2: Expand the understanding

TIRE: Expand the understanding

GOAL: Your dog jumps through the tire in all the various *Aim for it* and *Race to reward* setups.
Work in parallel fashion with both procedures—each will enhance the other.

Aim for it:	*Race to reward:*
1. Your dog spontaneously jumps through the tire from a few steps' distance.	1. Your dog spontaneously jumps through the tire to the reward.
2. Vary the angle.	2. Vary the angle.
3. Increase the distance.	3. Increase the distance.
4. Vary your own position and movement.	4. Vary your own position and movement.
5. Vary the spontaneous starts with start-line stays.	5. Vary the spontaneous starts with start-line stays.

Race to reward (continued):

In the beginning it's easiest to start from a collar transport, close to the tire. Then you can let go as you feel your dog aiming correctly.

Start varying the angle right away, making sure your dog is actively aiming for the tire from the very beginning.

Coming at the tire from an angle

With Race to reward, *start close to the tire and introduce slight angles right away (letting go when you feel your dog aiming correctly).*

Be a bit careful with angles: as the angle gets steeper, the round hole becomes more like a squished oval, making it trickier for your dog to jump through cleanly. Especially avoid setting up the tire so that your dog "slices" it (by going straight ahead, but through an angled tire) since he then risks injuring himself.

Since a larger dog might hit his back on the top of a low tire if he jumps through it at speed, make sure to raise the tire up to full height before you let a big dog approach from more than one stride away.

Step 3: Get the flow

TIRE: Get the flow

GOAL: Your dog keeps working ahead and jumps through the tire even when it appears in a sequence. Work in parallel fashion with both procedures—each will enhance the other.

Aim for it:	*Race to reward:*
Using *Aim for it*, you can practice the tire in Bermuda Triangle settings, speed circles, straight lines, and horseshoes.	Using *Race to reward,* you can practice straight lines and horseshoes.
Most people might not have access to more than one tire. You can still set up a version of the Bermuda Triangle, though, letting your dog repeat the tire several times for one reward. When he lands, simply turn him around you in a circle so that he gets to the same tire from the same direction again.	

If you have access to several tires, you can practice not only Bermuda Triangles but also speed circles, straight lines, and horseshoes with just tires. Usually, however, that's not the case, so you can use jumps and tunnels as well in your practice sequences. Mixed sequences will help your dog discriminate when he has to gauge his jump precisely to fit through the tire hole.

In the beginning, place the tire either first or last in the sequence. When you dog is successful practically all the time, try putting the tire in the middle of the sequence as well. If you get more than the occasional mistake at the tire in sequences, you need to break down tire training further. Does your dog need to practice a single tire at longer distances? Or with you running? Or with a distracting tunnel farther ahead (click and reward for the tire)? Remember, reinforcement builds behavior, so maintain a high rate of reinforcement at the tire until it feels just like any old jump to your dog.

On the agility course, obstacle performance and handling will come together seamlessly. Don't dwell on just "doing obstacles." As soon as your dog masters a certain version of an obstacle, bring it with you to the next chapter and start working with the various handling maneuvers on that obstacle.

Handling sequences

We want you to move on quickly to practicing your handling maneuvers with jumps and tunnels, so here we combine handling maneuvers with obstacle performance into sequences. The exercises we present will give you ideas on how you can both practice the various maneuvers and customize sequences to fit your training.

Combining handling maneuvers and obstacle performance

As soon as your dog is confidently performing a certain version of an obstacle (be it jump wings, a low jump, a short tunnel, or whatever) from various angles and distances (with spontaneous starts and start-line stays, with and without remote rewards), you can start introducing various handling maneuvers at that version of the obstacle.

Your handling maneuvers, in combination with your position on course, tell your dog exactly where to go. As your dog approaches an obstacle, your position and your general direction will clue your dog to where you're headed. At takeoff you'll provide precise information about where he should go next (for example, by rotating your shoulders away from your dog or starting a front cross). Make sure you always head for the next obstacle and stay out of your dog's path.

This chapter is all about integrating handling maneuvers with obstacle performance to do sequences. We opt to call everything a sequence—even if you're working with only one obstacle. The reason is that even with a single obstacle, your dog always needs to get *to* and *from* it.

Once your dog is confident with a certain obstacle, start using it in various handling sequences.

In this chapter, we present sequences featuring the following handling maneuvers:

- Straight ahead
- Regular turn
- Front cross
- Rear cross
- The wrap
- The threadle
- The serpentine

You and your dog know most of these maneuvers from working with them on the flat. Only the more advanced threadle and serpentine maneuvers, which both consist of consecutive front crosses, are new.

Although we present all the rest of the maneuvers one by one, we present *straight ahead* and *regular turns* together since they form the core of your handling. These are the most fundamental maneuvers—you'll use them all the time, and they are the ones you've been working with while teaching your dog jumps, tunnels, and the tire. Even though straight ahead and regular turns might seem deceptively simple, they deserve careful attention. Working on them as a pair also enables you to practice contrasts, which makes each of these handling maneuvers clearer to your dog as well as to you.

Front crosses and *rear crosses* are the methods we use to switch sides, from right-side handling to left-side handling or vice versa. Theoretically, you can always choose to do either a front cross or a rear cross when you need to switch sides. Practically, in a given sequence, you might find that one works better than the other. A skilled dog and handler team should be comfortable and confident with both since to get around a course smoothly and efficiently you'll most often need front and rear crosses.

A *wrap* is a tight turn back toward you after an obstacle. You'll use your stopping/standing still to cue your dog to prepare himself for the upcoming wrap by altering his stride on the approach, and then to wrap tightly back to you after the jump.

Threadles and *serpentines* are advanced handling maneuvers that require that both dog and handler have a solid understanding of the front cross. A *threadle* "threads" your dog in between two obstacles by using two abbreviated front crosses where you stop and face your dog. The *serpentine* also uses abbreviated front crosses, as an alternative to doing full front crosses before and after a certain obstacle.

We'll go through each maneuver in detail, outlining when you should use it, how you should perform it, and suggesting some sample sequences where you can practice it. The chapter ends with a section called "Further sequencing" where you'll learn how to apply your skills in slightly altered settings and how to take your training even further.

"RIGHT" OR "WRONG" DEPENDS ON YOUR HANDLING SYSTEM!

Now that we're starting to apply all the handling maneuvers in obstacle sequences, we urge you to remember that our descriptions of what to do (and what not to do) are based on the system of handling that we use. Different ways of handling aren't right or wrong in themselves—they are correct or incorrect in the context of a certain handling system.

Teaching your dog to follow your handling in sequences

Throughout this chapter our examples feature only jumps and tunnels, but the handling principles we discuss apply to all obstacles. Once you've thoroughly taught your dog other obstacles (including the contact obstacles, the table, and the weaves, which are discussed in later chapters), go ahead and incorporate these in your sequences as well.

- Work the sequences that you feel fit your and your dog's current level of understanding. We'll describe simple sequences for beginners as well as more advanced sequences. Don't try to do it all at once!
- Vary which obstacles you use in your handling sequences (the obstacles in our diagrams are merely examples).
- Vary the jump heights; there's nothing to be gained from working your dog on full height all the time.
- Remember that you can work with just the jump wings, to focus solely on your handling.
- Make up your own sequences according to what you and your dog need to practice.
- Enjoy yourself! Use our guidelines, but don't get hung up on them. Attitude is more important than precision, and that goes for you as well as for your dog!

From learning the obstacles, your dog already knows to follow the direction of your shoulders to get *to* the obstacle. He's also used to seeing your shoulders pointing in the direction where the reward appears after the obstacle. When working with sequences, you'll also vary where he should go *after* the obstacle. That way your dog will learn to pay close attention to your handling since that's how he'll know where to go to get his rewards.

At first, work with one handling maneuver at a time in very short sequences, continually rewarding your dog for following your handling correctly. There's no point in trying sequences that combine several different maneuvers before you can execute each of them separately.

When rewarding you can use a remote reward (so placed that your handling guides your dog to it), throw a toy, or deliver a reward from your hand. Choose whatever fits your purpose best in each situation. At first you might use your rewards as lures, to get the dog to exit in the correct direction. Soon your dog will start to predict where the reward will appear (in the direction your handling indicates). Voilà! Now you can let your rewards turn up as reinforcers only.

Multiple remote rewards are excellent for proofing your dog's understanding of your handling. Seize the opportunity when you have access to several helpers!

SEQUENCING FUSES *AIM FOR IT* WITH *RACE TO REWARD*

As you combine handling maneuvers and obstacle perfor-mance, the concepts of *Aim for it* and *Race to reward* will become less and less relevant since almost every exercise will incorporate elements of both. Nearly any sequence will be an *Aim for it* exercise, in that your dog should always aim ahead toward the obstacle your handling directs him to—and continue aiming for obstacles your shoulders point toward until there are no more. And every remote reward may—or may not—be for your dog to race to. Your han-dling will tell your dog which path to take, and rewards will appear somewhere along that path.

Just as when working with handling maneuvers on the flat, you can choose to set out one or several remote rewards; these remote rewards will function either as mere distractions (dummy rewards) or as actual rewards that you'll send your dog to. Helpers are useful to guard dummy rewards and to help throw rewards, thus keeping your dog guessing where the reward will come from and when it will appear.

For each sequence, you can either use spontaneous starts (letting your dog start directly as you finish the transport) or position your dog in a start-line stay and use your start cue. Starting from a stay is often most practical because it enables you to position yourself wherever you want before starting your dog. On the other hand, a spontaneous start better replicates what it feels like on course, coming into a sequence at full speed. We recommend varying between start-line stays and spontaneous starts, using what fits the situation best and what you feel you need to practice the most.

Always consider where to start and where to finish

Before you handle a sequence, always decide in advance not only where your dog should start but also where he should finish—in other words, where the reward should appear. That's equally important.

Even when you're working with just one obstacle—or when you get to the last obstacle in a sequence—always handle your dog's path *as if* there were yet another obstacle to handle your dog toward. Reward along the path toward that imaginary obstacle! By being consistent and always directing where your dog should go after each obstacle—even after the last one—you ensure that your rewards will always appear in accordance with your handling and thus constantly strengthen your dog's responsiveness to your handling cues.

Usually we don't use the clicker when working with sequences—we simply deliver the reward. But if there's a specific response that you wish to reinforce, feel free to use a clicker to precisely mark it.

Employ back-chaining

Back-chaining is an excellent way to build both your and your dog's skills; it increases your confidence in a certain maneuver or sequence because you and your dog are always working toward a highly reinforced final behavior.

You can often break down a maneuver or sequence into smaller pieces, practice them separately, and then put the pieces back together again, using back-chaining and beginning at the end. Sometimes you might find it beneficial to backchain a sequence or maneuver stride by stride, starting just one step from the end ("the end" being where your dog gets his reward, either a remote reward or a reward that is thrown or delivered by your hand). Then add one stride at a time.

Contrasts

The obstacles themselves can't tell your dog which way to go: He needs to learn to pay attention to your handling to know which path to choose. For that reason, training handling relies a lot on contrasts to develop your dog's ability to discriminate between your handling cues. First you practice one handling maneuver (for example, going straight). Then you practice another handling maneuver (for example, a regular turn). Then you contrast the two of them by varying between them in the same setup, generously rewarding your dog for following your handling. This way your dog will learn to truly cue off your handling maneuvers.

Make sure the contrasts are black and white. If your dog makes a mistake and chooses the wrong path, consider how you would handle the sequence if you *wanted* him to take the "wrong" path. Have you really made the contrast black and white? Usually when a dog misinterprets handling, it's because the contrast between the handling cues isn't stark enough.

Handling mistakes

You need to know what to do the second something goes wrong; otherwise you risk subjecting your dog to weirdness (such as odd handling that has nothing to do with your chosen system, or simply falling to pieces, like a bad soufflé). You can't reverse time anyway, and telling your dog he made a mistake doesn't help him. What he needs to know is where to go next so that he can earn some rewards!

When a mistake occurs, you have choices about how to carry on:

- Our preferred option is that you just continue handling your dog as seamlessly as possible. This means not only that you continue directing him, but that you continue to do so with focus and intensity—as if nothing happened. Then you'll get the opportunity to reward something he actually gets right.
- If you can't find a way to just continue, or if you for some reason really want to start over right away, handle your dog so that he ends up with you. You can then transport him to a new starting point for another go.

"Wahoo! See me RUN!" Enthusiasm, confidence and speed, all in one.

Yes, this means rewarding your dog for following your handling after a mistake. Does this risk reinforcing the mistake? Possibly. But you don't reward your dog *as* the wrong behavior happens—you reward him for following your handling *after* the mistake. You cannot stop handling since your dog has nowhere to go (*never ever* leave your dog in limbo on the agility course!), and since your dog follows your handling you should reinforce that. But you can always save the best rewards for the times when he actually gets the tricky part right.

We really encourage you to embrace your and your dog's mistakes! Mistakes are information about what the two of you haven't mastered yet, and that's information that *you* need to get, not your dog. You're the trainer! If the same mistake occurs over and over, you need to figure out how to set up for success so that you get the chance to lavishly reward the correct behavior.

Walk the course

When working on sequences, naturally you need to "walk the course" so you know your job before you bring out your dog. Here is a brief check list of what your course walk should include:

- Find your dog's path (straight ahead, turns of various degrees).
- Find your own path.
- Plan which handling maneuvers to use.
- Decide where and how to start (both your dog's starting position, and your own).
- Decide where and how to reward.
- Walk the sequence, getting a feel for exactly what to do, and where and when to do it.
- Test-run the sequence, performing everything just as if you had your dog with you.
- Go through it in your head right before actually running the sequence with your dog.

Practicing with a human "dog" is often very beneficial.

And yes, all this holds true even if "the course" is only a one-obstacle sequence! To set up your dog for success you need to plan exactly what to do when and where, and you need to remember that plan so that you can execute it.

There are quite a few tricks to help you memorize your plan:
- *Splitting:* Splitting the sequence into sections resembles what you do all the time with behaviors you want to train. Simply divide the sequence into more manageable sections.

- *Set points:* Set points help you keep on track. Look for where you need to be when your dog is at a certain spot. For example, "When my dog takes off at obstacle X, I should be next to jump Y."
- *Back-chaining:* Back-chaining your own walking of the sequence is tremendously helpful. Not only will you avoid the crowds at the beginning of the sequence (if, for example, you're training with other people or if you're walking a course at a competition), but you'll make your job a lot easier. By splitting the course into parts and beginning your actual walk-through with the last part, adding on the second to last part, and so on, you'll always be working toward something that you know better. When you begin to tire at the end of your run, you'll be in the parts that you've walked the most, which will help you keep on top of your game.
- *Virtual course walking (visualizing your run):* Close your eyes and imagine your actual run—either standing still and using your mind's eye, or moving around and going through all your motions. This will help you make sure that it's all in there. Don't forget to include your way to the start line and from the finish line. If you get stuck somewhere in your virtual course walk, you need to prepare some more before you bring your dog out—but when you nail it, you know you're ready to run! Visualizing has proven to be extremely effective. It takes some practice, but when done well it's as if you've already had your run when you finally get to the start line.

The handler's shoulder direction at takeoff tells the dog which reward to go for. If the handler faces south, the dog goes south!

Straight ahead and regular turns

While learning the various jumps and tunnels, your dog has experienced both going straight ahead and doing regular turns after the obstacles. In this section he'll learn to truly cue off your handling to know where to go.

What should straight ahead and a regular turn look like?

The direction of your shoulders when your dog is at takeoff at an obstacle tells him where to continue after that obstacle:

Straight ahead means your dog will continue in the direction he had at takeoff. You simply keep pointing your shoulders in that direction, toward the next obstacle, and move ahead yourself.

A **regular turn** requires your dog to turn to get to the next obstacle. When your dog is at takeoff, you turn your shoulders toward the next obstacle to cue your dog to turn with you in that direction.

Going straight (left) and turning (right). Note the handler's shoulders and general direction.

Looking at the handler (left) won't conjure the start cue, but looking straight ahead (right) will.

How can you train straight lines?

When practicing straight lines:

- Always set up your dog so that he has a perfectly straight line from start to finish.
- Position yourself so that your path, too, is straight.
- Give your start cue while your dog is looking ahead.
- Make sure the reward appears ahead of your dog, along the straight line, so that he keeps going straight all the way to his reward. You can, of course, use a remote reward to get the behavior of running straight, but you should also work with thrown toys to ensure that your dog really cues off your straight-ahead handling.
- Vary the number of obstacles and which obstacles you use. When using jumps you can also vary their angle. As long as your dog's path goes straight, it's a straight line! Employ back-chaining if you need to, starting with just the final obstacle and gradually adding more.
- Vary your position when your dog starts (parallel to him, a little bit ahead, or further ahead), your speed (running hard or moving a bit slower), and your lateral distance. Be rigorous about your handling, though—your shoulders must point straight ahead, and your forward momentum must carry forward all the way until your dog has reached his reward.
- Also vary the distractions (dummy obstacles and/or dummy rewards) that appear to the sides of the straight line.

By starting at a lateral distance, the handler can prepare for what's next on course. Remember: The handler's job is to show the way; the dog's job is to perform the obstacles and to follow the handling.

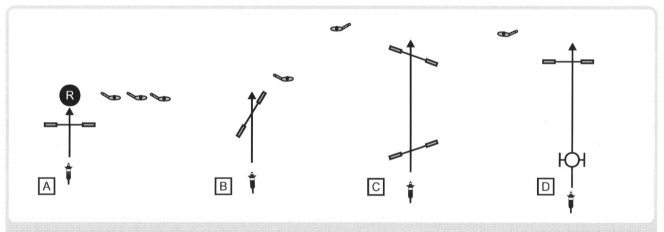

Here are some sequences to start teaching your dog to follow your handling straight ahead even when you're farther ahead at a lateral distance. Leave your dog in a start-line stay, position yourself beyond the last obstacle, and reward along the straight line, after the last obstacle. You can stand still throughout—your dog should still run along the straight line, because your shoulders are pointing that way and your shoulder plane is ahead of him. To make it really easy you can use a remote reward, positioned parallel to you after the last obstacle (as in A). However, to ensure that your dog really is aiming for the actual obstacles, it's best to reward with a thrown toy that appears as a surprise after the last obstacle. Start with easy sequences and successively increase the difficulty, for example, by varying the lateral distance (A), the angle (B), the number of obstacles (C), and the obstacles involved (D).

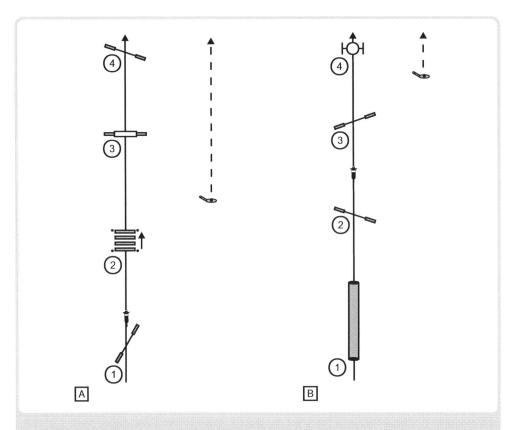

Note that in situations where your dog should blast past you, you need to move ahead when he approaches your shoulder plane (or, more precisely, when he approaches the last obstacle before reaching your shoulder plane—that's when he needs to know if he should prepare for turning or for continuing straight ahead).

A. If you stand still after jump #2 when your dog starts, start moving at the latest when he approaches #2

B. Similarly, if you stand still after jump #3, you need to move ahead at latest when your dog approaches #3.

AVOID LAYERING

To keep it simple for both dog and handler and to avoid confusion with other handling maneuvers (especially the serpentine, described on page 338), we opt to avoid "layering" (running with obstacles between the handler and the dog) in our basic handling. So when you add dummy rewards and dummy obstacles, make sure your path runs next to your dog's path, to the "inside" of the distractions.

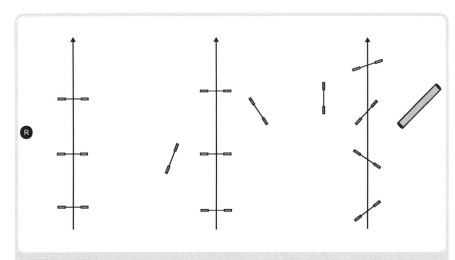

To practice distractions, you can add dummy rewards (the black "R") and/or dummy obstacles along either side of the straight-line corridor.

The first dog/handler shows how you send your dog toward jump #1 by pointing your shoulders toward it. The second dog/handler shows the regular turn: At takeoff, you rotate your shoulders away from your dog, toward jump #2, and start moving toward it.

How can you train regular turns?

When practicing regular turns:

- Stay out of your dog's way.
- As your dog takes off, aim your shoulders exactly in the direction you want your dog to go—no turning into him, and no over-rotating.
- Place your rewards precisely—in the direction your regular turn implies.
- Vary your speed and your position so that you can sprint ahead or hang back, or run close to your dog or far out laterally.
- Vary the degree of the regular turn and also vary with straight-ahead training.
- Also proof whether your dog can follow your shoulders in a turn, even if there are temptations (dummy rewards or obstacles) farther ahead.

Practice regular turns after all kinds of obstacles. Tunnels might deserve some special attention: Since your dog's vision is limited while he's in the tunnel (especially if the tunnel is curved), tunnels are one place where a verbal cue can be valuable from early on in the training, in addition to the handler's movement. We usually opt to have "continue straight ahead" as the default behavior, and to use the dog's name as a cue to "turn toward handler" at the exit.

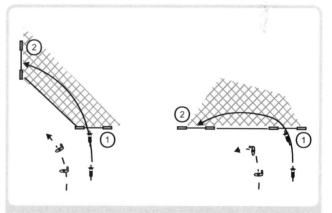

At takeoff, the dog notices where the handler's shoulders are pointing. Either a reward appears in that direction, or the dog continues toward the next obstacle.

Stay out of your dog's space (marked gray here; see also page 274) so that you make it possible for him to find the shortest path between the obstacles.

At tunnels (and other "long" obstacles) it can be helpful to imagine two jumps instead—one at the entry, and one at the exit. As your dog enters the tunnel, you point your shoulders toward the exit—and as he approaches the exit, you point your shoulders in the direction he should continue.

A verbal cue for "turn toward me," in combination with the handler's movements, tells the dog to turn at the tunnel exit.

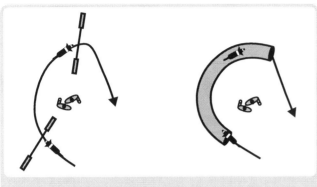

Regular turn at the long jump

REGULAR TURN WHEN TAKING AN OBSTACLE "FROM BEHIND"

Usually, you should turn your shoulders toward the next obstacle as your dog takes off. An exception is when you're directing your dog to take the obstacle "from behind" (as to jump #2 in these diagrams). In that case, you need to first send your dog past the plane of the jump, and then turn your shoulders to tell him to take it. You have already practiced this handling some when working with angles at jump wings (pages 270–271).

A: From jump #1 and to the plane of jump #2 (the dotted line) is a straight line, so as your dog takes off at jump #1, you keep pointing your shoulders straight ahead. When your dog passes the plane of jump #2, you rotate your shoulders to the right, which tells your dog to take the jump. As he takes off, he has a straight line to jump #3.

B: To get from jump #1 to the plane of jump #2, your dog needs to turn right, so as your dog takes off at jump #1, you rotate your shoulders in that direction. When your dog passes the plane of jump #2 you turn your shoulders right again, telling your dog to take the jump. He again needs to turn right to get to jump #3, so you perform yet another regular turn to the right as he takes off at jump #2.

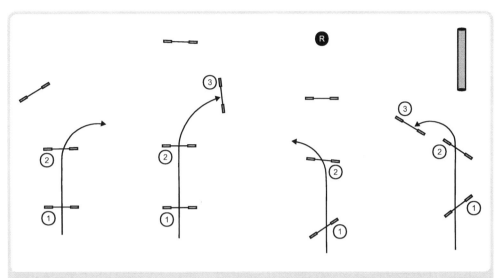

Regular turns with various distractions—when your dog gets to takeoff at jump #2, turn your shoulders and start moving in the new direction. Handle as if the distraction wasn't there (don't look at it or do anything differently), and lavishly reward your dog for following you. In the beginning you can place the distraction far away and/or a bit out to the side. Then gradually increase the difficulty by bringing the distraction closer and closer.

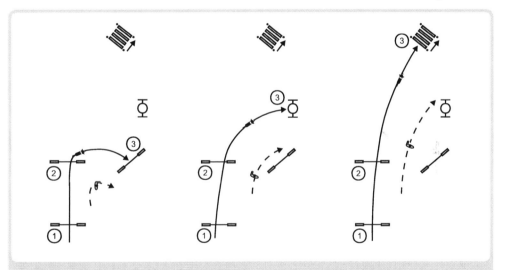

Sometimes there'll be several obstacles to choose from, each requiring a regular turn. So how will your dog then know which to aim for? To some extent he'll get that information from the degree of your shoulder rotation. But he'll also cue off your general direction—so make sure to distinctly aim for the correct obstacle yourself.

SOME FREQUENT REGULAR TURN SEQUENCES: 90°, 180°, AND 270° TURNS

You often encounter 90°, 180°, and 270° turns on courses. Handle them as regular turns: keep your dog on the outside, rotate your shoulders in the direction your dog should go, and use the near arm!

Sometimes you'll want your dog to come in between obstacles. Since we want the regular turn to mean "take the obstacle in the 90°/180°/270° turn," we do *not* use a regular turn to tell the dog to come in between obstacles. Instead, we use a *threadle* in these situations (you'll learn about threadles on page 332). This is a rule we follow for the sake of clarity, to make it as easy as possible for dog and handler alike to separate situations that otherwise might look very similar.

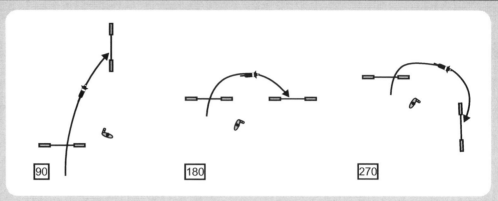

Some common regular turns: 90° turn, 180° turn, 270° turn.

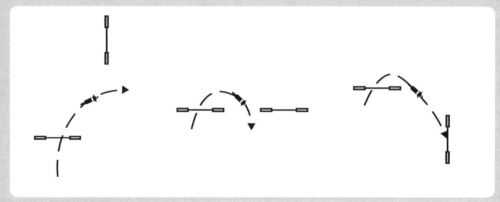

What we don't do with a regular turn! You should not use a regular turn to get your dog to come in between the obstacles, as the dotted paths show. Instead, use a threadle.

Contrast straight ahead and regular turns

Work a lot on straight ahead, regular turns, and variations between the two, constantly paying close attention to the direction of your shoulders (toward the next obstacle), the timing of your rotation in the regular turn (just as your dog reaches takeoff), and the placement of your rewards (in accordance with your handling, along your dog's path). Also remember to vary your own position so that you can be close or far away, ahead or behind your dog.

It's vital that you know whether your dog is going straight or turning after each obstacle—both for your straight lines/regular turns, and for the other maneuvers to come. Look through these sequences and test your understanding!

GOING STRAIGHT OR TURNING?

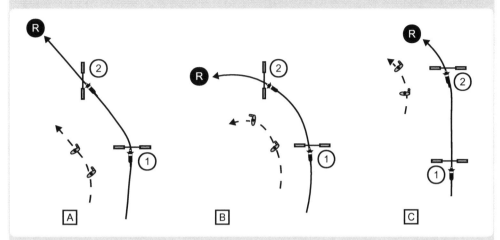

First an easy one. Where are the straight lines, and where are the left turns? Does the dog need to turn between jumps #1 and #2 in these sequences, or is he going straight? And, what about between jump #2 and the reward?

Answer:
A. Left turn from jump #1 to jump #2, straight ahead after jump #2.
B. Left turn from jump #1 to jump #2, left turn after jump #2.
C. Straight ahead from jump #1 to jump #2, left turn after jump #2.)

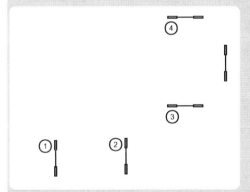

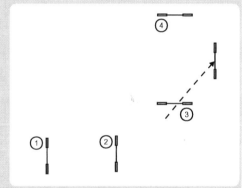

In this sequence there's a straight line between jump #1 to jump #2 and a left turn from jump #2 to jump #3. But what about from jump #3 to jump #4? Is that a straight line?

Answer: #3 to #4 is a left turn, not a straight line. When your dog has jumped #2 and his nose points toward #3, he has a straight line toward the dummy jump on the right. So to get to #4 you have to cue him to turn left (by rotating your shoulders toward #4) as he takes off at #3.

GOING STRAIGHT OR TURNING?

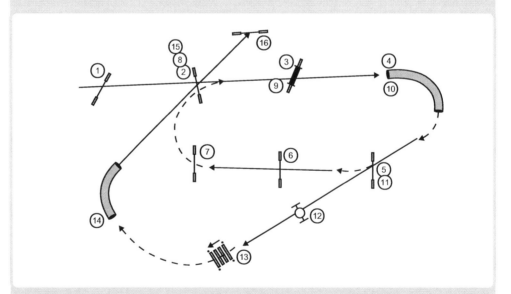

Follow the dog's path through this course. Between which obstacles does he have straight lines?

Answer: *The straight lines (shown with solid lines) are at: The beginning #1 through #4 (just position your dog correctly at the start line, so that he really has that straight line straight ahead of him). #6 to #7, #9 to #10, #11 to #12 to #13, and #14 to #16 (although the dog turns in the curved tunnels). The turns (shown with dotted lines) are at: #4 to #5, #5 to #6, #7 to #8, #8 to #9, #10 to #11, and #13 to #14. These all require your dog to turn (as opposed to going straight). You can test this—just see where your dog would end up if he didn't turn but kept going straight after #4, #5, #7, #8, #10, and #13!*

Work with your dog on contrasts between going straight and turning. As your dog approaches each obstacle, he'll cue off your general direction and position to get a first clue about where he's going next. As he takes off, he'll cue off the direction of your shoulders to get precise information.

Remember to be clear about where you're going after each obstacle—even after the last obstacle. Handle *as if* there were more obstacles to come, and place your reward in alignment with your handling. You can set out remote rewards if you like—both as distracting dummy rewards and as actual rewards.

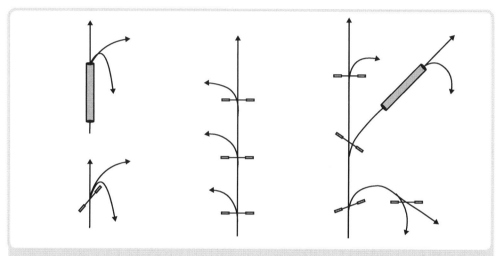

Set up sequences where you can vary between going straight and turning, and reward your dog lavishly for following your handling. It's a good idea to videotape your training or have a friend watching you carefully, to check your timing and the direction of your shoulders.

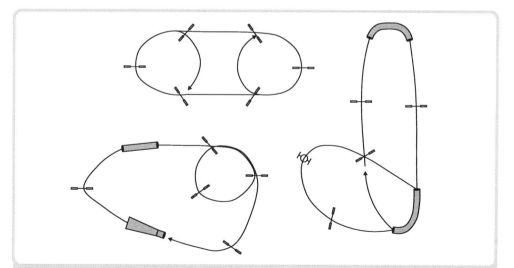

Never-ending sequences are valuable since you can begin wherever you want, reward whenever you want, and always keep going if something goes wrong. You can build a lot of fun, flowing sequences using just straight ahead and regular turns. Here are just a few examples! If you start in left-side handling you stay in left-side handling throughout (and vice versa), and all you really need to focus on is to point your shoulders toward the next obstacle when your dog reaches takeoff. And to reward along his intended path, of course.

Front cross

The front cross is one way to switch sides, from right-side handling to left-side handling or vice versa. (We present rear crosses, the other way we use to switch sides, on page 320). The front cross also turns your dog in your direction after an obstacle (if he is in right-side handling, he'll turn left)—just as a regular turn does.

Crossing in front

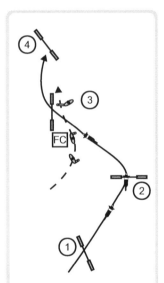

Front cross between #2 and #3

What should the front cross look like?

To explain the front cross clearly, let's begin with an example:

The jump sequence starts with right-side handling (dog on handler's right), and the dog's path looks like this:

1. Straight ahead #1 to #2
2. Left turn #2 to #3
3. Right turn #3 to #4

The handler needs to switch sides between jumps #2 and #3, and chooses to do so with a front cross. The front cross cues the dog to turn left after jump #2 and also switches the dog from right-side handling to left-side handling, so the dog is on the handler's left side for jump #3.

The front cross looks like this:

1. While your dog approaches the obstacle before the front cross (in this case, jump #2), you keep pointing your shoulders toward jump #2. This tells your dog to take that obstacle.
2. As your dog takes off at jump #2, you begin your front cross: Rotate your shoulders toward your dog, raise your outer (left) arm, and simultaneously start moving to the far wing of the next jump. *This tells your dog to turn toward you as he lands.*
3. You complete your front cross so that you end up by the far wing of jump #3, facing the new direction. *This tells your dog to speed past you, on your new outside, and take the next obstacle.*

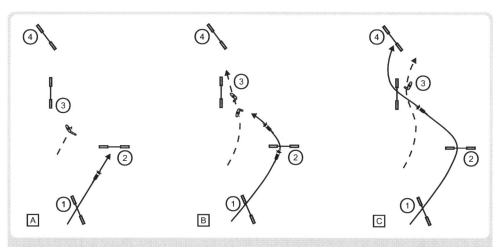

These diagrams show the front cross step by step. The handler sends the dog to jump #2 (A), crosses in front while moving toward #3 (B), and ends up by the far wing, sending the dog to #3 (C).

THREE-STEP REMINDER

Here are the details of your front-cross footwork (for more information, see "Handling maneuvers on the flat", page 250):

Before takeoff: Foot No. 0 (the foot nearest the dog, the right foot in this sequence) takes the last step before the front cross. Your shoulders are pointing toward the first jump.

At takeoff: Foot No. 1 (the foot farthest from the dog, here the left foot). The first step of the front cross—the "toe in" step, where you rotate your shoulders toward your dog while stepping in the direction of the next (#3) jump. Simultaneously, you switch arms.

Then: Foot No. 2 (here the right foot). The "toe out" step, where you step backward, continuing toward the far wing of the next jump.

Finally: Foot No. 3 (the foot that ends up nearest to your dog, here the left foot). The final step of the front cross, stepping to the wing. Your shoulders are now pointing toward jump #3.

How can you train front crosses?

You and your dog are already skilled in performing front crosses on the flat, so in this chapter we'll present an array of front-cross sequences where you get to practice your front crosses with obstacles.

To execute a successful front cross:

- Your dog has to be skilled at aiming for and performing obstacles at a distance from you. If you have to babysit him at each and every obstacle, you can't get to the correct front-cross position. So parallel to working on your front crosses, you should also continually reward your dog for aiming ahead and taking obstacles independently of you.
- Begin your front cross as your dog takes off—not earlier! Send your dog to the obstacle as usual (pointing your shoulders in the direction of the obstacle and using your nearest arm) and begin your front cross when he reaches the takeoff point. If you start your front cross early, you'll either pull your dog away from the obstacle (if that happens, reward your dog for following your handling!), or inadvertently teach him not to respond immediately to your front-cross cues.

WHAT IF I CAN'T MAKE IT TO THE FRONT CROSS?

When you perform a front cross you have to be closer to the next obstacle than your dog is. What if it feels as though you can't make it to the correct position?

• Go for it! If you just set your mind to it, you'll get much farther than you'd ever imagine.
• Check that you are truly heading straight for the farthest wing of the next jump. If you're dancing around elsewhere, you'll not only confuse your dog, but you'll also have to take many more steps.
• Check your footwork: Are you using the three-foot pattern? That is absolutely the fastest way to move through the front cross.
• Are you babysitting your dog at the previous obstacle? Let him work independently so that you can take a shortcut. If he isn't skilled enough yet, keep working on getting him to drive ahead at the obstacles, with you at a lateral distance, before involving front crosses.
• If you can't make it to the front cross, you can always switch sides with a rear cross instead. Don't sacrifice your dog's understanding of the front cross by performing it poorly or in the wrong place.

• Make sure you're close enough to the next obstacle when you begin your front cross. When your dog is at takeoff and you begin your front cross, you should be within three steps of the next obstacle. That way you'll stay out of your dog's way, and your position through the front cross clearly indicates which obstacle you're headed toward next. Practically, this often means that you have to be quite far away from your dog as he approaches the obstacle preceding the front cross.
• Throughout your front cross, aim for the farthest wing of the next jump (so that you don't pirouette away in any other direction).

First, work with just one obstacle and practice using a front cross to turn your dog in your direction after the obstacle. When practicing on one jump, it helps to imagine a second one after the front cross, so that you know where you're heading with your front cross and in which direction you should place the reward. And to vary the exercise, you can easily move your imaginary jump around.

Begin your front cross as your dog takes off, finish your front cross (so that you've switched sides and are facing the new direction), and reward your dog as he catches up with you. When rewarding, you'll be facing in the direction you would be going next if you were continuing. Either deliver the reward from your hand, or throw it ahead in the new direction.

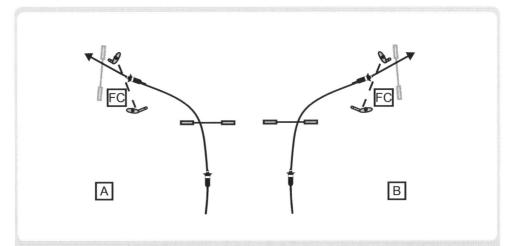

Front cross training with one jump allows you to practice your timing, your position, and your footwork. It also teaches your dog that front crosses mean "turn in your direction" on obstacles as well as on the flat. Of course you practice both changes from right to left (A) and from left to right (B).

The second, gray "jump" in these diagrams is just an imaginary jump, drawn to show where the handler is aiming to go next. The two dog and handler positions show where the dog and the handler are right before and right after the execution of the front cross.

When you and your dog are confident executing front crosses at one obstacle (using an imaginary jump to aim for), add an actual obstacle to send your dog to after the front cross. Just remember, you should be within three steps of the next obstacle when your dog is at takeoff. The more independently your dog can work on the obstacles *before* the front cross, the easier it will be for you to get to the right position.

Vary the angles and distances between the obstacles, vary the obstacles, and eventually add more obstacles to the sequence both before and after the front cross.

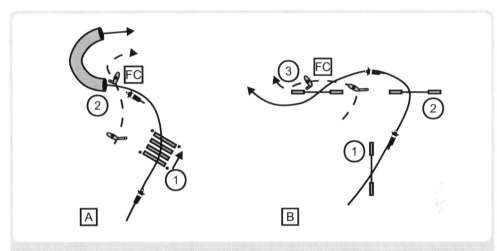

The variations are endless. Here are a few examples.

A: Cross in front as your dog takes off at the long jump. Aim for the tunnel!

B: Lead out a bit, and cross in front as your dog takes off at jump #2. On your third step you should be by the far wing of jump #3!

Front crosses with distractions

Test that your dog understands to turn toward you and come up on your new outside when you do a front cross, even if that means turning away from a dummy reward or a dummy obstacle. As always, handle as if the distraction wasn't there, and reward lavishly when your dog follows your handling.

With your front cross you can steer your dog through really narrow gaps—he "can't" take the off-course obstacle since that would mean ignoring your front cross and going behind your back, totally contradicting the direction of your shoulders.

Whenever you execute a front cross, your dog turns toward you and hurries to catch up!

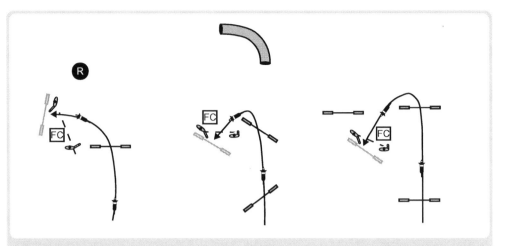

Here are some examples of front crosses with distractions. The imaginary jump at the end in the diagrams is merely to help you know where you are going with your front cross. The diagrams show where the dog and the handler are right before and right after the execution of the front cross. Begin your front cross when your dog is at takeoff. Reward right away!

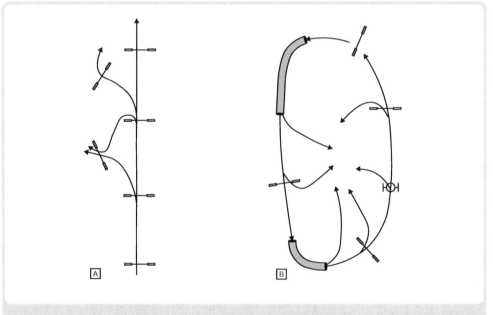

Here are two set-ups we often use for training front crosses—in this case, for starting with your dog on your right. Remember to mirror the setups!

A. Try out the various paths—three different front crosses, plus going straight ahead. For the front crosses, walk the course carefully to figure out where you need to be when your dog is at takeoff at the previous obstacle so you can reach the next wing with your three front-cross steps.

B. In the speed circle you can turn into the middle with a front cross at any obstacle. Reward as your dog comes up to your new outside. You can also choose to place a remote reward in the middle and aim for it with your front cross. Or you can add one (or several) jumps in the middle. Don't always turn into the middle, though—there's always the option of simply rewarding along the circle path.

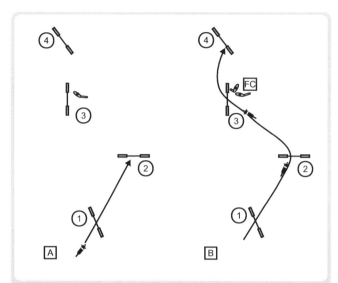

This is an example of what a lead-out pivot looks like:

A. Position your dog at the start line so that he has a straight line between jumps #1 and #2. Position yourself by the far wing of jump #3, facing the direction your dog should go over jumps #1 and #2 and looking at your dog over your shoulder. Give your start cue while your dog looks ahead, toward jumps #1 and #2, and keep your shoulders pointing in the direction your dog should go.

B. As your dog takes off at jump #2, begin your front cross. Pivot toward your dog, switching arms and doing all three steps "on the spot" so that you end up facing the wing. When you've completed your front cross, your dog will be on your left side, heading for jump #3.

Front cross in the start: "lead-out pivot"

If you're doing a front cross early on in a course, you can leave your dog at the start line and walk out to the front-cross position (close to the farthest wing) right away. The principle of this so-called "lead-out pivot" is just the same as in any front cross; the only difference is that you stand still as your dog starts and do the full front cross (all three steps) by pivoting on the spot.

Lead out pivot practice—here, the handler is standing in the lead out pivot position, ready to perform the front cross as the dog takes off.

Front cross on the outside of a 270°-turn

Sometimes you may want to perform a front cross at an obstacle that your dog takes "from behind," for example, on the outside of a 270° turn. In such cases, wait to begin the front cross until your dog is on the correct side of the next obstacle.

This is how you do it:

1. To send your dog past the plane of the jump, go around the wing yourself. This tells your dog to stay on your outside and will get him to the correct side of the obstacle.
2. As your dog passes the plane of the jump, begin your front cross. This tells your dog to turn toward you.
3. Complete the front cross, ending up by the far wing of the jump. This tells your dog to take the jump.

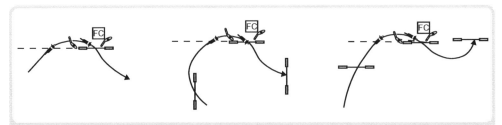

In these diagrams you can see where the dog and handler are right before and right after the front cross.

These maneuvers are easier than they look. Since your dog is skilled at working independently, you can be at a distance when he takes the first jump—this gives you a head start. And since your dog is skilled at keeping to your outside, you can run ahead around the jump while relying on your dog to keep up with you and not sneak behind your back. Then, as you and your dog are both on the correct side of the jump, you execute your front cross and your dog takes the jump.

Rear cross

The front cross is one way to switch sides; the rear cross is the other. In the rear cross, you send your dog ahead to an obstacle and switch sides behind his tail as he takes off. In our handling system, we only cross behind when the dog is taking off at an obstacle, and the dog then turns with the handler as he lands.

Crossing behind

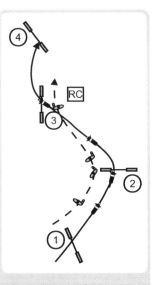

Rear cross at #3

What should the rear cross look like?

Here is the jump sequence you've seen before but executed then with a front cross (page 314). This time, we'll explain how to switch sides with a rear cross. The dog's path remains the same:

1. Straight ahead #1 to #2
2. Left turn #2 to #3
3. Right turn #3 to #4

The handler needs to switch sides between jumps #2 and #3, and now chooses to do so with a rear cross. The rear cross will switch the dog from right-side handling to left-side handling as the dog takes jump #3.

The rear cross looks like this:

1. As your dog takes off at the obstacle before the rear cross (in this case, jump #2), you point your shoulders toward the obstacle where you plan to execute your rear cross. *This tells your dog to aim for that obstacle.*

2. As soon as your dog aims for jump #3, you prepare for the rear cross by heading to the right (far) wing of jump #3, running along the diagonal line (you'll be behind your dog, still with him in right-side handling, but your converging on his path will push him toward the farther wing and prepare him for the upcoming rear cross). This is the tricky part of the rear cross: Dare to run that diagonal!. *This tells your dog to yield slightly while running ahead, so that he jumps close to the farthest wing.*

3. As your dog takes off at jump #3, you cross behind his tail, thus switching to left-side handling, and turn your shoulders toward jump #4. *This tells your dog to turn his head and follow the direction of your shoulders.*

Your change of arms isn't significant to your dog in the rear cross; you just use the nearest arm as usual, switching arms as you switch sides behind him.

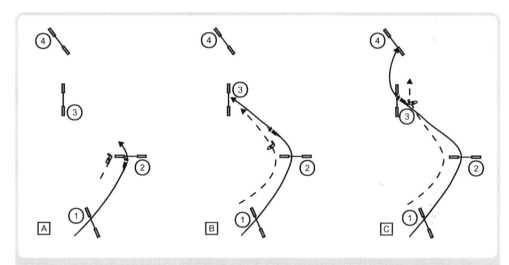

These diagrams show the rear cross step by step.

A. As the dog takes off at #2, the handler points her shoulders toward #3.

B. As soon as the dog's nose is pointing toward #3, the handler runs the diagonal toward the far wing.

C. As the dog takes off at #3, the handler crosses behind and turns her shoulders toward #4.

How can you train rear crosses?

You've practiced rear crosses with your dog sitting or standing still, so he already knows to turn his head when (and only when) you step behind him. In this section you'll practice your rear crosses at obstacles.

To execute a successful rear cross:

- Your dog has to be skilled at aiming ahead since rear crosses require him to drive past you and take obstacles ahead of you so that you can cross behind his tail as he takes off.

- You have to be behind your dog on course—in other words, you have to hang back so that your dog gets to the obstacle you'll be crossing behind.
- You need to get as close as you can to the previous obstacle (avoid lateral distance). This will put you behind your dog and make it possible for you to run the diagonal.
- As soon as your dog starts aiming for the obstacle you'll be crossing behind, head for the farthest wing and run along the diagonal, "pushing" your dog's path toward the far end of the obstacle. Again, your dog must be truly skilled at driving ahead and taking obstacles independently of you.
- As your dog takes off, cross behind his back, so as he lands, you have already switched sides. To continue you simply aim your shoulders wherever you're going next.

Since your dog is already skilled at following your shoulders and aiming ahead at obstacles, as well as turning his head when you cross behind him on the flat, one way to introduce the rear cross at obstacles is to simply go out and do it! Many dogs will get it right on the first try.

Naturally, you can also break down the rear-cross training into smaller pieces. In this case, we suggest working close to the rear-cross jump first—for example, like this:

Step 1: Send to the jump and cross behind, using *Race to reward*.
Step 2: Send to the jump and cross behind, using *Aim for it*.
Step 3: Add obstacles after the rear cross, exiting in various directions.
Step 4: Add obstacles before the rear cross, approaching from various directions.

Working on the rear cross using Race to reward. *Here the handler releases the dog at takeoff and crosses behind right away.*

Step 1: Send to the jump and cross behind, using *Race to reward*

We use *Race to reward* with a spontaneous start to introduce rear crosses at obstacles. The remote reward will function as a lure in the beginning, ensuring that your dog takes the right path and allowing you to focus totally on getting your part of the job right. And with the spontaneous start your dog will aim ahead from you while you're both moving, resembling the finished picture.

Set out the remote reward at an angle after the jump, creating the turn with the reward (so if you start with your dog in right-side handling, the remote reward should be a bit to the right of the jump).

In the first exercise you'll release your dog very close to the jump that you'll cross behind. This means that your dog will be at takeoff right away, so you'll simply cross behind him right after releasing him, aiming your shoulders toward the remote reward.

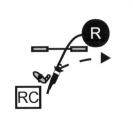

Point your shoulders at the far wing and release your dog. Cross right away as he takes off, and point your shoulders toward the reward.

Exercise 58: The first rear crosses (releasing your dog at takeoff and crossing right away)

In this example you'll begin with your dog on your right.

1. Set out a remote reward at an angle, creating a right turn after the jump.
2. Transport your dog to a starting point on your right, just one stride away from the jump, facing the far (right) end of the jump.
3. Point your shoulders at the far (right) wing, and release your dog.
4. As your dog takes off, cross behind him and point your shoulders toward the reward.
5. Your dog reaches his reward.

Then mirror the exercise, switching from left-side handling to right-side handling with your rear cross.

Suggested tag points:

- End transport one stride from the jump
- Aim shoulders at far wing
- Cross behind at takeoff

Next, increase the distance to the jump. Just as in the previous exercise, your dog's nose is already pointing toward the correct obstacle when you release him. But now you need to prepare for the rear cross by heading for the far wing, running the diagonal line. Your moving along the diagonal pushes your dog's path very close to the far wing and prepares for the rear cross. When your dog reaches takeoff, you cross behind him and aim your shoulders toward the remote reward.

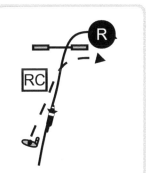

Point your shoulders at the far wing and release your dog. As your dog drives toward the jump, run the diagonal towards the far wing. As your dog takes off, cross behind him and point your shoulders toward the reward.

Exercise 59: Increase the distance to the jump (running the diagonal)

In this example you'll begin with your dog on your right.

1. Set out a remote reward at an angle, creating a right turn after the jump.
2. Transport your dog to a starting point on your right, a few strides away from the jump, facing the far (right) end of the jump.
3. Point your shoulders at the far (right) wing, and release your dog.
4. Your dog heads for the jump.
5. While your dog approaches the jump, run the diagonal toward the right wing (you'll almost crowd your dog but stay slightly behind him).
6. As your dog takes off, cross behind him and point your shoulders toward the reward.
7. Your dog reaches his reward.

Then mirror the exercise, switching from left-side handling to right-side handling with your rear cross.

Suggested tag points:

- Run the diagonal!
- Point your shoulders toward the reward at take off

Dare to really run the diagonal! Your job is to head for the far wing; your dog's job is to stay ahead of you and take the jump.

Expand the exercise by moving the remote reward farther out to the side, teaching your dog to really head for the obstacle first rather than taking the shortcut to the reward. Make sure you stay consistent in your handling, running the diagonal even though it might feel as if you're about to push your dog off from the jump! Have your helper remove the reward if your dog misses the jump, and go back to a shorter distance or an easier placement of the remote reward if you need to.

You can also progress in your training by angling the jump or changing to another obstacle. Just remember to alter one thing at a time. And since you're still starting your dog with his nose pointing toward the correct obstacle, he already knows which obstacle to take. Your job is simply to release him, run the diagonal, and cross behind at takeoff.

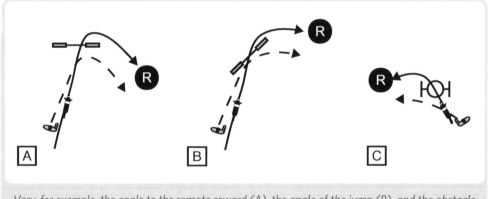

Vary, for example, the angle to the remote reward (A), the angle of the jump (B), and the obstacle you cross behind (C).

Step 2: Send to the jump and cross behind, using *Aim for it*

Work through the same process without the remote reward—either reward with a thrown toy, or reward from your hand after the turn. Decide in advance where your dog's path should go after the jump so that you handle and deliver the reward accordingly.

First, start close to the jump with a spontaneous start: Release your dog, cross behind as he takes off, and point your shoulders toward where the reward will show up.

Gradually add more distance to the jump, and run the diagonal. Remember, dare to push it on the diagonal! Vary the angle of the jump, and vary with other obstacles, but make sure your dog can go straight to the obstacle from where you release him. He should already be aiming for the correct obstacle when he starts, and you should be running the diagonal right away.

Contrast your rear crosses with going straight ahead or doing regular turns or front crosses, to ensure that your dog (and you) can differentiate the maneuvers. Working with contrasts helps you stay consistent in your handling and keeps your dog from beginning to anticipate the rear cross. Remember: Rear crosses happen only as you step behind your dog at takeoff after running the diagonal.

Dare to run the diagonal!

Step 3: Add obstacles after the rear cross, exiting in various directions

Now it's time to add obstacles *after* the rear-cross obstacle, varying the path you take. As usual, you turn your shoulders in the direction you're going next as you cross behind. But now, instead of getting to his reward, your dog will get to another obstacle.

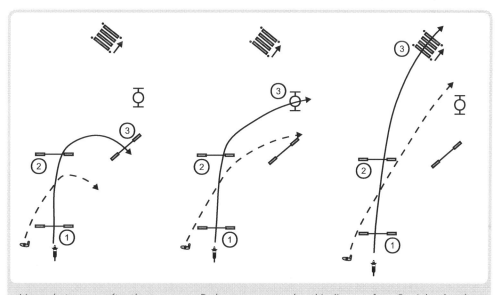

Vary what comes after the rear cross. Perhaps you remember this diagram from Straight ahead or regular turn (page 309)? If you start in left-side handling, it's a regular turn between #2 and #3, but here you start in right-side handling and cross behind at #2. Aim for the obstacle you want your dog to take!

Step 4: Add obstacles before the rear cross, approaching from various directions

Finally, it's time to add obstacles *before* the rear cross, coming to the rear cross from various paths. Now your dog doesn't always have a straight line to the rear-cross jump—so you'll first have to give him information about which obstacle to take by pointing your shoulders toward it. As soon as his nose is pointing toward the correct obstacle, you continue as usual: running the diagonal, and crossing behind at takeoff.

This means you'll do the whole "1-2-3" of the rear cross:

1. Point your shoulders toward the obstacle you plan to cross behind, until your dog's nose is pointing toward it.
2. Aim your shoulders at the far wing and run the diagonal.
3. Cross behind as your dog takes off, turning your shoulders in the direction your dog should go next.

When coming in to the rear cross from a turn, your dog really gets to show off his drive toward obstacles.

THE FINER DETAILS OF WHERE TO POINT YOUR SHOULDERS

At take-off at the previous obstacle, you'll point your shoulders at the obstacle you'll be crossing behind. That's how your dog knows to take that obstacle. To prepare properly for the rear cross, however, you should also be sending your dog to the correct part of the obstacle you'll cross behind! This is especially relevant at jumps, where there is a long bar to jump over: When you plan to cross behind, you should send your dog directly to the far end of the bar by pointing your shoulders at the middle of the jump.

Note: This distinction only concerns the moment during which you tell your dog which obstacle is next. As soon as he's aiming for the correct obstacle (in other words, as soon as his nose is pointing toward it), you turn your shoulders toward the far wing/far edge as usual, running the diagonal and crossing behind at take-off.

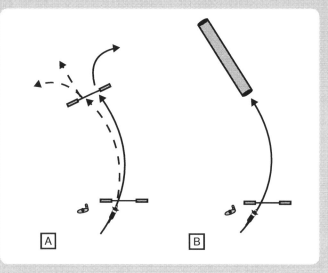

A

B

A: When you plan to perform a rear cross, you want your dog to run the solid line, aiming for the far (right) end of the jump. Thus you should send your dog to the jump by pointing your shoulders toward the middle of the bar. (To grasp the contrast, it helps to think of what you would do if you wanted your dog to run the dotted line, as you would if you were continuing straight ahead or turning left. Then you would point your shoulders at the near (left) wing as your dog takes off at the previous obstacle, and your dog would aim for the near (left) end of the bar.

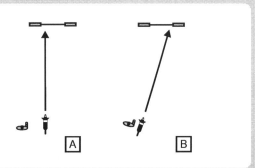

A

B

A: If the handler points her shoulders at the nearest wing, the dog will jump the bar close to the near wing.

B: If the handler points her shoulders at the middle of the jump, the dog will jump the bar close to the far wing.

B: If you're going to cross behind a "narrow" obstacle, there really is only one spot to send your dog toward. Thus you'll simply send your dog to the obstacle by pointing your shoulders toward the nearest wing/edge.

DRIVING AHEAD IS KEY

If you run into trouble in your rear-cross training, most often it's because your dog doesn't aim and drive ahead hard enough. Whatever you do, don't try to solve this problem by babysitting your dog! Face the problem head on and go back to basics. Work on your dog's skills and understanding of aiming ahead of you in all kinds of setups before going back to working on the rear cross again. Actually, one of the best preparations for rear crosses is training where you never cross behind your dog at all.

Vary the setup, adding one or several obstacles before the rear cross. You can switch between spontaneous starts and start-line stays; you can use remote rewards (both as actual rewards and as dummies); and you can give or throw rewards yourself or employ a helper. Always remember to plan your dog's path after the rear cross: As he takes off, the path you direct should lead him either to another obstacle or to where a reward appears.

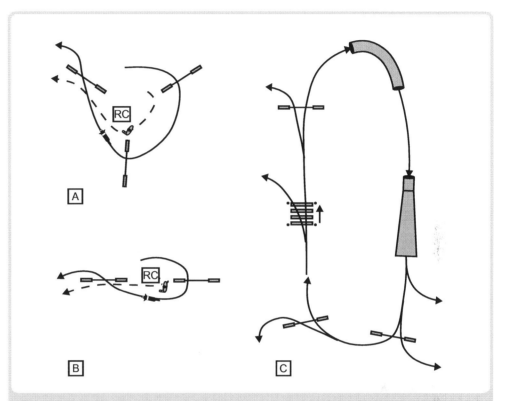

Here are some rear-cross versions of well-known setups. Remember to prepare your rear cross properly: Get yourself close to the obstacle prior to the rear cross, and push your dog's path toward the far wing by running the diagonal before crossing behind him.

A: The Bermuda triangle is excellent for rear-cross training.

B: With only two jumps you can set up tricky angles. Here you will truly test your dog's ability to aim ahead since you have to hang back to get behind him for the rear cross.

C: In a speed circle you can turn out of the circle with a rear cross anywhere.

Hugging the wing and turning back to the handler.

The wrap

Standing still or stopping (distinctly decelerating or halting completely) on the takeoff side of an obstacle while your dog approaches that obstacle is a cue for your dog to prepare for a tight turn back to you after that obstacle. Such a tight turn is also referred to as a *wrap*.

What's special about the wrap is that your dog has to prepare himself several steps in advance to execute it correctly. Your handling maneuver (standing still or stopping by the obstacle your dog is approaching) will tell your dog to prepare himself, take the obstacle, turn smartly, and come back to you as quickly as he can.

What should a wrap look like?

1. As your dog approaches the obstacle, you stand still (or stop) by the wing. *This tells your dog to adjust his stride (collect) and prepare for a tight turn after the obstacle.*
2. As your dog takes off, you can either stand still and reward your dog directly as he comes to you or do a front cross or a regular turn, depending on whether you need a change of sides or not. *If you stand still it tells your dog to come to you, and if you move, it tells your dog to continue in the direction given by your shoulders.*

Your dog has to adjust his stride

To make a tight turn, your dog needs to alter his stride as he approaches the obstacle, especially if he's the long-legged, long-strided type that flies ahead. To turn tightly, he must shift gears: Your standing still/stopping maneuver is what tells your dog to collect, add an extra stride, and make a short, rounded jump.

How can you train wraps?

The training process for wraps is the same as when you were working with stopping/ standing still on the flat—the only difference is that your dog now is supposed to take the jump and turn back to you.

For successful wrap training:

- Make sure you're ahead of your dog, so that you can get to your position in time. You need to be standing still by the wing as your dog approaches, so that he notices your maneuver in time and can adjust his stride accordingly.
- As your dog takes off, stand still and reward your dog immediately as he turns back to you, delivering the reward by your knees (just as you did when practicing stopping/ standing still on the flat).

When your dog is skilled at wraps so that he collects before takeoff and wraps tightly around the wing, you can start moving again as your dog takes off. Aim your shoulders in the direction you plan to go next, start moving in the new direction, and reward your dog for following your handling (either immediately, or a bit later in the sequence).

Jump and turn tight

The first step of the training teaches your dog to wrap around the wing and get back to you.

Exercise 60: The first wrap

Begin with just jump wings (or a very low jump).

1. Set up your dog at a start line just one stride away from the jump (so that he doesn't have the chance to build up any speed).
2. Position yourself by the wing, facing forward and standing still.
3. Give your start cue.
4. As your dog takes the jump, remain still.
5. Reward by your knees.

Suggested tag points:

- Stand still by wing
- Reward by knees

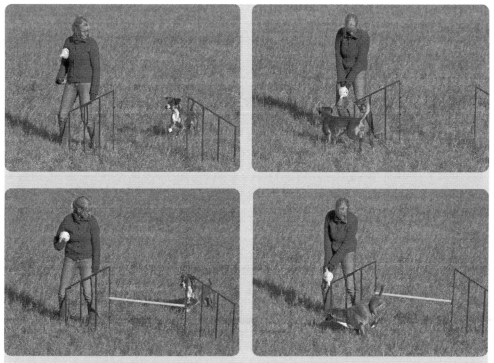

Stand still and reward by your knees. Practice first at jump wings (top), then with a jump (bottom).

At first you may use the reward as a lure, showing it as your dog lands off the jump, but then move on to presenting it as a reward as your dog wraps around the wing.

WHAT IF MY DOG HESITATES TO TAKE THE JUMP?

- At first, your dog might think he's supposed to stop with you without taking the jump. Starting him a short distance from the jump will help. Using your clicker to mark as he takes the jump will further reassure him that he is correct.
- You can begin the session with a couple of spontaneous starts, where you just release him "on the move" from the transport. That way he automatically will get ahead of you.
- Make sure you stand very close to the wing (within your dog's jumping distance). If you stand farther away from the jump, he should stop with you and refuse to take the jump.

Gradually add to your dog's distance, letting him come toward the jump with some speed. Also add some movement of your own—running up to the wing and stopping there as your dog approaches—but make sure you get to the wing before your dog does so that he sees you stopping as he comes up to the jump.

Contrast your wrap work with straight-ahead exercises where you send your dog ahead by moving forward. As long as you're moving ahead, he should continue forward and blast right by you.

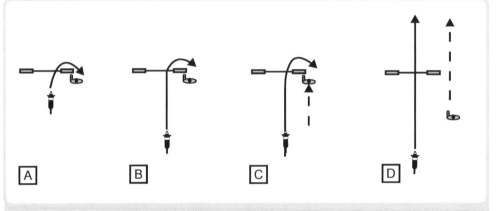

A. You standing still, starting the dog close to the jump
B. You standing still, starting the dog a bit farther away
C. Your moving and stopping.
D. Remember to contrast wraps with going straight ahead!

As the jump gets higher, the demands on the dog's physical and technical abilities increase. For a really tight wrap your dog needs to understand the task, he needs to know how to use his body, and he needs the strength and flexibility to actually do it.

When your dog is skilled at wrapping back to you when you stand still or stop at one jump, you can add distractions farther ahead (in the form of dummy obstacles, or dummy rewards). Alternate between stopping/standing still, rewarding by your knees, and moving forward, thus sending your dog to the obstacle or remote reward.

You can add obstacles before the one you want your dog to wrap and gradually raise the height of the jump. If your dog doesn't turn as tightly as you would like when you increase his speed toward the jump and/or the height of the jump, you may have moved ahead too fast in your training, *or* there might be a physical issue making it hard for him to turn tight, *or* he might not yet have the body control and technical skill necessary to do this kind of maneuver. To properly manage the wrap, your dog has to first measure the distance to the wrap jump, adjust his stride and collect before he gets there, take off close to the jump and really push off with his rear end, and turn to wrap the wing while he's in the air. This really is acrobatic work for your dog! Keep working at a level of difficulty where he's successful, increasing the difficulty only gradually.

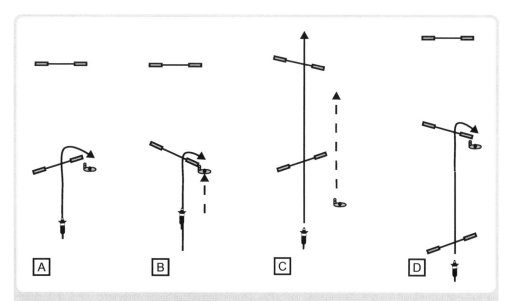

Here are some more standing still/stopping sequences:

A. Standing still by jump #1
B. Moving and stopping by jump #1
C. Going straight ahead
D. Standing still by jump #2

Wraps on course

In "real life", your standing still or stopping will be combined with other handling maneuvers.

- As your dog wraps toward you, you can make either a regular turn or a front cross. If you perform a front cross, you'll probably not be able to get to the next obstacle in three steps since you're starting from the wrap position—that's OK in this specific situation.

- If the wrap occurs in conjunction with a rear cross, you're per definition behind your dog and you need to cross behind him before he can turn toward you—so you can't really stand still or stop by the wing as your dog approaches it. Instead you decelerate as your dog approaches the obstacle (while you're behind him, running the diagonal).

WHAT IF I CAN'T MAKE IT TO THE WING?

Sometimes you might want to cue a tight turn after an obstacle but find yourself unable to get to that obstacle before your dog does. Then simply hit the brakes wherever you happen to be when your dog approaches the jump, coming to a complete stop as he takes off. Your dog will see your deceleration (dogs have great peripheral vision), and he'll also hear your footsteps slow.

You can also teach your dog a verbal cue for this behavior. Just go back to simple training situations and add your verbal cue as your dog approaches the jump (while you're stopping/standing still by the wing), and then gradually move yourself farther out of the picture.

Until your dog is truly skilled at wrapping the wing, however, make sure you get to that wing in time to cue him clearly!

The threadle

The threadle is a handling maneuver based on an "abbreviation" of two consecutive front crosses on the ground between two obstacles. Hence, before you start working with threadles, you and your dog *must* be skilled in executing all sorts of front crosses. You'll use a threadle when you want to pull your dog through a gap between two obstacles, having him take the second obstacle from the same side as he took the first, in other words, creating an S-shaped path between the obstacles.

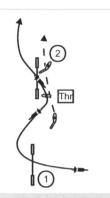

The threadle maneuver is an abbreviated version of two front crosses, creating an S-shaped path between two obstacles.

Left: To direct the dog through the gap between the jumps, the handler steps into the "threadle position" (next to the wing of the second jump, facing the dog) and points her "threadle arm" across her body.

Right: Once the dog is through the gap, the handler turns toward the second jump.

AN "ABBREVIATION" OF TWO FRONT CROSSES

To understand the handling maneuver referred to as a threadle, you first need to know where the front crosses go. To keep your dog on your outside throughout this sequence, you'd first do one front cross to get him between the two jumps, and then another front cross to switch sides and turn him back toward the second jump. Theoretically you could do the sequence this way, performing two front crosses in quick succession. But it would mean covering lots of ground, so you'd have to move fast, and your dog would turn wider than necessary.

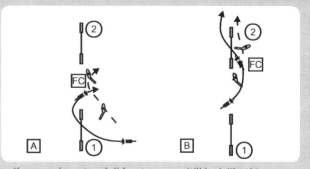

If you perform two full front crosses, it'll look like this:

A. The first front cross turns the dog right after jump #1 and brings him through the gap in right-side handling.

B. The second front cross turns the dog left and sends him to jump #2 in left-side handling.

Sending the dog to jump #1

Threading the dog between the jumps

Sending the dog to jump #2

What should the threadle look like?

Instead of doing the two full front crosses, you can "front cross" with your arms but stop halfway with your feet. The threadle maneuver is a form of shorthand that will save you steps, is conspicuous to your dog, and will give him the shortest possible path. In detail the threadle looks like this (in this example you're beginning with your dog on your left side):

1. As your dog approaches jump #1, you make sure you get as close to jump #2 as possible (to get into position for the upcoming threadle). You keep your dog in left-side handling, and your shoulders are pointing toward jump #1. *This tells your dog to take jump #1.*

2. As your dog takes off at jump #1, you step into "threadle position" by the nearest wing of jump #2.
   – Rotate toward your dog and switch to your right arm (just as in the beginning of a front cross).
   – Plant your feet parallel to the wing and stand still, facing your dog, your right side by the wing and your right arm pointing across your body to guide your dog past the wing of jump #2.

   This maneuver symbolizes the first front cross, switching from left-side handling to right-side handling, *and it tells your dog to turn toward you and aim in the direction your right arm is pointing.*

3. As your dog passes the plane of the jump #2 wing so that he's on the takeoff side of the jump, you switch arms and aim for the far wing of the jump:
   – Switch to your left arm.
   – Step back with your right foot and step to the far wing with your left foot.

   This maneuver symbolizes the second front cross, switching from right-side handling to left-side handling, *and it tells your dog to turn toward you again and aim for the jump off your left side, since that is where your shoulders are pointing.*

THREADLE FOOTWORK

Here is a description of where to place your feet in the threadle. In this example, you begin with your dog on your left side.

"The first front cross" in the threadle (actually, only the first two steps of a front cross):

1. Your right foot (the one farthest from your dog): Toe in, place your foot by the wing.
2. Your left foot: Place it next to your right foot, stand still by the wing, weight on the left foot.

"The second front cross" in the threadle (actually, only the last two steps of a front cross):

3. Your right foot: Toe out (stepping backward, in the direction of the far wing, to open up space for your dog).
4. Your left foot (the one nearest your dog): Step to the far wing.

To rehearse the footsteps in a full front cross, see page 250.

The right foot: Toe in, step to the wing.
The left foot: Place it next to the right foot, stand still by the wing.
The right foot: Toe out, step backwards in direction of far wing.
The left foot: Step to the far wing.

How can you train the threadle?

So how do you start with threadles? One way is to simply go out and do the full threadle. Many dogs will catch on right away as long as you do your job correctly (so make sure you're fluent—practice without your dog until you are!).

Another way to begin is to break down the threadle into smaller pieces, and gradually put them together. For example, you can work in four steps:

Step 1: Come to you in threadle position. Use only the second jump and teach your dog to come to you in the threadle position, rewarding there. Here your dog will not jump at all; he'll simply pass by jump #2 and come to you.

Step 2: The second arm change. Use only the second jump and add the second arm change: Stand still and bring your dog toward you in the threadle position, then do the "second front cross" (the second arm change), sending him over the jump.

Step 3: The first arm change. Use both jumps to do the first arm change: Send your dog over jump #1 and do your threadle as he takes off, bringing him toward you between the jumps.

Step 4: Do the full threadle. Put it together and do the whole threadle.

WAIT UNTIL YOU AND YOUR DOG ARE READY

The threadle—as well as the serpentine, which we'll discuss in the next section—are advanced handling maneuvers. If your dog is skilled at aiming ahead with full drive, at executing front crosses, and at coming straight toward you when you stand still, he's well prepared for learning threadles.

If your dog is not yet proficient in aiming ahead (or if he doesn't yet have full forward drive), don't introduce threadles yet since that could cause him to slow down. Keep doing sequences where you work on going straight ahead and doing regular turns, front crosses, rear crosses, and stopping/standing still. Once you and your dog are confident with these maneuvers in various sequences, the threadles (and serpentines) will be a breeze to learn.

Step 1: Come to you in threadle position

First, teach your dog to follow your threadle arm and come toward you when you stand in the "threadle position." If your dog hesitates even slightly, use a toy (or treat) as a lure in your threadle hand for a couple of repetitions.

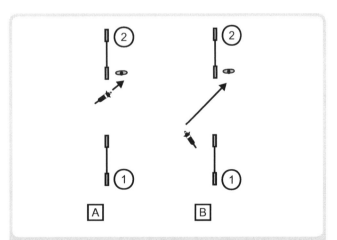

Use your threadle arm to pull your dog toward you between the jumps. First, do just the last couple of steps. Then, start from where he'd land off jump #1.

Exercise 61: Use your threadle arm to pull your dog past the jump wing

1. Imagine your dog's path from jump #1 to jump #2, and position your dog in a stay along that path just a couple of strides away from the wing of jump #2.

2. Position yourself in the threadle position (standing by the wing of jump #2, facing left with your feet parallel to the wing and your right arm pointing across your body in the direction your dog should go).

3. Give your start cue.

4. Your dog runs toward you (following the direction of your threadle arm).

5. Reward as your dog reaches you, using your threadle arm.

Reward your dog for coming to you in the threadle position.

Suggested tag points:

- Feet parallel to wing
- Stand still
- Threadle arm pointing across your body
- Reward with threadle arm

Gradually add distance to your dog's start position until you reach his landing position off jump #1.

Then, start from where he'd land off jump #1.

Step 2: The second arm change

Still using only one jump (the second one in a threadle setup), pull your dog in between the jumps and add the second arm change, so that you send your dog over the second jump.

Exercise 62: Pull your dog between the jumps, then send him ahead over the second jump

1. Position your dog in a stay, just a couple of strides away from the wing of jump #2, and yourself in the threadle position.
2. Give your start cue.
3. Your dog runs toward you (following the direction of your threadle arm).
4. As your dog passes the plane of the jump, switch to your left arm, step back on your right foot in the direction of jump #2, and step with your left foot toward the far wing of jump #2.
5. Your dog takes the jump.
6. Reward from your left hand (or throw the toy, or use a remote reward) after your dog takes jump #2.

Suggested tag points:

- Step toward wing
- Reward with hand nearest dog.

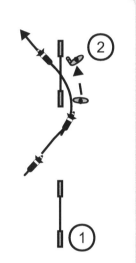

Stand in the threadle position and pull your dog between the jumps; then send him over the second jump.

As your dog passes the plane, switch arms and send to the second jump.

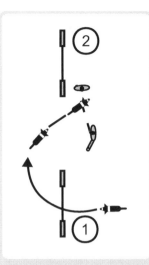

Send your dog to jump #1, then thread him between the jumps.

Step 3: The first arm change

Now, add the first jump so that your dog gets to respond to your change of arms and turn toward you. Reward when he comes to you in the threadle position.

Exercise 63: Send your dog over jump #1, then pull him between the jumps

1. Send your dog to jump #1. (Make sure you can quickly get to the wing of jump #2.)
2. As he takes off, step into threadle position next to the wing of jump #2, your right arm pointing across your body in the direction your dog should go.
3. Stand still in threadle position as your dog turns toward you and aims in the direction of your right arm.
4. As your dog reaches you, reward with your right hand.

Send your dog to jump #1 on your nearest arm. As he hits takeoff, switch arms and step to the familiar threadle position by the wing.

Step 4: Do the full threadle

Now you can easily do the whole threadle.

Exercise 64: Do a complete threadle

1. Send your dog to jump #1. (Make sure you can quickly get to the wing of jump #2.)
2. As he takes off, step into threadle position next to the wing of jump #2, with your right arm pointing across your body in the direction your dog should go.
3. Your dog runs toward you (following the direction of your threadle arm).
4. As your dog passes the plane of the jump, switch to your left arm, step back on your right foot in the direction of jump #2, and step with your left foot toward the far wing of jump #2.
5. Your dog takes the jump.
6. Reward from your left hand (or throw the toy, or use a remote reward) after your dog takes jump #2.

WHAT IF I CAN'T MAKE IT TO THE WING?

Most times you can make it to the wing to do a threadle if you just plan ahead, trust your dog, and set your mind to it. In extreme cases, where you simply can't get to the wing to do a proper threadle, get as close as you can and then stop and do your threadle maneuver where you are.

Vary the threadle setup: You can vary the obstacles, the angle and distance between the jumps, where you come from, and where you're going next. You'll find that the more independently your dog can work on the obstacles before the threadle, the easier it'll be for you to do a proper threadle.

Work with different kinds of obstacles. Here a spread jump and a tunnel.

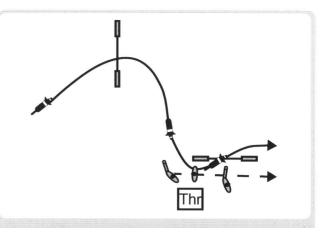

You can also alter the setup of the obstacles. The handler's job remains the same: Step to the wing, stand still with the threadle arm across the body. As the dog passes the plane, step back and toward the far wing and change arms.

Threadles in more open settings

If you ever want to turn your dog *between* two obstacles in 90° turns, 180° turns, and 270° turns, use a threadle. In these situations, the threadle is also known as a "false turn" or a "reverse flow pivot." The maneuver turns your dog off his path one notch toward you (with the first arm change), and then sends him ahead again (with the second arm change) on the altered path. The threadle maneuver looks basically the same, but usually you won't be as close to the second obstacle and won't bring your dog all the way to you before sending him again. Instead, stop and do your threadle maneuver between the obstacles, holding your first arm change until your dog has turned enough toward you, and then switch back, sending him to the next obstacle.

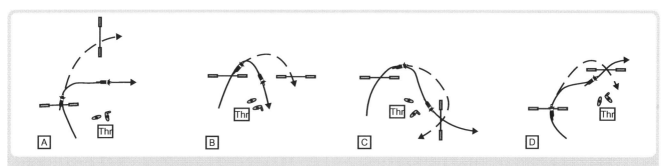

Make sure the contrast is clear! If you want your dog to run as the solid lines indicate and come in between the jumps, you need to use a threadle: As your dog takes off at the first jump you switch arms, rotate toward your dog, and stand still! When your dog has turned toward you, you switch back and continue ahead. If, instead, you want your dog to follow the dashed lines, you simply keep your dog on your outside and rotate your shoulders in a regular turn.

Practice contrasts! Here are the two paths at D in the diagram. above.
Top (left and right): Threadle (the solid path in the diagram)
Bottom (left, center, right): Staying on the outside (the dotted path in the diagram on the previous page)

The tricky thing with these threadles is that your dog may start anticipating the second arm change, which would weaken the threadle and—even worse—weaken your dog's responsiveness to front crosses. So make sure you follow the correct order of events:

1. You begin your threadle—stopping, facing your dog, and switching arms.
2. Your dog turns toward you.
3. You switch arms again and aim for the next obstacle.
4. Your dog heads for the next obstacle.

Your second arm change (where you aim for the next obstacle) will reinforce your dog for turning toward you, so make sure you switch arms while your dog is actually coming toward you. You can also surprise your dog with rewards as he comes toward you.

If your dog starts exiting your threadle too early (heading for the next obstacle before you have switched arms again), simply hold your ground and maintain your threadle position, making him turn back to you. Then, when he actually comes toward you, either reward right away with treats or a toy, or reward by switching arms and continuing to the next obstacle.

The serpentine

Like the threadle, the serpentine is an advanced handling maneuver based on two abbreviated, consecutive front crosses. In the serpentine you run along the landing side of an obstacle and your dog takes that obstacle on his way toward you, running an S-shaped path. Theoretically you can perform a serpentine wherever it's feasible to do a front cross both immediately before and immediately after an obstacle. Properly executed, the serpentine tightens your dog's path, but just as for the threadles, you and your dog need to be skilled in performing front crosses before starting to work on serpentines.

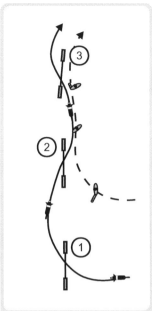

In the serpentine the handler runs along the landing side of the middle obstacle instead of doing two front crosses before and after that obstacle.

Center: To direct the dog's path over the middle jump the handler runs far ahead, close to the obstacle, and points her "serpentine arm" across her body.

Right: When the dog lands, the handler is out of the way, directing the continuing path.

TWO FULL FRONT CROSSES ON EITHER SIDE OF THE MIDDLE OBSTACLE

Serpentine handling is used to replace two full front crosses on either side of an obstacle. So, to understand serpentines, you first need to know where the front crosses go. Here is an example of a sequence where you can perform a front cross both before and after the middle obstacle. Note that it's perfectly OK to handle these sequences with two full front crosses. The serpentine maneuver is just another option.

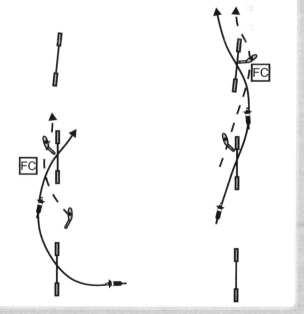

Instead of a serpentine you can simply do a front cross before and after the middle obstacle.

What should the serpentine look like?

Just as with the threadle, instead of doing those two full front crosses, you can handle these sequences with a kind of front-cross shorthand—by switching arms but not following through with your feet. In the serpentine you run *on the landing side* of the middle jump, close to the obstacle, switching arms to bring your dog toward you over the jump, and then switching back to turn your dog over the next jump.

Sending the dog to jump #1

Directing the dog over jump #2 with the serpentine arm.

Handler aiming for jump #3; dog following the serpentine arm.

Switching to the nearest arm, sending the dog to jump #3.

In detail the serpentine looks like this (in this example you're beginning with your dog on your left side):

1. While your dog approaches jump #1, you make sure you get as close to the far wing of jump #2 as possible (to get into position for the upcoming serpentine). Meanwhile, you keep your dog in left-side handling, and your shoulders are pointing toward jump #1. *This tells your dog to take jump #1.*

2. When your dog has a straight line toward you over jump #2 (or a fraction before that; see "Timing refinement in the serpentine"), you *switch* to your serpentine arm:
   - You should be by the far wing of jump #2.
   - Switch to your right arm and rotate your shoulders toward your dog.
   - Keep your feet facing forward, and keep moving forward.
   This maneuver symbolizes the first front cross, switching from left-side handling to right-side handling. *This tells your dog to turn toward you and follow your serpentine arm to you. Since you're on the opposite side of jump #2, he'll take the jump on his way toward you.*

3. As your dog takes off at jump #2, keep moving in the direction of the next obstacle so that you stay ahead of your dog, and keep your serpentine arm up across your body. *This tells your dog to keep following your serpentine arm, landing behind you.*

4. As soon as you can get a straight line toward jump #3 (which usually happens when your dog lands off the serpentine obstacle), you switch arms again:
   - Switch to your left arm.
   - Aim for the next jump.
   This maneuver symbolizes the second front cross, switching from right-side handling to left-side handling, and *it tells your dog to take jump #3.*

TIMING REFINEMENT IN THE SERPENTINE

Theoretically, your first arm change should happen when there's a straight line between you and your dog, over the second jump. The arm change turns him toward you and "draws" him over the jump.

Practically, your arm change should take place a split second earlier (because your dog will have to finish the stride he's at, which takes a few milliseconds). In instances when there's already a straight line between you and your dog over jump #2 as he lands after taking jump #1, you should actually switch arms as he takes off at jump #1: Once he lands you'll both be in perfect serpentine position.

How can you train the serpentine?

Just as with threadles, your dog already has all the basic understanding he needs (in the form of front crosses and keeping to your outside). So one way to begin teaching the serpentine is to simply go out and do it. As long as you do your part of the job, many dogs will get it right away.

Naturally you can break down the serpentine into smaller pieces, as in this one possibility:

Step 1: Come toward you over the serpentine jump. Use only the second jump (the middle, "serpentine" jump) and teach your dog to come toward you over the jump when you're in serpentine position, rewarding there.

Step 2: The second arm change. Use only the second jump and add the second arm change: From your serpentine position, bring your dog toward you over the serpentine jump, then do "the second front cross" (the second arm change) and reward your dog for following your handling past the wing.

Step 3: The first arm change. Add the first jump and do the first arm change: Send your dog over jump #1, do "the first front cross" by switching arms. Now you're in familiar territory, and your dog will come toward you over jump #2 on your serpentine arm. Then do "the second front cross" by switching arms again, and reward as he follows you past the wing.

Step 4: Do the full serpentine. Add the third jump to do the whole serpentine.

Step 1: Come toward you over the serpentine jump

First, teach your dog to follow your serpentine arm and come toward you over the jump when you're in the "serpentine position" (on the landing side of the obstacle, close to the wing, far ahead, and with your feet pointing in the direction you're going, but with your shoulders rotated toward your dog). *Note:* You should be so far ahead, and so close to the jump, that your dog actually lands *behind* you.

Use your serpentine arm (and your rotated shoulders) to bring your dog toward you over the serpentine jump.

Exercise 65: Use your serpentine arm to bring your dog toward you over the middle jump

1. Imagine your dog's path from jump #1 to jump #2, and position your dog in a stay along that path, on the takeoff side of jump #2.
2. Position yourself in the serpentine position (by the far wing of jump #2, your feet pointing forward but shoulders rotated toward your dog, and with your far arm—here the right arm—pointing across your body). Your dog should now have a straight line toward your serpentine hand over jump #2. Your body should be even farther ahead.
3. Give your start cue.
4. Your dog follows your serpentine hand and takes the jump toward you.
5. As your dog lands, reward with your serpentine hand.

Suggested tag points:

- Close to the wing while far ahead
- Stay out of dog's way
- Feet pointing forward
- Shoulders rotated toward dog
- Serpentine arm pointing across body

Reward your dog for taking the jump!

In this first step of the training, you'll deliver the reward with your serpentine hand as your dog lands. This is something we normally do only a few times, until the dog has got the picture—we don't want to spend too much time on rewarding the dog "behind the handler's back," so as soon as possible, move on to Step 2 where you'll do the second arm change and reward your dog for catching up with you.

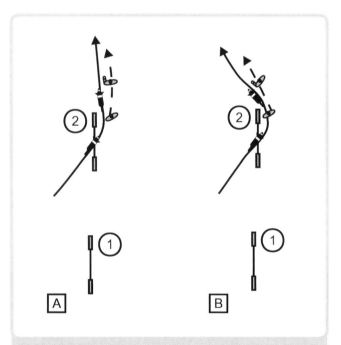

A. Bring your dog toward you over the jump with your serpentine arm, then switch arms.

B. You can make the maneuver even more salient (both for you and for your dog) by making a very tight turn around the second wing.

Step 2: The second arm change

Now add the second arm change. At this stage you'll switch arms as your dog lands, cueing your dog to go between you and the jump wing, and reward immediately as your dog follows your handling past the wing. (Later you'll use the second arm change to send your dog to the next obstacle.)

Exercise 66: Bring your dog toward you over the middle jump, switch arms, and reward

1. Imagine your dog's path from jump #1 to jump #2, and position your dog in a stay along that path, on the takeoff side of jump #2.

2. Position yourself in the serpentine position (by the far wing of jump #2, your feet pointing forward but shoulders rotated toward your dog, and with your far arm—here the right arm—pointing across your body). Your dog should now have a straight line toward your serpentine hand over jump #2. Your body should be even farther ahead.

3. Give your start cue.

4. Your dog follows your serpentine hand and takes the jump toward you.

5. As your dog takes off, keep your serpentine hand up and move ahead toward where the next obstacle would be.

6. As your dog lands, switch arms.

7. Your dog comes up between you and the jump wing.

8. Reward with your nearest hand (either deliver the reward directly, or throw it ahead).

Suggested tag points:

- Switch arms
- Reward with nearest arm

To help both you and your dog know where to aim for in that second arm change, you can set up the remote reward where jump #3 would be, or along your dog's path in that direction. The remote reward will give you a set point to aim for and will also help proof your dog's understanding of the serpentine handling (since he should take the serpentine jump first, and not just go straight to the reward).

When your dog jumps, aim toward where the next obstacle would be and switch arms. Your dog's path goes between you and the wing.

Step 3: The first arm change

Now it's time to add the first jump and do the first arm change, teaching your dog to truly cue off the beginning of your serpentine maneuver. Send your dog to jump #1 and run to your serpentine position by the far wing on the landing side of jump #2. As your dog takes off at jump #1, you should be in serpentine position. Switch arms to cue your dog to come toward you over the serpentine jump. Then switch arms again as he lands, cueing your dog to go between you and the jump wing, and reward immediately (in the direction of where the next obstacle would be), either delivering the reward from your hand or using a remote reward.

To send your dog to jump #1 you can either use a spontaneous start or start your dog from a stay. What's important is that you can get close enough to jump #2 while your dog approaches jump #1, so that you can get into the serpentine position in time. The secret is to get *close* to the landing side of jump #2, and *run* to the far wing.

In the setup we illustrate here, your first arm change should happen as your dog takes off at jump #1, since when he lands he can come directly toward you over jump #2.

Send your dog to jump #1, then bring him toward you over jump #2 with a serpentine.

Exercise 67: Send your dog over jump #1, switch arms, and bring him toward you over jump #2

1. Send your dog to jump #1 (with left-side handling).

2. As he takes off at jump #1, switch arms (pointing your right arm across your body) and rotate your shoulders toward your dog while moving forward along the landing side to the far wing of jump #2.

3. Your dog turns toward you and heads for jump #2, aiming in the direction of your serpentine arm.

4. As your dog takes off at jump #2, keep him on your serpentine arm and keep moving toward where the next obstacle would be.

5. As your dog lands, switch arms.

6. Your dog comes up between you and the jump wing.

7. Reward!

Suggested tag points:

- Run close to the serpentine jump
- Run far ahead at the serpentine jump

You can vary the angle and the distance between jumps #1 and #2, trying out various possible ways to come in to the serpentine. When you alter the setup of jump #1, you might also need to alter the timing of your serpentine arm. Remember: Your *switch* of arms will turn your dog toward you, so you should switch arms when there will be a straight line between you and your dog over the serpentine jump. Usually that happens as your dog takes off at jump #1, but sometimes you'll first have to send your dog around to the takeoff side of jump #2 before you can switch arms.

Make sure you get far ahead while sending your dog to jump #1! That way you'll be in a good position for your serpentine.

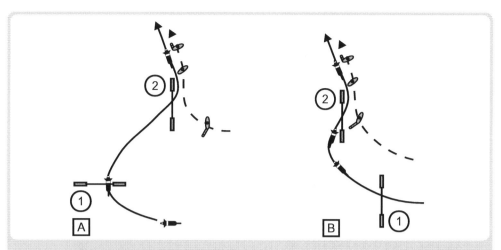

Vary how you come in to the serpentine.

A. Here your dog really has to work independently on jump #1 so that you can get to your serpentine position in time. Switch arms as he takes off at #1, since he'll then have a straight line toward you over jump #2.

B. Here you have to keep your dog in left-side handling until he is on the correct side of jump #2, and then switch arms (at the same time as you hurry to get to the far wing of #2, on the landing side). In situations like this you cannot switch arms as he takes off at jump #1 since he'd then come to you between the obstacles.

Step 4: Do the full serpentine

All that's left now is to add the third jump to do the whole serpentine. Instead of rewarding directly after the second arm change, you'll send your dog to jump #3.

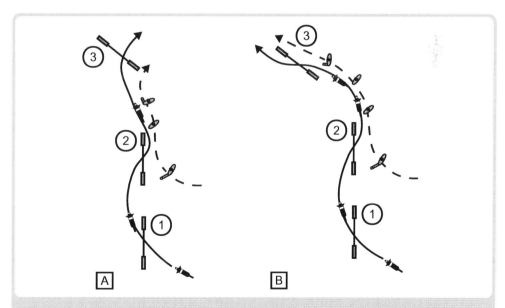

In serpentine A you can switch arms and send your dog to jump #3 as he lands off jump #2. Serpentine B is a tricky one! Here you have to keep your dog on your serpentine arm while "running around the corner." Yes, you'll be running the outer lap here, but with your dog on your right hand. Make sure you stay ahead of your dog, and switch arms as soon as you can send him straight to jump #3.

Normally you can do the second change of arms as your dog lands off the serpentine jump. What's important is that you have to be able to send your dog straight to the next jump as you switch arms—so in some situations, you'll have to keep him on your serpentine arm a bit longer (for example, if you have to "run around the corner" of the next obstacle before you can set him off toward it).

Keep varying the serpentine setup: Change the obstacles, vary the angles and distances, and begin doing serpentines in larger sequences where you'll come in with full speed. Keep in mind that your position is vital! You have to make it to the far end of the middle obstacle quickly, which means your dog has to be very good at working on his own at the previous obstacles, at a distance from you. If you can't make it to the serpentine position, don't do a serpentine! You can always perform the two front crosses instead.

Further sequencing

There are infinite possible sequence variations, but within all that variability, you and your dog will be comfortable since you both have all the necessary skills to deal with new and different sequence challenges. This section shows you how to apply those skills in slightly altered settings. As with everything else, remember to increase the difficulty one step—and one aspect—at a time.

Tailor your sequences to your level of training

Whenever you attempt a sequence with your dog, make sure your current level of training matches the challenge. This rule is true whether you or someone else constructed the sequence.

So that you and your dog stand a reasonable chance of being successful, each sequence you run should include only obstacles and handling maneuvers that you and your dog are happy and confident about because you've trained and practiced them thoroughly. For example, if you haven't sufficiently taught the tire yet, then wait to include it in your sequences. In the same way, if your rear crosses aren't yet up to par, then hold off on trying more advanced sequences that require rear crosses. Longer and more complex sequences are merely a continuation of your earlier work, so just keep working on the details and then put them together, piece by piece.

Set goals for each sequence

For each sequence you attempt, you also need to know what your goal is. Why do you want to run your dog through it? Which lesson do you want him to learn? Are you aiming to reinforce anything in particular? Your dog will learn something from each and every sequence, so make sure he learns what will aid your future agility training.

Occasionally you might be tempted to try your luck on a sequence that might be a bit over your head. As long as you remain fair to your dog, and as long as it happens only once in a while—sure, go ahead! Just throw yourself out there, give it your best, and see how it goes. Perhaps you and your dog are capable of more than you thought. If not, at least you'll learn more about where your strengths and weaknesses lie, and that knowledge can help you design your future training program.

Notice, however, the difference between testing and training: *Testing* is trying something out, checking if you can do it, if you both have the skills to get it right. It's like a pop quiz, thrown in to see where you both are. But the lion's share of your practice should be *training*, step-by-step building of your and your dog's skills. In a positive reinforcement regime "training your dog" reads as "reinforcing responses." For example, "training rear crosses at the tire" should mean "reinforcing rear crosses at the tire." The point of training is always to increase your dog's desire to do whatever it is you want him to do, in other words, to strengthen the responses you wish to see more of. This is what your sequences should accomplish! That means you should custom-fit your sequences, so that they match your goals and your and your dog's current competence level.

Minor adjustments, major progress

The first aspect to look at when progressing in your training is all the *minor adjustments* you can make in each setup. Often you'll practice a particular sequence only once or maybe twice. Then you'll change something, and each variation adds to your dog's knowledge and understanding. You can make minor adjustments to the setups from earlier in this chapter or you can design your own sequences and make adjustments within them.

- Build and run the mirror image.
- Alter which obstacles you use.
- Change the angles a bit.
- Modify the distances between the obstacles.
- Vary the details in your handling: how you start, your lateral distance, and so on.
- Vary between different handling maneuvers, for example from front crosses to rear crosses.

Make sure all sequences are at your dog's level (and your own!). In order to benefit your training the most, think about what you wish to accomplish and make up a sequence that fits your current training plan. By making successive approximations, for example moving an obstacle two inches at a time, you can stretch your dog's level of skill while maintaining a high success rate.

Longer sequences

The *length* of the sequence is another aspect to consider. Running a course with 20 obstacles is definitely different from practicing a two-obstacle sequence—for both you and your dog! Staying focused throughout a longer sequence requires stamina and high focus as well as the ability to quickly get back on track after minor mistakes.

To build the length of the sequences while keeping your dog on his toes, constantly hoping for his reward to appear, simply ping-pong the length back and forth: Constantly vary, but gradually increase the maximum length. The best way to ensure success in longer sequences is to do *lots* of short sequences and then randomly slip in a long one (for example, doing 1–3–2–5–1–15–2–3 obstacle[s]). Don't fall into the trap of constantly doing long sequences since you'd miss out on lots of great opportunities to reward your dog and thus risk weakening your dog's skills while inadvertently teaching him that rewards come only at the end of a run.

Perpetual drills (circles, figure eights, and other never-ending sequences) are terrific for building endurance, since they give you the opportunity to infinitely vary the length of the sequence while sticking to one or a few handling maneuvers that are repeated—and rewarded—again and again.

If your dog's enthusiasm ever drops as the sequences grow longer, it's a clear sign that you have gone too far too fast. Immediately review your training and take action to ensure maximum speed and intensity. The cure might be to reward much earlier (thus shortening the sequence and ping-ponging back and forth to build more anticipation, knowledge, and stamina). Or you might have to go back to kindergarten and work with each single obstacle or handling maneuver on its own, richly rewarding each correct attempt.

Complex sequences

Another aspect of training is increasing the *complexity* of sequences you run with your dog. Performing many different handling maneuvers in quick succession puts high demand on your footwork and timing and requires your dog to read your handling cues correctly.

As soon as you and your dog are comfortable with a certain handling maneuver in isolation, you can begin combining it with others. Gradually add to the complexity of your sequences, beginning with short series of just two or three maneuvers and eventually working your way up to full courses.

For example, you can set up sequences
- with many variations of the same maneuver (for example only regular turns, or only rear crosses).
- where you vary between two or more maneuvers (for example two front crosses, followed by a regular turn, followed by a rear cross).
- that shift from open, flowing sequences to tricky, crowded parts or vice versa.

Complex sequences are especially demanding for *you,* the handler. Practice a lot on your own, without your dog, before you run! Walk the sequence bit by bit, walk the whole sequence, run the whole sequence, have a friend act as your "dog" while you run the sequence. In short, make sure you're fluent before you bring your dog out. Running complex sequences with your dog is only meaningful if you do your job correctly.

Your dog's job is actually quite easy, even in complex sequences: He simply needs to follow your handling maneuvers (which he already knows well) and perform the obstacles (which he also knows well) on the path you direct him along.

Altering given sequences

Before running any given sequence, you need to decide whether it fits your training or whether you should alter something. This is particularly important if someone else has designed the sequence (since that person probably isn't familiar with your current training plan and/or your and your dog's skill level), but even if it's your own design, you'll often want to alter the sequence somehow. In particular, you often may want to add rewards within the sequence, to highlight and reinforce various behaviors.

Here are some options:

- Run the sequence just as it stands, trying to get it right on your first attempt.
- Move one or more of the obstacles, to alter distances and/or angles. By moving the obstacles you can easily adjust the sequence to fit your dog's current level of understanding. Then you can seamlessly stretch his proficiency by altering the obstacles little by little.
- Design a different path for yourself and your dog. The numbers might be out there, but you can always choose another path that suits you better.
- Do the full sequence but "break it off" with rewards. Either reward and continue from the same spot (#1 to #4, reward, #5 to #9, reward, #10 to #15, reward), or reward and start over at a previous obstacle (#1 to #4, reward, #4 to #9, reward, #7 to #15, reward).
- Backchain the sequence—all of it, or just the trickiest passages. For example, if #10 to #12 is especially difficult, start at #12 and continue until the end (say that's #15). Then do just #11 to #12. If that works well, do #10, #11, and #12. Repeat until the chain flows smoothly. Then, if you like, you can do the whole end of the sequence, #10 to #15—and finally you can also add the beginning of the sequence.
- Start later in the sequence. For example, if the sequence is #1 to #15, start at #12. To best mimic the full sequence, start along the path you would have taken if you had been running the full exercise (between #11 and #12).
- Reward earlier in the sequence. For example, if the sequence is #1 to #15, reward after #5. To best mimic the full sequence, reward along the path you would have taken if you had been continuing ahead in the sequence (between #5 and #6).
- Split the sequence into several parts, and then choose which part or parts you want to work on. You can do this within the full sequence, or you can build your own tinier sequences on the side.
- Walk the course (all or parts of it) as if you were going to run it, and perhaps run it with another human as your "dog," but leave it at that.
- Don't do it at all—walk away and do something else that suits your training better.

Now that you know how to work with your handling maneuvers in obstacle sequences with jumps and tunnels, it's time to train the rest of the agility obstacles.

The contact obstacles

A fast, reliable, and independent contact obstacle performance requires that your dog knows exactly what to do when he gets to the end of the obstacle. Therefore, you need to choose and train a specific behavior for your dog to perform in the "contact zone." In this chapter we give detailed instructions for training contact zones and contact obstacles, from choosing a behavior all the way to performing the entire A-frame, dogwalk, and teeter.

About contact training

With all the other obstacles on an agility course, the obstacle's construction and the competition rules dictate the goal performance. For example, your dog should *run through* the tunnels and *jump over* the jump bars between the wings, so these are the behaviors you teach him. The contact obstacles are different, however, since the stipulated "stepping on the colored zone" is way too vague an assignment for your dog to comprehend. Instead you need to choose a specific behavior for your dog to perform—one that has clear criteria that can be taught to proficiency and that is incompatible with jumping over the contact zone.

So when you're working with your dog, be it in training or on course, "correct" performance at the contact zone will be whatever you have decided on—it has nothing to do with that colored area, or whether a judge would fault you or not.

There are three contact obstacles: The dogwalk, the A-frame, and the teeter. Before you start training for these obstacles, you need to decide exactly what you want your dog to do at the contact zones.

THE CONTACT ZONES

The down contacts are our prime concern. To get an independent performance, all dogs at least need to have trained behaviors for the down contacts on the *dogwalk* and the *teeter*. Without training, most dogs leap over the dogwalk's contact zone and fly off the teeter prematurely, given enough speed and enthusiasm. Without training, most dogs also jump off the side—especially if the handler falls behind. With proper training, your dog will never miss a contact! On the teeter a trained contact zone behavior will also help your dog keep his balance as the teeter drops, since he knows exactly what to do as the board hits the ground. A great many dogs also need a trained behavior for the down contact on the *A-frame*, but some smaller dogs have a natural stride that lands them in the contact zone every time without training.

The up contacts are of lesser priority to us. Up contacts are problematic for several reasons, and we'd actually prefer if they weren't judged at all (as is the case in some agility organizations). Most dogs spontaneously step on the up contact, at least most of the time, as long as they know to ascend from the very end. But with a long-strided dog, you might need to teach a specific behavior for the up contacts as well. Using a specific up-contact behavior will cost you time, however, and it will also be harder on your dog's body. If you feel that you must have an up-contact behavior, teach the down contacts to perfection first. Then you can use the same methodology for the up contacts.

Teach your dog a specific task to perform at the very edge of the down contact. When he knows what to do (and can do it independently of you), he'll be drawn to the end like a magnet. Here, the dog is performing a two-on/two-off contact on the A-frame.

Aspects to consider when choosing your contact behavior

How do you choose which contact zone behavior to teach your dog? There are several aspects to take into consideration. We believe that no matter which performance you choose, you should make sure it is clearly defined, involves the edge of the obstacle, and is performed independently of you. We also recommend choosing a stop-and-go performance including a start cue, where your dog stops at a specific place and waits for your start cue.

You might choose the same behavior for all the contact obstacles, or distinct behaviors for the different obstacles. What's important is that you decide on a goal behavior for each contact zone, train for it, and stick to your training. When choosing your dog's contact zone performance, take the following questions into consideration:

Is it clearly defined? The goal performance must be black and white so it will be easy for your dog to understand and perform reliably, and easy for you to stick to your criteria. Poorly defined contact zone behaviors inevitably will frustrate and bewilder your dog.

Does it involve the edge of the obstacle? If you want your dog to drive forward over the obstacle on his own, he needs a specific spot to aim for. By choosing a behavior that involves the bottom edge of the obstacle, you ensure that your dog will always drive to the end of the zone to perform his behavior.

Can it be performed independently of you? If your dog's job is to perform each obstacle on his own, without help from you, he needs to know exactly what to do whenever he gets to a piece of equipment. When your contact zone behavior is fully trained, you should be able to sprint past your dog, hang back, do cartwheels, run out laterally, whatever—while he remains completely confident about his job and performs with speed and accuracy.

Some handlers teach a handler-dependent performance (either because they actually choose to do so, or because they forget to train for independence from the beginning). In a handler-dependent performance the dog performs his behavior in relation to you, not in relation to the obstacle. That means the dog learns to focus on what the handler does instead of focusing on the obstacle. If you choose a handler-dependent performance (such as following your hand, your body language, or verbal directions such as "slow down" or "stop"), notice that following directions is what generates rewards: If your dog is trained to follow your hand, and that hand is in the wrong place so he jumps off the top of the A-frame, he still would be doing what he was trained to do and should be rewarded accordingly.

To us the choice is simple: We opt to put a lot of work into teaching an independent contact behavior because we want the dog to work in relation to the obstacle.

Does the behavior include a cue to start off the contact? A stop–wait for cue–go behavior, where your dog stops and waits for a cue to start, is the easiest to train and maintain and produces a fast and reliable performance. With a cue to start you can do all the following:
- Vary how long your dog holds his position.
- Withhold your release cue if your dog makes a mistake.
- Add extra rewards while your dog holds his position.
- Use your start cue as a reinforcer each and every time—even at competitions.

A contact behavior performed without any release cue requires much more elaborate training because it's a complex behavior that involves setting and maintaining extremely precise criteria, without the advantages we just listed. But if you're a daredevil trainer you might want to give it a go! Examples are running contacts (where your criteria have to do with your dog's running style) or a "stop-and-go on-your-own" behavior (where your dog stops briefly to perform a chosen behavior, and continues ahead without any cue from you).

Two-on/two-off

The contact performance we generally recommend is the classic two-on/two-off, where your dog stops with his rear feet on the obstacle and his front feet on the ground and waits for your start cue before he continues ahead. The two-on/two-off is clearly defined, it involves the edge of the obstacle, it can be performed independently of you, and it involves a cue to start off the contact.

What should the finished two-on/two-off performance look like?

1. The dog zooms over the obstacle, aiming for the bottom edge of the down contact.
2. At the end he stops short with his front feet straight ahead on the ground (not to the side) and his rear feet on the obstacle.
3. He holds his position, waiting for the start cue.
4. When you give the start cue, he dashes off the contact, continuing in accordance with your handling.

While your dog is on the obstacle, he works independently of you—you can run past, hang back, do cartwheels, or whatever.

The down edge is the important part of the obstacle. Two-on/two-off (left); starting on cue (right)

TWO-ON/TWO-OFF WITH A NOSE TOUCH

A variation on the two-on/two-off contact is the *nose touch*, where the dog assumes the same position with his feet, but also presses his nose to the ground. Some handlers train a stationary nose touch (the dog presses his nose to the ground and waits for the start cue); others teach a "wood-pecker" nose touch (the dog repeatedly pecks his nose on the ground).

The nose touch can be advantageous since the dog gets a set position to place his nose (not only his feet). The "woodpecker" nose touch also has the benefit of being an active, repetitive behavior (compared to the more passive "just hold the position").

In this chapter we've chosen to focus solely on the regular two-on/two off, describing the training process in great detail. However, the same principles are valid if you wish to teach a nose touch contact behavior, with the addition that you first need to teach your dog to perform the desired nose touch behavior on a target.

With a nose touch, the dog is aiming for the ground with front feet and nose.

How can you train the two-on/two-off behavior?

Independent, reliable, and fast contacts are taught using back-chaining. The important part is to teach your dog what to do at the end of the obstacle, so at least 99% of your training will revolve around that bottom edge. When your dog truly knows what to do at the down contact he will be drawn like a magnet to that edge. At that point, adding distance and teaching your dog to actually run over the obstacle to get to the contact zone will be a walk in the park.

The edge of the contact zone calls for a chain of three behaviors:

1. Get into the two-on/two-off position.
2. Hold that position.
3. Start off the contact on cue.

Contact zone training bears many similarities to start-line stay training. First and foremost, your dog must excel in *starting on cue* since that is the last part of the chain. Second, he needs to know how to *hold his position* and wait for that cue to start. Both on the start line and at the contacts, inter-mediate rewards might be delivered while he's waiting, but the magic start cue is always what ends the stay behavior.

What distinguishes the contact zone training from the start-line stay training is that your dog is also required to get into the right position on his own. To teach the two-on/two-off position, we use two procedures separately but in parallel, away from the actual obstacles:

- **Use a foot target**, where your dog first learns to put his front foot onto something (like a mouse pad). You can then place the target where you want your dog's front feet. Eventually you can fade the target so that your dog keeps placing his feet where the target used to be.
- **Free-shape a two-on/two-off behavior**, teaching your dog to step down over an edge with his front feet without using any targets or prompts.

You can choose to work with only one of these procedures—they both lead to the same goal in the end: a two-on/two-off at the contacts. But we find it beneficial to work with both. The foot target is easy to practice everywhere, you can quickly get lots of repetitions, and you can use the target on the obstacle to help your dog find the correct spot even when you add difficult variations and distractions. Free-shaping the two-on/two-off teaches your dog

TRAIN YOUR CONTACTS METICULOUSLY, STEP BY STEP

Working on your dog's two-on/two-off performance is pretty straightforward, what you could call "cookbook training": Follow the recipe and the result will be good. Notice that this training requires a somewhat linear train of thought; your dog needs to excel at every step before you move on. Don't fall into the trap of advancing too quickly, since that would force you to yo-yo back and forth and thus jeopardize your dog's understanding.

Since you'll be employing back-chaining when training for your dog's contact performance with two-on/two-off, that means that each part needs to be trained to fluency before you chain the parts together. If the behaviors aren't fluent, the chain won't work.

The only jumping back and forth you should do is between the parallel paths of target training and two-on/two-off shaping. Even if you're well advanced in your target training and at a beginner stage in the two-on/two-off shaping, you still can move freely between them.

JUST FOR FUN, OR A COMPETITIVE EDGE?

If you're thinking, "Oh, but I don't need my dog's contacts to be that perfect—I'm just doing agility for fun," think again. Training your dog's contact performance properly will exercise his brain and help you create a happy and confident agility partner. In our experience those people who opt for less rigorously trained contacts usually end up either demanding far more from their dogs than they've trained for (leaving the dog everything but happy and confident) or having to completely retrain the contacts (and regretting they didn't train them properly from the start). If for some reason you choose to train your contacts sloppily, you have to take responsibility for that choice and not blame your dog.

From the competitive side of things, a well-trained contact performance will improve your dog's times since he will be driving into position and awaiting his release cue, enabling you to position yourself exactly where you need to be. Having a fast and independent contact performance will allow you to be the best possible handler for your dog, since you'll be able to do your job (the handling part of the agility dance) while your dog does his job. As a bonus, you'll avoid the disappointment of getting faulted for a missed contact on an otherwise perfect run.

to locate and work with just an edge, cements your dog's understanding of what to do, and transfers directly to the edge of the obstacle. By teaching both a foot-target and free-shaped two-on/two-off, you'll be able to vary between them for quicker and more solid progress.

The training process is pretty much the same for both. We suggest that you start with the foot target since that is a little bit easier in the beginning. As soon as you and your dog have become acquainted with the procedure, move on to free-shaping the two-on/two-off as well.

Contact zone training really is simple and straightforward—you just have to take it one step at a time and employ the principles of back-chaining! The whole training process is described in the following pages. In short, it looks like this:

AWAY FROM THE OBSTACLES

Use a foot target	Free-shape two-on/two-off
Get the foot target behavior	Get the two-on/two-off behavior; Reward in position, and include the start cue from the beginning
Add holding the position + start cue	Add holding the position
Add variations and distractions	Add variations and distractions
Increase the distance	Increase the distance
Step down to the target	

ON THE A-FRAME AND DOGWALK

Rehearse the same steps on the actual obstacles, beginning with the very end of the down contact and gradually increase the distance (starting from higher up on the obstacle) until your dog runs over the entire obstacle. Finally add handling and other obstacles before and after the contact obstacle.

ON THE TEETER

The teeter is a special case, requiring your dog to ride the obstacle to the ground first, but the contact work remains the same.

PREREQUISITES FOR TRAINING FOR THE CONTACT OBSTACLES

FOUNDATION SKILLS FOR YOU

What	Why
Remaining neutral while saying the start cue	Your start cue should be disconnected from your movement, so that your dog doesn't have to look at you to know when to start. If the dog has to look at the handler in order to know when to leave the contact, he'll soon start looking for body language cues earlier—on his way to the contact—and lose his independent performance.
Varying your own behavior	To get and keep an independent contact performance, you need to constantly vary your behavior slightly. The edge of the contact is the only thing that always remains the same! That's what your dog should focus on. If the dog can cue off the handler's body language, he'll do just that … and then all independence will be lost.

FOUNDATION SKILLS FOR YOUR DOG

Reward procedures	Your training will benefit from varying between treats and toys in the same training session (for example, treats for remaining still, and a thrown toy after leaving the contact).
Transport procedures	In the earliest two-on/two-off training, the treat magnet is especially useful for lining up your dog in precisely the right spot.
Start on cue, *Race to reward*, "Go" and throw	Leaving the contact on cue is the last part of the chain—it's what your dog will be working toward so your dog must be skilled at starting on cue—both toward a remote reward, and without having anything to aim for (just expecting a thrown reward).
Stay and wait for that start cue	If your dog knows to keep still to get that desired start cue and has some experience in getting intermediate rewards while keeping still, your training will proceed faster.
Aim for it	*Aim for it* primes your dog to look and work ahead (as opposed to curling back and looking at you for cues)—which is exactly what he'll be doing when aiming for that spot to put his feet in.
Stepping onto things	Experience in stepping onto things will make it easier for you to train both the foot target (where your dog will put a foot on a target) and the two-on/two-off (where your dog needs to stand up on something before you start shaping him to step down with his front feet).

Before you start working on the actual contact obstacles, your dog also needs to be skilled at stepping, climbing, and balancing on various objects, even high off the ground. |
| **Rear-end control** | To balance at full speed and stop and hold the position in a two-on/two-off, your dog will need both strong core muscles and an awareness of how to work that rear end, to keep it in the right spot. |
| **Create and demand noise and movement** | The teeter both moves and goes bang, and for successful teeter training your dog should love to create both noise and movement. |

When you teach the contact obstacles, your dog will make use of many previously learned skills, for example, balancing on narrow objects (left), creating movement (center), and starting on cue (right).

OUR ACTUAL CRITERION: AT LEAST ONE FRONT FOOT ON THE TARGET

Although we prefer the dog to hit the ground with both front feet, we usually set our criteria to be "at least one front foot on the target." Especially in the early training, we want to focus our training on the first foot hitting the correct spot as quickly as possible, and therefore we prefer the "at-least-one-foot" criterion. Once you place the target in front of the down contact, you can switch to a two-foot criterion if you feel the need for it (but then your focus will be "feet on the ground after the edge," not "two feet on the target").

Foot target

In this section we'll describe how you can teach a foot-target behavior to use in your contact training.

What should the foot-target behavior look like?

1. Your dog races to the target.
2. He hits it with at least one front foot, keeping his forward direction.
3. He holds the position on the target and awaits your start cue.
4. You say your start cue.
5. Your dog starts off the target.

Throughout the procedure, you and your dog are facing in the same direction.

Dash to the target (left), freeze, and listen for the start cue (center), and dash off on cue (right).

Equipment

You can use practically anything as a target when training this foot-target behavior (for example, a mouse pad, a plastic lid, or a paper plate). It's a good idea to get your dog used to several different targets right from the beginning. That way you can use whatever target you have available.

Contact training focuses on where to plant those front feet—and a well-taught target behavior is a great aid!

Why do you need it?

The foot target

- simulates the ground at the end of the contact zone obstacle.
- provides your dog with a specific spot to put his feet.
- helps you build the chain of "aim–place front feet–start on cue."
- helps build independent performance.
- can be practiced anytime, anywhere.
- provides a point of success that you always can return to and aids in problem solving.
- can eventually be transferred to the ground at the end of the contact.

How can you train it?

We'll go through target training for contacts in six steps:

Step 1: Basic foot-target work teaches your dog to put his foot on the target—actively, quickly, without hesitation, and independently of you. In the early foot-target training your dog will earn lots and lots of rewards for a simple behavior, building excitement and reliability from the very beginning. And for you, the basic foot-target work gives opportunities to improve your coordination, speed, and ability to vary your own position.

We teach your dog to immediately slam his foot on the target as soon as you put it down in front of him in three stages:

> **Stage 1:** Get the behavior: foot on target
> **Stage 2:** Make it fast and fluent
> **Stage 3:** Add variations and distractions

Step 2: Hold the position at the target, start on cue teaches your dog to bolt off the target on cue, and only on cue. Simultaneously, he learns to hold his position on the target and wait for the start cue. This training resembles teaching your dog to stay on the start line, except that now your dog must find the correct position (on the target) by himself.

We practice holding the position using two methods:

> **Method 1:** Using solely the start cue as reward
> **Method 2:** Using multiple rewards in position

Step 3: Add Further variations and distractions proofs your dog's understanding of hitting the target, freezing on it, and tearing off it on your start cue no matter what happens around him.

Step 4: Increase the distance to the target is an easy task once you have completed the rest of the training, but don't start it prematurely. When you start to add greater distances, make sure to work as often close to the target.

Step 5: Step down to the target from an elevated surface is the final skill to practice before you can start using the foot target on the obstacles.

Step 6: Fade the target explains how you can get rid of the target, transforming the target behavior into a two-on/two-off performance.

Step 1: Basic foot-target work

The goal of the basic foot-target training is that as soon as you put the target down in front of your dog, he immediately slams at least one front foot onto the target.

Thoroughly work through the outlined steps—the basic foot-target work is the most important part of your target training!

Stage 1: Get the behavior: foot on target

Stage 2: Make it fast and fluent

Stage 3: Add variations and distractions

Stage 1: Get the behavior: foot on target

Teaching your dog to put his foot on the target is just another variety of *Aim for it*; you've already shaped your dog to aim for and onto various objects, and here his job will be to step "onto" the target. What's great about the target is that you can easily move it around as you see fit. So instead of transporting your dog to a good starting position you can simply place the target right in front of him.

The tag point is: Treat toward target.

During the target training, strive to get yourself and your dog to face the same direction as much as possible. Stick to your system of handling, and avoid working face to face! Start off the session by using a treat magnet or collar transport to get yourself and your dog facing the same direction, and put the target down right in front of your dog.

When you put the target down, be ready to click and treat: You want your dog to start working right away. Begin by clicking and treating for nose pointing toward target, but shift to foot movement as soon as your dog starts to zoom in on the target. Reward downward, close to the target. During the session, if your dog happens to swing his rear end away from you, you can just move yourself parallel to him while delivering a reward. That way, when he continues working after the reward, he'll start from the correct position.

The criterion shifts through the shaping process (from "nose toward target" to "foot on target"). Intermediate criteria in the shaping process might be

1. glancing toward target
2. nose pointing toward target
3. slightly moving a foot
4. lifting a front foot
5. front foot touching target

Exercise 68: Get the foot-target behavior

1. Get out your target and the number of tasty treats that you'll need for one training session.

2. Start with your dog at your side (you can hold his collar, or have him on a treat magnet).

3. Put the target down in front of him.

4. Your dog looks at the target (or even moves toward it or puts a foot on it).

5. Click and reward low, close to the target.

6. Continue shaping, clicking, and treating for motion toward the target.

7. To end the session, pick up the target.

Suggested tag points:

- Until you're ready, keep the target away
- Face the same direction as your dog
- Hand on target when delivering treat
- Pick up the target while delivering the last reward

If your dog keeps using just his nose rather than his feet, you can pull the target away slightly (forward or to the side). He'll move to follow the target. Click and treat as the first foot moves!

If your dog still has a foot on the target when you reward him, you need to get the target out from underfoot before the reward is over so that he can step on it again. Either pull the target out from under his foot while he gets the treat, or use the reward as a treat magnet to get him to move a little bit (just enough to enable you to remove the target) so you can start again.

You can let the reward last while you free the target.

You (or your helper) can pick up the target and put it down again whenever you need to. For example, you can pick it up while rewarding and then put it down exactly where you want it for the next repetition. Or you can pick it up if you need a fresh start (for example, if your dog starts mouthing the target, or passes over it, or gets distracted and loses focus).

As rewards, tasty treats that allow many repetitions in a short time work best. But you can use toys as well. To help your dog focus entirely on the target (not minding you at all), let the rewards appear unpredictably from many directions, but always deliver them close to the target. You can use both hands to reward (even though it violates the "nearest hand" rule) if that helps you place the rewards quickly and wisely. Using helpers (different people rewarding your dog) "sets the reward free" from you and thus increases your dog's focus on the target. With several people rewarding, your dog simply cannot anticipate where the reward will come from, so he'll just do his job, anticipating that the reward will appear under his nose.

TIPS TO AVOID CURLING

Ideally you and your dog should face the same direction during the target work. If he curls toward you and/or swings his rear end out, it's usually due to habit (lots of face-to-face work) and reward management (the rewards making the dog curl). To fix this, you need to create new habits and manage the rewards cleverly. Here are some tips to help your dog keep his direction in the target work:

- To prevent your dog from curling toward you or even moving into a face-to-face position, train many different behaviors with your dog by your side so he gets used to working by your side facing forward.
- Your dog may curl toward you anticipating where the reward will come from. The more you vary the direction rewards come from and where they appear the easier it will be for your dog to stay straight during target training.
- Click and deliver the rewards quickly, so that your dog doesn't have time to curl toward you.
- Deliver the rewards close to the target to increase your dog's focus on the target.
- Reward in front of your dog or on the far side of his head rather than next to you.

- Use helpers, and take turns in rewarding so the reward always appears from the person that the dog isn't looking at.
- While you deliver the reward, move parallel to your dog so he always gets a correct starting position for the next repetition.
- After a reward and before your dog has time to move around, be quick to slap down the target again for a new repetition.
- All that said, please don't get too hung up about a little bit of curling. Top priority is that your dog learns to throw himself at the target!

You can help your dog focus only on what's important (the target) by employing a helper and alternating where the reward comes from.

CONSTANTLY VARY YOUR OWN BEHAVIOR A LITTLE BIT

From the beginning when working with contact preparation, varying your own behavior is critical. Trainers who forget to vary their behavior typically get dogs that rely on handler position or movement (which is the opposite of an independent contact performance).

In the earlier stages, use small variations that your dog can easily work through: work on the right and left side, step half a foot forward/backward/sideways, walk in place, wiggle your hands, and so on.

Stage 2: Make it fast and fluent

When your dog has learned to put his foot on the target, it's time to maximize the intensity and pace so that the behavior becomes fast and fluent. Work to get your dog lunging for the target, and present your rewards from various directions, constantly placing them close to the target, to help your dog remain straight so he doesn't curl around you.

Ideally your dog will try to slam the target as you are putting it down. To help your dog reach the borderline-crazy intensity he needs for developing a spectacular contact performance, warm up with some wild games, keep the training sessions short, and use high-quality rewards.

Exercise 69: Teach your dog to **Step on it!**

1. Put the target down.
2. Your dog slams his foot on the target.
3. Click and reward low, close to the target.
4. While you're rewarding, free the target by pulling it away or by using the treat reward as a magnet to get your dog to step off it.
5. End the reward.
6. Your dog slams his foot on the target again.
7. Click and reward, freeing the target while you reward.
8. Repeat a few times.
9. To end the session, pick up the target.

Intensity and speed are key. Your putting the target down, your dog stepping onto it, and your clicking and rewarding should all happen more or less simultaneously (within less than a second). And your dog should be facing forward (keeping straight, not curling or wobbling around) for the entire sequence. Either you can leave the target on the ground throughout the session, or you can pick up the target while rewarding and immediately put it down again. Always pick it up as the session ends, though.

Throughout the training, you should be facing the same direction as your dog, but work to keep yourself out of the picture to ensure independent performance. It helps to position yourself a bit behind—next to your dog's rear end (but still within reach so that you can deliver the rewards). That way you reduce the risk that your dog somehow will involve your legs in his visual picture of target training.

"I'm listening for my start cue—it can come at any time now!" Building duration on the target also means introducing the start cue. Your start cue tells your dog he'll be rewarded for leaving the target—so he'll leave the target if, and only if, he hears the start cue.

During the reward you can move around—to vary your position, and to remain facing in the same direction as your dog. By ensuring that your dog always is in a good starting position once the reward is over, you make it possible for him to work with maximum intensity throughout the session, focusing totally on the target.

Stage 3: Add variations and distractions

When you set down the target, your dog should be so focused on it that he doesn't even notice what is going on around him. Check that your dog can keep doing his job at top intensity while you vary your posture and position, wave your arms, distract with treats or toys, and so on. Add variations and distractions gradually, so that your dog keeps working with top intensity.

Step 2: Hold the position at the target, start on cue

When your dog knows to slam his foot onto the target and does so with gusto as soon as he gets a chance, it's time to add duration: teaching him to hold his position on the target. Simultaneously, you'll teach him to dash

WHY IS THE START CUE SO IMPORTANT?

Once you start to work on duration, you are teaching your dog to stick to his target. As in the start-line stay, you'll be teaching your dog to remain in position no matter what happens around him, and to leave that position only on your verbal cue. For your dog to figure out that he's supposed to stick to his target no matter what, you have to be clear about when he is supposed to leave it. Therefore, using a clear start cue is vital.

"GO" AND THROW OR *RACE TO REWARD?*

As in many other situations, you'll find both *Race to reward* and *"Go" and throw* useful.

Race to reward adds intensity and gives your dog a direction to work in, which will make it easier for him to focus ahead and keep his body straight. The *Race to reward* game can also help you get an explosive start on cue.

"Go" and throw ensures that your dog maintains his direction on the target and truly starts on your cue, even if there is nothing ahead for him to aim for.

off the target on cue. The goal now is that the instant your dog's foot hits the target, he freezes in position, poised for action. When you give your start cue, he dashes away.

The minute you start adding duration to the target behavior, you also have to start using your start cue. From now on, only your start cue can release your dog from the target. Until he hears his start cue he "can't" leave the target, so you shouldn't be able to lure him off no matter what you do!

There are two different methods you can use to teach your dog to hold his position on the target (you'll recognize both varieties from the start-line stay training described in "Starts and stays," page 197):

- Using your start cue as sole reward
- Rewarding your dog multiple times in position

You can choose one method or vary between the two, but you'll always end the stay on the target with your start cue and always reward the end of the chain—starting on cue—with either a remote reward or a thrown toy.

Method 1: Build duration using solely the start cue as reward

To teach your dog to hold his position on the target using solely the start cue as reward, you build directly on the target–start cue training. From your dog's perspective, he's making you give the desired start cue by putting his foot on the target. Sometimes you say "go" right away as your dog hits the target, sometimes you wait half a second, and sometimes you wait several seconds, and so on. Your dog will learn to hit the target and hold that position, because that's the only way to get that precious start cue. You're building a chain that looks like this:

1. Hit the target
2. + keep still
3. + cue to start
4. + start
5. + get treat or toy.

Exercise 70: Teach your dog to hold his position on the target, rewarding solely with your start cue

1. Put the target down right in front of your dog.
2. Your dog slams his foot onto the target.
3. Your dog sticks to the target for half a second.
4. Say "go."
5. Your dog races ahead (either to a remote reward or to a thrown toy).

Suggested tag point:

- Say "go" while your dog's foot is on the target

If your dog's foot leaves the target before you've said your "go" cue, quickly pick up the target and start over from the beginning. When using *Race to reward,* your helper will remove the reward if your dog goes for it prematurely. Your dog will get his start cue and the subsequent reward only if he keeps his foot on the target.

Build duration by letting your dog wait longer and longer for his start cue, just as you did with the start-line training. Since here you also want to constantly strengthen the target behavior, however, give the start cue quickly more often than making your dog wait. That way your dog will maintain his intensity, slamming his feet on that target and hoping to get his start cue right away.

Method 2: Build duration using multiple rewards in position

To teach your dog to hold his position on the target using multiple rewards in position, you first click as your dog's foot hits the target and instantly machine-gun treats to him while he maintains his position on the target (before he has time to curl toward you or move off). Place the treats so that your dog remains straight. Give your start cue to end the stay, and reward your dog (either with a thrown reward or a remote reward) as he leaves the target. The chain will look like this:

1. Hit the target
2. + click + eat treat
3. + keep still
4. + eat another treat
5. + keep still
6. + cue to start
7. + start
8. + get treat or toy.

CLICK OR NO CLICK?

When rewarding the dog for holding his position, we just deliver the treats. But when we wish to precisely reinforce the act of hitting the target (before freezing), we mark it with a click.

When clicking for hitting the target we do wish to reward in position—in other words, you don't want your dog to leave the target just because you click. But, on the other hand, the click marks the transition between your dog's job and his reward (so technically he's not making a mistake if he steps off after the click). To solve this dilemma we *hurry* to deliver the reward after the click, before he has time to move. If he manages to move between the click and the reward, he gets the treat anyway, and you learn to be even quicker next time.

Exercise 71: Teach your dog to hold his position on the target, rewarding with multiple treats in position (and ending with the start cue)

1. Put the target down right in front of your dog.
2. Your dog slams his foot onto the target.
3. Click and reward low, close to the target, machine-gunning treats while your dog's foot is on the target.
4. Say "go."
5. Your dog races ahead (either to a remote reward or to a thrown toy).

Suggested tag point:

- Say "go" while your dog's foot is on the target

WHAT IF MY DOG DOESN'T HIT THE TARGET?

When you begin adding the start cue to the target work, your dog might get so caught up by the thrill of starting that he forgets about his target behavior. Or, he might get locked into a stay, unable to move his feet at all.

Here are several suggestions to help him get the idea:

- Put the target down while you are both in motion—avoid "parking" your dog.
- If your dog doesn't hit the target right away, just wait for a couple of seconds to see if he figures it out.
- To break the mental impasse, pick the target up and put it down again.
- If you're working with *Race to reward,* try placing the target a bit to the side (so that there is an angle between the dog, the target, and the remote reward). This seems to make the difference between "forgetting the target and going directly for the reward" and "going for the target first" more obvious to the dog.
- With *Race to reward,* have your helper hide the remote reward behind his back, producing it after you have given the start cue.

WHAT IF MY DOG DOESN'T RESPOND TO MY START CUE?

If your dog doesn't respond at all when you give the start cue, you need to revisit your start cue training. But to solve the acute dilemma (dog standing still on target after the start cue has been given), we suggest you lure the start. If your dog doesn't respond immediately, throw your toy or have your helper bring the remote reward to life to get your dog's attention. As you know, luring is not our favorite solution, but we prefer it to leaving the dog in limbo.

To avoid inadvertently teaching the dog to stand still and wait for the lure: Add the lure immediately if your dog doesn't start on cue. Don't wait one or several seconds, since you then really would be rewarding your dog for keeping still after that start cue. By adding the lure immediately, you'll replicate the *"Go" and throw* procedure (see page 205 in "Starts and stays"), so that your dog learns to anticipate the reward.

Acknowledge that your dog needs more training in starting on cue. Do lots of start cue training away from the target training.

Build duration by waiting longer between each treat. You can vary the time before the first treat, and you can vary the time that lapses between the treats.

Handle mistakes the same way as when rewarding solely with the start cue. If your dog steps off the target while you are feeding him treats (that is, before you have said your "go" cue), pick up the target and start over from the beginning. Make sure you're successful this time, and end by giving your cue to start while your dog continues to keep still. But there shouldn't be many mistakes in this training; your dog simply should not have time to step off his target.

Step 3: Add further variations and distractions

You want your dog to hit the target with his foot, hold his position, and dash off on cue no matter what is going on around him. Variations thus are essential for an independent performance, so before you move on to adding distance to the target, you need to make sure that your dog can do his job no matter what happens around him.

Vary what happens

- as your dog puts his foot on the target.
- while he holds his position on it.
- as you say the start cue and he starts.

You can vary

- your own behavior (for example, movement and position).
- other distractions (for example, you can use potential rewards as distractions, proofing that your dog maintains position either until the reward reaches him or until you give your start cue).
- the time lapse before your start cue (cueing the start just as your dog hits the target, or after various periods of time).
- the intermediate rewards in position (none or various numbers of rewards appearing after varying periods of time).
- how you reward your dog for starting on cue (using a remote reward or a thrown toy).

DON'T JUST PROOF YOUR DOG FOR HOLDING POSITION!

It seems to be highly reinforcing for humans to test their dog's ability to remain in position, so watch that you don't just proof your dog's ability to stand still. Remember to add lots of different variations as he puts his foot on the target, so that he really learns to hurry up and slam that target no matter what happens around him. Often reward right away (either with the start cue or with a reward delivered directly to him), so that he gets instant reinforcement for his effort to hit the target as quickly as possible.

Also remember to vary what happens as you say the start cue, to ensure that he listens to your cue and doesn't pay attention to anything else. To further help you structure your variations, revisit "Starts and stays", page 218.

Never mind the person with the ball—I'm focusing on my target!"

Step 4: Increase the distance

Adding distance to the target is the last part of the chain. You can begin to work on distance once your dog is completely confident about the rest of the target work. When adding distance to the target we use the *Race to reward* procedure to ensure that the dog keeps straight. Your dog will always be able to see both the target and the remote reward. We always use a visible remote reward when adding distance to the target because, without a remote reward to focus on up ahead, most dogs would turn toward the handler as they hit the target—and you don't want that. Naturally, you could teach your dog to keep his direction on the target even at a distance from you, but that requires elaborate training and, frankly, you don't really need it. Once you start working on the actual obstacles, the obstacle itself will tell your dog where to keep that rear end, but until then the remote reward will set the direction.

Exercise 72: Hit the target from a distance

1. Set out the remote reward (so that your dog sees it).
2. Transport your dog to a starting position at least a few meters from the remote reward.
3. As you and your dog turn to face the remote reward, quickly put down the target a step ahead of your dog, and let go of him.
4. Your dog moves ahead, slams his foot onto the target, and holds his position.
5. Say "go."
6. Your dog races to the remote reward.

When starting to build distance, we find it easiest to just reward with the start cue (without giving any treats in position). You can also reward your dog in position if you like, before saying the start cue.

USING A CUE TO RELEASE YOUR DOG TO THE TARGET

Up until now, your dog has always offered the target behavior spontaneously, but now you sometimes can park him in a stay before releasing him to the target. For that you'll need a verbal cue, one that releases him from the stay and allows him to dash to the target. We simply use our start cue.

Place your target a bit ahead, hold on to your dog until he "parks" himself in a stay, and give your start cue, which tells him to work ahead toward whatever is there—in this case, the target. As he holds his position on the target, give another start cue to release him to his reward. If he forgets the target and goes directly for the remote reward, the reward just disappears. Soon he'll figure out that the start cue means "start and do your job" and not just "run directly to your reward."

Incrementally add more distance to the target, transporting your dog away up to 10 meters from the target before releasing him. Don't increase the distance until your dog confidently rushes to the target and slams his foot on it without hesitation. If you get any hesitation or other mistakes, immediately shorten the distance.

At first, stand still at the starting point where you released your dog until he has hit the target and you've given the start cue. Then you can run up to him at the remote reward. Eventually, start varying your behavior. You should be able to be anywhere (behind, ahead, very close, or at a lateral distance), tip-toeing, walking, or running—your dog should still do his job. To keep your handling consistent, make sure your shoulders are pointing ahead. And, if you're in a position where your dog should fly past you, also make sure that you are moving forward.

Step 5: Step down to the target

Up until now, your dog has been doing all his foot-target training on level ground. Now you'll teach him to do the same behavior over an edge, stepping down with the front feet to reach the target. For example, you can work off the last step of a stair, a plank, a curb, or a tree stump. If you have already free-shaped the two-on/two-off behavior parallel to the target procedure (see page 370), your dog will be familiar with the setting.

Either way, since you are now introducing a whole new concept to your target training (starting perched on an object and stepping down to reach the target), start at a short distance—just a few inches from the edge—and use a low, wide surface where it's easy for your dog to keep his balance.

Exercise 73: Target over an edge

1. Place the target directly on the ground by the edge.
2. Use a treat magnet to transport your dog up onto the surface, so that his front feet end up just an inch from the edge.
3. End the transport.
4. Your dog hits the target.
5. (Optional: Click and reward in position.)
6. Your dog holds his position.
7. (Optional: Reward in position while your dog keeps still.)
8. Say "go."
9. Your dog races ahead (to a remote reward or a thrown toy).

Suggested tag point:

Treat magnet transport to edge

For the very first repetitions, reward your dog just for hitting the target in this new situation. Then add "keep rear feet up" as a new criterion: reinforce hitting the target only when the rear end stays on the elevated surface. If your dog hops off with all four feet, simply pick up the target and start over again.

Work through the target training again from elevated surfaces—adding all kinds of variations, increasing the distance, and so on.

Treat magnet transport to a good starting position, close to the edge

Stepping down to the target

Reward!

Step 6: Fade the target

Now that your dog does a perfect target behavior and two-on/two-off behavior from various surfaces, the only thing left is to make sure you can get rid of the target. In your future contact training you'll sometimes want to use the target, sometimes not—so it's a good idea for both you and your dog to learn how to make the transition between target and no target.

If you've been free-shaping the two-on/two-off as well, your dog already knows the two-on/two-off behavior without the target. Then you can just start varying, even within a session, whether there is a target or not. Don't announce to your dog whether the target is in place or not—his job is to get to the edge and slam his feet to the ground, target or no target.

Even if your dog doesn't already know the two-on/two-off without the target, you can still transfer his target behavior to the ground, teaching him to slam his front feet where the target usually is. One way to fade the target is to gradually make it less visible (for example, make it progressively smaller, or partly cover it with dirt or grass). Another way is to do three to four repetitions with the target, then secretly remove it for one repetition—your dog will believe it's still there, so most likely he'll slam his feet where it usually is. Then you can slide the target back again for the next repetition.

Once you start fading the target your criterion will be "front feet on the ground." If your dog actually hits the target or not (when it's there) isn't what counts anymore. Be quick to reward as his front feet hit the ground—either giving your start cue directly, or first rewarding in position.

Rear feet "on," front feet "off"

"I know where to plant those front feet—on the ground."

Two-on/two-off

In this section we'll describe how you can free-shape the two-on/two-off behavior. The two-on/two-off skill exactly replicates what the final behavior will look like (front feet on the ground, rear feet on the equipment). You're just not working on the actual obstacles. No targets or other prompts are involved in this procedure.

What should the two-on/two-off behavior look like?

1. Your dog starts on an elevated surface.

2. He hurries to the edge, steps over it as fast as he can and stops short, front feet on the ground.

3. He holds his position and waits for his start cue.

4. When you say your start cue, he dashes away.

Equipment

What you need is an edge of some kind, and it doesn't need to be a high one at that. For example, you can work off a curb, the last step of a stair, a tree stump, a plank, or even a phone book.

Why do I need the free-shaped two-on/two-off behavior?

Free-shaping the two-on/two-off

- teaches your dog to step down to the ground with his front feet.
- provides a solid foundation that you can transfer directly to obstacle training.

How can you train it?

When free-shaping the two-on/two-off we use the *Aim for it* procedure to get the behavior of stepping over the edge. You will find that two-on/two-off training closely resembles target training. But there is one big difference: Your dog will now be working *off* a piece of equipment (and not working on the ground with a target that you can easily move). That means you have to be particular about your transport so that he gets to start working close to the edge. It also means you need to make use of your start cue from the very beginning since we never want your dog to experience leaving his two-on/two-off position without being cued to do so.

Step 1: Step down, reward in position, and start on cue teaches your dog to hurry over the edge and plant his front feet on the ground. Just as with the target, your goal is for him to find the right position actively, quickly, without hesitation, and independently of you.

At the same time, your dog gets accustomed to getting multiple rewards in the two-on/two-off position and to starting away from it on cue. This basic step includes three stages:

Stage 1: Get the behavior: step down
Stage 2: Make it fast and fluent
Stage 3: Add variations and distractions

Step 2: Hold the position is about teaching your dog to actively hold his two-on/two-off position until you give the start cue.

Step 3: Add further variations and distractions will proof his performance.

Step 4: Find the edge from a distance is the last step. Increase the distance incrementally, ensuring that your dog always drives into his position without hesitation.

We'll go through the first step in detail but only briefly comment on the other steps, since the process follows what we described for the foot-target behavior (see page 359).

WHY DOES THE FIRST STEP OF THE TWO-ON/TWO-OFF TRAINING DIFFER FROM THE FIRST STEP OF TARGET TRAINING?

When working with the foot target we begin with just "foot on target" and then introduce the stay and the start cue.

With the two-on/two-off training we opt to reward in position (getting the dog to hold his position) right away. Then the start cue becomes a necessity, to tell your dog when it's time to leave that position. There are two main reasons for this difference:

- It simply isn't possible to get the same quick repetitions of two-on/two-off as you got with the first step of your target work. In the target training you can move the target around, but in training two-on/two-off, you have to move the dog. So instead of focusing on many quick repetitions, we choose to focus on rewarding many times in position.

- In the two-on/two-off position, your dog has to work his front and rear end simultaneously. The novel "bottoms up" position requires your dog to control his rear end while stepping down with the front end—a balancing act not required in target training. By rewarding many times while your dog holds his position, you help him get control over that rear end.

Step 1: Step down, reward in position, and start on cue

This is the goal of Step 1 in the two-on/two-off training:

1. As soon as the transport ends, your dog steps over the edge and puts his front feet on the ground while keeping his rear feet on the equipment.
2. You reward in position (maneuvering the rewards so that your dog remains in position).
3. From there, he starts off on your cue.

The basic two-on/two-off training mirrors the basic target training—the main difference is that in the two-on/two-off training you'll make use of your start cue from the very beginning. Thoroughly work through the three stages:

Stage 1: Get the behavior: step down.
Stage 2: Make it fast and fluent
Stage 3: Add variations and distractions

Stage 1: Get the behavior: step down

Before you begin, rehearse starts on cue. Your start cue will appear at the end of the first session.

To begin the first two-on/two-off session, transport your dog onto the object to a starting position just a finger's length from the edge. To minimize how far you have to transport your dog, simply bring your dog up on the object from the side, facing the edge. We suggest using a treat magnet transport since that enables you to place your dog's nose exactly where you want it. As you remove the treat magnet, be prepared to click and treat for any movement toward the edge.

Intermediate criteria in the shaping process might be:

1. glancing forward
2. nose pointing toward the edge
3. reaching with nose toward the ground
4. slightly moving a foot
5. lifting a front foot
6. front foot on the ground

Exercise 74: Shape your dog to step over the edge

1. Use a treat magnet to transport your dog to a starting position, his front feet just an inch from the edge.
2. End the transport.
3. Your dog glances ahead (or lowers his head or even lifts a foot).
4. Click and reward low by the edge.
5. Continue the shaping, clicking, and treating for motion toward the ground.
6. Your dog puts a front foot on the ground (either he offers it, or he happens to put it there when reaching for a reward).
7. Click and then machine-gun treats to your dog while he remains in position.
8. Give your start cue.
9. Your dog starts.
10. Reward ahead of him!

Suggested tag points:

- Reward low by the edge
- Machine-gun treats for correct position

Be scrupulous about your transport so that your dog gets a good starting point to begin working from (left and center left). When you've ended the transport, click for nose pointing down (center right), and reward low (right).

Click for foot over the edge (left) and machine-gun treats to keep your dog in that position. You can maneuver your treat deliveries so that he ends up with both front feet on the ground (center). To end, give your start cue and reward further ahead (right).

During this first stage of the training, while you are shaping forward/downward movement in order to get the front feet to step to the ground, many different things can happen. To cover all eventualities, let's go through the various possibilities.

Getting on the equipment: First of all, you may or may not be successful in transporting your dog up onto the equipment.

- If your dog happily follows the treat magnet or whatever transport you use, end the transport as his front feet are close to the edge.
- If your dog hesitates to follow your treat magnet up onto the equipment, switch to training mode and reward him several times during the transport, to reinforce the transport behavior. If necessary, do several sessions just working with the transport before moving on to the two-on/two-off training. Once the transport is in order, end it when your dog's front feet are close to the edge.

Staying on the equipment: Then, once you've started clicking and treating for forward movement, your dog may or may not stay on the equipment.
- If your dog stays on the equipment, keep shaping forward/downward motion.
- If your dog steps or jumps off the equipment, just transport him back onto it (using a collar transport or a rather boring treat magnet).

Foot on the ground: During the first sessions your dog may or may not offer to place a foot on the ground.
- If your dog puts a foot—or both feet—on the ground, click and reward! Try machine-gunning treats while he is still standing in his two-on/two-off position, using the placement of the treats to help him keep his balance and remain in position. End with a start cue, and reward him for starting on cue. In actuality, however, your dog has three options once he has placed a foot on the ground:
  - In the best-case scenario, he remains in position while you keep delivering rewards, dashes off on your start cue, and gets a thrown toy or remote reward for starting on cue.

– Or, he might remain in position while you deliver several rewards but then jump off or slip off with his rear end. As he bails, you end the reward ceremony. If you wish to continue, start over from the beginning by transporting him to the starting point on the equipment again.

– Or, he might jump or slip off just as you click, before you've had time to deliver a reward. Since you've clicked, quickly reward anyway. Then, if you wish to continue, start over from the beginning by transporting him to the starting point on the equipment again.

- If your dog doesn't offer placing a foot on the ground, you can use reward placement to get that foot on the ground. Click for aiming forward, and place the reward so close to the ground that your dog accidentally puts his feet down to reach the treat. Yes, this is luring (thus your dog won't learn too much about where to put his foot), but you'll then be able to send him away from the two-on/two-off position with your start cue—and that will aid your back-chaining.

- Or, if you wish to end the training session before your dog has placed a foot on the ground, just transport him off the equipment after the last reward (lift him off, or use a treat magnet). In this situation, don't use your start cue to get him off. Say your start cue only when your dog is actually standing in his two-on/two-off position. Remember: Starting on cue is the last part of the chain. So every time you give your start cue, reward your dog for starting!

TIPS FOR GETTING YOUR DOG TO STEP DOWN STRAIGHT AHEAD

On the actual obstacles you'll want your dog to put his feet *straight ahead* of the edge, not off to the side. So just as you should try to avoid curling when working with the foot target, you should strive to get your dog to do his two-on/two-off behavior straight ahead rather than drifting toward you. Here are some tips:

- Start with objects where there is only one edge (for example, use stairs or a curb), so that your dog cannot step off to the side.
- Be particular about your transport so that your dog's nose is pointing forward and his body is straight when he starts working.
- Make sure you're next to your dog or slightly behind him, facing forward, when the transport ends.
- Vary where the rewards come from. Helpers are helpful!

- Deliver the rewards close to the ground.
- If your dog habitually aims toward one side or tends to curl toward you, place most rewards a bit to the opposite side (for example, if your dog is aiming too much to the left, place the reward slightly to his right).
- Deliver the reward for "starting on cue" straight ahead. The anticipation of going straight after the start cue will help your dog keep straight when stepping down.

Of course, you can also use shaping to teach your dog to adjust himself and get into the right spot. But if you're careful about your transports and your reward management, your dog usually will straighten out on his own. Remember: The top priority is that your dog hurries to slam his front feet on the ground.

ONE OR TWO FEET ON THE GROUND?

In the two-on/two-off, our goal is two feet on the ground. Especially in the early stages of training, however, we want to focus on the first foot hitting the ground. In our experience, most dogs automatically start using both front feet as they gain intensity. If your dog doesn't, just switch to a two-feet criterion, shaping your dog to put both feet on the ground.

You can also vary the height of the surface. In the beginning it's often easiest to use a low edge, but using a higher edge produces a more distinct behavior and pushes your dog to place both front feet on the ground simply because that is more physically comfortable. Once this becomes a habit you can lower the surface again.

Stage 2: Make it fast and fluent

Once your dog has gotten the idea of putting a front foot on the ground, minimize the number of clicks and treats you use to get him there, and, as quickly as possible, make "foot on the ground" your only criterion. Fast and fluent is your goal!

Make sure you always transport your dog to a starting position *close* to the edge. That way he just has to step down to get his click and treat.

Continue to machine-gun treats to your dog as he hits the ground, and end with your start cue. Your dog's job is to hit the ground; your job is to manipulate the rewards so that he remains in that position until you give the start cue. To further increase your dog's intensity you can vary between rewarding solely with your start cue and saying the start cue as his front foot hits the ground.

Stage 3: Add variations and distractions

When the transport ends and your dog sees the edge, he should be totally focused on his task and barely notice anything else. Gradually add variations and distractions, constantly monitoring to make sure that your dog keeps diving into position with full intensity.

A tempting toy placed a bit ahead first is a distraction. After the start cue, it transforms into a reward. Once your dog has gotten used to it, it also functions as an aid, giving your dog something to aim toward. Then remember to treat it as an aid: Use it but be aware that you also need to teach your dog to work without it.

Step 2: Hold the position

Up until now, you've been machine-gunning treats to your dog so that he has remained in position until you've given your start cue. Now it's time to give him the responsibility to hold his position, by incrementally increasing the time between the rewards. The goal now is that the instant your dog's feet hit the ground, he freezes in that position until you release him with your start cue.

To build duration, you can

- continue to reward in position, varying the period between the rewards and always ending with a start cue,
- or you can skip the rewards in position and just vary the time before the start cue.

Either way, keep ping-ponging the time up and down so that your dog stays on the edge—and don't get too obsessive with getting long durations. Your dog throwing himself into the two-on/two-off position is always your main focus.

Step 3: Add further variations and distractions

Just as in the target training, you can ensure independent and reliable performance by varying what happens as your dog starts working and steps down, while he stands frozen in position, and while he starts on your cue—no matter what is going on around him. Make sure you often reward just as your dog's feet hit the ground (either by clicking and treating, or by giving the start cue right away), to continually boost your dog's motivation to dash into position.

Step 4: Find the edge from a distance

As a final step before introducing the actual obstacles, teach your dog to get to the edge from a distance. Here we usually don't build up to more than a few steps (as compared with the target training, where it's simple to add many meters on the ground). You'll build greater distance on the obstacles.

To increase the distance, simply end the transport a bit farther from the edge. To keep boosting your dog's motivation to hustle into position, often reward quickly (within half a second from when the front feet hit the ground), either with a click and reward in position or with a cue to start. If your dog *ever* hesitates before stepping over the edge, immediately revisit earlier steps to ensure that your dog always dives right into position.

A-frame and dogwalk

You and your dog now have the requisite skills to take on the A-frame and dogwalk: You know how to constantly vary your behavior and remain neutral while giving your dog's start cue. Your dog has learned targeting and two-on/two-off skills, has good rear-end control (to maintain his position), can hold position until cued and start on that cue, and is comfortable with negotiating elevated, narrow objects and with creating and demanding noise and movement.

With all your contact preparation work, introducing the A-frame and the dogwalk will be simple! Just rehearse the same steps on the actual obstacles (or on objects that look just like the last part of the obstacles), starting at the end and gradually increasing the distance until your dog runs over the entire obstacle. This way, the first time your dog goes over the entire obstacle, he'll know exactly what to do at the end and zoom right into his two-on/two-off position. Remember: Back-chaining is key to successful contact-obstacle training!

What should the finished A-frame and dogwalk performance look like?

1. Your dog zooms over the obstacle, aiming for the bottom edge of the down contact.
2. His front feet hit the ground and he freezes in a two-on/two-off position.
3. On your start cue, your dog explodes off the contact, continuing in accordance with your handling.

While your dog is on the obstacle, he works totally independently of you.

The obstacles

The obstacles are built in accordance with competition rules, and each has specific requirements related to the following characteristics:

- Height
- Width
- Angle to the ground
- Surface (for example, carpet or sand-painted wood)

You can start directly on the competition version of the obstacles, or you can work through successive approximations and start lower, wider, or at a wider angle. At first, you'll work only at the end of the obstacle, so you can use other objects that simulate the last meter or so of the A-frame or dogwalk. This way you don't need so much space, you don't have to drive to the dog club for all your training, and you can arrange any height, width, angle, and surface you like. For example, you can run a plank from a table or from a rock, or you can build miniature versions of the A-frame and the dogwalk.

When we talk about obstacles in this chapter, we're referring either to the actual competition dogwalk or A-frame or to any other object that simulates the end of the obstacle. Use what is most convenient for you and what best fits each stage of your training.

How can you train it?

Continue with your target training and your free-shaped two-on/two-off training on the actual (or simulated) obstacles. Before each session

- choose whether you're going to work with or without a target, or if you're going to vary (sometime repetitions with target, some without);
- choose how you're going to reward the behavior (solely with your start cue, or first delivering one or several rewards in position);

- choose how you're going to reward the start off the obstacle (remote reward or thrown toy);
- decide how to vary your own behavior (for example, right or left side, behind or ahead, close or farther out to the side, standing still or moving, and so on).

Be scrupulous about your transport, making sure that your dog is really hanging on to his treat magnet or that you're holding his collar all the way until you want him to start working on his own. You can end the transport as he places his front feet up on the obstacle (facing the right direction) or, *at the earliest,* just before he hops onto the obstacle. *Never* end the transport several feet or more away from the obstacle. You don't want to teach your dog to run by himself to the down contact and hop on.

The handler ends the transport, and the dog immediately aims for the ground.

A-frame and dogwalk training in six steps

Steps 1–3: Get the behavior, vary the duration, and add variations and distractions means working through exactly the same training as in the preparation training away from the obstacle. First you need to get the behavior fast and fluent at the end of the obstacle, then begin to vary duration and add variations and distractions.

Step 4: Vary where you are going after the obstacle means adding some handling after your start cue.

Step 5: Increase the distance means starting your dog farther back on the obstacle, incrementally adding to the distance he needs to zoom to get into position, until eventually he is performing the entire obstacle from the beginning.

Step 6: Vary where you come from before the obstacle means adding handling from different directions and from different obstacles that you've already taught.

Work through all possible varieties on the down contact. Can your dog do his job even though you're behind him? Or if you're jogging in place and waving an arm?

Steps 1–3: Get the behavior, vary the duration, and add variations and distractions

Before the first session, start with some repetitions away from the obstacle (for example, some target work on the ground, or some two-on/two-off on a familiar object). Then move on to the actual/simulated obstacle and begin at the end (just a step from the edge). To get your dog up on the end, transport him in a small circle around your legs so that he approaches from the side, facing the end of the obstacle. Even a small dog can easily jump up from the side onto both the dogwalk and the A-frame.

Get the behavior fast and fluent at the end, vary the duration before the start cue (with or without intermediate rewards in position), and work through lots of different variations and distractions.

WHAT DO I DO IF MY DOG DOESN'T PUT HIS FEET WHERE I WANT THEM?

When you start working on the actual obstacles (or other sloping equipment), your dog may try stepping down to the side. To teach him to put his feet straight ahead, try the following:

- Use your target: Place the target where you want your dog's feet, building a good habit; then fade the target.
- Redo the free-shaping process on the actual obstacle, to explain to your dog exactly where he should place his front feet. If he steps down to the side, shape him to adjust himself and get into the correct spot (clicking and treating for any tendency to move the front end in the right direction).

- Make the edge a bit higher (more visible), for example, by placing a brick under it. Successively lower it.
- Temporarily use some kind of markers at the edge's corners to make sure your dog's feet land ahead of the edge instead of the side. The markers will both help you set your criteria (only reward for feet on the correct side of the markers) and function as prompts for your dog. (Note that markers are an aid that needs to be faded.)

For further ideas for how to keep your dog straight when working with the target and the two-on/two-off, review the suggestions on pages 360 and 362.

Step 4: Vary where you are going after the obstacle

After the contact you can exit straight, execute a regular turn (at various angles), or perform a front cross. Notice, though, that you're still working only with the last part of the obstacle; your dog is merely stepping down over the edge and waiting for your start cue. Give your start cue, direct your dog where you want him to go, and either reward him directly for following your handling, or continue on to other obstacles. Continually vary when you give your dog's start cue and what you are doing so that he learns that the start cue can happen anytime while he's holding his position on the contact.

You might need to put some work into maintaining the perfect performance when your dog anticipates a tight turn after the contact. Here your target can come in handy, to help your dog put his feet in the correct spot (and not step off to the side).

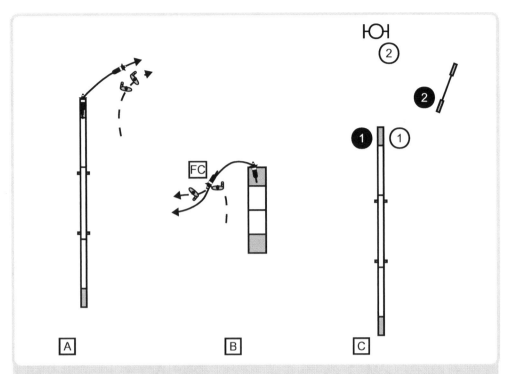

Vary where you're going after the contact. Here are a few examples:

A. Doing a regular turn off the dogwalk
B. Doing a front cross off the A-frame
C. Adding two obstacles means endless opportunities! You can for example follow the white numbers, start in right-side handling, and cross behind at the tire. Or you can follow the black numbers, start in left-side handling, and do a front cross between the dogwalk and the jump. Or, also following the black numbers, you can start in right-side handling, cross behind the dogwalk, do a regular turn to the jump, and cross behind again at the jump. Or... (find your own versions!)

Step 5: Increase the distance

Increase the instance inch by inch, ending the transport farther from the edge so that your dog has to take one or several steps to reach the edge. When you increase the distance that your dog moves down the plank or A-frame, eventually he won't be able to hop on from the side anymore. To start even higher up, you can lift him up (if you both are comfortable with that), or you can place something to step on (for example, a table) next to the obstacle.

You don't necessarily have to add inch by inch all the way to the beginning of the obstacle. If your dog is fast and fluent at a meter's distance from the down contact, you can often just start from the beginning. Do the whole obstacle *once,* rewarding lavishly, then immediately ask for several shorter repetitions before going for the whole obstacle again.

Remember:
- Continue to terminate the transport only when your dog is in position to shoot down toward the edge (don't end the transport prematurely).
- Ping-pong back and forth between longer and shorter distances—that'll help you keep top speed and intensity driving into position.

- Keep varying everything. When you introduce new difficulties, momentarily go back to a shorter distance.
- If your dog ever hesitates before he hits the ground, immediately go back to kindergarten at shorter distances.

Step 6: Vary where you come from before the obstacle

You can now add handling *from* different directions (approaching straight or from an angle, in a regular turn or with a front cross, or performing a rear cross as the dog ascends the contact obstacle). Let your dog handle the ascent himself—he'll soon learn how to approach from an angle and still keep his balance over the obstacle.

You can also add obstacles your dog knows before the dogwalk or A-frame. Put the A-frame or dogwalk into different kinds of sequences—just remember to add one new difficulty at a time.

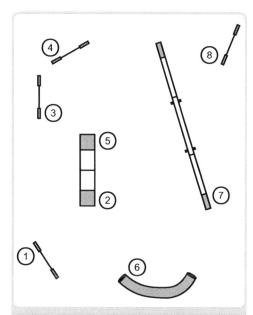

Try this sequence with all front crosses (at #2 to #3, #4 to #5, and #6 to #7) and with all rear crosses (at #3, #5, and #7). It's a good idea to reward all the down contacts (either rewarding in position or rewarding right after the start cue).

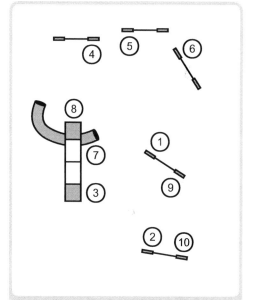

Now that your dog can do the contacts in sequences, the benefits of an independent contact behavior become obvious. In this sequence, for example, you'll want to hurry to get to the threadle position close to #5—and, you want to get close to #9 to cue the wrap back to #10. No problem, since your dog will do his job on the A-frame while you move toward the next obstacle!

WHAT IF MY DOG DOESN'T ASCEND THE OBSTACLE CORRECTLY?

If your dog ascends from the side (not taking the obstacle all the way from the beginning), you can

- work lesser angles to get him into the habit of ascending correctly.
- make sure your handling is unambiguous.
- keep working a lot with the downside contact—if your dog really aims to drive with full speed over the obstacle, he's more likely to ascend properly.
- try using some kind of barrier to help your dog get the right approach (this is an aid to build a better habit; it works for some, not for all).

If your dog ascends from the end but often leaps over the up contact, you need to make a choice about perhaps teaching a specific behavior for the up contact. If so, work that separately—for example, up a plank that ends on a table or on a rock. We prefer not to train the up contacts, but if we have to, we usually choose to use the two-on/two-off for the up side as well. Easiest is to use your target, simply placing it where you want the front feet and starting your dog off it with your start cue. On the dogwalk and the teeter your dog can easily stop and start on his way up. Since climbing a full-height A-frame from a stop at the bottom is quite hard, we recommend that you give your start cue before your dog comes to a full stop (or let him stop, reward in position, and transport him off without sending him over the obstacle).

The teeter

It ends in the middle of nowhere, it moves, and it makes noise—and on top of that, it has contact zones! The teeter is unique among the agility obstacles. Proper training will make your dog think it's a roller coaster designed to amuse him!

What should the finished teeter performance look like?

The competition rules say that the dog should step on the up contact, run over the teeter plank so that it tips, step on the down contact, and leave only when the board has hit the ground. But just as with the other contact obstacles, the rules only set the framework for your training: You need to set your own goal for your dog's teeter performance and train accordingly.

For the teeter, we recommend teaching your dog a two-on/two-off down contact with a cue to start, just as on the dogwalk and A-frame. We also recommend you teach him to run far out on the teeter—farther than gravity actually dictates. Your dog should learn that the teeter moves only when he has reached your chosen point (the "start button").

The final performance is a behavior chain:

1. Your dog races onto the teeter.
2. When he reaches the "start button" (the point you've chosen, far out on the teeter),
3. … he sets the teeter moving,
4. … which causes the teeter to hit the ground,
5. … which gives your dog the opportunity to perform his contact behavior.
6. As quickly as he can, he plants his front feet on the ground, where he freezes in a two-on/two-off position,
7. … which causes you to give your start cue,
8. … which allows him to dash off the teeter, continuing on course in accordance with your handling.

"FOUR ON THE CONTACT" ON THE TEETER

If your dog is very small, the teeter might bounce his rear end up in the air while he's in his two-on/two-off position, possibly causing pain or injury. His weight simply might not be enough to keep the board down.

One possible solution is to teach a four-on performance instead, skipping the potentially more harmful two-on/two-off, and giving your start cue while your dog is standing *on* the contact. However, then you lose the benefit of having the edge involved in the contact performance. What we usually do in these cases is to first teach a two-on/two-off teeter contact behavior (to get full drive toward the edge), and then, if it seems as though there might be a recoil problem, we switch to rewarding and giving the start cue while the dog still has his front feet on the obstacle.

For a larger dog, a recoiling teeter might present a problem if he is off balance, hasn't shifted his weight back, or doesn't actively push the teeter down. Proper teeter training solves these issues; if your dog really knows what to do at the end and strives to get to the ground and into his two-on/two-off position as fast as possible, he'll automatically keep his balance.

How can you train it?

The main principle behind teeter training is back-chaining: We want the dog to constantly strive to get to the end where he can perform his contact behavior, get his start cue, and start off. But, since the teeter performance involves so many different behaviors (making it quite a complicated chain) we practice several of the pieces separately before putting them together.

Driving to the end of the teeter.

This is how we go about the training:

Step 1: Learn what to do at the end of the teeter teaches your dog to ride the board to the ground and make it slam, get into the two-on/two-off position, wait for the start cue, and start. We teach this in four stages:

> **Stage 1:** Teeter movement
> **Stage 2:** Teeter impact
> **Stage 3:** Rehearse the two-on/two-off + freeze + start cue
> **Stage 4:** Add movement + impact to the chain

Step 2: Run to the "start button" teaches your dog to run far out on the teeter—all the way to your chosen "start button." This includes three stages:

> **Stage 1:** Run all the way to the start button
> **Stage 2:** Hit the start button and make the teeter move
> **Stage 3:** Perform the whole obstacle "competition style"

TEETER CAUTIONS

Don't let your dog bounce around the agility course unsupervised. Agility is something you do together; the dog can putter about elsewhere. An inexperienced dog must never get onto the teeter unaided; if the teeter were to tip, it could scare or even hurt him. Furthermore, his experience—even if he wasn't frightened—would clash with what you want him to learn, so your training would become more difficult than necessary, and your dog would have to relearn instead of starting from scratch.

Be attentive to your dog's reaction when other teams are training on the obstacle. Some dogs find the sound disturbing; still others react in a negative way to the sudden movement. Dogs pay attention to one another, so your dog should be allowed to watch only brilliant teeter training. Watching another dog that seems unsure or scared on the teeter or a stressed trainer using a cautious or angry tone of voice could affect your dog and instill negative associations. So make sure that your dog forms positive associations with the teeter from the beginning. Connect the sound the obstacle makes with a nice treat (for example, treat your dog every time another dog executes the obstacle), and give him positive teeter connotations by watching teeter training only where the dogs are having fun with the teeter and their trainers.

PRESSURE-FREE TEETER TRAINING

When we first introduced teaching your dog to like and create noise and movement (page 173), we cautioned you to watch your dog carefully for signs of stress—if a noise was too loud or a movement too big or sudden—and to back off as necessary. If your dog chooses to jump off the teeter, he's letting you know it's too much too soon. Let him continue working, but reward him only when he's on the teeter. This way he'll make an effort to stay on the board, but if he feels uncomfortable, he knows he can jump off if he wishes. Giving your dog that control will build his confidence.

Step 3: Vary where you are going *after* **the teeter** incorporates continuing in different directions and *toward* different obstacles.

Step 4: Vary where you come from *before* **the teeter** incorporates approaching *from* different directions and from different obstacles.

When you start training on the teeter, it's practical (but not essential) to have two helpers—one to maneuver the teeter according to your instructions and one to act as a treat machine. This way you get to concentrate on watching your dog and decide what to reinforce.

In early training, it'll be you and your helpers that decide how and when the teeter "acts"—not your dog. Always remember to vary your own position and to deliver the treats in the direction you want your dog to be facing.

Step 1: Learn what to do at the end of the teeter

Fully trained, Step 1 (the end of the teeter) should look like this:

1. When you begin the session, the teeter needs to look as though it has already hit the ground. One option is to hold the end to the ground—another, easier way is to work on what really is the up contact but pretend it is the down contact (since that end is already on the ground).
2. You transport your dog onto the end of the teeter, facing the edge.
3. While your dog is busy with a treat magnet, your helper lifts the teeter up in the air with the dog on it.
4. When your dog is up in the air, you end the treat magnet.
5. Your dog looks expectant and prepares for a ride down.
6. Your helper lets go of the teeter, which drops to the ground (with a large dog, the helper softens the drop a little).
7. As the teeter hits the ground, your dog gets into his two-on/two-off contact position and freezes there.
8. You give your start cue (possibly after one or several intermediate rewards in position).
9. Your dog starts off the teeter.
10. You reward the start.

Throughout the Step 1 work, your dog will work only on the very end of the teeter, and you'll let the treat magnet transport continue until the end of the teeter is lifted off the ground.

We'll describe the training in detail, in four stages:

Stage 1: Teeter movement teaches your dog that being on the end of the teeter when it moves is a fabulous thing. He'll learn to like the movement, and that he can create it (through you).

Stage 2: Teeter impact teaches your dog that the board's impact—as well as its movement—is fabulous.

Stage 3: Rehearse the two-on/two-off + freeze + start cue lets your dog practice his two-on/two-off contact at the end of the teeter.

Stage 4: Add movement + impact to the chain teaches your dog to happily and confidently ride the teeter to the ground, eventually from full height, ending with the two-on/two-off contact and the subsequent start cue.

If your preparation work is really, really well done so that your dog truly loves all kinds of noise and movement underfoot, you can start on Stage 3 right away. We recommend working through the first two stages too, however, to make sure your dog is enjoying the movement and the noise on the actual teeter. Perhaps you can accomplish it in one training session; perhaps it'll take a lot longer.

Stage 1: Teeter movement

In your foundation work you've already made sure your dog likes movement, and you've worked to the point where he eagerly creates movement himself, demanding whatever object he's on to move. This first stage of your teeter training functions as a reminder, teaching your dog that movement is fun on this peculiar object, too. At the same time, your dog will learn to stand close to the end of the teeter, to stay on the teeter when it moves, and that he can "start" the teeter himself, by appearing to want it to move.

When introducing the teeter, first do a couple of repetitions where you simply pair teeter movement with tasty treats, *classically conditioning* your dog to enjoy the teeter movement. Simultaneously, these treats will function as rewards for staying on the teeter.

Move the board when your dog looks expectant.

Exercise 75: Rock the boat (teeter movement equals treat)

1. Use a treat magnet to transport your dog onto the down end of the teeter, facing the edge.
2. Your helper barely lifts the end of the teeter.
3. Reward as the teeter moves.
4. Your helper rocks the teeter slightly (without letting it touch the ground).
5. Reward immediately.
6. Repeat the pairing of rock—reward a few times.
7. To end the exercise, your helper gently eases the teeter down until it hits ground.
8. Reward this last teeter movement (and the ever-so-slight impact).
9. Use that last reward to transport your dog off the teeter for a break.

Suggested tag points:

- Reward when teeter rocks
- Treat magnet to get off

Once the end of the teeter is raised off the ground in these exercises, it rocks up and down but never hits the ground until you've finished the training session. Rock the teeter briefly with a little bit of stillness in between (where your dog doesn't get a treat) so that he really makes the connection: Moving teeter equals treats.

For the first few repetitions, deliver a treat for each movement (both raising and lowering). This is the sequence: stillness—teeter tips down—reward—stillness—teeter is raised—reward—stillness—teeter tips down—and so on. Reward low, close to the teeter's edge. The best placement of reward is for the treat to "emerge" from under the teeter, just ahead of the edge.

What you're aiming for, however, is for your dog to learn that *going down* is the really fun part! So as soon as you see your dog enjoying this new game, reward only the downward motion and extend that reward while the teeter is lifted up again. The sequence then becomes: stillness—teeter tips down—reward while teeter is raised—stillness—teeter tips down—and so on.

At first, move the teeter slightly, and gradually build up to about 10–30 cm (up to a foot) of rocking.

As you work through this training, watch for your dog pricking his ears, or "making himself heavy" to get the teeter to move. As soon as you start seeing such expectant behaviors, progress to letting your dog *create the teeter movement through you* by letting some sign of anticipation be the behavior that causes teeter movement. (This training replicates what you did when teaching your dog to create movement; see page 180.)

Exercise 76: C'mon, make it move! (create teeter movement through you)

1. Use a treat magnet to transport your dog onto the down end of the teeter.
2. Let the treat magnet continue while your helper gently lifts the end of the teeter a bit.
3. End the treat magnet and observe your dog for signs of anticipation.
4. Your dog "looks expectant" (perhaps pricks his ears, or looks downward).
5. The teeter drops a little bit (guided by your helper). Note: The teeter doesn't touch the ground.
6. Reward! Let the reward continue while your helper lifts the teeter again.
7. Repeat a few times.
8. To end the session, your helper gently eases the teeter to the ground and you use the last reward to transport your dog off the teeter.

TO CLICK OR NOT TO CLICK?

In teeter movement and teeter impact training, the clicker is optional. You can simply rock the teeter and deliver a reward, making the movement (and later, the impact) the equivalent of a click. Your dog acts, the teeter rocks, you treat.

If you wish to use your clicker as a precise marker, you can begin with a few repetitions of clicking as your dog acts (for example, click for "looking down" and deliver the reward while you rock the teeter). Soon, however, you should move on to marking *the teeter movement* rather than the dog's action. The teeter rocks, click, treat. "Being on a rocking teeter" should be what earns the click and treat—"acting to get the teeter to rock" is how to get there.

WHAT ABOUT THE CONTACT PERFORMANCE?

At this stage you won't be asking your dog for a contact performance. Instead, you'll use the last reward to transport him off the teeter.

The reason for adding the contact performance later is that you need to get some rapid-fire training here. You need your dog to learn to really like the teeter's movement and impact, and to get him to try and make the teeter move and hit the ground. If you were to add a contact performance every time the teeter was lowered to the ground, you wouldn't get the rapid repetitions you need for the training to work.

Once your dog is happy and confident about staying on the teeter as it moves and hits the ground, you'll reinstate your contact and actually begin the back-chaining procedure proper. Until then, use your last reward to transport your dog off the teeter—make sure your treat magnet is up to par so that your transport works smoothly.

Suggested tag points:

*   Treat magnet while the teeter is lifted up
*   Reward the drop
*   Treat magnet to get off

Vary how high you raise the teeter: Sometimes rock the teeter close to the ground; sometimes hoist the teeter high up in the air and rock it up there. You want your dog to be completely comfortable with being close to the end of the teeter at whatever height, and you want him to crave it to move whenever your helper holds it still. Gradually build more abrupt "drops," both high up in the air and low to the ground.

Quite a few dogs choose to crouch or lie down during this training, which is just fine. The dog is lowering his center of gravity, which makes it easier for him to stay balanced. Whatever position your dog chooses, however, reward low and close to the edge—that's where you want your dog to focus.

Stage 2: Teeter impact

Your dog has already experienced the mild impacts that ended each movement training session on the teeter. Now it's time to make the rewards conditional on the impact, teaching your dog to really strive to make the teeter hit the ground.

This training is a continuation of the "C'mon, make it move" training—the only addition is that you let the teeter hit the ground before you reward. Begin low, with a dampened impact. Your helper will guide the teeter's movement, regulating how far and how fast it drops and how hard it hits the ground. If you opt to use your clicker, click for the impact.

Rollercoaster training!

Exercise 77: C'mon, slam!

1. Use a treat magnet to transport your dog onto the down end of the teeter.
2. Let the treat magnet continue while your helper gently lifts the end of the teeter a bit.
3. End the treat magnet and observe your dog for signs of anticipation.
4. Your dog "looks expectant" (perhaps pricks his ears, or looks downward).
5. The teeter drops a bit (guided by your helper).
6. The teeter hits the ground (guided by your helper).
7. Reward! Let the reward continue while your helper lifts the teeter again.
8. Repeat several times.
9. To end the session, use the last reward to transport your dog off the teeter.

Gradually increase the impact and height, but make sure that your dog maintains a positive attitude. Your dog should always strive to get back to the teeter! If he seems the least bit hesitant, the previous repetition was probably too difficult and not enough fun (even if your dog seemed to enjoy it while he was in the midst of it). Note that his attitude toward the next attempt reflects how he perceived the previous attempt. So if he ever hesitates, immediately return to an easier step, progress more slowly, and use even better rewards.

Work your way up to full height. If your helper simply lets go of the teeter, both the speed and the impact will increase with the height. To work on these aspects separately, have your helper adjust the speed of the drop and the severity of the impact by continuing to hold on lightly to the teeter. Throughout the training, keep a close eye on your dog's attitude. This should be fun, fun, fun!

IT DEPENDS ON YOUR DOG'S SIZE

If you have a small dog, he needs to learn to stand on the very edge of the teeter when it drops to the ground from full height. That's just what it'll look like in his final teeter performance!

If you have a bigger, heavier dog, you don't have to work all the way to full impact from full height. You can soften the "fall" by having your helper gently hold on to the teeter as it drops (but letting go completely before it hits the ground), you can dampen the impact by practicing on a pliable surface (for example, a thick and soft mat or horse stall mat), and you can let the really big dog stand a bit farther from the end (which will make the drop a bit slower).

TEETER WOES

If your dog suddenly becomes wary around the teeter and the training you're doing, you might simply have progressed too fast. But the problem could also have a physical cause. A dog with a sore neck or back might show his injury by acting strangely, either on the teeter or subsequent obstacles. To risk training with an injured dog is dangerous. Be sure to have the dog examined by a vet to rule out physical causes for teeter problems before you start to fix things in your training.

Also always remember to do a proper warm-up before training, even if you are just training some small detail. The teeter does produce strain on the dog's back from its recoil, and the dog's muscles must be warm enough to be able to handle the stress. Your agility dog is an athlete and must get proper physical care.

Stage 3: Rehearse the two-on/two-off + freeze + start cue

Since your dog's two-on/two-off and start cue are what will glue together this chain, rehearse his contact performance, freeze, and start cue on the actual teeter. Transport your dog to the end of the contact facing the edge, and let him offer a two-on/two-off (with or without a target). Reward in position if you like, but always end with your start cue and reward. Before moving on, make sure your dog reliably shoots down into position, holding it until you release him with your start cue, and reward his start.

Stage 4: Add movement + impact to the chain

Now it's time to chain the last part of the teeter performance together, so that your dog performs his contact as the teeter hits the ground. Begin the session with a couple of two-on/two-off contacts without movement; then add movement and impact. When you plan to work with movement and impact, your transport must carry on until you've lifted the end of the teeter up with your dog on it! If you end the transport prematurely, your dog should dive into his two-on/two-off position right away. By now, when you end the transport up in the air, your dog immediately should show signs of anticipation and "wanting the teeter to drop." So, practically, you'll drop the teeter as you end the transport.

Exercise 78: Two-on/two-off after movement and impact

1. Use a treat magnet to transport your dog onto the down end of the teeter.
2. Let the treat magnet continue while your helper gently lifts the end of the teeter a bit.
3. End the treat magnet.
4. The teeter drops (guided by your helper).
5. The teeter hits the ground (guided by your helper).
6. Your dog offers his two-on/two-off behavior.
7. (Optional: Click and treat in position.)
8. Give your start cue.
9. Your dog dashes ahead.
10. Reward!

Work until your dog's performance is fast and fluent when your helper drops the teeter from various heights.

Here, a target is placed on the ground.   Left: Treat magnet transport up in the air.   Center left: When the teeter hits the ground, the dog hits the target.   Center right: A distracting toy flies by.   Right: Start cue: "Grab that toy!"

"Look, mum, I found my edge!"

Step 2: Run to the start button

Now that your dog knows exactly what to do at the end of the teeter, it's time to teach him to mount the teeter and run far out on the plank to start the fun. We want the dog to run farther out than the actual pivot point of the teeter, so we choose a "start button" point on the teeter, and teach the dog to run all the way to it. From the dog's perspective, the teeter moving and hitting the ground should have nothing to do with gravity: As far as he knows, the teeter starts moving as a result of his "hitting that start button."

To teach the start button, we make sure the teeter moves when—and only when—the dog reaches the start button. The training follows these three stages:

Stage 1: Run all the way to the start button
Stage 2: Hit the start button and make the teeter move
Stage 3: Perform the entire obstacle "competition style"

During the first two stages, your helper (or you) is always holding on to the teeter while the dog ascends. Either put a foot on the up contact so that it's held to the ground, or hold the down contact up in the air.

Stage 1: Run all the way to the start button

Now, for the first time, your dog will get to ascend the teeter from the "correct" end. He'll get to run all the way to the end that's held up in the air and stop there to get his reward (not continuing into thin air). To get the behavior of running all the way to the end, you can use a foot target (placing the target at the end of the teeter) or you can simply click and reward as your dog reaches your chosen spot.

Hold on to the teeter so that it can't move, transport your dog to the beginning of the teeter, and let him ascend. Click and reward generously as he reaches the start button (if you need to, shape him there by clicking and rewarding during the ascent the first couple of times). When your dog has reached the start button and earned his reward, end the first repetition (lifting your dog off, or letting the reward last while your helper gently lowers the teeter so that you can transport your dog off). Repeat a couple of times if you like, but as soon as your dog confidently runs right to the edge, move on to the next stage.

Stage 2: Hit the start button and make the teeter move

You've already taught your dog that he can "start" the teeter by his own actions. Now he'll learn that running to the start button is what starts the teeter.

First, add movement after the reward: Let your dog ascend, reward as he reaches the start button, and then just wait and allow your dog to notice that he is on familiar ground (close to the edge, high up in the air). Wait for him to look expectant (looking down, pricking his ears, or whatever you've been working with), and reward him with teeter movement. Do just a short "drop" at first, reward immediately, and wait for another expectant look before dropping the teeter again (eventually to the ground). Once the teeter has hit the ground, your dog should do his contact behavior, possibly earn a reward for getting and staying in position, and definitely earn one for starting on cue.

Then, let the movement be the beginning of the reward: Skip the treat at the start button—instead, reward your dog for reaching the start button by dropping the teeter a bit and then delivering the reward. Now the movement functions as a click! The teeter moves if, and only if, your dog "pushes the start button"—and the movement leads to the actual reward. You can drop the board in stages or let it go all the way to the ground. As before, if the movement ends up in the air you reward immediately—but after impact, your dog first performs his contact behavior. Then either you can reward in position, give your start cue, and reward the start, or you can simply give your start cue and reward.

SECURE THE TARGET

If you opt to use a target to mark the start button and get the behavior, make sure to secure it (with duct tape, for instance) to make training safe for your dog. A dog that's happy and confident on the teeter is enthusiastic and will be moving with speed and intensity. You don't want that target to slide out of place.

Exercise 79: Push the button, make the teeter move!

1. Prepare: Make sure the teeter is steady. If you're using a target, secure it where you want your dog's start button to be.
2. Transport your dog to the beginning of the teeter.
3. End the transport.
4. Your dog races all the way to his start button.
5. The teeter drops a bit (guided by your helper).
6. Reward!
7. The teeter drops and hits the ground (guided by your helper).
8. Your dog hurries into his two-on/two-off position.
9. He freezes in position.
10. (Optional: Reward in position.)
11. Give your start cue.
12. Your dog starts ahead.
13. Reward!

USING A LOWER TEETER

If you like, you can practice the entire teeter behavior chain at a lower height. You can either use a very low teeter or rig a regular teeter between two tables (so that your dog starts on one table and ends up on the other). The same rules apply: The teeter moves when (and only when) your dog reaches his start button, far out on the teeter. Begin low and gradually advance to regular height.

This approach reduces the height of the drop: Instead of your dog having to ride the teeter all the way from high up to the ground, the impact comes right after your dog has reached the start button—and so does the opportunity to perform the contact behavior—so your dog will earn his ultimate reward faster.

Finally, link the whole chain together: Move on to letting the teeter drop all the way to the ground (without any intermediate reward). Now the start button behavior leads to movement, which leads to impact, which gives your dog an opportunity to perform his contact behavior, which earns him a start cue upon which he speeds away—and then, the actual reward appears. Voilà—a teeter performance extraordinaire!

If you've properly trained the movement and impact portion, these features will reinforce your dog's behavior on the teeter. Remember: The teeter starts if (and only if) your dog pushes the start button, in other words, if he gets to the right position on the teeter.

The teeter starts moving when the dog reaches the "start button" point, then drops all the way to the ground where the dog finds his two-on/two-off position.

Stage 3: Perform the whole obstacle "competition style"

The final stage is to fade your helper so that your dog performs the entire teeter, working the obstacle on his own. Now gravity will gradually come into play again—but by now, your dog is running all the way to his start button so fast that the teeter won't have time to drop until he reaches it! First have your helper let go of the teeter a little bit earlier (while your dog is still moving, right before he reaches his start button). Then gradually remove the helper totally.

JUST TRYING TO GET THERE

In the finished teeter performance, your dog might not reach his start button point, but he'll be working hard to get there and that will keep him aiming ahead beautifully. A small dog might get to the end of the board, but a heavier dog (although taught that his start button is a decimeter from the end) might not. Keep an eye on your dog's performance to make sure that he does really work toward his start button. Try a training session every now and then where you (or a helper) simply hold on to the teeter so that gravity once again is out of play, and your dog really has to work his start button.

This doesn't mean that you'll never use a helper ever again! Especially with small dogs, using a helper to hold the teeter every once in a while helps maintain the brilliant performance you want by ensuring that your dog actually runs all the way to his start button. Remember: Your dog should never know that the teeter has a pivot point—he should believe that he is making the teeter start by dashing out to the right spot on the board.

Make sure that your dog gets to experience different teeters during his training. However much we claim that gravity doesn't have anything to do with your dog's perfor-

THE TEETER CUE

We suggest adding a cue to your dog's teeter performance, for the sole reason that the teeter and the dogwalk look much the same to a dog approaching straight on at high speed, and you don't want to surprise your dog with a teeter when he thought he was dashing up the dogwalk. We want the dog to always be certain when he is attempting the teeter, to keep his performance brilliant, clean, and safe.

So when you're absolutely happy with your dog's teeter performance, add a cue for the obstacle. Simply say your teeter cue while your dog aims for the teeter, and your dog will soon make the association. Having added the cue doesn't mean you have to use it all the time, though—just practice it often enough so that your dog keeps associating it with the teeter, and make use of it whenever your dog might mistake the teeter for a dogwalk.

The finished product: Aiming for the end!

mance, pivot points might vary, surfacing might vary, and so on. Your dog needs to know how to do his job regardless.

Step 3: Vary where you are going after the teeter

After the teeter, exit in different directions and toward different (well-trained) obstacles. You can also set up distractions (dummy obstacles and dummy rewards) to make sure that your dog really follows your handling after being released off the teeter. Always vary when you give your dog his cue to start and what you're doing when giving the cue so that he learns that the start cue can happen any time when he's in his two-on/two-off position.

Step 4: Vary where you are coming from

Add handling from different directions as well as different obstacles on your way to the teeter. You want a dog that correctly ascends the teeter, zooms into position for his start button, rides the teeter to the ground, gets into his contact position, waits for his start cue, and dashes off the contact—in all kinds of sequences.

Maintaining brilliant performance on the contact obstacles

Teaching the contact obstacles is a straightforward process. So is maintaining brilliant performance, but it does require some work! The key is to never stop training. Constantly monitor both your dog's behavior and your own, and constantly keep working toward the goal of perfect performance.

Here are a few guidelines to help maintain brilliant performance:

- Stick to criteria.
- Use your start cue as a reward.
- Go back to basics whenever you need to.
- Vary, vary, vary.
- Keep it fun and exciting.

"My job is always the same!"

Stick to your criteria

Remember, *you* judge "correct" performance; it never has anything to do with that colored area or whether or not a judge would fault you. So first of all, make sure you know exactly what your criteria are. By being crystal clear about what you expect, you'll be consistent all the time—and that will make your dog confident of his task.

To maintain the behavior you *must* stick to your criteria. Rewards (tangible rewards as well as start cues) appear when, and only when, the dog's performance is up to par. If he makes a mistake (stopping too early, starting before your cue, or whatever), transport him back to a new starting point and give him another chance to get it right. Then evaluate your training to ensure that the mistake doesn't grow into a habit.

Your dog should perform the same behavior in training and in competition. If you were to change the rules at competitions, your dog would of course learn to change his behavior accordingly. Stick to your two-on/two-off criteria and remember to vary the duration before the start cue, even in competitions. Yes, letting your dog wait on the contact for a second or two will cost you time, and it might ruin your chances of winning that class—but it'll increase your chances at winning the really important classes, and it'll definitely increase your chances of having a long career of brilliant contact performances.

Use your start cue as a reward

Remember, your start cue always functions as a reward (whether you have also rewarded in position or not). Your start cue should be just as well-timed as a click.

Your start cue is your most precious reward.

Give your start cue when, and only when, your dog's performance meets your criteria. If your dog doesn't perform his behavior correctly, you can't give your start cue. And if you haven't given your start cue, you can't continue ahead.

Often reward starting to ensure that the start cue maintains its reinforcing effect. Let phenomenal rewards appear just as your dog starts off the contact, especially in situations where your dog might not be expecting it. This way your dog will keep listening carefully for his start cue.

Go back to basics whenever you need to

Remember, reinforcement is what builds behavior. Continually ping-pong back and forth between easier and more difficult trials, ensuring that your dog is heavily rewarded for correct performance. Whenever you like, you can rehearse the work you did away from the obstacles and/or work short distances on the obstacles.

If you see any signs that a contact performance is deteriorating, immediately go back to earlier stages in the training. Mediocre performance must never become a habit. Pay special attention to the last links of the chain (especially the start on cue), since they're what reinforce the earlier parts and hold the entire chain together.

Vary, vary, vary

Remember, independent performance means that your dog does his contact behavior no matter what happens around him. To maintain an independent behavior you have to keep

EXAMPLE OF VARIATIONS FOR CONTACT PERFORMANCE

By combining variables and writing down combinations you can get a precise list of what to do for each repetition. Here's an example:

Rep No. 1: Start your dog one foot from the end of the contact, sprint ahead, give your start cue after one second.

Rep No. 2: Start some distance before the obstacle. As your dog ascends, cross behind him and run out laterally. Click as his front feet hit the ground and run back to deliver three treats in position before giving the start cue.

Rep No. 3: Recall over the entire obstacle; stand still several meters ahead. Give your start cue after two seconds, and reward the start with a tug toy..

Rep No. 4: Start your dog a meter from the contact's end and run backward as your dog hurries to his position. Go up to him and deliver one treat in position, then give your start cue and send to a remote reward.

Rep No. 5: Let your dog do the entire obstacle; jog forward and perform a front cross while your dog approaches the down contact. Give your start cue after two seconds and reward with a game of tug.

In this example we have varied only your own behavior, the duration, and the rewards. You can come up with other variations and add all kinds of distractions. Make sure that your dog keeps his speed and intensity throughout. If you notice any variations or combinations that your dog isn't sure of, break down the training and do isolated work with just that tiny part, if possible away from the obstacle. For example, if your backing away while your dog approaches the edge seems to be an issue, you can practice that in a target-training setting, away from the obstacle. Or if your dog starts as you throw his ball (instead of waiting for the start cue), build that skill in start-line stays first, without involving contacts. Then, as your dog's skill advances, put the parts back together again.

Continually reinforcing the behavior away from the obstacles will strengthen the obstacle performance.

varying everything—or your dog will pick up patterns and lose his independence. Always keep in mind that for a handler, it's terribly easy to get stuck in patterns.

To avoid such patterns, we suggest you make lists of factors to vary. This way you can keep track of which variations you do and which you should do more of. See pages 218 (starts line stays) and 366 (target training) for ideas. Merely *thinking* of all the different variables will actually make you a better trainer since it alerts you to all these factors. *Working through* them will make both you and your dog truly skilled.

Keep it fun and exciting

Remember, attitude is always your first priority. Yes, your training should be very methodical, but at the same time it should be tons of fun. There is no contradiction between perfection and having a blast every training session!

Handle mistakes lightheartedly. Your dog mustn't be afraid to make mistakes! He just doesn't get his favorite reward that time. If your own attitude goes sour for some reason, break off the training and go do something else. Remember, it's just a game.

Keep your dog alert with new challenges to work through and great rewards to boost his excitement. Surprise him with fabulous rewards when he least expects it!

Not only will the two-on/two-off training give you brilliant contacts—it also provides you with all the tools you'll need for training the obstacle we present in the next chapter: the table.

21

The table

Teaching the table is just like teaching the contacts. It's all about your dog getting into position, holding that position, and starting on cue.

Down on the table, waiting for the start cue

Teaching the table

Some organizations put the table to frequent use; others use it sparingly or not at all. The dog's required position also varies: Some organizations stipulate that the dog merely has to get on the table; others require that the dog remain on the table for five seconds—either in any position, or in a sit or a down. At competitions, the judge or a beeping tone (if the table is equipped with an electrical mat) signals the handler when the five seconds are up.

Since most organizations accept (or require) a down position during the table performance, we opt to teach the dog to dive into an instant down as he jumps up on the table. If you need a sit as well, you can teach that afterward.

What should the table performance look like?

What you're after is a dog that zooms onto the table and gets into position, eagerly awaiting your start cue. Since a down is accepted by most organizations, the training here will describe teaching the dog to fly onto the table into an instant down.

The final goal is:
1. Your dog jumps onto the table.
2. He lands lying down.
3. He remains lying down until you give the cue to start.
4. On your start cue, he explodes off the table in the direction your handling tells him.

Resemblances to contact training

The table resembles the contacts, and the same basic principles apply: Your dog needs to know how to get into position, stay in position, and start on cue, and you'll be able to reward those behaviors. Contacts and tables both consist of behavior chains and are preferably taught using back-chaining.

The table, however, presents a new obstacle for your dog to get onto, and a new behavior (lying down) for him to offer on it. On the table—unlike the contacts—direction isn't really an issue; it's OK if your dog turns toward you as he jumps onto the table … as long as he instantly dives into his down.

The process: table training in eight steps

The prerequisites for table training are the same as for the contacts:

You need to be skilled at remaining neutral while giving the start cue and at varying your own behavior. This will help you build independent table performance.

Your dog needs to be skilled at getting onto different surfaces, at starting on cue, and at keeping still awaiting his start cue.

To teach your dog to spontaneously land on the table lying down and remain glued to the table until he hears your start cue, you first need to teach him to offer a voluntary, instant down (without any verbal cues) and then put the parts together in a chain.

Step 1: Lie down teaches your dog a lightning-fast down.

Just as in the contact preparation training, the first step includes three stages:

>**Stage 1:** Get the down.
>**Stage 2:** Make it fast and fluent.
>**Stage 3:** Add variations and distractions.

Step 2: Hold the position + start on cue teaches your dog to hold his down until you give the start cue.

Step 3: Get onto (+ down + hold the position + start on cue) introduces the first part of the chain: finding the right spot to lie down on. Begin on a low object (a target mat, for example) and gradually raise the height until your dog is on the actual table.

Step 4: Add further variations and distractions to to ensure that your dog can do his job no matter what.

Step 5: Vary where you're going after the table so that your dog learns to respond to your handling after the start cue.

Step 6: Increase the distance gradually and only when the behavior is solid.

Step 7: Vary where you're coming from, approaching from different angles and different obstacles, so your dog learns to adjust his table performance accordingly.

Step 8: Maintain the brilliant performance throughout your dog's agility career.

Step 1: Lie down

At this step, the training is all about teaching the action of diving into a down. So once your dog is in a down, reward immediately, and get him back on his feet for another repetition. For example, you can toss the reward away a little bit so that your dog needs to get up to get it. Then he can throw himself down again.

TEACHING A SIT, TOO

If you plan to compete in an organization that also requires a sit, we suggest that you use the down as your dog's "default behavior" (what he does spontaneously, if you don't give any other directions) and use a "sit" cue when you want your dog to sit. To accomplish this, begin by teaching the automatic down as we describe it in this chapter. Then, teach him to sit on cue away from the equipment. Finally, begin saying your "sit" cue as he gets onto the equipment. If you don't say anything, he should continue diving into a down—but if you say "sit" as he jumps on the table, he should sit.

The sit training process looks like this:

1. Get a voluntary sit. (This is Step 1 and Step 2 of the training described in this chapter, but using a sit instead of a down.)

2. Add the "sit" cue. (First saying the cue as he sits, then just before he offers the sit. Finally, quit rewarding the spontaneously offered sit—reward only if the sit occurs after your "sit" cue.)

3. Add the equipment. (This is Step 3. Say your "sit" cue as your dog gets onto the equipment. Vary with saying nothing—then your dog should dive into a down).

Stage 1: Get the down

First you need to get your dog to offer the down position on the ground. Even if your dog already knows a down on cue, you still need to begin here, ensuring that your dog *voluntarily* offers an instant drop from a stand.

There are many ways to get the down:

- Capturing: simply rewarding whenever your dog spontaneously lies down.
- Free shaping: reinforcing downward motion, incrementally getting an actual down.
- Luring: using treats or toys to prompt your dog to lie down.

No matter which method (or combination of methods) you choose, use your clicker to instantly mark the actual act of getting into position. For once, it's OK to be face-to-face with your dog if you like.

Capturing a down just requires watching your dog. He lies down many times during the course of a day, and you can easily reinforce a few of these, thereby increasing the chances that your dog will offer the behavior. If you think your dog is likely to offer a full down in a clicker training session, try that. Simply wait and let your dog experiment, and click and reward as soon as he offers a down.

Free-shaping a down can be a bit tricky—naturally not impossible, but if your dog has never been reinforced for a down before, it might take a while to get there. Devise a criteria plan with tiny steps and prepare to work through it as quickly as you can so your dog doesn't get stuck (not getting past the bow is a common song of woe …). Some of the steps might be: looking down, shifting his weight back, stretching his front legs, bowing, lowering his rear end, and so on until he's actually lying down. Clever placement of reward will help; for most dogs that means rewarding in between his front legs, quite far back.

Once your dog has gotten the idea of lying down, minimize the number of clicks and treats needed to get each down. As quickly as possible make your only criterion (the only thing he gets clicks and treats for) "elbows, rib cage, and heels on ground."

Trying things out.

"How can I get those treats?"   "A kiss?" Nope, that's not it.   "Leaning back?"

Yes, that earns a treat! The treat   "A down?"   Absolutely!
is delivered low to the ground.

A reinforceable moment: a bow, offered while playing around with a toy hidden in the hands.

Luring isn't something we normally advocate, but for the down we sometimes use a playful version of luring where the dog gets to solve a puzzle independently. To get some downward movement, sit down on the ground and play around with something really fabulous (a treat or a toy) in your hand. Hold your hand on the floor, and let your dog try to get that fabulous something. Make it a game, where your dog gets to be a bit naughty and try to pry the treat off you. Once you've got your dog going, he'll most likely try lying down so he can nudge and paw at the hand more easily. Great! Click and open your hand. If you don't get a perfect down right away, just shape the down by rewarding any downward motion during the play (crouching, bowing, and so on) and gradually tighten your criteria until your dog instantly throws himself to the ground.

Once your dog happily throws himself down in order to get to his treat or toy, start fading the lure. We find it easiest to do this by gradually hiding the treat or toy—first keeping it invisible in your hand, then hiding it between your knees, and eventually removing it altogether (for example, hiding it behind your back or putting it in your pocket). When you start fading the lure, start free shaping. Let your dog work on his own; don't lure more if he doesn't get it right away! He has already learned that he can get to his treat by lying down, so most likely he'll try some kind of downward movement. From your dog's perspective the rules of the game remain set; he can still pry the good stuff off you by diving into a down!

For table purposes it's important that your dog knows how to lie down from standing up. To give your dog a good starting position, start the session with some play close to the ground so that he's already standing up with his head quite low as the play ends and the training begins. If your dog occasionally sits before he lies down it's no big deal, but strive to reward downward motion right from the stand. If the sit seems to be built in, you can extinguish it by not rewarding downs that happen after a sit. Meanwhile, reward your dog for every form of standing, bowing, or downing. Remember that you're not just looking for the final product of a "dog in a down"; you're teaching the entire process of "lying down from a stand."

Stage 2: Make it fast and fluent

However you've chosen to get your down on the ground, you need to get it fast and fluent: you want your dog to fly into that down as soon as he gets a chance! Move on to clicking only for the full down, and remember to work with high intensity and lots of enthusiasm, altering the down sessions with energetic play. This will automatically increase the speed of your dog's down.

You can also shape for speed in diving into the down: tighten your criteria even more and reward only the fastest downs, so if your dog doesn't get down fast enough, you simply don't reward. He'll have to figure out that he must get back up on his feet and offer a new down. Since offering two downs in a row will be new for him, at first reward him immediately for trying again. Soon you'll be able to start selecting for the fastest downs. By being clear about your criteria, and letting your dog figure out for himself what to do if he doesn't get his click and reward, you'll get an eager and persistent dog that throws fast downs at you.

Stage 3: Add variations and distractions

Test your dog's skill by adding some variations and distractions: Will he still dive into his down with full intensity if you wave your arms, clap your hands, or wave his toy around?

When adding these new difficulties you might get some hesitation and some slower downs. That's OK for a few repetitions. Whenever you add a new challenge, you need to ease up on other aspects a bit, but then gradually sharpen your criteria again.

Lying down earns multiple rewards: first treats, then a start cue followed by a toy.

Step 2: Hold the position + start on cue

When you're happy about how your dog offers his down, it's time to add duration, teaching him to hold his down (freeze in that position) and only get up on your start cue.

As usual, either you can deliver several rewards in position and end with your start cue, or you can use your start cue as the sole reward. Whichever way you reward, you'll gradually build duration.

We usually opt to begin by machine-gunning treats while the dog is lying down. In the very beginning, your dog's job is just to hit the ground and to start on cue; your job is to manipulate the rewards so that he remains in that position until you give the start cue. End with your start cue, and reward your dog for starting on cue (for example, by throwing a toy). Soon you can start teaching your dog to actively hold his down until he hears the start cue. You can reward in position (varying the time between the rewards, always ending with a start cue) or you can skip the rewards in position and just vary the time before the start cue (which will then be the only reward). *Always reward the behavior of starting on cue,* since that's the end of the chain.

Step 3: Get onto (+ down + hold the position + start on cue)

Now it's time to introduce the first part of the chain: finding the right spot to lie down on. You want your dog to get onto an object before slamming into his down and to hold his position until you give the start cue. We suggest beginning with a mat (or some other flat material).

You'll be combining two separate skills: (1) getting onto something, and (2) lying down + holding position + starting on cue. Actually, all that means is that you add another criterion to the down: Now only downs *on the object* will count and generate rewards.

This is how you can introduce the concept in one session:

1. Practice getting onto something: Bring out your chosen object and do just a few repetitions of *onto* training, to ensure that your dog directly gets onto the object as soon as he gets a chance. Use a reward to transport him off the object for another repetition. (Revisit "Between, around," etc., pages 158 and 161, for the details of teaching *onto.*)

2. Practice instant downs: Remove the object and reward a few downs on the ground.

3. Combine the two behaviors: Bring out the object again, and reward your dog for spontaneously getting onto it, this time positioning your reward so that he stays on the object. Then shape the down on the object. Wait and see what your dog tries, and reward anything that might lead to a down. He might try a full down right away, or you might need to shape the down starting with the tiniest downward movement. When your dog is lying down, reward in position and then give your start cue. And, of course, reward him for starting on cue.

4. Keep practicing until your dog flies onto the object and into a down every time he gets the opportunity.

Getting onto and lying down earns a reward!

You can introduce new objects to jump up onto and lie down on in two ways:

- If you have used a mat in the first stages of table training, you can use the mat as a target and place it on your chosen object. Eventually, you'll need to fade the mat: Either randomly slide it away and put it back, or gradually make it smaller and more invisible (just as when fading the target in the contact training, see page 369).

- Or, you can simply repeat the training procedure over again on new objects, teaching your dog that jumping up and lying down works, for example, on mats, on a low box, on park benches, on rocks in the woods, and on the agility table.

Once you have started working with downs on objects, you can also introduce remote rewards that first serve as distractions then transform into rewards as you give your start cue and handle your dog toward them.

To set up for perfection at the actual table, wait to introduce the obstacle until your dog performs the whole behavior flawlessly on another object. Then just let him do the same thing at the agility table.

Flying onto the table, lying down, and starting on cue

Step 4: Add further variations and distractions

To get a dog that jumps up onto the table and slams into a down, holds that position, and explodes away on cue no matter what is going on around him, vary what happens as your dog dives into his down, holds position, and starts on cue. Your dog will learn that the start cue can happen any time while he's down on the table, and that he should lie down and listen for the cue regardless of what you do. See discussions of starts (page 218) and contacts (page 394) for ideas about what to vary.

Step 5: Vary where you're going after the table

Vary where you're going after the table: Either indicate a direction and reward right away, or continue to well-trained obstacles after the table. Of course, you can set up various dummy obstacles and dummy rewards that function as distractions to ensure that your dog truly follows your handling off the table.

If you want your dog to pay close attention to your handling as he jumps onto the table (so that he lands facing where he'll go next), make sure you cue the new direction as he jumps up. Continue straight ahead, do a regular turn, a front cross, or whatever—your dog's job still is to jump up and lie down on the table, but he'll notice your handling as well. Then quickly give your start cue and reward him for starting in the direction your handling tells him. Consistent handling in combination with quick releases will soon teach your dog to pay attention to where you're going next as he hops up. Once he's gotten the idea, you can let him wait longer for his start cue again.

Step 6: Increase the distance

You can begin to work on distance once your dog is completely confident about the rest of the job. Increase the distance in sync with your dog's confidence, so that he happily zooms to the table, slamming into his down without the slightest hesitation. Gradually add more and more distance, transporting your dog up to 10 meters or more away from the table before letting him go. If there's any hesitation, immediately shorten the distance to the table.

TABLE CUE?

The very presence of the table along your dog's path will be his cue to jump up and dive into a down. When starting toward the table from a stay, your start cue will tell your dog to go. If you also want a specific cue for the table, we suggest you wait to add it until your dog knows to aim for the table (without any cue other than your handling) in various sequences. To add the cue, go back to simple "onto + lie down" exercises (see Step 3). Start close to the table and give your table cue just as you end the transport. Eventually start saying the table cue as you send your dog toward the table in sequences.

Remember to keep the off-cue behavior as well; you still want your dog to do the table when you quietly handle him to it, so don't always use the cue!

Just as when adding distance in the contact preparation training, at first just release your dog to the table and stand still until he has landed in a down on the table. Eventually start varying your movements, hanging back, sprinting past him, and so on. In addition, vary between spontaneous starts and start-line stays with starts on cue.

Step 7: Vary where you're coming from

Finally, vary where you come from before the table so that your dog will zoom onto the table and into his down, waiting for his start cue, in all kinds of sequences. Now you can put the table into all different kinds of sequences. Just remember to add one new challenge at a time.

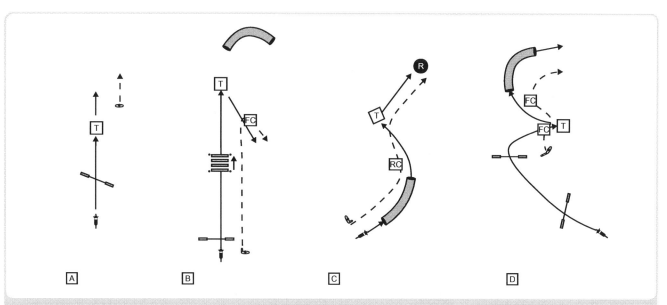

Here are some table sequences, just to spark your imagination. Design your own according to what you and your dog are ready for.

A. Start from a stay. Position yourself ahead of the table, and release your dog to race straight ahead over the jump to the table. Go straight ahead after the table.

B. Start from a stay. While your dog is on the table, do a front cross. Reward your dog for starting off the table in the new direction.

C. From a spontaneous start with your dog on your right, cross behind him as you approach the table (cross your dog's path as he takes off for the table). While your dog is on the table, turn your shoulders to the right. As he starts off the table, reward his turning right.

D. Start from a stay; position yourself by the second jump. Cross in front of your dog to get him to turn right to the table. When your dog lands on the table, he'll be on your right side. While he's on the table, do another front cross so that he's on your left side to head into the tunnel, and reward.

Step 8: Maintain the brilliant performance

To maintain your dog's great table performance throughout his agility career, use the same guidelines as with contacts:

- Constantly monitor both your dog's behavior and your own, and constantly keep working toward the goal of perfect performance.
- Stick to your criteria.
- Remember that your start cue functions as a reward for whatever your dog is doing when you say it.
- Go back to basics whenever you need to.
- Vary, vary, vary.
- Keep it fun and exciting.

Now you only have one more obstacle to teach your dog: In the next chapter we'll discuss how you can teach a fabulous weave pole performance.

The weave poles

The weave poles consist of an even number of poles standing in a straight line. Normally there are up to 12 poles, standing on a metal base. Your dog's task is to zigzag through the poles as fast as possible, always entering to the right of the first pole. In this chapter we'll discuss what's important in weave pole training, describe how we teach the weaves, and give you tools for both early training and refinement and problem solving.

"The weave poles are my happy place!"

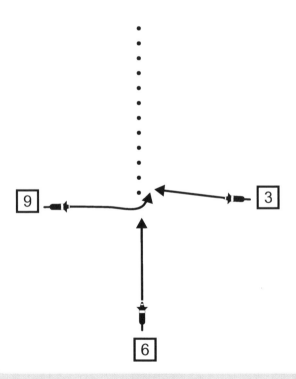

3 o'clock, 6 o'clock, and 9 o'clock weave pole entries

About training the weaves

Ultimately you want your dog to reliably weave all the way through the poles no matter what, with bulletproof entries and lightning-fast speed. Your job is to direct your dog to the poles; his job is to perform them correctly.

Fully trained, the weave pole performance looks like this:

1. No matter where he's coming from, your dog aims for the correct entry—to the right of the first pole.

2. As he enters, he aims forward in the weaves and zig-zags through all the poles.

3. While your dog is weaving, he works independently of you all the way through the poles—you can run past, hang back, do cartwheels, run in another direction, or whatever.

Weave pole entries around the clock

When talking about weave pole entries, we usually use the hand positions of a clock to describe the various angles of entry. For example, when your dog is coming straight toward the weave poles, it's a "6 o'clock entry."

Depending on which angle your dog is coming from, he'll get a different picture of the entry. Objectively (from a bystander's view), his job remains the same: Go to the right of the first pole, then go to the left of the second pole, and so on. Subjectively, from your dog's point of view, however, the weave poles present a different task depending on his approach angle. For example, when approaching at 6 o'clock, your dog sees only the first pole—the rest of the poles are hidden behind the first one. At a 9 o'clock entry, he sees all the poles, and should aim for the first pole in the row, head to the right side of it, and wrap around it. At a 3 o'clock entry, he also sees all the poles, but here he should aim between the first and second poles, going directly to the left side of the second pole and wrapping around it.

In the 9 o'clock entry, the dog aims to the right of the first pole and wraps left to enter.

In the 3 o'clock entry, the dog aims to the left of the second pole and wraps right.

Entering from 1 o'clock: This is a really tough one! The dog has to run by the whole line of poles and enter to the left of the second one from the start.

Weave pole training strategies

Along with the contacts, weave poles are the most complex obstacles on the agility course. With the contacts, first and foremost you have to choose *which contact behavior* to teach your dog (for example, an independent, two-on/two-off with a start cue). Then the training process is pretty straightforward (employ back-chaining, teaching the end first). With weaves, on the contrary, the behavior by and large is set by the competition rules (enter to the right of the first pole and zigzag through the poles). Your main choice is instead *which training strategy* to use: How are you going to set up the poles, and how are you going to get the behaviors you're after?

The weave pole setup can vary (and be adjusted) in regard to

- the number of poles (Using a full set of 6 to 12 poles? Working with pairs of poles? Adding one or two poles at a time?)
- the placement of the poles ("Closed" in a straight line along the middle, or "open" to the left and right of the middle, either with straight or slanted poles?)
- the distance between the poles (Regular distance of 60 cm [24"] between the poles? Closer? Distance between pairs of poles?)
- guiding props (No props? Guide wires or fences somewhere?)

We most often teach the weaves using Aim for it, *beginning with one pair of poles.*

Which setup to use is mainly a matter of taste. There are lots of "methods" out there using various setups, and most of them work well. We usually opt to work with pairs of poles, beginning with just one pair, in a "closed" or slightly "open" setup with regular distance and no helping aids, but this strategy is not set in stone.

How to get behavior can also vary. Regardless of which weave pole setup we use, we prefer to work with some version of *Aim for it* (where you reward your dog for aiming in the correct direction, without using any lures or prompts) and perhaps *Race to reward* (where a remote lure/reward gives the dog a direction to work in). As usual, we avoid luring or prompting with hands or body gestures since we want to build independent behavior from the very beginning.

How to succeed with your weave pole training

No matter which method(s) you use, successful weave pole training is mostly a function of

- training according to the list of priorities: attitude, direction, and precision.
- focusing on independent entries around the clock.

"Hey, look at me!"

Attitude, of course, always should be your top priority, but with the weaves it's especially important to remember, since those poles sometimes trigger the most fastidious tendencies in humans. If your dog's gung-ho attitude is lacking, take *immediate* action to fix it. Alter the setup, change your criteria, make your weave sessions even shorter with greater rewards, or take a break from weaving and train something else. There's no point in trying to practice weaving with a dog that isn't truly enthusiastic about the game. You're looking for a "Wahoo, Mum! See me do this!" attitude.

Direction is of utmost importance in the weaves. The obstacle may require a lot of bending, but the general direction is forward! If your dog lacks a sense of direction in the weaves, he'll be totally lost. We work with direction by always rewarding along the dog's intended path and by *always* continuing ahead to the end of the set of poles, even if the dog makes a mistake somewhere. Imagine that the weave poles are standing in a glass tunnel—if something goes wrong, your dog still needs to get to the end before he can exit the weave poles. As far as your dog should know, the only time it's possible to leave the weave poles prematurely is if you've clicked and rewarded, and he's busy with his reward. You're looking for your dog to understand, "I'm working in *this* direction until I get my reward!"

No matter what the handler does, the weaves go in one direction: Forward!

Precision is the very nature of weaving. Through your clever setups, your wise criteria, and your brilliant rewards, you need to explain to your dog exactly what he's supposed to do with those poles. At most other obstacles (except for the precise contact behavior, of course), your dog can pretty much figure out by himself what to do, but he probably would never guess what the weaves are about. You're looking for him to realize, "I'm actually making sure to negotiate these sticks in a certain fashion."

The entry requires a lot of attention since weaving consists of both entering correctly and zigzagging, and independent weave pole entries are a must! A dog that doesn't understand how to enter the weave poles will get frustrated, stressed, and/or shut down when he gets to the obstacle, and this lack of understanding often sparks a vicious circle where dog and handler frustrate each other. Acknowledging the complexity of the weave pole entry and committing to truly teaching your dog to handle it on his own are vital steps toward a happy and confident weaver.

Aim for the weaves

Our weave pole training method is built on the *Aim for it* procedure, teaching the dog to find the correct path through the weave poles by rewarding him for aiming at and moving along that path. This process is familiar to you and your dog—you've been working with *Aim for it* throughout this book. Our training begins with just one pair of poles, set slightly open to resemble the setting from the *between* training, making that, too, familiar for your dog.

In the first section, "One pair of poles," we'll describe how we work with just one pair of poles:

Step 1: Get the behavior at 6 o'clock.
> **Stage 1:** Get the behavior at slightly open poles.
> **Stage 2:** Get the behavior at closed poles.

Step 2: Get the behavior around the clock.
Work through the entries from different angles.

Step 3: Expand the understanding.
> **Stage 1:** Add handler variations and other distractions.
> **Stage 2:** Vary the distance.
> **Stage 3:** Let your dog do several pairs of poles for one reward.
> **Stage 4:** Introduce *Race to reward*.
> **Stage 5:** Introduce start-line stays.

In the next section, "Further weave pole training," we'll explain how we go from one pair of poles to a full set of weaves:

Step 1: Work up to four poles.
> **Strategy 1:** Put two pairs of poles together.
> **Strategy 2:** Shape three to four poles.
> **Strategy 3:** Channels: Advance from open to closed poles.

Step 2: Get all angles at four poles.

Step 3: Expand the understanding.

Step 4: Work up to a full set of poles.

Step 5: Vary where you are going after the poles.

Step 6: Vary where you come from.
At the end of the chapter, there is also a section about "Troubleshooting in your weave pole training."

In each section we present one aspect at a time, but weave pole training isn't necessarily a linear process: You'll often benefit from moving back and forth between different steps (you can also move back and forth between one pair and more poles), and your dog's understanding will benefit from every bit he learns. Varying which aspect you work on and continually introducing new bits of information will also help you avoid getting stuck

("Yes, it's correct to go to the right of the first pole when coming from 9 o'clock!" "Yes, it's correct to aim the nose to the left of the second pole—no matter where you're coming from!" "Yes, it's correct to keep aiming for more poles after the first one—even if I wave my arms!" And so on). If you run into problems, working on another aspect of weaving for a while can make the old problem disappear or at least make it easier to solve once you get back to it.

The only must: Always set up exercises that your dog can do independently! Don't go longer, more difficult, or more complex until your dog has a good shot at getting it right on his own. Resist any temptation to "help" your dog with body cues! Training is all about teaching your dog what to do with the poles, not about what to do when you wiggle your rear or move your hand in a zigzag pattern. Such "helping" attempts are a sure way to draw your dog's attention from the poles to you, and that's precisely what you don't want to do. If you feel the urge to "help" your dog, alter the exercise to make his job easier, or pace yourself and let him figure it out. Either way, he needs to be successful on his own.

One pair of poles

When introducing a beginner dog to the weaves, we start by teaching him to work with just one pair of poles. When refining a more experienced dog's performance or problem solving, we also typically begin with just one pair of poles. There are several benefits to working with one pair of poles:

- One pair of poles is a simple way to introduce the weaves.
- One pair of poles simulates the entry; building competence at all angles with one pair of weaves builds a solid foundation for further entry training.
- Doing all the work with one pair of poles cements your understanding for the training process.

What should the performance at one pair of poles look like?

- As soon as your dog gets a chance he flies through the pair of poles.
- He always enters to the right of the first pole, passes to the left of the second pole, and exits in the direction of the imaginary third pole.
- He enters correctly from all angles around the clock.

How can you train it?

A single pair of weave poles is *going between* with a twist! Free-shaping the first pair of poles using the *Aim for it* procedure from spontaneous starts will feel familiar for both you and your dog. At Step 1 you get the behavior at 6 o'clock entries, first with slightly open poles, then with closed poles. At Step 2 you get the behavior around the clock by working entries from all angles. At Step 3 you expand the understanding by varying your own position and movement, varying the distance, and introducing *Race to reward* and start-line stays.

You can either work with just one pair of poles or set up three pairs of poles in a Bermuda Triangle. As always we're fond of working with the Bermuda Triangle configuration because it shortens transports and gives you an easy way to keep working ahead if something goes wrong. Our triangular setup actually originated from weave pole training, and so did the name (referring to the mysterious triangle where all weave pole problems disappear ...).

We divide weave pole training with one pair of poles into three steps:

Step 1: Get the behavior at 6 o'clock.
> **Stage 1:** Get the behavior at slightly open poles.
> **Stage 2:** Get the behavior at closed poles.

Step 2: Get the behavior around the clock.
Work through the entries from different angles.

Step 3: Expand the understanding.
> **Stage 1:** Add handler variations and other distractions.
> **Stage 2:** Vary the distance.
> **Stage 3:** Let your dog do several pairs of poles for one reward.
> **Stage 4:** Introduce *Race to reward*.
> **Stage 5:** Introduce start-line stays.

Step 1: Get the behavior at 6 o'clock

Use the *Aim for it* procedure to introduce your dog to the 6 o'clock weave pole entry. Our main reason for starting at 6 o'clock is that it makes it easy for *you* to know in which direction the weave poles go, which means that it's easy for you to move around correctly and to reward along your dog's intended path.

Left: Ending the transport, letting the dog aim between the poles. Right: Rewarding along the line in the dirt.

Stage 1: Get the behavior at slightly open poles

In the very beginning, set up the poles so that they are slightly open—that way it'll be a simple *go between* exercise that your dog easily recognizes. To set up the poles correctly

1. imagine (or draw) a line on the ground, about two meters long. This line mimics the weave-pole base, showing the direction of the weaves.

2. place pole No. 1 by the beginning of the line but slightly to the left of it.

3. place pole No. 2 a bit farther ahead (50–60 cm, 20"–24") and slightly to the right of the line. (If you're using a setup with two poles on a base, rotate it a bit so that your dog can go straight between the poles.)

Now there's a straight line for your dog to run along, between the "open" poles. This will give him his first weave pole experience: passing to the right of the first pole and to the left of the second pole. The line also helps you, telling you in which direction the weaves go. All rewards should also appear along this line.

If something goes wrong, keep the forward momentum and transport your dog to a new starting position. You can use a treat magnet to transport your dog to a new starting point after a mistake—just make sure your actual rewards are more valuable than the transport treat.

THIS GOES FOR ALL YOUR WEAVE POLE TRAINING

The directions for Stage 1 are equally valid throughout all your weave pole training:

- Transport your dog to a good starting position.
- End the transport and let him start spontaneously.
- Reward him for aiming correctly along the intended path (your criterion can be anything from "nose pointing in the correct direction" to "passing the last pole correctly).
- All rewards appear ahead, along the intended path.
- The reward procedure might end just a step ahead, so that your dog can continue working through the poles from there, or it might bring your dog away from the poles, thus ending that trial.
- No matter what happens, keep working forward. If possible just let your dog keep working—if not, transport him to a new starting point. Either way, head forward.
- Work on both your left and your right sides from the very beginning.
- Always remember your priorities: (1) attitude, (2) direction, and (3) precision.

To begin training, transport your dog to a starting position at 6 o'clock within a meter of the first pole. Using a treat magnet or a collar transport is the easiest way to get your dog to exactly the desired starting position. End the transport and use the familiar *Aim for it* procedure to shape your dog to go between the poles. Since the dog's path just goes straight here, we suggest you click for any forward motion and deliver just one exciting reward far ahead along the intended path, building lots of anticipation and forward drive. Another option, of course, is to click and treat many times along the path. Either way, each click should be for looking or moving forward, and each reward should appear ahead along the intended path. The trial is over when your dog's front feet have passed the second pole; have a party and then transport yourselves back to the starting point for a new repetition (or, if you're using a Bermuda Triangle setup—which is a very good idea—transport yourselves to the starting point before the next pair of weaves).

Exercise 80: Get the behavior of "going between slightly open poles"

1. Transport your dog to a starting point within a meter from the first pole, facing the intended path.
2. While your dog is still moving, end the transport.
3. Your dog points his nose forward (or even moves forward, between the poles).
4. Click and hurl the reward ahead, along the intended path between the poles.
5. Your dog dashes to get his reward.

Suggested tag point:

- Reward straight ahead

If something goes wrong, keep working forward. Never hit the brakes, never turn your dog back! This is a central principle in all our training, but it's especially important with the weave poles where we really want the dog to get a feel for the direction of the obstacle. If your dog can't keep working from where he is, simply transport him to a new starting point—but do so with a forward motion, not by abruptly turning him back.

Stage 2: Get the behavior on closed poles

Alter the setup so that both poles stand along the line, looking just like the first two poles in a regular set of weaves. You can change from "open" to "closed" poles in one step, or you can do so gradually.

Now place the poles along the line.

Repeat the training process with this new setup: Transport your dog to a starting position at 6 o'clock and shape him through the poles using the *Aim for it* procedure. What will be different is that your dog's intended path now goes in zigzag, giving you many possible moments to reward, for example:

- nose pointing to the right of the first pole
- moving toward the right side of the first pole
- nose passing the first pole
- body wrapping around the first pole
- nose turning left after the first pole
- nose pointing to the left of the second pole
- moving toward the left side of the second pole
- nose passing to the left of the second pole
- front feet passing the second pole

Click for "nose to the right of the first pole," and place the reward along your dog's intended path through the poles.

The dog is aiming independently for the weave poles, and at the exit the reward appears, dancing ahead.

You can still choose either to do many clicks and treats for each repetition, or to click and reward once, placing the reward farther ahead along the intended path, inviting the dog to exit the poles correctly while chasing after the reward.

You can keep working until your dog is fluent at the 6 o'clock entry, spontaneously flying through the poles as soon as he gets the chance, *or* you can do just a few repetitions on your left and right sides respectively so that you and your dog start to get the picture, and then skip ahead and start working with various angles or distractions. What's important is that you've got the picture so that you know where the dog's path goes and feel confident about the procedure.

Step 2: Get the behavior around the clock

Now the real fun begins! Teaching proper weave pole entries is all about teaching the various angles of entry. Each new angle presents your dog a new picture—and a new path to take. There's a difference between adding angles to your weave training and adding angles to the route toward other obstacles. With other obstacles, the dog's job remains the same: He just approaches the obstacle from different directions. With the weave poles, adding angles means that the dog has to adjust his entry behavior: Each different approach presents a new job for your dog. Acknowledge that the various entries can be a tricky concept for your dog to grasp—and get down to business and start teaching them!

The *Aim for it* procedure makes it easy for you to break down the task into manageable pieces. You can always transport your dog to the starting point, reward him for "nose pointing in the correct direction," and work from there. To us humans it might make sense to begin with the almost-straight angles (between 5 and 7 o'clock) and then move to more severe angles, but actually, you might as well begin with the harder angles right away; as far as your dog's concerned, the degree of difficulty doesn't necessarily have anything to do with the degree of the angle.

When practicing angles, follow this protocol:

1. First, make sure *you* know which way the weaves go! When working with angles, it's vital that you remember which pole is number one and in which direction your dog's intended path goes.

2. Choose an angle and transport your dog to a good starting position. Remember to always keep your dog on your outside—this is how *he* can know the direction of the weaves. On the 1 o'clock to 5 o'clock angles, your dog will be on your left side, aiming directly to the left side of the second pole. On the 7 o'clock to 11 o'clock angles, he'll be on your right side, wrapping right around the first pole.

3. Shape your dog through the poles, rewarding along his intended path. We opt to use mostly high-energy rewards here to keep the dog's happy-go-lucky attitude and drive and to avoid his becoming overly "thoughtful."

4. Vary the angles until your dog is confident around the clock!

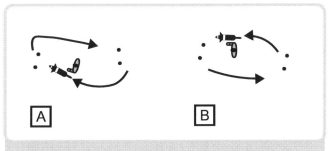

The Bermuda Triangle makes your transports easier: Just move ahead after rewarding (with your dog still busy with his reward), and you'll be at the next starting point.

A. Left-side handling
B. Right-side handling

At sharper angles, it's easiest to use a 2-pair-Bermuda.

A. Left-side handling (3 o'clock)
B. Right-side handling (9 o'clock)

Various entries at two poles: 3 o'clock (left), 8 o'clock (center), and 11 o'clock (right). Start close to the poles!

HOW WILL MY DOG KNOW WHICH DIRECTION THE WEAVES GO?

At a longer set of weaves, you'll send your dog to the beginning by pointing your shoulders in that direction. Then it's easy for your dog to see where the weaves start, and in which direction the obstacle goes. But with only two poles at tricky angles, how can the dog know the direction? The answer is twofold.

First of all, the training procedure sets the direction: You'll be rewarding for aiming in a certain direction, and you'll place the rewards along your dog's intended path. That'll tell your dog to work in that direction.

Second, and in the long run more important, your dog will learn to cue off your handling to figure out the direction of the weaves. The reason he can do this is that he knows to keep to your outside. If he's on your left side, he'll be turning right as he enters the weaves (in other words, it'll be an entry somewhere between 6 o'clock and 1 o'clock). And if he's on your right side, he'll be wrapping left around the first pole as he enters the weaves (the entry will be between 6 o'clock and 11 o'clock).

USING A SET DIRECTION AS A HELPING AID

Sometimes we opt to use the environment as an aid to tell the dog where the weaves go. For example, we might set up the weaves in the corner of the garden, decide that the exit is in the direction of the apple tree, and then practice in that set direction all the time. By giving the weaves a set direction that remains the same for each repetition, you remove one factor (deciding which way the weaves go), thus making the dog's job easier. This might be an approach to use for just an occasional training session or for a longer period of time. Like all helping aids, however, eventually you'll have to remove it and then you might have to go back to kindergarten for a while, making other aspects as easy as you can.

Step 3: Expand the understanding

By varying the angles and your own position and movement, you build independent weave pole entries and a solid understanding of the first pair of poles. Eventually add further variation in the form of distractions, distance, remote rewards, and start-line stays. Remember, the order of training aspects of weave pole performance isn't set in stone. Work with what you feel you need (or want) at the moment, and make sure your dog stays successful and happy! Moving back and forth between different aspects usually aids the training process.

Stage 1: Add handler variations and other distractions

At the weaves your dog's sole focus should be working the obstacle, confident in knowing that his reward will eventually appear ahead of him. He shouldn't pay attention to you at all—nor should he notice other potential distractions. Once your dog is fluently performing a certain two-pole setup, it's time to start adding variations and distractions.

You can vary your own behavior, for example:

- Your posture: Stand up straight, crouch down, stand on one foot.
- Your movement: Stand still, move slightly, wiggle some fingers, jog in place.
- Your position: Hang back, move ahead, increase lateral distance.

You can vary other aspects of the environment:

- Work in different places.
- Add distractions of other people, other dogs, and so on.
- Add stuff around the poles, so that there are other objects around than just the poles.
- Use potential rewards as distractions (wave them about, place them on the ground, and so on).

Keep the rate of success high! Do challenge your dog, but do it in ways that build his confidence. His attitude should be "Ha! You might be able to trick me once … but not twice!"

Environmental distraction: A pair of shoes next to the weave poles.

You can do all sorts of handler variations. Here the handler is running.

Stage 2: Vary the distance

There's no need to do a lot of distance work with just one pair of poles. We suggest that you introduce some minor variations, up to three to four meters, to avoid patterning a set distance. Building distance means shortening the transport, ending it earlier and earlier. In the Bermuda Triangle you'll soon get to a point where you reward your dog right after one set of poles, rotate your shoulders, end the reward, and let your dog go to the next pair of poles (without any transport in between).

Once your dog is happy about that distance you can make use of the Bermuda Triangle's full potential: If your dog makes a mistake at one pair of poles, you can simply turn your shoulders and let him continue to the next pair (without any transport in between). All correct attempts are rewarded, and all incorrect attempts are ignored; your dog simply continues ahead and gets a new shot at the next pair.

Increase the distance to the weaves by ending the transport earlier and earlier. Note that your dog should drive ahead by himself! If you have to prompt him with your movement, you have added too much distance too soon.

Here, the handler ends the transport close to the poles.

Here, the handler ends the transport quite a distance away (left) and the dog happily dashes all the way to the poles (right).

If no reward appears after the first poles, the dog aims for the next pair.

Negotiating the poles correctly on the way toward the remote reward

Stage 3: Let your dog do several pairs of poles for one reward

When your dog is confidently hurrying through one pair of poles at a certain angle, doing it correctly all the time even from a distance, you can start letting him do several pairs for one reward. Use the Bermuda Triangle, where you can simply skip one reward. When your dog doesn't get his reward immediately after one pair of poles, the next pair will draw him like a magnet. Voilà, your dog will race through two pairs of poles for one reward!

Let your dog do multiple pairs of weaves for one reward only as long as he's getting it right all the time. If you get mistakes, immediately go back to rewarding each correct attempt. The mistakes tell you that your dog needs more information (read "reinforcement") about which behavior is correct.

Stage 4: Introduce *Race to reward*

When you're well on the way with your weave pole training using the *Aim for it* procedure, you can set out a remote reward, turning it into a *Race to reward* exercise. The remote reward, set a bit ahead along the line, will have several functions: It'll serve as a distraction (so make sure you have a helper who can remove or cover it), as a reward, and as a direction indicator (as long as you place it beyond the last pole).

Make sure you give your start cue at the right moment. Not now (left)...but now (right)!

Stage 5: Introduce start-line stays

By introducing start-line stays you'll be able to vary your own position and movements even further. Park your dog at your chosen starting point and give your start cue as he points his nose in the correct direction, toward the poles.

Further weave pole training

One pair of poles is the core of weaving. But don't dwell on one pair too long; you can always go back to working with one pair again if you need to. Further weave pole training begins with adding more poles (usually up to four) and working all angles again. Everything we said about entry angles for a single pair of poles still holds true when working with more poles—but you're adding both complexity and more aspects to the task:

Finding the entry (the first pair of poles) in a bunch of poles is different from finding the correct entry in one pair. Now your dog has to "count" the poles, always entering to the right of the first pole and to the left of the second.

- Getting to the third pole requires your dog to collect himself and bend as he enters, which is quite a challenge, both physically and mentally.
- You need to find a good balance between reinforcing the entry, the negotiation of all poles, and the exit.

THE CLICKER AND THE WEAVES

When working with more than two poles, use a marker whenever you wish to reinforce some detail within the weaves. You want to be able to reward within the weaves, but you don't want your dog to quit weaving just because you wave some toy around. When you use a marker, your dog can easily distinguish between rewards and distractions.

Here are our rules for potential rewards in the weaves:

- Within the weaves (no click), the treat or toy is a distraction—so your dog should ignore it.

- After the exit (no click), the treat or toy is a reward—so your dog should just go for it!.

- After a click (within the weaves or beyond), the treat or toy always is a reward.

CONTINUE TO THE END OF THE WEAVES EVEN IF YOUR DOG MAKES A MISTAKE

The weaves go in a set direction, and you want your dog to work his way to the end no matter what. A click and reward can "break off" his weaving, but anything else that might happen while he's in the weaves should be regarded as a distraction. That means you must never pull your dog out of the weave poles to start over. If you try, your dog should ignore you and continue forward. You don't want your dog to quit weaving because you do weird things with your handling, so keep going to the end of the weaves!

But, someone might say, if I let my dog continue to the end after a mistake, then how will he know he's making a mistake? Our answer is, as always: If you feel the need to tell your dog when he's doing something wrong, you're most likely not reinforcing the correct behavior enough! Go back to the drawing board and find ways to convey information to your dog by rewarding what's right and ignoring what's wrong! Set

up situations where you can easily reward every correct trial while ignoring all mistakes—for example, a Bermuda Triangle where you can easily just continue to the next set.

The only exception we can think of is for an advanced dog and handler team, in a late stage of the weave pole training when the dog is very confident and generally has solid weaves, and the handler has really good arguments for wanting to be able to stop the dog under certain specific conditions. Under such circumstances, we'd advise the handler to teach a verbal "break off" cue (and still only use it very sparingly, solely in situations where she has decided in advance she definitely wants to break off the weaving). Note all the "ifs and buts" here, though! Our general guideline is still that you always continue to the end no matter what, rewarding the behaviors you want and ignoring the ones you don't want.

We present the further weave training in six steps:

Step 1: Work up to four poles.
    Strategy 1: Put two pairs of poles together.
    Strategy 2: Shape three to four poles.
    Strategy 3: Channels: Advance from open to closed poles.

Step 2: Get all angles at four poles.

Step 3: Expand the understanding.

Step 4: Work up to a full set of poles.

Step 5: Vary where you are going after the poles.

Step 6: Vary where you come from.

Step 1: Work up to four poles

There are several possible ways to get to four (or more) poles. You can take two pairs and successively put them together, you can shape the path all the way through more poles, or you can use some kind of channel with open poles that you gradually close. If you like, you can even vary between strategies (perhaps focusing on different aspects with the different strategies).

Strategy 1: Put two pairs of poles together

Put two pairs of poles in a straight line, and gradually close the gap between them.

Our favorite strategy is to gradually put two pairs of poles together in a line of four. Once your dog is confidently doing several pairs of poles for one reward in the Bermuda Triangle, you can rearrange the setup and put two pairs of poles in a straight row, gradually narrowing the gap between the pairs and thus going from two pairs to one four-pole set of weaves:

1. First put two pairs in a straight row, start at the first pair, and vary when the reward appears. Sometimes reward after the first pair, end the reward, let your dog do the second pair, and reward again. More often, let your dog do both pairs in a row and reward only after the second pair.
2. Then successively bring the pairs closer together until you have a set of four poles.

This is the strategy we use most often. It's simple and straightforward, fits well with how we work with pairs of poles in the Bermuda Triangle, and it's easy to use high-energy rewards to rev up your dog's attitude and speed.

Strategy 2: Shape three to four poles

Another strategy is to shape the dog through three or four poles. Add one or two poles to the first pair and shape your dog through the whole string, clicking and treating several times along the path. Start by reinforcing every tiny movement in the right direction, constantly placing the reward a little bit ahead along the intended path and letting the dog continue working from there. Gradually you'll be able to get more behavior for each reward until your dog negotiates the whole set without intermediate rewards.

Since you'll click and reward for many different behaviors (for example, for nose in the right direction, moving toward the poles, choosing the correct entry, moving along the path correctly, choosing the correct side of each pole, exiting the poles correctly, driving ahead out of the poles, and so on), you can really provide your dog with a lot of information about all the tiny details.

This strategy doesn't build much speed, but it's a fascinating process! It makes a good complementary strategy since it teaches your dog to look for entries and to continue ahead along the path in the poles at the same time as it tests your shaping skills. Often we play around with this strategy on weave pole substitutes, like bottles or figurines in the living room.

Strategy 3: Channels: Advance from open to closed poles

You also can add more poles in a *channel*. Channel training usually starts with a longer set of weaves (usually 6 to 12 poles). At first you open the poles so that your dog can run straight through them, and then gradually close them so that your dog eventually zigzags through a straight line. Channels can

- use straight or slanted poles.
- be placed along a middle base or stuck in the ground.
- come with or without guiding props such as wires.

Channel with slanted (v-set) poles

We're not going to discuss all possible versions of channels here. Instead, we want to discuss the basics of this strategy.

Get the behavior of running straight through the channel. You can use either *Race to reward* or *Aim for it,* or vary between the two. What's important is that your dog drives through the channel at full speed. To advance in the training

1. incrementally close the channel.
2. if you have been using guiding props, gradually remove them.

Channels are great for building speed, since the dog at first just races through them. They can also help with establishing the desired footwork where your dog either single-steps (left front foot steps left, right front foot steps right, and so on) or bounces in a two-footed zigzag through the poles (no trotting). It's important, however, to begin closing the channels as soon as you can, so that your dog gets used to bending in the weaves, not just running straight ahead. We usually don't use channels "from start to finish" ourselves, but we sometimes make use of "open poles" as a complementary tool in our training.

A COUPLE OF BRAND NAMES

The *Weave-A-Matic*® is a brand-named equipment for channel training. There are other factory-made channel weaves out there as well.

2x2 is a detailed training method designed by Susan Garrett, teaching the weaves with pairs of poles—at first opened up and then gradually closed. To learn about the 2x2, take a look at her *"2x2 Weave Pole Training"* DVD set.

9 o'clock entry at four poles. Click for the entry (left) and reward along the path (right).

Nailing the 2 o'clock entry. Using three poles leaves only two "gaps" to choose between, which can make it easier in the beginning. Note that the third pole is mostly a distraction—the dog's job is to aim to the left of the second pole and wrap around it.

DISTRACTING HANDLING IN THE WEAVE POLES

When approaching the weaves, the direction of your shoulders—pointing toward the poles—tells your dog that those are what to work with. As soon as your dog is committed to the poles, you should be able to do whatever. Just as with the dogwalk, for example, executing the poles correctly is your dog's responsibility; it's your responsibility to move to wherever will benefit your team the most after the weaves. That means you can add any distractions, including contradictory handling cues (such as turning away or running in the opposite direction): Your dog will learn not to pop out of the weaves before the end, no matter what.

Step 2: Get all angles at four poles

As soon as you've introduced your dog to the concept of more poles (be it three, four, or more poles), start working with angles around the clock. Do *not* wait until your dog is doing four poles perfectly from a 6 o'clock entry! Angles need to be an integral part of the training.

Remember, there are always many possible reinforceable moments. For example, reinforce "nose pointing toward the correct entry" (from looking at the entry from the starting point, to approaching the entry), "nose passing the correct side of a pole," "wrapping around a pole," and so on all the way to "exiting the poles." Throughout, we recommend using high-energy rewards to maintain your dog's attitude and drive.

Also remember the possibility of altering the setups. For example, you can vary among two, three, and four poles. Especially when working with 1 o'clock to 5 o'clock entries, three poles can be valuable since there are only two "gaps" to choose between. You can alter between Bermuda Triangles and just one set of poles. You can choose to open the poles slightly (at the beginning and/or at the end). You can do some work in a set direction (where the dog knows in advance which way the weaves go). There are many possible options!

Step 3: Expand the understanding (working through all variations)

Just as when working with one pair of poles, expand your dog's understanding by

- adding handler variations and other distractions.
- varying the distance.
- letting your dog do several sets of four-pole weaves for one reward (we suggest using the Bermuda Triangle).
- using *Race to reward*.
- varying between spontaneous starts and start-line stays.

Work through all variations at all angles, and reward either within the poles or as your dog exits. At this stage, we usually either reward at the entry (for entering correctly) or at the exit (for performing the full set).

"Hey doggie, can you do the weaves if I flap the toy (left)—or if I run the other way (right)?"

A remote reward can help your dog keep his direction when you start adding weird distractions.

Add more poles by closing the gaps between your sets. Remember to continue rewarding the entries sometimes! Here are some possible set-ups.

Step 4: Work up to a full set of poles

When your dog is doing several sets of poles for one reward in the Bermuda Triangle correctly nearly every time, adding more poles after the first four is easy! He's already experienced at doing 8, 12, 16 poles, but with small gaps at every fourth pole, so now you just need to bridge the gaps.

Set up a straight line of poles—you can either add two more poles at a time, going from 4 to 6 to 8 poles, and so on, or you can put two sections (4+2 or 4+4 poles) in a straight line with gaps between and successively close the gap. Build up to 12 or even 14 or 16 poles: Your dog's job is to keep weaving until there are no more poles.

Step 5: Vary where you are going after the poles

Until now you've always rewarded your dog right after the poles, teaching him to drive to the end. Now it's time to teach him to also follow your handling out of the weaves. Begin at four poles and simply alter the placement of the reward, so that it happens in alignment with your handling. If you aim straight ahead, the reward appears straight ahead. If you do a regular turn or a front cross, the reward appears in the direction of the turn. You may very well be early with your handling maneuvers—your dog "can't" exit prematurely, so even if you turn away when he's in the middle of the weaves he needs to continue until the end before turning with you.

Vary the number of poles, so that your dog learns to look for the end. When your dog is confident in following your handling as he exits the poles (but ignoring it while in the poles), add various obstacles to go to after the weaves.

Reward your dog for following your handling after the poles!
Left: Here the handler is performing a front cross at the exit.
Center: The dog is rewarded for following the handling.
Right: Sometimes it's good to deliver the reward at the very exit—so here the handler throws the toy back to the dog.

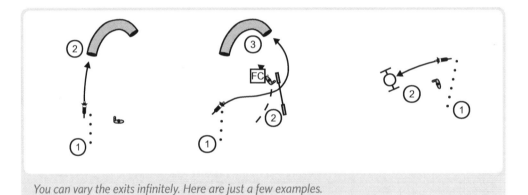

You can vary the exits infinitely. Here are just a few examples.

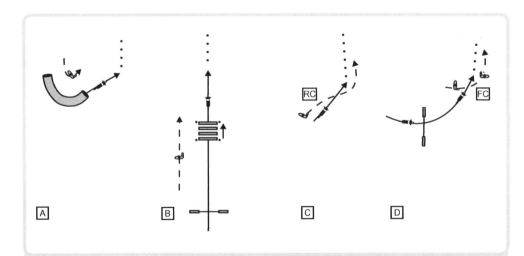

You can vary the weave pole approach endlessly—here are a few examples. To switch sides you can either cross in front before the weaves (begin your front cross as your dog takes off at the previous obstacle), or you can send your dog to the weaves and then cross behind him.
A. Coming from a tunnel at 7 o'clock   B. 6 o'clock entry at full speed   C. Doing a rear cross.
D. Doing a front cross.

Step 6: Vary where you come from

Practice different approaches to the weaves: putting various obstacles before the weaves, doing front crosses before the weaves, and doing rear crosses as the dog enters the weaves or while he's weaving. And practice all your variations around the clock.

SENDING TO THE WEAVES FROM THE "WRONG" SIDE

Normally you send your dog to the 1 o'clock to 5 o'clock entries from left-side handling, and to the 7 o'clock to 11 o'clock entries from right-side handling (since that's when your dog is on your outside). But what if you come upon, say, a 3 o'clock entry with your dog on your right side?

Our solution to this dilemma is:

- Only send your dog to the poles from the "wrong" side when it's a long set of poles and it's obvious which end of the poles you're sending him to.
- Be extremely clear about aiming your shoulders at the first pole.
- And then do a rear cross as the dog enters the poles: The rear cross cues your dog to head in the direction of the weaves. If you need to switch back to the original side, you can cross behind again as your dog weaves.

In the beginning you can start close to the weaves and use a remote reward to set the direction, getting your dog used to this new concept. Never practice this maneuver on short sets of weaves, though. For the shorter set, the "old rule" (figuring out the direction by staying on your outside) holds true.

3 o'clock entry with right-side handling: The handler crosses behind as the dog enters.

Troubleshooting in your weave pole training

In your weave pole training, as everywhere else, troubleshooting and training are the same thing. Focus on what it is you want your dog to learn and how you can teach him that, and remember: A happy attitude is priority No. 1!

If your dog seems to get stuck in the wrong pattern somewhere, you need to do something about it by altering your training so that you get some reinforceable responses. Here are some components you can work with:

- Alter the setup of the poles—for example, change the number of poles, how open/ closed the poles are, or whether you use one or several sets of poles (in a Bermuda Triangle or in some other setup).
- Alter your dog's starting point—for example, change the distance or the angle of approach.
- Alter how you start—for example, switch your method of transport (collar? treat magnet? tug?), vary between spontaneous starts and start-line stays, or change your own starting position.

- Alter your criteria—for example, by rewarding earlier along the intended path, before the mistake happens, and then gradually shifting your criteria.
- Alter the reward—for example, switch to an even more thrilling reward, let the reward appear either closer to your dog's nose or farther away, change where the reward comes from, and/or change where it's presented.
- Go for classical conditioning—if your dog's happy attitude has gone AWOL for some reason, make the weave poles into your happy place. Forget about formal training for a while. Never mind criteria; don't even think about precision; just make sure your dog has a blast every time he comes near the weave poles.
- Take a break and do something else—either something that has nothing to do with weaving, or a completely different aspect of weaving. The problem might just disappear if left alone for a while.

One of the beauties with the Aim for it *strategy is that you can always go back to rewarding your dog for pointing his nose in the right direction. Set up for success, reward the slightest tendency toward the correct behavior, and build from there!*
Left: Here the handler uses a collar transport, simply waiting to let go until she feels that the dog is aiming correctly.
Right: Here the dog is rewarded for taking one step to the right of the first pole.

Look at what it is that you want, and set up situations where your dog is likely to learn that. For example, if you want more speed, use high-value rewards in simple settings (for instance, use just two poles coming from a distance, do many poles but open them up slightly, and set out a remote reward). If you want higher precision at tough angles, constantly vary the angles and often reinforce the entry (either with just two poles or with more poles). If you want more independence, work in simple settings where your dog can easily get it right and add all sorts of variations in your own behavior. In short: focus on whatever aspect you wish to strengthen, and build it, bit by bit.

Mistakes and misunderstandings

In weave pole training, expect some mistakes and misunderstandings along the way. This is true in all training, but the weaves present so many elements, and your dog's job differs depending on his angle of approach. So if things seem to go wrong, don't panic! Just notice what happens, and adjust your training.

For example, imagine you've been doing a couple of sessions at 9-to-11 o'clock angles, and your dog has grasped the concept of wrapping around the first pole. Then you switch sides, starting at a 4 o'clock angle—and your dog goes to the wrong side of the first pole! You try again, and he repeats the same behavior, looking as if he really believes he's correct. What happened? Probably your dog now thinks the game is "wrap around the first pole," so that's what he does. Take notice, but don't worry. Simply switch focus for a while to teaching (re-teaching) the behavior of going to the right of the first pole and to the left of the second (for example, going back to two poles, to a 6 o'clock, left-side handling approach, and/or to holding onto his collar and simply clicking and treating for looking at the correct entry). Then start shifting back and forth between approaches around the clock, checking that your dog understands that wrapping around the first pole is for 7-to-11 o'clock entries only, while the 1-to-5 o'clock approaches require nailing the space between the first and second poles and wrapping left around the second pole.

Or, imagine you've clicked and treated for "nose to the left of the second pole in a row of four" a couple of times. Then you withhold the click (wanting your dog to continue weaving)—and your dog stops at the second pole! Clearly, he's waiting for his click, thinking the game now is "nose to the left of the second pole." Again, take notice, but don't worry. If possible, simply wait for any movement along the correct path and reward that. Or start over, switching focus to "forward movement along the path." For example, click earlier, before your dog stops, and then start varying when you click. Perhaps do some work with many clicks and treats in each session, rewarding all forward motion. Or lessen your dog's anticipation of the click by going back to two poles and simply toss the reward as your dog enters correctly, without clicking first.

Whatever your dog does, it's merely behavior and thus you can alter it through training. The best-case scenario would be to foresee all these possible misunderstandings and take action before they occur. But interesting things tend to show up in weave pole training, and when they do, don't be too alarmed. Smile, think, plan, and take action!

To see your dog take off and blast through the weave poles with confidence and joy is truly exhilarating! It also means you've done an excellent job of training independent performance of the most complex agility obstacle. Your job as a trainer and handler, however, is forever evolving—but that is the challenge and delight of agility, as we discuss in our last chapter.

23

Parting thoughts

That's it—the gospel according to E & E! There are two ways you can read the title of this book, *Agility Right from the Start*, and we hope we've succeeded on both counts: giving you a solid introduction to the sport, from the very beginning of foundation training and onwards, and also helping you getting your training "right" in the sense of making it good training, following clicker training principles and Good Agility Practices. We want you to experience the winning feeling that comes from witnessing your teammate happy and confidently playing the game with you.

Happy training!

Here's what we want to leave you with:

- Know your goals.
- Work on one tiny bit at a time.
- Reward what you like, ignore what you don't like, and set up for success.
- Let the spirit of Good Agility Practices soar over all your training.
- Above all, have fun with your dog.

This is how you build a great foundation. It's also how you move on—and how you solve problems that may arise along your way.

Know your goals: Know what you're striving toward. "What does that look like?" is one of the most important questions you can ask yourself. When you know your goals, you're well on your way in training. This goes for both the big picture and the little details. Every little detail that you want you or your dog to master is a miniature goal in itself (for example, "your dog points his nose at a piece of equipment," "you end the transport as you reach your chosen starting point," or "you keep going after a mistake").

Keep in mind: *You* set your own goals—both large and small. Do get input from others (through friends, seminars, books, magazines, DVDs, and so on), but remember to keep your thinking cap on! Ask yourself: Does what is being presented fit into my training? Do the handling maneuvers fit into my system of handling? Does the obstacle training fit with what I wish to teach my dog? You're never obligated to do what someone else says just because she or he says so. Make your own decisions!

Advancing in your training means continually setting new goals. Problem solving means finding new ways to reach your goals—and perhaps refocusing for a while, finding intermediate goals to work toward. Neither you nor your dog is supposed to get everything right from the start, but when you pay attention to the details and set clear goals, you'll constantly have reasons to pat yourselves on the back.

Work on one tiny bit at a time: Set the tiniest, clearest goals possible. When you focus on one small aspect at a time, you and your dog are both likely to be successful—both with that detail, and with the big picture. For your dog, this means ample opportunities to earn great rewards in the form of treats, toys, and other joyful events. For you, the rewards come in the form of seeing your dog's and your own progress, reaching goal after goal while experiencing the joy of interspecies teamwork.

Foundation training is all about splitting, working through each skill separately. Spotlighting one skill at a time is also the way to go when building, maintaining, and fixing behaviors. As your training advances, you'll continually discover new components to work on and new problems to solve. Keep splitting, going back to basics, and focusing on one aspect at a time. The beauty lies in the details!

Reward what you like, ignore what you don't like, and set up for success: These principles form the core of clicker training. When you use your rewards as your dog's prime source of information, you maximize both the learning and the fun!

Since both you and your dog are constantly learning, the training process never ends. The laws of learning are as valid when you start training with a puppy as when you prepare for the world championships. Whether you're teaching a new skill, refining an old one, or solving some problem that has arisen, you apply the same principles.

Let the spirit of Good Agility Practices soar over your training: Give yourself and your dog the best possible place to begin. Your short and sweet sessions, your distinct transports, your cleverly delivered rewards, and your ability to keep working even if something goes wrong all contribute to the clarity and consistency of your training.

Whenever you wish to sharpen up your training or solve a particular problem, remember the tiered cake:

- Bottom tier: Only nice things happen around agility training. This sets the tone for your training and classically conditions your dog to expect pleasant experiences.
- Middle tier: Good Agility Practices strengthen general agility behaviors. When you maintain your focus and intensity and stick to your handling system, you keep your dog busy and give him a direction to work in—which, in turn, strengthens his focus, intensity, and ability to follow your handling.
- Top layer: Explicit reinforcement of particular responses enables you to build precisely the skills you want.

Above all, have fun with your dog! Approach yourself, your dog, and the process of learning with a joyous frame of mind. Attitude is always top priority! Be happy and proud of all your successes, big and small, and embrace all errors as merely reports about what you have yet to master.

We wish you truly happy and inspiring training days, and we look forward to meeting you and your dog on the agility field some day!

Resources

A list of recommended books, DVDs, and web pages could easily run many pages. Here are our personal favorites, along with brief comments.

Positive reinforcement, clicker training, and TAGteach

Don't Shoot the Dog: The New Art of Teaching and Training, by Karen Pryor (1999) Bantam Books. First on our list comes this groundbreaking book about positive reinforcement, which helped launch the clicker training era when it was first published in 1983.

Clicker training: The 4 Secrets of Becoming a Supertrainer, by Morten Egtvedt and Cecilie Köste (2008) Canis (available as an e-book on www.canisclickertraining.com along with their upcoming dog obedience book): Our favorite clicker training book! It earns a spot on every clicker trainer's reading list.

Click for Joy: Questions and Answers from Clicker Trainers and their Dogs, by Melissa Alexander (2003) Sunshine Books. This excellent book is based on topics and questions asked on the Clicker Solutions mailing list (www.clickersolutions.com).

Animal Training: Successful Animal Management Through Positive Reinforcement, by Ken Ramirez (1999) Shedd Aquarium Society. Intended as a training manual for animal trainers in zoological settings, this book is a goldmine for anyone wanting to learn more about training. The principles remain the same, regardless of which species you're working with!

Reaching the Animal Mind: Clicker Training and What It Teaches Us about All Animals, by Karen Pryor (2009) Scribner. A fascinating investigation into the past, present, and future of positive reinforcement.

www.tagteach.com: The TAGteach webpage features information, videos, FAQs, upcoming seminars, and an online TAGteach course. TAGteach International also has an inspirational and informative blog at www.tagteach.blogspot.com.

www.clickerexpo.com: Yes, we know it's not a book, nor a DVD. It's a webpage for an event. But it's not any event—it's ClickerExpo! It's the greatest resource, giving you the opportunity to listen to fascinating lectures and socialize with clicker trainers from all over the world.

Behavior and Learning

How Dogs Learn, by Mary Burch and Jon Bailey (1999) Howell Book House. An informative guide that helps you understand the principles governing learning.

Control Unleashed, by Leslie McDevitt (2007) Clean Run Productions. Your canine teammate needs to be able to relax and focus in arousing and possibly intimidating settings. *Control Unleashed* is a coherent program for helping dogs handle the features surrounding training and competition venues.

The Culture Clash, by Jean Donaldson (2005) James and Kenneth Publishers. This book offers a great perspective on the lives of our dogs in human society. Indeed it's quite the culture clash.

Agility Training and Handling

"Great Dog…Shame About the Handler," "Great Dog Great Handler—A Winning Combination, " and "On Course to Excel," by Greg Derrett (2003, 2007, 2008) available at www.gtagility.com. These DVDs detail Greg Derrett's handling system. Greg and Laura Derrett's webpage links to their YouTube channel and provides information about online tuition. If you get the opportunity to attend one of Greg's seminars, go for it!

"Success with One Jump," and "Crate Games," by Susan Garrett (2006, 2007) Say Yes! Dog Training. The one-jump DVD offers handling drills based on Derrett's handling system while "Crate Games" presents Garrett's widely popular program of nurturing self-control and motivation.

"Foundation Jumping," "Advanced Jumping," and "Puppy Jumping," by Susan Salo (2008, 2009, 2009) Clean Run Productions. Jumping guru Susan Salo's DVDs teach you how to train jump technique. The "Advanced Jumping" DVD set includes an instructional PDF with exercises and previously published articles.

Clean Run magazine, published monthly, focuses solely on agility and is available in both paper and digital editions from www.cleanrun.com, where you also can find various agility resources and a web shop.

Your Secret Coach, by Christine Smith (2002) Clean Run Productions. Training and competing well also has to do with your mental state. When it comes to working on improving your mental attitude, this small but inspirational book helps you become the trainer and competitor you want to be.

The companion website

Please visit visit www.AgilityRightFromTheStart.com for a detailed overview of our whole program and one-sheet versions of the exercises you can take with you to practice.

…and us!

www.carpemomentum.nu: Last but not least, we welcome you to our own website, which offers information about us, our dogs, and our seminars as well as articles and other information about agility, clicker training, and TAGteach. You also can contact us directly at info@carpemomentum.nu.

About the authors

Emelie Johnson Vegh and Eva Bertilsson live in Sweden and run Carpe Momentum ("seize the moment") together. Appreciated for their systematic approach that focuses on joy and success for both dog and handler, they give agility seminars as well as clicker training seminars all over Sweden and Norway. They also offer TAGteach Primary Certification seminars, being the first in Europe eligible to do so.

The two colleagues regularly contribute to the Scandinavian clicker training magazine *Canis*, (owned by Morten Egtvedt and Cecilie Køste) and have been published in *Clean Run*. They are part of the 2010 Clicker Expo faculty, presenting their application of clicker training principles to agility. This is their first book.

The two best friends and colleagues live 400 km apart. Eva resides in Munkedal on the west coast (100 km north of Gothenburg, Sweden's second-largest city); Emelie lives in Malmö in the very south of the country with her husband and two sons.

Although you may be surprised that Swedish authors would write their first book in English, we can assure you that no stunt writer has touched this. In Sweden everybody studies English from an early age, and media in all forms contribute to English being a language that most Swedes are quite comfortable with. English also happens to be Emelie's second mother-tongue, since her father comes from an English-speaking country.

Emelie Johnson Vegh

Emelie is a high school teacher with degrees from Lund University and Malmö University but works solely within Carpe Momentum. Other than pure agility classes, she also offers private lessons, clicker training classes, and freestyle classes.

Emelie began training dogs as a teenager, after many years of involvement with horses. She was convinced by a neighbor to try dog training when her parents said no to buying her a horse of her own. Heartbroken, Emelie got to borrow a Labrador named Kicki, and the rest, as they say, is history. When her parents saw her commitment to taking care of and training Kicki, she got permission to get her first dog—Nilla, a mixed breed that Emelie refers to as "a once in a lifetime dog" that competed successfully in both agility and obedience.

Her first Border terrier came into her life in 1994; all in all she's had three terriers, with My still sharing her life. The Border terriers have mostly been involved in agility, but also in some freestyle and ground work. In 2009, a Kelpie—Scout—entered the family. With her, Emelie is working in agility, obedience, and freestyle, with the hope of adding some search work or tracking.

Both as a youth and an adult, Emelie and her dogs have won medals at the Swedish Nationals, with a silver team medal as the best placement.

Eva has a degree in psychology and education and used to work as a teacher before devoting all her time to Carpe Momentum. She also has worked within the Swedish Kennel Club for many years, educating agility instructors and future instructors' teachers as well as offering pet dog classes and campaigning for clicker training at local clubs.

Eva Bertilsson

A born animal lover, Eva grew up with horses, rabbits, and cats but always yearned for a dog. When beloved Nova Scotia Duck Tolling Retriever Sickan finally joined the family, dog training became Eva's lifestyle, and a new world opened. Soon Sickan and Eva were competing successfully in obedience, and the dog club turned into a second home.

Then a tiny bundle of pure energy made her entrance. For the last 16 years, Misty (a Phalène—the drop-eared version of the Papillon) has shared Eva's life and her passion for training. Together they've excelled in agility, won the individual Swedish Agility Nationals, and competed for the Swedish national team at the FCI World Championships. They've also earned titles at the highest levels in obedience and conformation and have enjoyed several other dog sports as well.

Over time, Eva's pack has expanded to include Misty's son Soya (Phalène), and Border Collie Tizla. Tizla is still a novice at playing agility, obedience, and rally obedience, while Soya is a seasoned agility competitor with an individual silver medal at the National Championship as his finest merit.

For more information about Carpe Momentum and Emelie and Eva, check out their web site at www.carpemomentum.nu.

Acknowledgements

First and foremost, our gratitude goes to all our students for all the inspiration and feedback you give us. Without you guys, this book would never have come to be.

To our American sisters Theresa McKeon and Beth Wheeler: Thank you for introducing us to TAGteach and for generously sharing thoughts and insights. And for giving that copy of our article to Karen Pryor—that's what set this production off!

To our dear friends Morten Egtvedt and Cecilie Köste: Thank you for getting us writing in the first place, and for inspiration and great discussions over the years!

To Karen Pryor: Thank you for believing in us and in our book, and for all the sound advice during the process.

To Nini Bloch: Thank you for bearing with us during a long and tough editing process. We made it!

To our photo wizard Nina Mortensen: Thank you for the countless hours you've spent working with the photos, both behind the camera and in front of the computer screen.

To all our photographers: Thank you for letting us use your wonderful photos in our book!

To all the people and all the dogs that appear through the pages of this book (Angela, Ann, Anna, Annica, Annsofi, Carola, Enar, Janne, Karin, Kerstin, Lone, Louise, Maria H, Maria L, Maria O, Marie, Mia, Michaela, Peter, Tina, Tommy, Armani, Arn, Axl, Buffy, Csilla, Eema, Eo, Fen, Gaia, Gessi, Heaney, Jason, Kia, Kis, Lady, Lira, Love, Ludde, Lukas, Miro, Misty, My, Ozzy, Rex, Scout, Soya, Tom, Tizla, Troppy, Vilda, Virvla): Thank you for lending us yourselves to illustrate our text!

To Dag Brück, who came up with "Good Agility Practices" as a translation of our Swedish term "Agilitymässighet," thanks for your creativity.

To all our instructors over the years: Thank you for sharing your insights! Our special gratitude goes to Irene Stjärnås, who early on showed us truly independent obstacle performance and sparked our thinking on rewards and reward placement, and to Greg Derrett who bravely returns to Sweden every winter (despite the risk of frost injuries), teaching us the ins and outs of his handling system and the importance of clarity and consistency.

Last but not least, our warmest thanks go to our families and friends: Thank you for your patience, love, and constant encouragement. We couldn't have done it without you!

Photography credits

Unless noted below, all images were taken by Nina Mortensen, www.ad-meliora.se.

Front cover: cynoclub, istockphoto.com

Back cover: Johanna Strandner

Eva Bertilsson: 2, 10, 16, 18, 20, 22 (left), 28, 38, 41, 54, 57, 58 (bottom), 60 (bottom pair), 71 (all), 75, 76, 77 (all), 80 (left), 81, 84, 87, 89, 93 (bottom right), 96 (all), 101, 102, 106, 107, 109 (all), 112 (bottom), 118, 120, 121 (left), 123 (all), 128 (bottom), 129, 133, 140 (right), 141, 143 (bottom pair), 144, 150, 152 (top left, middle left, bottom right and center), 155, 156, 160, 161 (bottom left), 164, 167, 168, 170 (all), 171, 178 (far left), 180 (bottom left), 184, 185 (center and right), 186, 188, 189 (top), 190, 191, 192, 193, 194 (all), 195 (left and right), 199 (middle left and right), 200 (bottom far left, bottom center left), 212, 222 (all), 227 (top), 245 (left), 247, 248, 252, 254, 261, 267, 268 (left and center), 304 (bottom pair), 352 (left), 355, 358 (top left), 360, 361, 363, 369, 370 (all), 378, 379, 401, 414, 416 (top pair, bottom far left and center left), 423

Mette Björne: 4, 11, 90, 95, 111, 143 (top), 153 (top left), 264 (center), 277 (all), 282 (top two), 283, 291, 302 (top), 308 (top), 408, 437 (top)

Annika Clerselius: 23

Tommy Hagström: 36, 406

Lone M. Hellesvik: 189 (bottom right), 354

Tom Espen Hellesvik: 245 (right), 296

Jenny Johansson: 153 (bottom center)

Emelie Johnson Vegh: 56, 63, 99, 113, 115, 128 (top), 253

Michaela Kartler: 152 (top right), 196, 204, 262, 264 (right), 266, 285 (all), 287, 358 (top right), 394 (top)

Gunnar Lindgren: 430

Johanna Strandner: 7 (right), 27, 29, 32, 50, 70, 88, 117, 153 (top right, middle left, bottom left), 176, 189 (bottom left), 195 (center), 201, 223 (bottom), 232, 234, 238, 286, 288, 307, 319, 332, 333 (vertical series), 339, 352 (center), 353, 358 (bottom series), 359, 383, 385, 389, 390, 396, 404

Hans Wretling: 437 (bottom)

Lotta Larsson: Illustration, page 24